Liberation Struggles

in International Law

Liberation Struggles
in International Law

Christopher O. Quaye

Temple University Press
Philadelphia

Temple University Press, Philadelphia 19122
Copyright © 1991 by Temple University. All rights reserved
Published 1991
Printed in the United States of America

The paper used in this publication meets the minimum
requirements of American National Standard for Information
Sciences—Permanence of Paper for Printed Library Materials,
ANSI Z39.48-1984 ∞

Library of Congress Cataloging-in-Publication Data

Quaye, Christopher O.
    Liberation struggles in international law / Christopher O. Quaye.
        p.   cm.
    Includes bibliographical references (p.   )
    ISBN 0-87722-712-8 (alk. paper)
    1. Self-determination, National.   2. National liberation
movements—Africa.   I. Title.
JX4054.Q39   1990
341.26—dc20   90-10857
                                                      CIP

Dedicated to Mom and Dad,
Madam Emelia A. Lomo and Mr. Daniel Quaye Tawiah

Contents

Liberation
Struggles
in International Law

Chapter

1

The Nature of Liberation Movements

LIBERTY IS ONE of those traditional concepts that are easily pressed into the service of many different causes. It has served as a battle cry for people fighting against domination by others as well as for expansionists seeking to extend their territories. It has been used to justify struggles against dictatorial governments and colonialists and by incumbent authorities and colonialists against their adversaries. The concept of liberty has also proved convenient to rival factions struggling to capture control over the affairs of their countries, and it has served as the basis for intervention and counterintervention by rival states to help their favorites in intrastate conflicts. It is no wonder, then, that often the same cause that is applauded as "liberationist" is described as "terroristic" or "criminal."

In the past, "liberation" movements were pursued mostly by individual factions motivated by personal idiosyncrasies, whereas contemporary movements enjoy some communal and legal support from the international system. Featured as one of the cornerstones in the U.N. commitment to preserve international peace and security, this support has been articulated in many U.N. documents, providing blanket permission for people struggling for self-determination to use any means at their disposal; encouraging states to give moral, material, substantial assistance to liberation movements; forbidding states to give any assistance to the authorities against whom the struggles are directed; and characterizing struggles within states as international conflicts.

With the branding of all liberation movements as international conflicts—even the intrastate ones—those that were treated under the traditional law as falling outside the purview of international law are made a relevant concern for the international community. In effect, liberation movements have become one of the most prominent and thought-provoking subjects of international relations. This book examines the various responses of the international community—especially its highest politico-legal organization, the United Nations—to

3

problems posed by liberation movements to see how the commitment to use liberty as a cornerstone of the pacific mission is observed in practice.

Recent activities of certain members of the international community, notably those of the United States in Nicaragua, the Soviet Union in Afghanistan, Great Britain in its conflict with Argentina over the Falklands, and France with regard to its independent nuclear policy (the celebrated *force de frappe* concept), have called into question the potency of the international legal system. Examples like these may appear to support the positivists' argument that the term "international law" is a misnomer, but this book argues against that position.

Yet the justification of the legal nature of the contemporary international order is not the only jurisprudential question confronting us. We must examine the contradictions in the international legal order—a system based on sovereign equality of states, with each state having as much power and freedom to determine which laws are relevant to cases affecting it, the content thereof, and how to apply them; a system wherein rules are incepted at different points in time and under a variety of circumstances; a system in which there is very little indication as to how the rules should apply in relation to one another; and a system in which there are so many tools for determining the significance of conflicts that the conclusions in one case are not always the same as those reached in similar cases. By the use of the canons of construction, we will explore questions regarding the parameters of the U.N. Charter's clause prohibiting the use of force and compare it with the rather controversial provision on self-defense in the same document, or even the relationship of these two provisions and that on self-determination, which hardly mentions force. We will also examine why the same conflict-resolution body, namely, the International Court of Justice (I.C.J.), has provided different answers for similar cases and sometimes even for the same conflict, as exemplified by the South-West Africa cases.

Finally, we confront the question of the exact contours of liberation movements. Although the literal meaning of the term "liberation" and the U.N. Charter's provision on self-determination and human rights make it nearly impossible to restrict the subject to any particular type of conflict, virtually all contemporary documents relevant to "self-determination" seem to confine it to decolonization cases. Nor is it difficult to explain why, from its inception, the United Nations has shown unflinching interest in the crusade against colonialism. Partly because of the invaluable assistance of most of the colonies to the Allied forces in the two world wars, the Allies made certain promises to their colonies. One such promise was independence. Thus, one way to rationalize the support for the anticolonial movements is to see it not only as a fulfillment of the promise to the colonies, but also as a way of bridging the credibility gap that has been fostered between the colonies and their masters by some of the evils of colonialism.

But confining liberation movements to the anticolonial struggles is too parochial. Can it be said that after achieving independence a state can do whatever it wants to its subjects and yet be free from movements against it? What of citizens who struggle against dictatorial or unrepresentative leaders? Does the word "liberation" not apply to the causes of the oppressed against their oppressors? And what about people of a particular ethnic group who become victims of discrimination or of genocide from their government? It is conceded that even those who succeed in "liberating" their countries from oppression often face the same criticisms made against their predecessors. These problems clearly reveal the difficulty of defining exactly what constitutes "liberation movements"; sometimes similar questions arise even when decolonization cases are included in the subject. One example of this difficulty is the controversy at the Hostages Convention about whether a cause ceases to be a "liberation movement" if the champions employ certain tactics to achieve their aims. Another conceivable problem is how to choose between two rival factions when each claims to be the legitimate champion for the liberation of the countries from the throes of colonialism.

At this point, it may be appropriate to present a brief outline of this work. Chapters 1 and 2 focus on the definition and characterization of liberation movements; whether the struggles in the intrastate category are relevant subjects of international law; and the legal implications of the use of certain terms, notably "terrorism," "communism," and "rebellion," to describe causes professedly pursued as liberation movements.

Chapter 3 deals mainly with the legal nature of the international order and the various mechanisms by which the system can be used to resolve problems arising from liberation movements. Among the issues considered here are the various techniques of construing norms and the means for choosing between norms of equal relevance to the same or similar issues. Also considered is the relevance of international adjudication to liberation movements: whether liberation movements that lack the status of statehood can appear before the I.C.J. or arbitral tribunals; the relevance of judicial techniques like *res judicata* and *stare decisis* to liberation movements, particularly in view of the requirement of consent for jurisdiction in international cases and the I.C.J. Statute's provision that the court's decisions apply solely to the particular parties over whom they are given; and the significance of advisory opinions of the I.C.J. and the circumstances under which such opinions are given and become part of international law.

Chapters 4 to 6 deal with the legal ramifications of the colonial cases. In Chapter 4 the focus is on colonialism as traditionally defined by the "salt and water" dichotomy. Chapter 5 examines the few remaining vestiges of colonialism, such as those in the South African apartheid system, and Chapter 6 explores the issues of historical claims, notably those by Morocco and Indonesia over Spanish Sahara and East Timor, respectively. Though technically noncolonial, the cases in Chapter 6 are so reflective of some of the despicable features of colonialism that they warrant consideration as to whether they cannot be treated as new versions of colonialism.

Chapters 7 through 9 discuss the noncolonial struggles. We examine whether the struggles against existing governments and those that merely seek to achieve secession for their champions can be considered as liberation movements. We further consider the legal significance of the noncolonial struggles by subjecting them to the principles of effective control and self-determination.

Chapters 10 and 11 focus on the legal ramifications of the use of force by liberation movements. Finally, suggestions are made about how the international legal system can be improved to respond squarely to the challenges posed by liberation movements. Broad though the scope of this work is, it cannot cover everything. The book covers only contemporary cases and thus ignores the French and American revolutions, the American Civil War, and the decolonization of the Spanish territories in the Americas, even though the champions of contemporary movements draw much of their rhetoric from these historical examples.

Even within the terms of the chosen subject, the research is restricted in some ways. The exposition of the susceptibility of conflicts to intervention and counterintervention by states and their consequent effects on international peace and security, for instance, says little about the perennial struggles in the Middle East or about the Korean crisis. Yet this stance is not difficult to explain. The issue of peace is not the sole subject of this inquiry, and the causes for the intervention in some of those cases and the law relating thereto are essentially the same as those studied in the cases discussed in this work. While the failure to discuss them in detail is to avoid repetition, it is interesting to note that the chosen cases, particularly those of Africa, provide a wider aperture for the study of contemporary legal and political issues on international relations. First, because of Africa's richness in minerals and its strategic importance to global politics (notably, South Africa and its cape), none of the major powers, particularly those engaged in the Cold War, would favor a rival's acquisition of substantial advantage. Thus, any serious intervention in any African country is likely to trigger a counterintervention to maintain the balance of power. Again, as the newest continent with some territories yet to be liberated from colonialism, Africa is an interesting aspect of the Cold War politics, particularly because the protagonists in the Cold War have been scrambling for African allies. With the continuation of some vestiges of colonialism and because leaders of independent countries have poor human rights records, the cases there represent most of the challenges for which the contemporary system was built, and thus make it difficult to overstate their importance in studies on international relations.

WHAT IS A LIBERATION MOVEMENT?

There is no unanimity about the precise scope of the subject "liberation struggles."[1] Only a few works on the subject have tried to define it. The most favored approach is simply to list the phenomena commonly considered to be liberation movements.

Nor is this general attitude entirely unrealistic. "Liberation," as is well known, is a value-laden term that lends itself to exploitation by opposing factions in an armed conflict. What, for instance, is the exact content of the liberation movement that is being pursued, and who defines that content? How far can a struggle for freedom go, and would it cease to be a freedom movement as soon as it goes beyond that threshold? What about the people against whom a liberation movement is pursued? Do they have the freedom to fight to maintain what they have achieved and have long enjoyed? What terminology should be used to describe methods used by those targets to maintain the status quo? In the contemporary international system where the initiation of, or participation in, any armed conflict has become the exception rather than the rule,[2] the seriousness of this problem cannot be exaggerated.

Baxter discusses the correlation between self-determination and liberation movements:

> The right of self-determination can, however, mean different things in different contexts. It is all very well to speak of anticolonialist struggles in Africa, but does a similar right of self-determination exist in the metropolitan territory of other countries? . . . States which have had experience with secessionist movements, such as Nigeria, Pakistan and Indonesia . . . , react with some surprise and resentment to the suggestion that they have been guilty of a violation of the Charter. . . . It is quite clear that one man's war of national liberation can be another man's war of national secession.[3]

In another study the problem has been demonstrated by how states often apply double standards in their relations with liberation movements:

> The dilemma posed by these questions is not Cuba's alone. The General Assembly majorities . . . have shown an equally schizophrenic approach to the problem of attempting to define the proper bounds for states' conduct with regard to wars of national liberation. The states of the majority view have

championed movements against regimes they abhor. But they have shown
little hesitancy in suppressing movements for self-determination within their
own borders. . . . Domestic political considerations, an ever-present element
in international policy rationalizations, undeniably explain a large part of the
dilemma.[4]

But perhaps the most intriguing problem is the confinement of the concept
to anticolonial struggles.[5] The main consideration apparently influencing this
approach is the U.N. practice of invariably equating "liberation movement"
with struggles against colonial domination. Thus, in the words of Baxter:

> The discussions that have taken place in recent years in the General Assembly
> of the United Nations, in the two conferences of Government Experts on the
> Humanitarian Law of War, and in other bodies make it clear that wars of
> national liberation are thought of in two ways: The first is the waging of
> hostilities by "freedom fighters" struggling for liberation and self-determina-
> tion in territories under colonial domination. The second is resistance activities
> conducted against unlawful foreign occupation.[6]

Is the apparent restriction of the concept of liberation struggles to the anticolonial cases merited?[7] One writer interprets the language of Protocol I to the
Geneva Convention of 1949 to mean that only colonial struggles can be called
liberation movements.[8] The protocol reads as follows:

> The Protocol, which supplements the Geneva Convention of 12 August 1949
> for the protection of war victims, shall apply in the situations referred to in
> Article 2 common to those conventions.
>
> 1(4) The situations referred to in the preceding paragraph include armed con-
> flicts in which peoples are fighting against colonial domination and alien occu-
> pation and against racist regimes in the exercise of their right to self-deter-
> mination, as enshrined in the Charter of the United Nations.[9]

But it is doubtful whether the writer's interpretation is defensible. The proceedings that culminated in the adoption of the protocol were not set up to find
an exhaustive definition of "liberation struggles." Nor did the provisions of the
resulting convention make any pretense of doing so. The word "include" also
suggests that the provision is not intended to be exhaustive.

Of course, this conclusion may run afoul of the U.N. Declaration on the
Granting of Independence to Colonial Countries and Peoples, Resolution 1514,
particularly its paragraph 6, which categorically excludes secessionist movements from the definition of self-determination.[10] But this problem can be easily
dispelled when Resolution 1514 is read together with the famous U.N. Declara-

tion on Principles of International Law Concerning Friendly Relations and Cooperation Among States in Accordance with the Charter of the United Nations, Resolution 2625, which clearly recognizes the right of peoples to exercise their right of self-determination against their own governments if such governments are unrepresentative of or discriminate against them.[11] Since both resolutions cite the Charter as their main source of support, there may be some questions about their interrelationship—whether they are reconcilable with one another or which one should have priority over the other. Unfortunately, the Charter does not provide any direct answers for these questions.

Obviously, this may reduce the value of the Declaration on Friendly Relations as the most appropriate statement of the principle of self-determination and, a fortiori, the law about the definition of "liberation movements." However, based on the circumstances in which the document was adopted[12] and the fact that it was adopted years after the inception of the Charter and the Declaration on Colonialism,[13] it may be argued that the document still supports the notion that the concept of "liberation struggles" encompasses some noncolonial struggles as well.

It should be obvious, then, that just as the approach to the study of liberation movements through the ordinary meaning of the word "liberation" is not expedient for this book, the model generally followed for identifying the subject is not entirely problem-free, either. But because the latter has one advantage over the former—it narrows the focus of the study to a few test cases—that is the approach followed in this book. However, because excluding the noncolonial cases, as do most works pertaining to liberation struggles, would narrow the field of study too far, I have added some of the noncolonial conflicts for discussion in this book.

The following are the cases examined in this study:

The Anticolonial Cases

This category comprises: (*a*) the struggles against colonialism as traditionally understood—regimes and troops of metropolitan powers that deny statehood to their overseas territories; (*b*) the struggles against the authorities created under the League of Nations' mandate system that have so far refused to give up those territories in spite of incessant entreaties from the United Nations; (*c*) the struggles against racist regimes in independent or quasi-independent countries; and (*d*) the struggles against neighboring countries that seek to annex former colonies after the demise of their original colonial systems. Examples of the struggles in group (*a*) are the Algerian war of independence against France and the struggles of Angola, Mozambique, and Guinea Bissau against Portugal; (*b*), (*c*), and (*d*) may be illustrated by the Namibians' struggles against the apartheid regime of South Africa, the Rhodesian and South African blacks' struggles against the racist minority regimes in those countries, and the struggles of the Sahraouis and East Timorese against Morocco and Indonesia, respectively.

Irredentist Struggles

This group includes struggles for the recovery of lost national territories—as in the conflict between the Palestinians and the state of Israel.[14]

Secessionist Struggles

The cases in this category comprise: (*a*) struggles by people who have been incorporated into the political structures of larger states against their will; and (*b*) struggles by people who, though not seriously opposed to their initial incorporation into the states against which their movements are directed, are later faced with experiences that leave them no other choice than to fight for separation. Examples of the former category are the Eritreans and Somalis in Ethiopia, the Katangas in Congo, and the Greeks in Finland; the latter category is represented by the Nigerian-Biafran and Pakistan-Bengali conflicts.

Struggles to Effect a Change of Government

The struggles in this group professedly seek to eradicate corruption, dictatorship, or the ineptitude of the governments in their countries. They are illustrated by the cases of Ghana, Nigeria, Liberia, Uganda, Dahomey, Nicaragua, and El Salvador.[15]

Many issues have to be clarified to reveal fully the advantages of the approach I have chosen. For instance, from what exactly do the champions liberate their participants? According to one writer on the nature of revolutions, the same people whose revolutionary propaganda includes appeals to human rights and the ideals of freedom, liberty, equality, and justice often employ "abominable methods" once they are in power.[16] This phenomenon is nowhere more evident than in the struggles against existing governments. Lee describes the process:

> Although it may figure prominently in explanations given for their action, the desire to provide efficient administration does not seem part of the normal African military make-up. There is little evidence to indicate that African

armies make better instruments of "modernization" than their civil servant counterparts. Indeed, all the organizations of the state appear to face a common set of problems.[17]

Again, according to Zolberg:

As a category, the military governors of Africa are unlikely to rule better, more justly, or more effectively than their (overthrown) civilian predecessors. Beneath their uniforms, the Gowons, Lamizanas, Bokassas, and Mobutus are men with the same range of virtues and vices, wisdom and foolishness as the Balewas, Olympios, Yameogos, and Nkrumahs they replaced.[18]

This would seem to call into question the classification of some cases, particularly those relating to change of government, as liberation movements. For the moment, we should suspend judgment and examine each situation on its own merits.

Another problem with the definition of liberation movements is that sometimes struggles professedly undertaken as liberation movements are described perjoratively as "terrorism," "communism," and "rebellion." Since we must distinguish the struggles that are privileged under the present system from those that are not, at least in order to know what law to apply in any given situation, we must examine the role such perjorative terms play in the general understanding of liberation movements.[19]

CHARACTERISTICS OF LIBERATION MOVEMENTS

Naturally, liberation movements share common attributes. These include the element of force, the right of self-determination, and intervention from outside in favor of any of the belligerent factions.

The Element of Force

One must be cautious not to seem to say that the use of force is a sine qua non for any venture involving decolonization, change of government, or separation of territory from what once was a single unit. Indeed, numerous colonial structures, notably those in Guinea, Ghana, Nigeria, and Gambia, have been dismantled with little or no force, just as many changes of government and dissolutions of federations and confederations of states have been effected amicably.[20] Nevertheless, the violent nature of the cases selected is the basis of their treatment as "liberation movements," to the exclusion of the nonviolent ones. And there is a reason for this distinction: the liberation movements use force because their adversaries have closed all avenues for amicable dissolution of the oppressive structures maintaining them in power.[21]

In the contemporary international legal system where the use of force is prohibited,[22] the crucial question is whether this violence is defensible. Within the U.N. Charter—the principal document embodying the present law on the subject—the provision outlawing force, however, is not absolute or unambiguous.[23]

The Provision on Self-Defense

Except where the United Nations may employ or authorize the use of force to prevent threats to or breaches of the peace, article 51, which provides for self-defense, is the only express qualification to the U.N. Charter's prohibition of the use of force.[24] But this article has many problems. The specification of "a Member of the U.N.," for instance, has raised an intense controversy as to whether nonstates also have the right of self-defense.[25] Second, the phrase "if an armed attack occurs" is undermined by the term "inherent right of self-defense," raising questions as to whether the traditional right of preemptive self-defense is still a legitimate recourse under international law.

Third, notwithstanding the Nuremberg ruling[26] that the legitimacy of the use of force in self-defense is a question to be answered solely by an international body, not only does article 51 seem literally to preserve the right of states to decide for themselves, but in practice the actors see themselves as the sole judges of when to use force in self-defense. Direct cases in point are the U.S. intervention in Vietnam on the pretext of the Vietnamese right of collective self-defense, the Soviet action in Hungary and Czechoslovakia pursuant to the so-called Brezhnev Doctrine, the British and French invasion of Egypt to keep the Suez Canal free from blockade, and the Indonesian and Indian invasions of East Timor and Goa, respectively.

The way the self-defense argument has been invoked in some cases, notably those involving colonialism, deserves particular attention. The strugglers premise their attacks on the force by which their colonial experiences were initiated.[27] According to this argument, the inception of colonialism was grounded on illegal aggression; its continuation is consequently a perpetuation of that illegality and thus entitles the strugglers to use force to eradicate it. India's position on this subject is spectacular. It points to the 450 years of Portuguese occupation of Goa and contends that that perpetual aggression warrants its invasion of Goa to rid the territory of the Portuguese colonial overlordship.[28]

That the acquisition of most colonies was effected by violence is indisputable. Yet it is difficult to support the tenets on which the alleged right of self-defense against the so-called illegal aggression is based. Here it must be re-called that at the time of the so-called aggression, not only was the use of force a legitimate instrument of international relations, but it was recognized as a legitimate means of acquiring territory. Again, one can cite the doctrine of prescription, according to which an occupation of a territory (regardless of how that occupation was brought about) matures into title for the occupier after a considerable length of time. Hall has stated the doctrine succinctly: "Title by prescription arises out of a long continued possession, where no original source of proprietary right can be shown to exist, or where possession in the first instance being wrongful, the legitimate proprietor has neglected to assert his right, or has been unable to do so."[29] The interesting thing to note about the traditional law is that if India had attacked Goa at any time before the birth of the United Nations (or arguably before the League of Nations period), the suc-cess of its venture would undoubtedly have validated the act.

In the contemporary system, the Indian argument is unmerited unless it can be sustained by any exception to the provisions against the use of force. The Indians have not been unaware of this; indeed, they sought to bolster their argument by appealing to the principle of self-defense. But according to the most celebrated authority on this concept, for the use of force to be a legitimate exercise of self-defense, the act occasioning it must be "instant, overwhelming, leaving no choice of means, and no moment for deliberation."[30] Since India's long period of inaction suggests that the alleged aggression was not "instant," but something that India could cope with, a situation that India long had the opportunity to deliberate, it is submitted that the Indian invocation of the self-defense argument was untenable.

Nevertheless, this case has one implication for many contemporary cases. Notwithstanding the palpable weakness of India's position, not only was its fait accompli in Goa left to stand, but it also stood uncondemned by the interna-tional community.[31] This outcome, to say the least, clouds the legal significance of the invasion, for it is still recognized in international relations that the legit-imacy of a revolution sometimes depends on its efficacy.[32]

In a sense, this aspect of the law is difficult to comprehend, for interna-tional law has long maintained—even before the U.N. regime with its more comprehensive provisions against the use of force came into being—that the fruits of aggression are illegitimate, abominable, and unrecognizable.[33] Among the most significant documents expressing this principle are the League Cove-nant, the Kellogg-Briand Pact, and the Stimson Doctrine.[34] Of course, the ap-plication of this principle in the era before the United Nations was fraught with considerable inconsistency. An obvious example was the lukewarm attitude of the League toward the Italian invasion of Ethiopia. Yet this response does not explain the apparent confusion now. Although in content and in scope the present system is more ambitious, it is nonetheless imperative that the United Nations not only learn and develop from the accomplishments of its predecessors but also from their shortcomings, particularly those pertaining to the use of force, which led to the demise of the League and to the consequent creation of the present system.

The Principle of Self-Determination

In the U.N. system and the international literature generally, the most widely used concept to assert the legitimacy of liberation movements is the principle of self-determination.[35] Indeed, this principle is the basis of all "liberation movements." Yet numerous questions must be examined to clarify the relationship between the concept and the liberation movements themselves.

First, there is the question of what exactly is meant by the principle of self-determination. The U.N. Charter does not shed much light on this. Consequently, authorities strongly disagree not only on the scope of the principle but on whether it is a legal principle or a mere political theory.

Another problem concerns the legitimacy of the force employed by the "liberation fighters." While the adversaries of the strugglers frown upon the force employed by the strugglers, the strugglers justify their resort to it by the principle of self-determination.

Considering that the Charter of the United Nations is the primary legal document on contemporary international relations, and considering also that in its entirety the Charter does not prescribe a hierarchy of rules and purposes, it may seem safe to treat with equal weight the provisions on the principle of self-determination and the prohibition of the use of force. From this it may be suggested that those who view the principle of self-determination as a way to evade the Charter's prohibition of the use of force may not be entirely wrong. The point that makes the position almost incontrovertible is that in most U.N. resolutions on the subject, the language leaves no doubt that the use of force in self-determination is legitimate.[36]

But there are scholars who dispute this view. Thus, according to one critic:

> The question of the relation between self-determination and the rules relating to the use of force has been neglected: . . . That there is, in all probability, a significant connection between the two legal principles is apparent from the Charter itself. Article 2 paragraph 4 includes an undertaking not to use force "in any other manner inconsistent with the purposes of the United Nations," and "respect for the principle of equal rights and self-determination of peoples" is one of those purposes. It might, however, be argued that the use of

force contrary to the Purposes of the United Nations is only a subordinate aim of Article 2 paragraph 4 (cf. the word "other"); that is the prevention of the use of force against the territorial integrity and political independence of States is the primary aim of the paragraph, and that the protection or advancement of the other purposes is legal only where it does not involve the use or threat of force against the territorial integrity or political independence of any State. To put it at its lowest, this is a plausible interpretation of Article 2 paragraph 4: moreover the development of Article 2 paragraph 4 in practice has tended to emphasize the prevention of overt aggression rather than, for example, the use of force by an incumbent against insurgents claiming for a territory a right of self-determination.[37]

Ingenious as this opinion may seem, it fails to convince. Not only is it undercut by the fact that the Charter does not prescribe a hierarchy of norms, but it fails to take into account the array of U.N. resolutions that encourage liberation movements to pursue their cause "by any means" but prohibit their adversaries from suppressing them.

Another criticism[38] points out that the Charter does not say anything to suggest that force may be used in pursuit of the right of self-determination. Most significantly, this view can draw support from the very argument that equates the status of the provision on the use of force with that on self-determination—the lack of hierarchy among the Charter's provisions. For, if self-determination is equal in status to the prohibition of the use of force mainly because the most important document on the two subjects fails to put one above the other, simple logic suggests that each provision should be taken *proprio vigore*. From this it is reasonable to infer that regarding the relative implications of the two provisions on matters involving the use of force, the one with a specific provision on the subject should have priority.

Nevertheless, the argument faces certain difficulties that ultimately make the majority position more persuasive. Here it suffices to focus on the Charter's silence on the use of force for self-determination. Notably, the Charter's failure is not only in not mentioning force but also in neglecting to indicate how the struggles for self-determination should be pursued. If the failure to mention force for self-determination is cited as an argument that the Charter forbids use of force for self-determination, then, a fortiori, the failure to shed any light on how self-determination is to be pursued would reduce the principle to a dead letter—a conclusion that is unsustainable by the principle of effective construction, according to which parties to a treaty are not to be presumed to have intended to nullify it by making its performance impossible. One need only observe that self-determination is a fundamental purpose by which the United Nations seeks to achieve its all-important goal of maintaining the peace.

Intervention

It is generally agreed that intervention by one state in the affairs of another is illegal. But just how this norm is applied defies definitive answers because the term "intervention" is elusive and shrouds any interference or interaction with any faction in conflict with illegality. In the contemporary international system where it is nearly unimaginable that events in one state can be insulated from all others, it is obvious that hardly any state can claim to have fully adhered to the rule against intervention.

Realizing the virtual absurdity into which the law is thus cast, most authorities have taken a narrow definition of the term. According to them, intervention is forbidden only if it amounts to a "dictatorial interference in the domestic or foreign affairs of another state [and] impairs that state's independence."[39] Although by this definition any interference that violates the independence or territorial integrity of a state is illegal, there is still no conclusive information as to how that law should apply in specific situations. Of primary significance in this respect is the disagreement over what is "dictatorial interference." Even more problematic is that under traditional international law, assistance to the incumbent government in a conflict-stricken country is considered legitimate. Moreover, not only are there ambiguities in determining what is the incumbent government and when the rule releasing states from the obligation to assist only the incumbent government comes into operation, there are other ambiguous principles, including intervention to protect national security, intervention to protect the lives and property of nationals, and intervention to uphold territorial integrity—all of which raise intense controversy.

Since the U.N. Charter is the ultimate document by which legal issues are resolved in the contemporary system, it seems reasonable to consider the issues from that document's pronouncements on the subject. Though the Charter contains a provision on "intervention" *expressis verbis*, that provision refers specifically to acts of the United Nations rather than to actions permitted of individual members. It is therefore doubtful whether it is relevant here. Conceivably, the provision against the use of force might have some relevance to the issue of intervention. But, the problem with that article is that it also indicates that the proscribed force is one that impairs the political independence or territorial integrity of a state. Inasmuch as an intervention in aid of the ruling government may arguably not compromise the independence or territorial integrity of the beleaguered state, the issue may elude solution.

Quite apart from the inconsistency of U.N. resolutions on the status of intervention—some sanctioning intervention in favor of strugglers for self-determination, others forbidding any type of intervention—there is some controversy about the place of the traditional law in the present system. Again, some authorities have suggested that the traditional law of intervention has fallen into desuetude and is therefore no longer part of international law. From the records, particularly state practice, it will be observed that this position is untenable. Finally, there are vexing questions about whether the failure to assist a government that had hitherto been assisted by a particular state can be described as a neutral act or as an intervention against that government. A corollary is whether a preexisting treaty for assistance to a particular government lapses as soon as that government faces an uprising from its people, in which case the issue becomes one between the two opposing principles of *pacta sunt servanda* and *rebus sic stantibus*. As demonstrated later in this study, these questions so defy objective solution that they leave one in a quandary about the real state of the law.

Finally, it should be observed that despite the apparent similarity of the selected conflicts, their legal significance varies. Among the factors explored in the next chapter to elucidate this possible discrepancy is that under customary international law, which still forms part of the present legal system, the legal significance of an armed conflict depends largely on its characterization as either an international or internal conflict.

COMPLICATIONS IN DEFINING LIBERATION MOVEMENTS

"Liberation Struggles" and "Terrorism"

There can be no confusing the legal consequences of terrorism and of liberation movements, for the two are not comparable. Liberation movements have a special status under contemporary international law: in pursuit of their rights of self-determination, such movements are entitled to employ "any means" at their disposal; they may seek and receive support from other states; their adversaries are forbidden to use force to suppress them; and they are to benefit from the laws of war, to mention but a few of their important privileges. Terrorists, on the other hand, have no advantages at all. Indeed, they are an object of the principle *aut dedere aut punire*,[40] and not only are their acts considered as crimes against humanity—*hostes humanis*—but they are so abhorrent to the community of nations that there is a strong consensus for their suppression.[41]

Simple as the distinction may seem, its practical significance is difficult if not impossible, to analyze objectively. For when it comes to figuring out the cases that qualify for the rubric "terrorism" in order to determine the applicable rules, the results are often more subjective than objective. The issue is complicated by the fact that although there are norms clearly defining the corresponding legal consequences of liberation and terrorism, there is no criterion or independent machinery by which acts that are terroristic can be distinguished from those that are dubbed liberationist. The natural consequence is that each faction and its sympathizers in any conflict, to paraphrase the apt statement by Baxter, characterize their causes and conducts as an epitome of righteousness, and they decry their adversaries' by using terms with perjorative connotations.[42] Realizing the enormity of the problem, Falk deems it inexpedient to attempt to distinguish the two. Thus, in his commentary on the Beirut raid he advisedly used the two terms interchangeably.[43] There are, of course, few authorities who do not favor this approach.[44]

It is important to realize why there is such a problem as mixing the treasured word "liberty" with a term that denotes abominable acts. According to one view:

> The word "terrorism" . . . carries with it a strong perjorative meaning. The term is often used by one side in a conflict to characterize the other side . . . Use of the term implies a moral judgment and if one party can successfully attach the label to its opponent, then it has indirectly persuaded others to adopt its moral viewpoint.[45]

Similarly, Daniel Haradsveit observes:

> The term "terrorism" is highly ambiguous and several meanings can be attached to it. It must be pointed out, however, that the word itself tends to be used to propagate certain opinions about a conflict often implying a moral judgment designed to put more blame on one party compared with another.[46]

Nor have efforts to find a working solution been very successful. At the Hostages Convention, where the issue was raised as to whether liberation movements can be condemned for terrorism if they engage in certain acts, the responses were inconclusive. Resuscitating the "just war" theory, one group—mostly Third World delegates—urged that there is no comparing the actions of terrorists and liberation fighters,[47] while the other—mostly Western delegates—dwelt on contemporary international values to dispute that position.[48]

It is not to be inferred from this that there is no way to determine what constitutes terrorism. Indeed, the international literature abounds in definitions of the concept.[49] And although the definitions differ, they all share certain values by which a working distinction between liberation movements and terrorism can be considered. For our purposes, it may be possible to confine the investigation to those that have been advanced at international conferences.

"Terrorism" as Defined by International Bodies

At the International Conference on Terrorism and Political Crimes, held in Syracuse, Italy, in 1973, terrorism was defined as follows:

> Individual or collective coercive conduct employing strategies of terror violence which contain an international element or are directed against an internationally protected target and whose aim is to produce a power-oriented outcome. Such conduct contains an international element when:
>
> (1) the perpetrator and victim are citizens of different states or
> (2) the conduct is performed in whole or in part in more than one state.
>
> Internationally protected targets are: . . .
>
> (5) members of non-belligerent armed forces.
>
> A power-oriented outcome is: an outcome which is aimed at changing or preserving the political, social or economic structures or policies of a given state or territory by means of coercive strategies.[50]

Obviously, this definition raises a number of questions. The emphasis on the international element, for example, poses problems as to whether the term cannot apply to reprehensible intra-national acts. Again, there may be questions as to what is meant by "non-belligerent armed forces," "strategies of terror," and what status is to be accorded to an act that is planned by a state against its subjects.

Nor is this the only example of definitions that limit the concept to international and individual cases.[51] Such an approach seems surprising, since it would logically seem to exclude state terrorism, the phenomenon from which the term "terrorism" originated[52] and which is considered to be the "most dangerous brand of violence in the world."[53] But the relationship between state and individual terrorism has been an irritating issue encountered in virtually all international forums dealing with the definition of liberation movements. At the Hostages Convention, for instance, most delegates, notably those from the Third World, found the convention unacceptable if it condemned hostage taking by "liberation fighters" but excluded those massively done by colonial, racist, and alien oppressive regimes.[54] Indeed, the opposition was even more vehemently expressed in the U.N. Ad Hoc Committee on International Terrorism, wherein most of the representatives—those from Africa and the Middle East—took a stand against the exclusion of state terrorism from the definition. According to the representative of Syria, state terrorism is the principal problem, and individual terrorism becomes an international concern only when it is employed for personal gain or caprice, as distinguished from a political cause, especially against colonialism and for national liberation. He referred to the so-called state terrorism as "the most dangerous brand of violence, the most often practiced at the most comprehensive scale,"[55] and included in that terminology the Israeli diversion of a Lebanese aircraft from Beirut, the kidnaping of a Korean politician in Tokyo, the Israeli killing of an Arab in Norway, and such other acts as aerial bombardment of civilians and apartheid.

Resistance to the restriction of terrorism to individual acts is not expressed in international arenas alone. Abu-Lughod, for instance, recently propounded a similar view. According to him, the proscription of the right of individual subjects to use the only instrument by which they can defend themselves against their states is not only unjust but exposes liberation fighters to double jeopardy when state terrorism is not equally proscribed. To buttress this view, he points out that, apart from being generally more hellish than individual terrorism, state terrorism enjoys overwhelming military advantage over liberation fighters.[56]

Clearly, the position of the Third World countries is not without merit. The crucial point, however, is that the position of their opponents (mostly Western countries) does not derive from callousness about state terrorism. Rather, their concern is that the issue of state terrorism has already been a subject of numerous international instruments, notably, the U.N. Charter, the Geneva Conventions of 1949, the Genocide Convention of 1948, the Hague Codification of Customary Rules of Warfare, and the Nuremberg principles.[57]

Given the need for the law to be certain, coherent, and effective, this concern may at first seem reasonable, especially since the inclusion of the same subjects that are regulated in other legal provisions may promote uncertainties and infractions of the law in situations where the prescriptions may be inconsistent. Its simplicity, however, is that not only is the problem of inconsistency applicable to all the different legal documents listed as having already dealt with state terrorism, but virtually all these documents apply as well to individuals. One merely needs to observe the implications of self-determination and human rights, which, as evident from the U.N. Charter and documents like the Genocide Convention and the Nuremberg Charter, apply to states and individuals alike.

Even assuming these instruments are not applicable to individuals, it is still arguable that a convention is not precluded from adopting and developing principles embodied in previous documents. Again, it is arguable that the basis on which state terrorism was excluded is indefensible. For the coherence and effectiveness of the law—the principal arguments on which the exclusion of state terrorism is pivoted—might be easier to achieve if there were uniformity in the law than if there were two different categories of law to apply respectively to state and individual terrorism.

One assumption about the confinement of the provisions of the international convention to international terrorism is that domestic terrorism has already been covered by criminal legislation of any state. But obviously, this is not a good explanation for excluding state terrorism from international legislation, for domestic criminal legislation passed by individual states is not subject to international scrutiny. Moreover, while such laws certainly apply to criminals as defined by the individual states—sometimes even covering people struggling for self-determination—they hardly apply to heinous acts of states. Surely, to the extent that states can treat and punish any conduct as treasonable, terroristic, or subversive, the only inference from leaving state legislation to define and deal with terrorism is to render nugatory the so-called privileged status given to liberation movements under the contemporary international legal order.

It is evident, then, that the troublesome issue of defining terrorism in these conferences is not so much about whether both individual and state acts can constitute terrorism, but whether state terrorism should be included in international conventions. Since it is common knowledge that the term "terrorism" can apply to individual and state acts alike, it is obvious that a great deal of the difficulty will be avoided if the two are treated by the same standards.

The General Features of Terroristic Acts

Elusive as the concept of terrorism is, authorities do seem to have certain criteria for determining whether an act is terroristic. These tests include the targets or victims, motives of the actors, and the methods used. At the Jerusalem Conference on International Terrorism, one U.S. senator applied them thus:

> The idea that one person's "terrorist" is another's freedom fighter cannot be sanctioned. Freedom fighters or revolutionaries don't blow up buses containing noncombatants; terrorists do. Freedom fighters don't set out to capture and slaughter school children; terrorist murderers do. Freedom fighters don't assassinate innocent men, women, and children; terrorist murderers do."[58]

According to Lador-Lederer, what is typical of terrorism as opposed to such other movements as guerrilla warfare is that "recurrent attacks on school buses, air and bus terminals, restaurants and market places are favored as a means of striking at innocent persons, a great part of them children, women and the elderly. Again terrorism attacks persons incapable of defending themselves."[59]

Considering the need for belligerents to confine conflicts to their localities and to abide by the laws of war, particularly those postulating that civilians and nonparticipants (innocent people) should not be attacked, some of these criteria seem to be appropriate. But in practice they are not very useful. Take, for instance, the target or victim test. Often, the victims are not known till after an act has been committed. Thus, as a tool for determining the status of a given phenomenon, the target test is useful only as an ex post facto device—an attribute that does not provide certainty in any legal system.

Another problem with the target test is that it is difficult to determine who is innocent, particularly in conflicts involving the use of armed force. For, as aptly pointed out by one writer, "law and philosophy meet on marshy grounds" on the issue of who is innocent, and all who have any connection with the adversaries of a struggling faction are taken by that faction to be guilty in one way or the other.[60] Recall the Lod Airport incident, where many Christians from Puerto Rico happened to be the victims of the attack of the Popular Front for the Liberation of Palestine (P.F.L.P.). There, the P.F.L.P. considered the victims to be guilty merely because, by traveling to Israel on Israeli visas, the victims had tacitly recognized Israel—the declared enemy of the Palestinians—and consequently become enemies too.[61] Likewise, Arabs who killed thirty-two people in Rome during an attack on a U.S. airliner in 1973 did not consider the victims innocent; in their view, the victims not only did not sympathize with their cause in the Middle East conflict, but by associating themselves with the group's adversaries made themselves part of the enemy.[62]

Certainly, inasmuch as the issue of innocence is subjective, it is difficult, if not impossible, to use the victim test. Yet there is another rationale for the use of the victim test. According to Beres, the apparent randomness of the selection of targets of terrorism is designed to foster fear on the part of anyone who is aligned against the terrorist.[63] As he puts it, if the alleged enemies of terrorism are made aware that everyone, not only statesmen and political figures, is a proper object of terroristic violence, then fear and terror may become so exceptionally widespread as to drive away those who would otherwise be aligned with the enemy of the terrorist. This technique has another advantage to the terrorists: it enables them to turn worldwide attention to their demands, enhancing their chances of being favorably responded to through negotiation or as a result of the pressure of world opinion.

But the motive test, which focuses on the reason why the actors want to employ techniques of unlimited killing capabilities and why they kill and injure indiscriminately, is not useful either.[64] Although sympathizers with the victims who find fault with the techniques see no reason to consider the motives of the actors, those who favor the objectives of the actors have few qualms about the legal sanctity of the acts. Revelations made at the Hostages Convention provide a case in point. Another case was the Entebbe episode; most Third World countries found serious fault with the Israeli rescue venture but sympathized with the hijacking that occasioned it.[65]

Note that motive is subjective, psychological, and too elusive for analyzing legal issues.[66] The only area of the law where it plays any role is after the criminal liability of an actor has been determined by the twin tests of *mens rea* and *actus reus*—the intention to do a forbidden act and actually doing it—at which time it is used to determine whether there are extraneous circumstances to justify mitigating the sentence.

No doubt, in most international instruments, notably the Draft Articles on the Prevention and Punishment of Crimes against Diplomatic Agents and Other Internationally Protected Persons, although the element of intentionality was recognized, motive was ruled out.[67] The commentary to draft article 2, for instance, reads:

> While criminal intent is regarded as an essential element of the crimes covered by article 2, the expression "regardless of motive" restates the universally accepted legal principle that it is the intent to commit the act and not the reasons that led to its commission that is the governing factor.[68]

Likewise, the Inter-American Convention on the Kidnapping of Diplomats provides:

> For the purposes of this Convention, kidnapping, murder, and other assaults against the life or personal integrity of those to whom the State has the duty to give special protection according to international law, as well as extortion in connection with those crimes, shall be considered common crimes of international significance, *regardless of motive*.[69]

Other tests for determining whether an act is terroristic are whether the actors are organized, whether they pursue a public purpose or are merely acting for private ends, and whether they aim at producing a power-oriented outcome. Although none of these factors can be ruled out completely from recent cases, it is submitted that none is conclusive as to what terrorism is. To take the organizational factor, for instance, it has been suggested that for an actor to be a terrorist, the act must not only be systematic but must also be perpetrated through an organization.[70] Obviously, this view cannot be taken as a substantive element in the definition of terrorism, and it has aptly been refuted by a more plausible observation that terrorism can occur in isolated cases and within a few seconds. Nor can a power-oriented outcome really provide any basis by which liberation movements and terrorism can be distinguished. The power-oriented outcome, it should be observed, is as much a feature of liberation movements as it is of any armed conflict (including terrorism) that seeks to change the existing state of affairs.

Clearly, writers and international organizations have not succeeded in differentiating between liberation movements and terrorism. Nor is much light cast by the instruments in which liberation movements have been accorded the special status. A brief look at the 1977 Protocol II to the Geneva Convention of 1949 will elucidate the point.

Significantly, the protocol does not mention liberation movements per se. Nor does it mention terrorism *expressis verbis*. Reliance on it as a test for distinguishing between the two is thus disputable. Considering its provisions in their entirety, particularly the values for which it stands, it will appear, however, that its use as a test for the two will not be too far-fetched. The crucial problem, then, is how decisively it can provide a distinction between terroristic and liberationist actions.

According to article 1, the protocol does not apply to all internal conflicts, but only those that are prolonged and of great intensity. It is also clear from the article that the actors must be "an organized armed group" operating under a "responsible command," and from a part of the beleaguered territory over which they exercise considerable control. Under paragraph 2, the protocol does not apply to "situations of internal disturbances and tensions such as riots, isolated and sporadic acts of violence, and other acts of similar nature." At first sight, these criteria may seem unreliable, at least insofar as there can be organized as well as unorganized terrorism. Their strength as tests lies, however, in the requirement for territorial control. For it is evident from the records that, whereas some of the phenomena listed in the chosen definition have considerable degree of territorial control, such an element may be hard to satisfy in most other cases. Yet it is equally evident that not all the cases listed have territorial control. Taking the struggles for change of government, for instance, one clear attribute thereof is the very transient nature of their operation. Almost all of them lack any sort of territorial control until the outcome of the conflict is determined.

Another point worth considering about the protocol is its humanitarian principles. Evidently, the only cases that can benefit from the protocol are those in which innocent people are not attacked. But it has already been indicated that the establishment of innocence is not easily done. Once again, on the issue of indiscriminate attacks on objects without military necessity, mere reflection on the complexities of the modern world and the possible risks that might be entailed in any rigorous attempts to sort out military targets from nonmilitary ones will readily show that such a test is as vulnerable as the others.

The convention also provides for certain conditions to be satisfied before its benefits can be reaped. These conditions are, inter alia, an appreciable organization of the actors, some distinctive marks by which the actors can be identified, and the application of the laws of war, which include humanitarian treatment and trial of enemy prisoners. Since most of the phenomena constituting liberation movements do not acquire the status of statehood until after the end of the conflict, it is surely difficult to imagine how they could satisfy all these conditions—a predicament that would definitely strip such struggles of the designation liberation movement and hence categorize them as terrorism. But even assuming all the tests were met, as in the Nigerian-Biafran situation,[71] it still would be doubtful whether these conditions can provide any solution to the problem since by focusing on how the struggles are organized and pursued, the convention shies away from the main issue—the substantive goals of the protagonists.

Another problem raised by virtually all the provisions of the protocol is that they do not specify a way to determine whether its conditions have been satisfied. It thus, arguably, solves no issue, inasmuch as the problem of objectivity—the tendency for each faction to accuse its adversary of having transgressed the conditions—remains. It has, of course, been argued brilliantly that because the protocol was meant to "develop and supplement" the provisions of the Geneva Convention of 1949, the supervisory system of the latter is still extant and hence applicable to the issues arising from the provisions of the protocol.[72] The difficulty with this view, however, is that, apart from the fact that the provision in question did not expressly call for supervision to determine whether or not the conditions have been satisfied, the provision is permissive, thus making it doubtful whether the so-called supervision would be employed in all cases.[73]

As can be seen, distinguishing between liberation movements and terrorism is difficult. Thus, unless the international community devises a clear definition and objective machinery by which that definition would be applied to cases as they arise, the issue is likely to trouble students, scholars, statesmen, and experts alike. Not that there should be no individual efforts to find a solution to the problem. Since it is the research and work of experts, students, and statesmen that provide the means by which the law of the international community is clarified and understood, continuing study of the issue by all in the international arena will be valuable. For the purposes of this inquiry, we must leave the issue of definition for future studies and proceed with discussion of the chosen cases.

"Liberation Struggles" and "Communism"

Another term used to denigrate liberation struggles is "communism." Here, "communism" is used in a perjorative sense—implying aggression, and as if it were synonymous with "liberation struggles." The most frequent manifestation of this usage is in Western or pro-Western literature and political statements. South Africa uses it interchangeably with the term "rebellion" against its anti-apartheid foes, and the United States employs it as a cloak for assistance to the El Salvadoran government and the anti-Sandinistas in their respective ventures against the El Salvadoran "rebels" and the Nicaraguan "communists." Indeed, nowhere is the equation of communism and liberation movements better highlighted than in the following: "What is 'war of national liberation?' It is in essence any war which furthers the Communist world revolution. . . . It is used to denote any effort led by Communists to overthrow by force any non-communist government."[74]

The difficulty is that the equation of liberation movements with communism treats liberation movements as if they were a communist preserve. The reasons for this are not difficult to find. In bracketing the two concepts together, the literature merely echoes what the communists themselves say about their ambitious or aggressive ventures around the world. Higgins observes:

> The traditional doctrine of non-interference has little appeal either for the revolutionary Marxist or for the newer nations that see no pacific method for altering the status quo in certain areas. The Communist nations have made it clear both in word and practice that they regard themselves as free to assist in what they term "wars of liberation."[75]

Likewise, another writer recounts:

> "War of national liberation" has become, then, one of those accordian-like terms which can be given either a strict or broad construction. Even states which have achieved independence by the most innocuous and pacific means may qualify as members of the anti-imperialist camp so long as they express the correct attitudes toward U.S. imperialism. A fortiori, Peking is likely to apply the term "war of national liberation" to almost any revolution or rebellion anywhere in the third world on the assumption that any violent disturbance can only propel the Chinese wave of the future and weaken the United States.[76]

Nor does the picture emerge from Western literature alone. In announcing the necessity for an alliance between the liberation movements in the colonies and the struggles of the proletariat in Europe, Stalin noted: "Leninism has proved . . . that the national question can be solved only in connection with and on the basis of the proletariat revolution and that the road to victory of the revolution in the West lies through the revolutionary alliance with the liberation movements against imperialism." [77]

As to their practice, one merely needs to recall the various events culminating in the installation of communist leaders in Afghanistan and Kampuchea, and their activities in Angola, Mozambique, Ethiopia, El Salvador, and

Nicaragua either by the major communist powers themselves or through such client parties as Cuba and Nicaragua.

Clearly, the temptation to label the communist ventures as liberation movements may be irresistible. But the crucial question is why the hallowed concept "liberation" should be equated with the activities of one state, especially in this instance where the state in question is the archrival of the very countries to which the writers belong. Nor is the equation supportable by history and the practice. Liberation movements are pursued by communists and noncommunists alike and do not fall within the province of any one state. In the struggles in the Horn of Africa, for instance, it is an open secret that the question as to which faction's cause is liberation-bound cannot be answered by either the communist or the anticommunist philosophy. Thus, whereas the Soviets and the United States took sides with the opposite factions in the Somali-Ethiopian conflict and in that between the Eritreans and Ethiopia—the Soviets relying on the "liberation" slogan and the United States defending the "territorial integrity" concept—no sooner was the pro-Western regime of Ethiopia overthrown than the two superpowers in the ideological conflict switched sides to support the factions against which they had been furnishing assistance. In the Angolan crisis, the factions with anticommunist sympathies—the Uniao National Para Independencia Total de Angola (U.N.I.T.A.) and the Frente Nacional de Libertação de Angola (F.N.L.A.)—were given various kinds of assistance by the United States in much the same way as the Soviets did to their protegés, the Movimento Popular Liberação Angola (M.P.L.A.), although the amount of assistance might not have been the same. Again, in El Salvador and Nicaragua, it is a common knowledge that the United States and the Soviets have been assisting the factions with which they see eye to eye, and which they thus label as the champions of righteousness or legality. Finally, some struggles have no ideological coloration at all. The Castro and Che campaigns against the Batista regime of Cuba, for instance, did not become ideological until well after the overthrow of that regime.[78] Similarly, the Iranian revolution that ousted the shah and has been raging since has no more communist tendencies than did the Argentine struggles over the Falklands.

Considering the universality of the concept "liberation movement," especially evident in the fact that such movements are supported by both communists and noncommunists, it should be obvious that the equation of communism and liberation movements is unsupportable.

But there is another explanation—perhaps a more plausible reason—why the Western literature apparently puts communism and liberation movements in the same bracket. Evidently, one of the consequences of the Cold War is to make the rival superpowers very sensitive about their national security and hemispheres. Thus not only is any development that is likely to impair the ideological hegemony of any of the superpowers intolerable, but it attracts the strongest possible response from the rival power. The implacable Soviet responses to the minor deviations of Hungary and Czechoslovakia from the communist club—which in the Czechoslovakian situation received a strong condemnation under the so-called Brezhnev Doctrine—are dramatic examples. In the noncommunist camp, parallel cases are the United States' enunciation of the Truman Doctrine[79] in assisting Greece and Turkey against subjugation in the Eastern hemisphere, and the invocation of the Monroe Doctrine in the Cuban Missile Crisis, the Bay of Pigs expedition, and such other cases as the 1954, 1965, and 1983 interventions in Guatemala, the Dominican Republic, and Grenada, respectively.

Since the great decolonization revolution and given the appreciation that the strength of any state depends on the number of its allies, the tendency for the superpowers to be sensitive to events falling outside their hemispheres has intensified. Thus, the use of the label "communists" in Western political statements is intended to arouse nationalistic sentiments, to cultivate support for governmental activities to forestall the infiltration of the rival ideology. Thus, in spite of the worldwide revulsion against the apartheid system in South Africa, the communist factor has been repeatedly invoked in the U.S. political arena to block Western support for the victims of apartheid. In the Philippines, despite the virtual tyranny and gross corruption of the Marcos regime, the United States used the communist factor to downplay the regime's vices. It applied the usual double standards in favor of Marcos even when the overwhelming majority of Filipinos supported the credible cause of the opposition. The veil of the anticommunist rhetoric was pierced only after the struggle reached a point where nothing could save Marcos and his few Filipino cronies. Likewise, in spite of the poor human rights situation in El Salvador, the U.S. government has been assisting the failing government from being overthrown by the gallant El Salvadorans. In support of its assistance, the United States has employed several tactics, ranging from those branding the strugglers as communists/or communist-sponsored, to those about the U.S. national security and those that suggest that the human rights situation in El Salvador has improved. It is no wonder, then, that one critic explains the occasional use of communism to describe liberation movements as mere propaganda:

> Apart from resorting to a stereotyped tactics of depicting the actions of the Salvadoran opposition parties as the "intrigues of international communism" the American administration has decided to test another provocatory ploy. . . . It has declared the struggle of the Salvadoran patriots . . . as part of "organized international terrorism." Here one immediately becomes aware of two goals which the White House wants to attain. The United States wishes to

discredit the Salvadoran patriots, and to deny them international support. Moreover Washington intends to prepare the American public for a wider interference by the Pentagon and the CIA in the affairs of El Salvador and other Latin American countries.[80]

But even assuming that liberation movements and communism were really correlated, does that attribute affect the legal implications of liberation movements? International law does not specify any particular ideological or political system to be followed by all states.[81] To the extent that there is thus nothing illegal about the ideological orientation of any movement that is not inspired or fomented from outside, it should be obvious that in strict legal terms the reference to a movement as communist does not carry the stigma suggested in the literature.

"Liberation Struggles" and "Rebellion"

Another term often associated with "liberation struggles" is "rebellion." Traditionally, this term has implications that are difficult to reconcile with the privileges supposedly enjoyed by liberation movements. Since traditional international law is part of contemporary international law,[82] it is necessary to study the traditional implications of the term "rebellion" to see the extent to which that term affects the understanding of liberation movements.

Traditionally, the term "rebellion" is used with "insurgency" and "belligerency" to describe different stages of intrastate conflicts. Belligerency, the highest status in that "continuum of ascending intensity," is the stage that formalizes the rights of the opposing factions vis-à-vis other states and virtually puts the conflict on the same footing as one between two sovereign states.[83] It upgrades a conflict to the level of interstate war and thus entitles all states to choose whether to be neutral or to support any of the factions. In short, the recognition of conflict as belligerency transforms an otherwise civil war into an international one with all its legal consequences, including the right of the belligerents to impose blockade against foreign states and seize their goods as contraband, the right of the protagonists to enter foreign ports, their right to engage in visit-and-search procedures, and their right to obtain credit abroad. Kotzsch presented the position concisely: "the recognition of belligerency gives rise to definite rights and obligations under international law."[84]

As distinguished from belligerency, insurgency is considered as a partial internationalization of an internal conflict, or, to put it concisely, as a via media between belligerency and rebellion. It constitutes a more sustained and violent intrastate conflict than that dubbed "rebellion." Though the difference between insurgency and belligerency has been described by reference to the fact that, unlike insurgency, belligerency gives rise to definite rights, insurgency has certain important consequences lacking in any conflict characterized as rebellion. For not only is there nothing against recognizing insurgents as a de facto government over the territory under their control, but states are free to assist any of the parties at this stage of insurgency. In the eyes of the law, they are contestants at law and not mere law breakers.[85]

Rebellion, on the other hand, has no favorable consequences whatsoever for its participants under international law.[86] Thus, whereas states are forbidden to give any form of assistance to the rebels, the law permits foreign assistance to the beleaguered authorities. Moreover, rebels have no right to operate beyond the afflicted territory,[87] and, if they operate on the high seas, the law treats them like pirates: they are considered as *hostes humanis*, and any favorable treatment given them is illegal and considered an act of hostility against the afflicted state.

Given the different consequences arising from any of the designated stages, it is not surprising that the law has certain criteria by which to distinguish the stage of belligerency from the others:

1. The armed conflict escalates from being one of a purely local character to a general character.
2. The strugglers occupy and administer a substantial portion of the national territory.
3. The hostilities are conducted through armed forces and under a responsible authority in accordance with the rules of war.
4. There exist hostilities of such magnitude that foreign states find it necessary to define their attitude toward the contesting factions by according to them the belligerent status.[88]

The law does not stipulate the way to distinguish rebellion and insurgency. The only way to distinguish them is to consider the factual circumstances of each situation to see:

1. whether the conflict is transient in its operation;
2. whether it is a sporadic uprising; and
3. whether it is susceptible to swift suppression by the ordinary security measures of the beleaguered state.

Generally, writers are skeptical about the usefulness of any of these criteria. Although some, notably Higgins, have observed that "the criteria for the recognition of 'insurgency' are elusive,"[89] others like Lauterpacht have been quick to urge that "any attempt to lay down conditions of recognition of insurgency lends itself to misunderstanding." As he indicates realistically, "recognition of insurgency creates a factual relation in the meaning that legal rights and duties as between insurgents and outside states exist only insofar as they are expressly conceded and agreed upon for reasons of convenience, of humanity, or of economic necessity."[90] The important question is whether the use of the term "rebellion" in reference to the cases dubbed "liberation movements" is appropriate. Evidently, the crux of the matter is that the use of the term "rebellion" for cases considered to be liberation movements is not only self-contradictory but also tends to cause threats to and/or breaches of international peace and security. The reason is that the indiscriminant use of the term "rebellion" may in given conflicts attract assistance from foreign states to the battered authority as well as assistance from other foreign states to the supposed "liberation movement."

In addition, it is difficult to sustain the application of the term "rebellion" to most of the phenomena explored in this research. Take, for instance, the conflicts in El Salvador, Nicaragua, Chad, and southern Africa, to mention only a few of the cases in which the strugglers have occasionally been referred to as "rebels." By their scopes and perennial natures, it is demonstrably clear that they are too serious to be quelled by the ordinary police measures of the afflicted states. Accordingly, the use of "rebellion" to describe some of them has no legal foundation whatsoever.

Moreover, as for the struggles of transient nature—those resulting in coup d'état—the fact that most of them succeed even before the issue of foreign assistance arises is a clear indication that the reliance on the traditional criteria for the characterization of conflicts as "rebellion," "insurgency," or "belligerency" can be very misleading. In most of the cases occurring in the present system, it is not even clear whether the term "rebellion" is employed with the same understanding as that conceived in the traditional system. For often, states, which refer to the strugglers in certain cases as "rebels," show no scruple in going to the assistance of those "rebels" or in using the terms "rebellion," "patriots," "liberation fighters," and "insurgents" interchangeably.

Chapter

2

Conflict and International Law

CHARACTERIZATION OF THE STRUGGLES

One of the legacies inherited by the contemporary international system is the principle of sovereignty.[1] According to this concept, all matters occurring within a state are the concern of that state alone and are to be regulated solely by its municipal laws. States are thus forbidden to interfere with the events in another state, and international law is considered to be applicable solely to interstate matters. One question posed in this study, then, is the extent to which liberation movements can be regulated by international law since most liberation movements are pursued by nonstates. Because there are many varieties of liberation movements, this question would be answered according to the classification of the movements.

The Anticolonial Cases

The status of anticolonial movements engaged international attention in the first decade after the United Nations was formed. Hitherto, colonial issues had been held to be a matter within the domestic jurisdiction of colonial masters, because the colonies were considered as integral parts of the territories of their metropolitan powers.[2] On virtually all the occasions when the colonial question was raised, the colonial powers not only invoked the notion of inseparability of the colonies from their respective metropolitan territories but also leaned on the domestic-jurisdiction clause of the U.N. Charter.[3] In all these cases, however, the United Nations failed to accept these age-old colonial arguments. This position has been confirmed in the famous 1970 Declaration on Friendly Relations, which confirms the obsolescence of the domestic-jurisdiction argument by branding the colonies as separate from their masters and enjoining the latter to

32

comply with the international regulations relating to human rights and self-determination in their dealings with their dependent territories.[4]

The Secessionist Cases

Since the main objective of any secessionist movement is to subvert the constitutional arrangement of the state of which the strugglers have been a part, it is possible to characterize secessions as internal conflicts. This characterization might, however, raise some questions. First, there is the issue of self-determination—whether the international nature of that concept does not give the secessionist struggle an international character. Although this question has proven difficult, especially because of ambiguities in the U.N. Charter and the 1960 General Assembly Declaration on the Granting of Independence to Colonial Countries and Peoples,[5] the 1970 Declaration on Friendly Relations has made it clear that the right of self-determination may apply to secessionary cases as well. Thus it may not be entirely incorrect to treat secessionary cases as international conflicts. However, this conclusion must be qualified, because the declaration's authorization for secessionist self-determination is not absolute: it holds only where the parent state is not representative of the people who seek to secede, or deprives them of their right to self-determination, or discriminates against them. Thus, secessionary cases that are not prompted by the transgression of the Charter's principles of human rights and self-determination may not be classified as international conflicts. Of course, the question as to whether a government is representative of its people or discriminates against some of them cannot be answered by objective criteria. However, there are certain clear-cut cases whose characterization as international conflicts cannot raise much controversy. The West-East Pakistani case, for instance, is one such case, given the refusal of the Pakistani government to allow the Bengalis to be led by their constitutionally elected leader. The issue here was clearly one of self-determination as enshrined in the Charter and, a fortiori, the Declaration on Friendly Relations.[6]

One set of cases whose characterization should not pose any difficulty is that involving more than one territory. In the struggle between the Somalis in Ethiopia and the state of Ethiopia, for instance, there is no question about the international nature of the conflict since the struggle is virtually between two sovereign states—Ethiopia and Somalia.

The Irredentist Struggles

The Somali-Ethiopian and Somali-Kenyan struggles in the Ogaden are good examples of the irredentist struggles. As has been shown, the fact that there is more than one state involved in each of these cases puts them into the international category. Another example is the Palestinian struggle against the Israelis in the Middle East. Given the fact that there is no state of Palestine, and considering also that the Palestinians and almost all the Arab states have refused to recognize the state of Israel, there may, of course, be some debate about the nature of the Arab-Israeli conflict. However, it is not inappropriate to characterize that conflict as international. First, the origin of the case is noteworthy: the conflict arose from the League mandate system[7] and therefore has an international character. Moreover, the Arabs' refusal to recognize Israel is not decisive about the status of Israel, because not only is Israel a member of the United Nations—an international organization whose membership is open to states alone—but a considerable number of states have recognized it as a state, and state practice and some authorities—the declarationists—do not accept recognition as a sine qua non for statehood.[8] Third, the fact that most of the Arab states consider themselves to be at war with Israel dispels any doubt about the international nature of that conflict. Finally, the United Nations has confirmed the international nature of the Arab-Israeli conflict by urging that the combatants be regulated by the international laws of war.[9]

The Struggles Against Existing Governments

Since these struggles are essentially against the constitutional governments of the states in which they are pursued, it is possible to characterize them as internal conflicts. However, the development of the principles of self-determination and human rights has complicated the issue. Although struggles against existing governments thus defy conclusive analysis, it may be safe to classify the cases that end within a short period and do not involve acts that can be labeled genocide, as internal conflicts. Thus, whereas struggles like those leading to the overthrow of Kwame Nkrumah, Kofi Busia, and I. K. Acheampong of Ghana, those ousting the regimes of A. T. Balewa, Yakubu Gowon, and Shehu Shagari of Nigeria, and those bringing Captain Thomas Sankara and Gnassingbe Eyadema into power in Upper Volta and Togo, respectively, can be treated as internal conflicts, others like those still raging in Chad, Nicaragua, and El Salvador—the more protracted cases—can be classified as international conflicts, since the latter not only raise human rights issues but also pose threats to, or cause breaches of, the peace by their susceptibility to intervention and counterintervention from other states.

Before considering the implications of classifying liberation struggles as international and internal conflicts, it may first be useful to consider the relative frequency of the two kinds of cases.

THE RISING INCIDENCE OF INTRASTATE CONFLICTS

Those who cling to the interstate-intrastate dichotomy as the means to categorize conflicts as international or internal have been alarmed by the rising number of cases now considered international that would formerly have been treated as internal conflicts. According to them, the intrastate conflicts have become the most threatening recurrent phenomena in the world.[10] Given the international commitment to eradicate all threats to and breaches of world peace and security, we must investigate the causes of these developments to find out where the emphasis of the pacific mission should be placed.

Reasons for the Relative Rarity of International Armed Conflicts

Among the factors cited to explain the decline in international conflicts are these:

1. the U.N. Charter's provision against the use of force;
2. the apprehension of the possible escalation of interstate conflicts into a nuclear war;
3. the existence of well-defined geographical borders; and
4. the unfashionability of war in the contemporary world.[11]

The Impact of the Provision against the Use of Force

The main provision against the use of force is article 2, paragraph 4, of the U.N. Charter. Since almost all members of the international community are parties to the Charter and thus are bound by the principle of *pacta sunt servanda* to comply with all the provisions of that document, it is difficult to dismiss the relationship between article 2(4) and the apparent decline in international armed conflicts. Upon further reflection, particularly in light of states' application of the provision, it is evident that the influence of the article on the occurrence of interstate conflicts is very slight.

First, consider the scope of the article. There is no indication in the Charter as to what is meant by the "force" it prohibits. The Charter authorizes the use of armed force in self-defense. The question, then, is, when is a state released from the prohibition under article 2(4)? Can it employ force to preempt an impending attack, and if so, what type of force can it use? Before the advent of the Charter, not only was it legitimate for states to use any type of reasonable force to dispel an imminent attack, but states were their own judges as to whether they were entitled to use force against other states. In its provision on self-defense, the Charter permits states to use force if there is "armed attack" against them. Although it can be argued, therefore, that armed attack is what article 2(4) prohibits, the provision on self-defense uses the word "inherent" to qualify the right of self-defense. Naturally, this patent contradiction between the provision against the use of force and that on self-defense has triggered controversy, raising doubts about whether the provision against the use of force can explain the decline in interstate conflicts.

The weakness of article 2(4) is even more obvious considering that, as in the past when states determined for themselves whether or not they should act in self-defense, the present system still uses that subjective way of determining when to use force. There is, of course, the principle established by the Nuremberg trials, that the issue as to whether a state should use force in self-defense is one of which an international body must be the sole judge. But what constitutes an international body on this matter? When is it to decide on the merits of the particular case—is it to make the decision while an attack is imminent or decide after an attack has been consummated? Again, what would be the status of a situation in which the international body is unable to reach a decision? And will not the concept of self-defense be compromised if an international body rather than the beleaguered state determines when an act in self-defense is warranted?

Obviously, not only is the so-called objective principle of the Nuremberg trials impractical, but it is too simple to have much credibility. Its practical bankruptcy was eloquently displayed in the U.S. intervention in Vietnam, where the virtual "escape route" from the Charter's proscription of the use of force[12] was illustrated in the State Department's invocation of the concept of collective self-defense:

> However, the Charter expressly states in article 51 that the remaining provisions of the Charter—including the limitations of article 2 paragraph 4 and the creation of United Nations machinery to keep the peace—*in no way diminish the inherent right of self-defense*. . . . Thus article 51 restates and preserves, for member states in the situations covered by the article, a long recognized principle of international law. The article is a "saving clause" designed to make it clear that no other provision in the Charter shall be interpreted to impair the inherent right of self-defense.[13]

Considering that the principle of self-defense was one of the most convenient rationalizations for the use of force by one state against another in the past, it should be obvious that the main consequence of the retention of the principle in the present system is to make current practice almost indistinguishable from that of the past.

Nor has the international system achieved much in getting the situation under control. Among the numerous situations exemplifying the virtual anarchy are the Soviet invasion of Afghanistan, the U.S. intervention in Lebanon, and the Indian use of force in Goa. In the Goan situation, the Indians said in defiance of article 2(4):

> This is a colonial question. It is a question of getting rid of the last vestiges of colonialism in India. That is a matter of faith with us. Whatever anyone else may think, Charter or no Charter, Council or no Council, that is our basic faith which we cannot afford to give up at any cost.[14]

A comparison of these cases with such others as the British position in the Falklands crisis, the Soviet invasion of Hungary and Czechoslovakia, the U.S. intervention in Guatemala and the Dominican Republic, the U.S. mining of the waters of Nicaragua and its invasion of Grenada, and more recently, the Iraqi invasion of Kuwait makes it clear that the Charter's prohibition of force is not really an obstacle for a state that wants to use force against another.

The Fear of Escalation into Nuclear War

The argument that attributes the rarity of interstate wars to general apprehension about nuclear weapons has been echoed in many contemporary writings, and its thesis is that the fear that the human race will be annihilated if an interstate conflict results in a nuclear war has restrained states from waging war with one another. Indeed, in some works the nuclear argument has even been advanced to rationalize the "happy ending" of the Cuban missile crisis.

It suffices to mention only a few of the scholars who share the argument about nuclear weapons. According to Firmage:

> The threat of nuclear war has produced sufficient restraint upon war-makers that the level of violence has been sub-nuclear since the end of World War II. In addition, formal wars between major states have been few due to the ever-present danger of conventional world war escalating to a nuclear level.[15]

Likewise, Luard remarks:

> Furthermore the strategic balance, and the development of nuclear weapons, meant that governments were less than ever prepared to risk the dangers of an all-out conflict by open war, even with conventional weapons, when they

could obtain similar ends by far less dangerous means. With hot war now so costly, cold war became the only alternative.[16]

In practical terms, these views are supported by the efforts of the major powers to reduce or slow down the arms race—the race that is considered worldwide to be the surest route to Armageddon. Further support for the argument comes from the numerous efforts by individuals and human rights organizations all over the world against the proliferation of nuclear armaments.

Yet the nuclear argument is not without flaw. First, the people who advance it to rationalize the decrease in interstate warfare use the same factor to explain the relative increase in intrastate warfare, and indeed, even contend that the superpowers pursue their interests through the latter.[17] Since nuclear war can occur by accident or miscalculation and in any context—interstate or otherwise—it is contradictory to say that the same people who fear the consequences of nuclear war will resort to intrastate warfare as a means of avoiding nuclear confrontation. The difficulty is particularly obvious if it is recalled that any assistance or intervention in an intrastate conflict by a superpower may lead to a counterintervention by other states—most particularly, the rival superpower.

Here the Berlin and the Cuban missile crises of the early 1960s are particularly relevant. A close look at the Cuban case will make the point. Although the legal implications of Cuba's importation of offensive weapons into the Western hemisphere depends on whether one places greater emphasis on the right of every sovereign state to get arms from whatever source it chooses or on the provisions of the Rio Pact[18] to which Cuba was a party,[19] the circumstances of the case make the nuclear argument virtually indefensible. First, the authority under which the United States imposed the quarantine is noteworthy. After deciding that the Cuban situation endangered the peace and security of America within the meaning of article 6 of the Rio Pact, the Organ of Consultation of the Organization of American States (O.A.S.) invoked the authority to take one or more of the measures listed in article 8 of the pact, with little or no regard to the pacific courses postulated by the Charter. It declared:

> The Council of the Organization of American States, Meeting as the Provisional Organ of Consultation, Resolves:
>
> 1. To call for the immediate dismantling and withdrawal from Cuba of all missiles and other weapons with any offensive capability;
> 2. To recommend that the member states, in accordance with Articles 6 and 8 of the Inter-American Treaty of Reciprocal Assistance, *take all measures individually and collectively, including the use of armed force, which they may deem necessary* to ensure that the Government of Cuba cannot continue to

receive from the Sino-Soviet powers military material and related supplies which may threaten the peace and security of the continent.[20]

The resolution was directed against Cuba—a nonnuclear power. Yet there is no question that the ultimate object of the resolution was to prevent the Soviet Union—a state that was not only a nuclear power but also the archrival of the United States—from fulfilling an obligation it had assumed in favor of its ally. Since it is impossible to say whether the O.A.S. could have achieved its objective without using force, including nuclear weapons if "necessary," against the Soviet Union—a possibility that could have led to a nuclear confrontation between the two superpowers—the O.A.S. resolution exposes the weakness of the nuclear-war argument.

But there are other arguments against the nuclear-war thesis. In justifying the quarantine, President John F. Kennedy cited, among others, the concept of pacific blockade. Without examining all the ramifications of that concept,[21] we can nevertheless point out that the U.S. position would definitely not have been adopted by a state that really dreaded a nuclear war. The following extract from the president's response is revealing:

> Any vessel or craft, which may be proceeding toward Cuba may be intercepted. . . .
> In carrying out this order, force shall not be used except in case of failure or refusal to comply with directions. . . . *In any case, force shall be used only to the extent necessary.*[22]

The weapons in question were missiles being shipped by a nuclear power. There was no guarantee that the "trespassing" nuclear power would not use nuclear force to back its position. The president's commitment to use only such force as was required was therefore not a secure indication that the conflict would not escalate into a nuclear war. What rendered the situation even more threatening was that the United States had made it clear on previous occasions that it would furnish any weak state with weapons to defend itself against communist aggression, and to prove the seriousness of this commitment, it had installed middle-range missiles in Turkey and other countries close to the Soviet Union—acts that surely suggest that the Soviets might violate the quarantine and face the possible consequences. Recall also the North Atlantic Treaty Organization (N.A.T.O.) policy that leaves the nuclear option open—another factor suggesting that the fear of the escalation of a conventional into a nuclear war is probably not as strong as the argument suggests.

Finally, it must be noted that only a few states presently own nuclear weapons. Those that do not have the weapons or the know-how to apply them make up more than 90 percent of the world community. Nor are conventional weapons now so obsolete as to be considered irrelevant in interstate warfare. Since conventional war still occurs without reaching the nuclear threshold, it is easy to conclude that the threat of nuclear war cannot account for the decrease in interstate warfare.

Well-Defined Geographical Boundaries

Some writers have argued that the borders between states are so well-defined in contemporary international relations that states feel less inclined to go after the territories of others.

> But there was another reason why external wars became less common. They were less necessary. The frontiers of the world were now more clearly and definitely drawn than in any earlier age. . . . In Asia and Africa, illogical though many of the frontiers inherited from colonialism were, in practice they were accepted by new governments as having a legally binding status. . . . The effect of this change was that, since territory was not coveted, external attacks became far less relevant to national aspirations. At the same time with the greater firmness of frontiers, such attacks could far less easily find justification.[23]

It is indeed true that although there are many boundary problems causing numerous armed confrontations between states in Asia, Africa, the Middle East, and Europe, the incidence of border warfare is now insignificant when compared to that of the past. It is difficult, however, to talk about the definite geographical borders without also mentioning the commitment to respect the territorial sanctity of states. Obviously, this requires some analysis of the U.N. Charter's provision on the inviolability of the territorial integrity of states, the O.A.U. Charter and resolution that urge members to accept the African continent as it is and its existing borders as "a tangible reality," and the Stimson Doctrine against the recognition of fruits of aggression. The problem with the argument, however, is that, being treaty based, it suffers from some of the problems that characterize the provision of the U.N. Charter prohibiting force. The most notable of these problems is the fact that states are free to make their own decisions as to what is in their national interest and when their resort to force against others is legitimate.

The Unfashionableness of War

The argument that war has lost its attractiveness has been presented effectively by Firmage:

Prior to this century, the law had ceased its earlier efforts to proscribe war. It is no longer fashionable to glorify war as a means of civilization or colonization. While some ascribe this in part to the civilizing effects of a changed regime of law, it is more likely that the law—like the fashionability of war—is more basically a reflection of the perception of war altered by its modern nature.[24]

At first glance, the argument seems unexceptionable. It is plausible because most of the values that triggered international wars in the past are now considered obsolete in international relations. These include religion (except the few isolated cases in the Middle East and Eastern Europe), which led to many of the religious wars in the Middle Ages; desire for aggrandizement by pursuit of "civilizing missions" and colonization, which led to wars between European states over colonies and to others like the Napoleonic wars of the late nineteenth century, as well as the Italian invasion of Ethiopia and Hitler's adventures in Europe of the twentieth century. But the argument has fatal weaknesses. Although it eloquently states that the ideas that led to war in the past are no longer cherished, it fails to explain the recent decrease in interstate warfare. The old motives no longer spur nations into war because they are no longer considered important in contemporary state practice. But their disappearance has not left a void; for experiences in Czechoslovakia, Hungary, Afghanistan, Grenada, Yemen, Lebanon, Gabon, Chad, the Falklands, the Dominican Republic, Goa, and more recently Panama, Iraq, and Kuwait—to mention only a few—all indicate that states are as prepared as ever to go to war over things they find worth pursuing. The old-fashioned values have been replaced by a new fashion that is more compatible with current realities.

None of the foregoing arguments is entirely irrelevant to a thorough explanation for the decrease in interstate warfare, yet no conclusive explanation can be gathered from any one of them. They can explain the relative dearth of interstate conflicts if they are combined with contemporary state practice, which, after all, is determined more by the interests of the states concerned than by the stipulations of international law.

Internal Conflicts

It remains to be seen whether the factors allegedly accounting for the decrease in interstate conflicts have any effect on the occurrence of intrastate conflicts. It is useful to start with the U.N. provision prohibiting the use of force. Because of its ambiguities, most writers view it as having little effect on intrastate conflicts. Judith Pinkard, for instance, argues: "Since the paragraph refers directly to international relations it only applies to force used by one state against another state and does not extend to the use of force by a state to suppress an internal disturbance."[25] Since states have an inherent right to use force to maintain order in their societies, this interpretation is obviously not without foundation. Nevertheless, the caveat in the same article, to wit, "or in any other manner inconsistent with the Purposes of the United Nations," raises doubt as to whether Pinkard's interpretation is not too parochial. Nincic puts it well:

> Less complicated might, at first sight, appear the question of the significance of the terms whereby the prohibition of the use and threat of force is confined to the "international relations" of a State. The meaning of this proviso was, of course, that States were not precluded—as they obviously could not be pre-cluded—from protecting their internal order by force if necessary in the event of a revolt or of any other attempt to subvert it by forceful means. . . . Were these relations to be regarded as "interntional" or "domestic"? Did the use of armed force by a colonial power against liberation movements in its colonies, fall, accordingly, under the prohibition of Article 2 (4)? To this question, existing realities have provided a compelling reply. . . . Suffice it to observe here that Article 2 (4) prohibits the threat and use of force, not only against "the territorial integrity and political independence of states" but also "in any other way [sic] inconsistent with the purposes of the United Nations," and that Article 1 (2) of the Charter proclaims it to be one of the basic purposes of the United Nations to "develop friendly relations among nations based on respect for the principle of equal rights and self-determination of peoples".[26]

It should be clear, then, that the problem with the scope of article 2(4) cannot be overemphasized. What makes it even more conspicuous are the many U.N. resolutions that at one and the same time forbid states to use force against their subjects who pursue their right of self-determination but fully approve those subjects' use of "any means" against their states. It is contended, how-ever, that ambiguities in the provision against the use of force cannot pose any serious problems in the determination of the effect of the Charter on the inci-dence of intrastate conflicts. For if article 2(4) cannot preclude states from fighting against each other, neither can it prevent states from using force against their subjects.

The effect of the fear of nuclear war is also uncertain. For not only does one seldom hear about intrastate conflicts in the states that own nuclear weapons, but it is also well known that the nuclear powers have been doing everything possible to prevent nonnuclear states from acquiring nuclear tech-nology and its know-how. It should be noted, however, that some writers argue that the inhibition placed by nuclear weapons on interstate warfare has led to an increase in intrastate warfare because the nuclear powers now prefer to foment conflicts in foreign states and fight through client parties.[27] Although this argument seems to be supported by practice, it is inherently self-contradictory insofar as it ignores the fact that intrastate conflicts may lead to nuclear confrontation if the superpowers are involved.

As for the impact of well-defined geographical borders, it should be obvious that the only intrastate conflicts to which this argument commonly applies are those involving the issue of secession. But, again, one cannot attribute the occurrence of secessionist conflicts solely to disagreements over the arbitrarily conceived boundaries of the afflicted states. For if the conflicts are studied closely, it will be clear that in spite of the gross ethnographic problems of most states, notably Nigeria, Pakistan, and Sudan, serious armed conflicts were not contemplated between the different ethnic units until one ethnic group was exposed to gross mistreatment by another.

Reasons for the Rising Incidence of Intrastate Conflicts

The factors responsible for the spate of intrastate conflicts are (1) the effects of World War II; (2) improvements in technology and communication systems; (3) the Cold War; and (4) the dramatization of politics.

The Effects of World War II

World War II gave rise to widely accepted values that made gross inequalities among people or wholly autocratic regimes less acceptable than they once were. According to many writers, the concepts on which these values were based—human rights and self-determination—spurred people on to rise against injustices in their societies; some asserted that even "the simple peasant, so beloved of Western writers, accepting destitution as a law of nature, became less common."[28] The war led to the creation of many weak and poor states, with the consequence that the inhabitants of those states not only looked for brighter opportunities to improve their circumstances, but found it easier to challenge their governments.

Improvements in Technology and Communications

The improvement in communication systems exposed people to developments in virtually every part of the world. Information disseminated via the radios, television networks, newspapers, and cinemas about successful revolutions encouraged people to take their destinies into their own hands and fight against existing authorities, in the hopes that their circumstances would improve. Moreover, with modern technology, particularly the use of aircraft and submarines, it became possible for the more developed countries to go to the assistance of revolutionaries in the less fortunate states at relatively little expense and with almost no likelihood of detection. Under these circumstances, people naturally grew to feel that their conflicts would not be fought by them alone—a notion that made participation in armed conflicts less risky than it had been.

The Cold War

One consequence of the Cold War was to increase the sensitivity of the superpowers to the need to maintain a balance of power in the world. To do this with minimal risk of getting into serious confrontations with each other, the superpowers resorted to the use of client parties to insure that unfriendly governments were replaced by more congenial ones.

The Dramatization of Politics

The dramatization of politics by the use of distinctive uniforms, salutes, revolutionary catch-words, and private armies made people grow to see revolution in a more attractive light. Moreover, the disappearance of foreign rule destroyed the facade of political unity in places like Africa and Asia, with the result that the underlying tribal and religious differences surfaced, causing severe tensions, conflicts, and, often, struggles for supremacy.[29] The post-independence experiences of Congo, Chad, Lebanon, Nigeria, Sudan, and Pakistan are but a few examples of this tendency.

A Critique of the Explanations for the Increase in Intrastate Conflicts

Obviously, intrastate conflicts are caused by a combination of sociopolitical and economic factors. The political factors may be external or internal. Most prominent among the external causes is the Cold War, by which the rival superpowers encourage factions with congenial ideological motivations to eject leaders who are unfriendly or difficult to manipulate. Examples are the Bay of Pigs expedition; the events that led to the overthrow of Salvador Allende of Chile, Kwame Nkrumah of Ghana, and the Benez Messaryk regime of Czechoslovakia; and the quelling of the coups in Gabon, Chad and, recently, Grenada.

Let there be no misunderstanding: not all contemporary intrastate conflicts are fomented or inspired by the superpowers. Most of the conflicts started as internal struggles before the superpowers stepped in. The struggles in the Horn of Africa, for instance, had virtually no external impetus or ideological coloration until it was in full swing. Similarly, the ongoing conflict in Iran was not initiated by the conflict between the superpowers, nor has its character changed because of their influence. Indeed, there are even cases where assistance to a faction from the superpowers is given merely for humanitarian, not political, reasons. A good example is the Algerian war of independence; evidently, apart from the main struggle between the Algerians and the French government, there was a collateral struggle between people of communist and capitalist biases for political control. Assistance to the respective factions, however, did not follow ideological lines. The French communist party, for instance, aided the noncommunist faction, and assistance from noncommunist countries was not necessarily directed toward the noncommunist faction. To understand such apparent contradictions, it is important to understand the underlying motivations for superpower intervention.

Superpowers intervene in order to establish a balance of power, but this is not the only reason. The primary motivation of the superpowers is their respective national interests—interests construed in terms of political, economic, and geostrategic importance of the state in which the conflict occurs and of the issues involved. In the Hungarian and Czechoslovakian cases, where the Soviet geostrategic and ideological interests were threatened, there was absolutely no hesitation on the part of the Soviets in stepping in to maintain their hegemony. In the case of the Cuban revolution, the United States adopted a wait-and-see attitude in the struggle between Fidel Castro and Fulgencio Batista so long as the struggle was nonideological. Its change in attitude occurred only when Castro exhibited hostility against the United States and gave the impression that Cuba was going communist. The Bay of Pigs incident was a mild demonstration of the United States' sensitivity to the establishment of hostile regimes in places where it has geostrategic interests. In the events that led to the Cuban missile crisis, where the threat to U.S. security was greater, the imposition of the quarantine clearly illustrates the extent to which the United States would go to protect its security. One must also cite the superpower politics in the Middle East, particularly those in the Persian Gulf states. There, the United States made it clear that it will do anything necessary to preserve its economic interest, although everybody knows that political and economic interests in the area are inseparable. On the other hand, in situations where the interests of the superpowers are insignificant, their involvement has been minimal.

But contemporary intrastate conflicts cannot be explained by sociopolitical factors alone. Evidently, every intrastate conflict has some economic undercurrents.[30] In the developed countries, where economic conditions are relatively sound, the incidence of intrastate conflict is almost unheard of. Conversely, in the developing areas in Africa, Asia, and Latin America, where economic conditions are not very good, the news is replete with actual or threatened intrastate conflicts in one place or another. But even in developing countries the frequency of these events varies with the degree of economic buoyancy.

LIBERATION MOVEMENTS AND INTERNATIONAL LAW

International law may or may not apply to liberation movements, depending on whether they are characterized as being involved in international or internal conflicts. Parties in conflicts in the international category are readily tagged as subjects of international law, but those that are involved in internal conflicts are far less easily categorized. These cases require critical analysis. Is it possible to treat a conflict between a state and nonstate, as in the anticolonial or secessionist cases, as interstate conflicts? Can a nonstate make legal claims under international law for injuries inflicted by their countries or others? Under international law, the rights enjoyed by nonstates are not co-extensive with those that benefit states. Under the Statute of the I.C.J. for instance, the most important legal right—that of international adjudication—can be pursued only by states.

But the judicial process is not the only means for determining the status of international cases. The laws of war also apply to states and nonstates, to varying degrees. A nonstate can qualify for its application under several landmark instruments, notably, The Hague Rules, the Geneva Convention of 1949, and Protocols I and II to the Geneva Convention of 1977. The latter are the bases on which authorities like Baxter have outlined the difference between interstate and intrastate conflicts.[31] However, even in the so-called revolutionary document—the 1949 Geneva Convention—which for the first time brought intrastate conflicts within the purview of international law, different sets of rules were devised for interstate and intrastate conflicts.[32] There may, of course, be debate as to whether the specific mention of "conflicts of non-international" nature in the 1949 convention implies that the conflicts that have been accorded an international status—the colonial cases for self-determination—now belong to the international category, thus making them a subject of the entire convention and not just the provisions for the internal category as defined above. But the recent reaffirmation of the convention in the two protocols, respectively, for international and internal conflicts have made it clear, however, that the difference lies in whether a particular conflict is between two states or within a single one. In the Protocol II, the criteria for international conflicts exclude almost all, if not all, intrastate conflicts from the purview of the Geneva Convention.

The Relevance of International Law to Internal Conflicts

The question of the applicability of international law to intrastate matters is not peculiar to the issue of liberation movements. Nor is it an issue of recent vintage. It is rooted in the concept of sovereignty, suggesting that states are the sole subjects of international law:

> Since the Law of Nations is based on the common consent of individual States, and not on individual human beings, States solely and exclusively are the subjects of international law. This means that the law of Nations is a law

for the international conduct of States, and not for their citizens. Subjects of the rights and duties arising from the Law of Nations are States solely and exclusively. *An individual human being is . . . never directly a subject of international law.*[33]

In recent times, the traditional position has been the subject of controversy among three groups of scholars. The first group, which comprises authorities like L. Oppenheim, G. Schwarzenberger, D. Anzilotti, and Torsten Gihl, clings to the notion that states are the sole subjects of international law. The second, represented by L. Duguit, H. Krabbe, and Georges Schelle, claims that individuals are the sole subjects of international law; and the third school, including Hans Kelsen, A. Verdross, and P. Guggenheim, deems both states and individuals to be subjects of international law.[34]

Evidently, in taking their respective positions, the experts are influenced by the expression "subjects of international law." In a critique of the positions of the three schools, one writer has defined the "subjects of international law" as those having "rights" and "duties" under international law. However, although he included what he termed the "substantive rights and duties" in the definition, he excluded the "procedural rights," which he defined as the right to sue and be sued.[35] Since in most cases the rules of procedure are necessary preconditions for the enjoyment of substantive rights, the definition leaves a lot to be desired. Another writer provides a wider definition that covers both the substantive and procedural rights:

> The subjects of international law, or international legal persons, are those entities that have the capacity to enjoy rights and assume obligations under international law. Independent nation-states are subjects in the most complete sense of the word; they are universally recognized as having full rights and duties under law. States have the capacity, for example, to enter into treaty relationships, appear as plaintiffs or defendants before international tribunals, join international organizations and press claims against other states.[36]

Before we can endorse this definition, however, we must clarify one point. This author emphasizes the rights and duties of states, thus raising the question as to whether his definition rules out the possibility that nonstate entities like organizations and individuals can have rights and duties—the sole attributes of "subjects"—of international law. In using the term "states," however, he emphasizes that states "are subjects in the most complete sense of the word," thus implying that other entities—those lacking statehood—could also be subjects of international law, even though they may not have the full-fledged status of states.

The crucial question is whether liberation movements are subjects of international law, whether they have rights and duties under international law. For simplicity, this discussion is limited to the intrastate cases.

Are Liberation Movements Subjects of International Law?

The issue as to whether nonstates can have rights and responsibilities under international law has been considered in many recent cases and documents on international law. In *United States v. Smith*, Justice Storey, for instance, ruled:

> The Common law, too, recognizes and punishes piracy as an offense, not against its own municipal code, but as an offense against the law of nations.
> . . . The general practice of all nations in punishing all persons, whether natives or foreigners, who have committed this offense against any person whatsoever . . . *is a conclusive proof that the offense is supposed to depend, not upon the particular provisions of any municipal code, but upon the law of nations*, both for its definition and punishment.[37]

Again, in rejecting the argument that individuals are not direct subjects of international laws of war, the Nuremberg International Military Tribunal held: "Crimes against international law are committed by men, not by abstract entities, and only by punishing individuals who commit such crimes can the provisions of international law be enforced."[38]

Clearly, what these cases suggest is that, not only do individuals have obligations under international law, but they can be tried by adjudicatory bodies and punished for their illegal acts. These cases satisfy one aspect of the definition of "subjects" of international law and suggest that liberation movements do not need to qualify as states—by having territory, a government, population, and the capacity to enter into international relations[39]—to be accountable for their acts under international law. Yet it remains to be seen whether liberation movements can satisfy the other aspects of the definition: do they have rights under international law, and if they do, can they pursue their claims under that law?

It is evident from most international legal documents that individuals have rights under international law. In the U.N. Charter, this is reflected by the guarantee of human rights and self-determination for all peoples.[40] In 1948 the General Assembly clarified the meaning of "human rights" by indicating unequivocally in the Universal Declaration of Human Rights that the right of the individual is a value that cannot be ignored in international relations.[41]

Of course, doubts exist as to the significance of the declaration.[42] Nevertheless, it has become increasingly clear from recent state practice and many U.N.

documents that the principles in the declaration are binding on all members of the international community. In the 1960 U.N. Declaration on the Granting of Independence to Colonial Countries and Peoples, for instance, there was consensus that "all States shall observe faithfully and strictly the provisions of the Charter of the United Nations, the Universal Declaration of Human Rights and the present Declaration."[43] In the 1963 Declaration on the Elimination of All Forms of Racial Discrimination, article 11 states in part:

> Every State shall promote respect for and observance of human rights and fundamental freedoms in accordance with the Charter of the United Nations, and shall fully and faithfully observe the provisions of the present Declaration, the Universal Declaration of Human Rights and the Declaration on the Granting of Independence to Colonial Countries and Peoples.[44]

Again, in the two 1966 covenants—the International Covenant on Civil and Political Rights and the International Covenant on Economic, Social and Cultural Rights [45]—the rights of the individual are apparent in the provisions on the freedom of speech, press, assembly, and religion; the freedom from inhuman treatment and arbitrary arrest; the right to fair trial; and the rights to education, medical care, and other socioeconomic benefits—all of which suggest clearly that statehood is not a sine qua non for the enjoyment of international rights.

The final question is whether and how these rights may be pursued by the individual. Arguments based on the twin concepts of sovereignty and domestic jurisdiction are often advanced in opposition to the assertion that individuals may make any claims under international law. Although the U.N. response to some of these arguments in such cases as the *Treatment of the Indians in South Africa*, the *Russian Wives*, and the *Observance of Human Rights in Bulgaria, Hungary and Rumania*, as well as the ruling of the Permanent Court of International Justice (P.C.I.J.) on the *Tunis Morocco Nationality Decree* case,[46] may deflate some of these arguments, the heart of the issue remains: whether an individual can pursue a claim as an individual.

One landmark case reflecting this question is the advisory opinion *Concerning the Jurisdiction of the Courts in Danzig*. Squarely confronted with the issue of whether a treaty between two states could confer rights upon individuals to enable them to pursue their claims by themselves, the P.C.I.J. ruled:

> According to a well established principle of international law, the Beamtenabkommen [i.e., the treaty, as interpreted by the Court], being an international agreement, cannot create rights and obligations for private individuals. But it cannot be disputed that the very object of an international agreement according to the intention of the parties may be the adoption by the parties of

some definite rules creating individual rights and obligations and enforceable by the national courts. That there is such an intention in the present case can be established by reference to the terms of the Beamtenabkommen.[47]

The opinion indicates that individuals can have enforceable rights under international law, but it also suggests that those rights can be acquired only if they are conferred specifically by interstate agreements. It is thus arguable that under international law individuals ordinarily may not have rights or the capacity to pursue them on their own. The case *Concerning the Jurisdiction of the Courts in Danzig* is not the only relevant case. In the *Mavrommatis Palestine Concession* case, the court held:

> It is an elementary principle of international law that a State is entitled to protect its subjects, when injured by acts contrary to international law committed by another state, from which they have been unable to obtain satisfaction through the ordinary channels. By taking up the case of one of its subjects and resorting to diplomatic action or international judicial proceedings on his behalf, a State is in reality asserting its own right. . . . Once a State has taken up a case on behalf of one of its subjects before an international tribunal, in the eyes of the latter, the State is the sole claimant.[48]

Indeed, the point is made even more succinctly in the *Barcelona Traction, Light and Power Company* case:

> Within the limits prescribed by international law, a State may exercise diplomatic protection by whatever means and to whatever extent it thinks fit, for it is its own right that the State is asserting. *Should the natural or legal person on whose behalf it is acting consider that their rights are not adequately protected, they have no remedy in international law.* All they can do is to resort to municipal law, if means are available.[49]

In *United States ex rel. Keefe v. Dulles*, where the State Department's refusal to espouse the claims of a U.S. national who had been detained in a foreign country was challenged, the court gave its imprimatur to the traditional position, ruling that the secretary of state

> was not under a legal duty to attempt . . . to obtain Keefe's release. Quite to the contrary, the commencement of diplomatic negotiations with a foreign power is completely in the discretion of the President and the head of the Department of State, who is his political agent. The Executive is not subject to judicial control or direction in such matters [citing *United States v. Curtis Wright Export Corporation*]. Accordingly we hold the petition [which the court regarded as seeking affirmative injunctive relief against the secretary of state] was properly dismissed.[50]

Nor has it been difficult for jurists to rationalize this position. In explaining the necessity for circumscribing the capacity of the individual to seek redress from foreign governments, Sir Arnold McNair opined:

> It must be remembered that the litigation of a claim between a private individual and a foreign Government before an international tribunal is capable of exciting national feelings between two States, and I submit that *an individual uncontrolled by his Government ought not to be allowed to make that possible.* I think that is the main reason in favor of the view that, if any machinery is to be created for enabling individuals to bring claims against foreign Governments before international tribunals, their own Government must ought to be in position to give or withhold its imprimatur, for one of the main preoccupations of Governments must always be to avoid international friction.[51]

Although the I.C.J. 1966 decision on the South-West African case[52] is of doubtful validity and, indeed, has been criticized vehemently by many renowned authorities,[53] it is possible to cite it as a further example of cases elucidating the prosecutable rights of the individual under international law. That the South-West African liberation fighters have rights under international law is a fact that cannot be disputed.[54] But the crucial question is: how enforceable were those rights at the time of the 1966 decision? Since article 34 of the I.C.J. Statute makes statehood a sine qua non for appearing before the court in contentious litigation, it is obvious that the South-West Africans could have no *locus standi* to pursue their so-called international rights in the International Court. Interestingly, however, the League Covenant had a clause authorizing any former member of the defunct League to institute contentious actions in the I.C.J. to enforce the rights granted under the South-West African mandate. Needless to say, absent this provision, most of the so-called international legal rights of the South-West African liberation movement would be rights without remedy and thus would negate the well-established maxim *ubi jus ubi remedium.* Yet the provision was of no avail to the victims; the court held in the 1966 case that the applicants—Ethiopia and Liberia—lacked the requisite legal interest in the case. But one thing about the case is certain: a supposed international legal right was denied because the ultimate beneficiaries lacked the requisite legal capacity—statehood—to claim it. Even in the political organs of the United Nations, where some liberation movements have been permitted to appear and make their cases, such appearances are merely honorary: the liberation movements even here are not given the rights generally enjoyed by states; they participate only in the discussions, not in the voting.

Nevertheless, there are a number of reasons why the individual's apparent lack of procedural capacity cannot determine the issue as to whether the individual has direct rights under international law. First, as to the pursuit of claims by nationals against foreign states: there is a precondition that the individual must have exhausted all the available domestic remedies in the foreign state before the mother country can seek its so-called redress against the latter.[55] If the right to pursue a claim were really that of the state of the national in question, why could that state not have the capacity to make its claim without bringing in the national? The flaw in the theory is that in situations where the individual fails to exhaust the domestic remedies, the so-called right of the individual's state becomes nonexistent. Second, if in exhausting the domestic remedies the individual is adequately compensated, not only does the person pocket all without rendering an account to the state, but the state has no further legal recourse against the other state in that particular case. Third, when a state pursues the so-called derivative right after domestic remedies have been exhausted, the damages are computed on the basis of the injury caused to the individual, not to the state.

Recently, the issue of the individual's capacity to put forth a claim in international forums has gained increasing attention in certain international quarters. Under the European Convention for the Protection of Human Rights and Fundamental Freedoms, which went into effect in 1953,[56] for instance, there is a commission—the European Commission of Human Rights—which is entrusted with studying and reporting alleged violations that may be called to its attention by member states or by individuals. The convention also has a court—the European Court of Human Rights—which deals with cases arising from states that are parties thereof. Although an individual cannot appear before the court, any member state or even the commission itself can institute a claim on behalf of an individual without encountering the problem that faced Ethiopia and Liberia in the South-West African case.

Although there may be some procedural problems regarding the rights of liberation fighters, there are instances where their rights can be pursued without much ado. The situation could be improved if the practice of the members of the European community was adopted by the world community at large, or at least by the various regional blocks constituting the world.

The International Legal System

POSITIVISM AND THE CONCEPT OF LAW

According to the positivist tradition,[1] the "law properly so called" is a command of a determinate superior, and no law can exist unless there is a supreme lawgiver with a coercive enforcement authority. To the positivists, therefore, insofar as the international order lacks an ultimate lawgiver whose behests are enforceable by threats of sanction, it is inappropriate to use "international law" to describe the way states deal with each other. In their view, what is generally called "international law" would be more properly labeled "international comity" or "positive morality." Thus, in *Queen v. Keyn*, Lord Coleridge, C.J., stated:

> Strictly speaking, international law is an inexact expression, and it is apt to mislead if its inexactness is not kept in mind. Law implies a law-giver, and a tribunal capable of enforcing it and coercing its transgressors. But there is no common law-giver to sovereign states; and no tribunal has the power to bind them by decrees or coerce them if they transgress.[2]

In defining law solely as a command from an ultimate sovereign, the theory approximates the teachings of the natural-law theorists, who treat as law only orders emanating from God. Under this definition, no regulation in any human society can qualify as law because there is no government in any society that is entirely above the laws.

But there are more direct ways to expose the fallacy in the theory. To begin with, as suggested in the label "positive morality," there is no doubt that most norms of the international system have moral overtones. Invariably, state practices, which through international pacts, judicial decisions, or custom crystallize into what is generally referred to as international law, are dictated by the

53

necessity for orderliness in international relations through inter alia an appreciable respect for humanity.[3] Yet the moral elements in the norms of the international order cannot bolster the argument that the expression "international law" is a misnomer. For, just as there are international norms that do not fall within the strict definition of morality, so, too, are there many norms of municipal legal systems with moral overtones.

Whereas "comity" is used in reference to practices that are observed by states as a matter of courtesy or convenience,[4] the term "international law" is used for conducts that are generally considered as binding in international relations. A useful illustration juxtaposes an example of comity with a norm of international relations. Thus, whereas as a matter of courtesy the United States and Canada allow each other's nationals to enter their countries for short visits without passports—a practice that does not apply in their respective relations with other countries—their treatment of each other's diplomatic agents is governed by a different arrangement, namely, rules that apply with the same force to all other diplomats in the world.

To construe law merely in terms of command and sanction is to see it solely in terms of the cops-and-robbers model of the criminal justice system, and thus to ignore entirely the extensive variety of laws—enabling statutes, commercial law, tort law, contract law, and resolutions of international bodies—whose existence does not depend on enforceability. The parochialism of positivism was pointed out by Hart when he commented that the positivist concept "plainly approximates closer to a penal statute enacted by the legislature of a modern state than to any other variety of law."[5]

Again, in the *Prometheus* case, Sir Henry Berkeley, C.J., deflated the thesis of the positivist tradition:

> It was contended on behalf of the owners of the Prometheus that the term "law" as applied to this recognized system of principles and rules known as international law is an inexact expression, that there is, in other words, no such thing as international law; that there can be no such law binding upon all nations inasmuch as there is no sanction for such law. . . . I do not concur in that contention. In my opinion a law may be established and become international, that is to say binding upon all nations by the agreement of such nations to be bound thereby, although it may be impossible to enforce obedience thereto by any given nation party to the agreement. The resistance of a nation to a law to which it has agreed does not derogate from the authority of the law because that resistance cannot, perhaps, be overcome. Such resistance merely makes the resisting nation a breaker of the law to which it has given its adherence. . . . *Could it be successfully contended that because any given person or body of persons possessed for the time being power to resist an established*

municipal law such a law had no existence? The answer to such a contention would be that the law still existed, though it might not for the time being be possible to enforce obedience to it.[6]

But to affirm the legal character of the international order is not to suggest that international issues can always be settled conclusively. If the realists' jurisprudential thought—that which postulates that the life of the law is experience rather than logic—has any relevance to contemporary practice, it is probably best reflected in the way the international community is regulated. For, unlike most municipal legal systems wherein the technique of legal reasoning that requires like cases to be treated alike is rigidly applied, the international system is by nature so loose that it affords wide opportunities for treating even similar cases differently.

This is not to suggest that there are hardly any two cases that attract a similar treatment or comparable results. As a system premised on established institutions and techniques, there are, of course, instances where previous cases are not only alluded to but also used in solving subsequent problems. The I.C.J. record, for example, is replete with instances where preexisting rules enunciated by the court itself, its predecessor the P.C.I.J, and arbitral tribunals are used to bolster the *ratio decidendi* or the *obiter dicta* of later cases—the express provisions of the I.C.J. Statute to the contrary,[7] notwithstanding. Similarly, most U.N. resolutions draw tremendous support from previous decisions of the court and/or past resolutions of the U.N. political organs, and sometimes even from cases with different factual backgrounds. One example of this is the U.N. application of the precedents established by the operations in Lebanon and Egypt to the Operation des Nations Unies, Congo (O.N.U.C) in the Congo crisis.[8] Yet, because of the complexities of the international system, the tendency to resolve cases in accordance with precedents is more the exception than the rule.

A comparison of the Goan situation and the more recent conflict over the Falkland Islands may provide a convenient starting point. As in Goa, one of the crucial issues in the Falklands was whether an irredentist claim could be made against a colonial master that for all intents and purposes had become the owner of the beleaguered territory. Although U.N. conflict-settlement devices were employed in both cases, none could provide a basis for determining the legitimacy of any of the protagonists. Yet the outcomes of the conflicts differed. Whereas the objectives of the invaders (the Indians) were realized in the Goan situation, the objectives of the invaders (the Argentines) in the Falklands ended in a fiasco. The difference raises an interesting issue: whether it would be appropriate to use the principle of effectiveness to brand the successful one as legitimate and a fortiori the abortive one as illegitimate. This question not only leads to the deferment of the legal significance of each case till after its outcome is reached but also results in the absurd conclusion that the same case can be legitimate or not, depending on whether or not it is successful. It is therefore difficult to imagine how useful the U.N. conflict-settlement devices can be in solving the emergent legal issues.

The international responses to the Congolese and Nigerian crises also illustrate the discrepancies that might be entailed in the outcomes of similar cases. Admittedly, there were certain significant differences between these cases,[9] yet their fundamental issues were similar. Like the Congolese case, the Nigerian case involved a struggle by an ethnic group that sought to secede from a country of which it had been a part since independence. In both cases, the issue was thus about how to resolve the conflict between the principle of secessionist self-determination and that of sovereign equality or territorial integrity of states. Nor did they attain different results; both the Congolese and Nigerian secessionist movements were suppressed. Yet it would be impossible to use their common outcome to determine the legality of the movements. In the Congolese case, the suppression of the secessionist movement was effected largely by U.N. intervention;[10] in the Nigerian case, however, the United Nations did not intervene. Considering that the United Nations is the highest legal body representing the conscience of the international community, these differing actions are surely not without significance. Was one antisecessionist movement legitimate while the other was illegitimate? But there can be no simple answers. The crux of the matter is that in spite of its involvement in quelling the Congolese movement, the attitude of the United Nations was too equivocal to suggest that the secessionist movement was illegal. We need only recall the organization's professed neutrality and the later casualties and financial problems that left it with no other choice than to suppress the rebellion.

Nor is it right to construe the U.N. failure to intervene in the Nigerian crisis as an indication of the international community's support for secessionist movements. The secretary general's statements at Addis-Ababa and Accra, and the U.N. agreement to leave the conflict with the African regional organization, the Organization for African Unity (O.A.U.), notwithstanding the latter's strong antisecessionist stance, are just a few of the considerations bolstering this conclusion.[11]

But even if one were to conclude that the failure of both cases was a manifestation of their common legal consequence, one has yet to reconcile that conclusion with the outcome of the Bengali movement, which succeeded in realizing its goal.

Sometimes it is even possible for the same case to receive different resolutions under the same dispute settlement machinery. In the Goan situation, for instance, it has already been observed that the response in the Security Council was conspicuously different from that in the General Assembly. The same thing occurred with the East-West Pakistani conflict. But perhaps the best example is the I.C.J decision on the South-West African (Namibia) dispute. Notwithstanding the strong support for the court's 1962 decision in which the Ethiopian and Liberian claims against South Africa were found to be justiciable,[12] the same court issued a startling verdict in 1966, urging that the applicants in the South-West African case lacked the requisite legal and material interest by which they could have *locus standi* in the case.[13]

The crucial question is how to reconcile the discrepancies in each of these sets of cases. Unfortunately, there is little information to go by. Nor is it possible to determine which cases were soundly decided and which were not. In the secessionist cases, for instance, arguments of equal persuasion can be made for territorial integrity and self-determination since there is no unanimity on the scope of the relevant law. But even if the more popular position were heavily emphasized—that which suggests that the principle of territorial integrity holds no weight in cases of gross violation of human rights[14]—a question remains as to its applicability in a case like the Nigerian one, where the battered government was able to suppress the movement.

Clearly, legal issues arising under the international system lack certainty. Considering that certainty and coherence are the crucial tenets by which a legal system achieves its twin objectives of justice and order, the value of the international system as a vehicle for settling disputes would seem to be questionable. It is conceded that to accept the lack of certainty as a predicament of the system and yet affirm its legal credibility is to accept an uncomfortable paradox. Yet the paradox is inevitable. Indeed, that paradox provides the central theme of this research, viz., that the international legal significance of liberation struggles is an issue that cannot be disposed of with any finality or objectivity. Here, it is sufficient to note simply that the international legal system is invariably a system sui generis. It has peculiar attributes and is beset with unique challenges that make broad generalizations on its modus operandi very misleading. Thus, the soundest way to understand the international legal system's responses to issues is to study the peculiar circumstances of each issue rather than to analogize from the more compact legal system of the individual states.

This, of course, is not to imply that the international legal system and those that regulate intrastate affairs are to be visualized in two water-tight compartments. Surely, the international legal system and most municipal legal systems dovetail in a number of ways. For example, not only do certain constitutions, notably the U.S. Constitution, have international law as one of their principal sources, but municipal courts are sometimes the main vehicles by which certain principles of international law (e.g., that on extradition) are rendered meaning-ful.[15] Conversely, it is well established that the sources of international law include customs and usages of civilized nations, which, no matter how restric-tively construed, will embrace almost all the municipal legal systems of the contemporary international community.

INTERNATIONAL LAW AND THE CONFLICTS RELATING TO LIBERATION MOVEMENTS

The international system has many ways to settle conflicts. It has a large edifice of rules; it has adjudicatory bodies like the I.C.J. and the European Court of Human Rights as well as arbitral tribunals, which can be ad hoc; it has regional bodies like the O.A.U. and the O.A.S.; and it has the political or-gans of the United Nations, namely, the General Assembly and the Security Council.

The first question is how to reconcile conflicting resolutions rendered by these multiple devices and how to decide which resolutions have priority. In a system whose members are all organized under one common organization, the norms recognized by all would provide a common denominator by which to reconcile conflicting dispositions. Yet it is doubtful whether these norms can carry much weight in the determination of legal issues. The resolutions are often post hoc, thus leaving legal significance of cases in abeyance until after the particular body or bodies have made a determination. Moreover, the resolu-tions are of little use in instances where a conflict is not brought before an international organization, as in the Vietnam situation, or in instances where even if the conflict were brought, the particular body is unable to pass a resolu-tion.

The Rules

The rules of the international legal system have evolved from many sources. Some result from multilateral or bilateral treaties. Others spring from customary practice of states, while others arise from resolutions of international organizations[16] and the determinations of arbitral tribunals or adjudicatory bodies. Although the peculiarities of the circumstances in which they evolve—different times, different parties, and the particular challenges to which they respond—affect their relative scope and significance, there is little, if any, indication as to their interrelationship. Nor is there any objective or comprehen-sive formula by which norms emanating from one particular source can be applied to the exclusion of norms from other sources. *Arguendo*, the fact that a particular rule might emanate from different sources is of no practical significance in cases where the formulation of it under one source entails no marked inconsistency with how it is formulated in the other relevant sources. But the problem that has so far defied solution is how to determine the priority between different sources whose formulations of a particular rule are not consistent with one another. Take, for example, the principle of self-defense, or even that of intervention in intrastate conflicts. As will be seen below, a controversy that still rages in international relations is whether the traditional laws of preemptive self-defense and intervention in favor of the ruling government in a conflict-stricken state have, respectively, been superseded by the more restrictive provision of the U.N. Charter and recent U.N. resolutions on self-determination.[17] Similarly, in a struggle involving secession, the ongoing controversy is between the traditional rule of sovereignty, which has been reincarnated by the principle of territorial integrity of the U.N. Charter, and the more recent U.N. resolutions that consider the traditional rule to be of no avail when the struggles are triggered by gross discrimination against or the violation of the human rights of the strugglers.

The problem has not been ignored. Within the framework of the international legal order there are documentary provisions and devices that provide information on how conflict between norms can be resolved.

The Normative Prescriptions on Choice of Law

Article 38 of the Statute of the I.C.J.

One possible test for choosing between norms in the international legal system is that provided in article 38 of the I.C.J. Statute:

> 1. The court, whose function is to decide in accordance with international law such disputes as are submitted to it, shall apply:
>   a. international Conventions, whether general or particular, establishing rules expressly recognized by the contesting states;
>   b. international custom, as evidence of a general practice accepted as law;
>   c. the general principles of law recognized by civilized nations;
>   d. subject to the provisions of Article 59, judicial decisions and the teachings of the most highly qualified publicists of the various nations, as subsidiary means for the determination of rules of law.[18]

One difficulty with the use of this provision as a formula for choice of law is that, apart from the fact that it is not designed to formulate how priority between norms should be resolved, an express proposal by the 1920 committee of jurists that the application of the various categories in its predecessor was to be in successive order failed adoption.[19] Yet the article is not entirely valueless:

in case of a conflict between the norms in paragraphs *a–c* and those in paragraph *d*, the former apparently have priority over the latter.

Yet the expressions "the court" and "such disputes as are submitted to it" suggest that the formula is solely for the court and is to be applied only in cases brought before it. Since the court is not the only machinery for settling international disputes, this surely raises problems as to how useful the statute can be for cases that are determined elsewhere. It may be argued, of course, that because the I.C.J. is the highest adjudicatory body for the international community, the values governing its operation would be emulated by any other machinery that seeks to achieve justice. But the fallacy in this reasoning is apparent: In the Model Rules of Arbitration, where the listed sources of law are essentially similar to those in the I.C.J. Statute, there is great leeway for parties to any conflict to determine what law is to be used by an arbitral tribunal in settling a conflict between them. Thus, the formula may be useful only if the parties to the conflict have not chosen the law to be applied to them.[20]

Nor is it possible to say that the court is required to give priority to paragraphs *a–c*. According to article 38(2), the preceding paragraph, article 38(1), "shall not prejudice the power of the Court to decide a case *ex aequo et bono, if the parties agree thereto*." Although there is little information in the statute or the *travaux preparatoires* as to what exactly this means, it has been suggested convincingly that the caveat "enables the Court to go outside the realms of law for reaching its decision." In other words, "the provision relieves the Court from the necessity of deciding according to law" and makes it possible for it to follow its own understanding of what is "fair" and what is "good faith," to render its decisions independently or even contrary to the law.[21] Considering the diversity of cases occurring on the international level, not to mention also the innumerable factors influencing the judges of the I.C.J. in their decisions, it is only fair to say that in cases where this provision is applied, the significance of the so-called formula in article 38(1) would be greatly undermined.

But even if these difficulties could be treated lightly, there would yet be the question of how the choice should be made between the different norms of the primary sources—those in paragraphs *a–c*—or those featured under the subsidiary sources, paragraph *d*. At first sight, it may seem possible to resolve this by determining whether the particular sources whose norms conflict with one another are mere evidences of the existence and content of the particular laws or the sources from which the norms originate. But it is difficult to say how useful this approach can be in the choice of law, for, quite apart from the fact that the distinction between sources—qua origin of norms—of international law and mere evidence of the existence of, or content of, any norms thereof is very fluid, it is evident that in accepting the court's jurisdiction, states can indicate what laws should govern the proceedings. Again even on the doubtful assumption that the document can be an objective tool for choice of law, it would be questionable whether conclusive answers can always be found for issues to which the formula is applied, because the norms of the system are so fraught with ambiguities that even one and the same norm may be susceptible to many conflicting interpretations.

Jus Cogens

There is near unanimity on the view that *jus cogens* have precedence over any other norms in the international system.[22] In the Vienna Convention on the Law of Treaties, article 53 states the general principle thus: "A treaty is void if, at the time of its conclusion, it conflicts with a peremptory norm of general international law."[23] In article 64 the convention stipulates further that "if a new peremptory norm of general international law emerges, any existing treaty which is in conflict with that norm becomes void and terminates."[24]

It is possible to raise questions about the scope of these provisions. The specific mention of "treaty," for instance, leaves one in the dark as to whether the instrument can be applied to norms that do not arise from treaties. Questions can also be raised about the relevance of the instrument to conflicts between treaty *jus cogens* and norms that are anything but *jus cogens*.[25] Difficult as these questions may seem, they are not beyond solution. As a convention seeking merely to codify the law that had existed from time immemorial, the provisions cannot eradicate any law *sub silento*. Thus the question of whether a norm is *jus cogens* can be useful as a test for choosing between treaty norms as well as between those of treaty and nontreaty origin.

Granted that *jus cogens* have priority over other norms in the system, a number of questions are inevitable: How is priority between two *jus cogens* to be resolved? What about that between two or more non-*jus cogens* that may be relevant to the same issue? Are they to be treated *pari passu*, or should one have priority over the other? If one is chosen to the exclusion of the other, will the excluded one not provide grounds to question the conclusiveness of any ensuing determination?

To be sure, the system has no answers for any of these questions. Nor is there a workable formula by which a norm can be spotted as a *jus cogens* for purposes of rendering the concept meaningful as a test. In the *travaux preparatoires* of the U.N. Charter, although considerable effort was made to determine the relationship between the well-established *jus cogens*—that which is expressed in the maxim *res inter alios acta nec nocet nec prodest*—and the Charter's article 2(6), which obviously conflicts with that norm, there was no direct discussion of what *jus cogens* really is.[26] The test that thus seems to be popular with authorities is the Vienna Convention's definition of "peremptory norm." It reads: "For the purposes of the present Convention, a peremptory norm of general international law is a norm accepted and recognized by the international community of states as a whole as a norm from which no derogation is permitted and which can be modified only by a subsequent norm of general international law having the same character."[27]

But in practice, this is not very helpful either. Not only is it manifestly circuitous, but it also begs the question because it does not provide the system with any means by which the *jus cogens*—the general norm recognized by the international community as a whole from which no derogation is permitted—can be identified. It is not surprising, therefore, that although there are a few norms that are generally taken as *jus cogens*, the ostensible consensus is not only isolated but takes the semblance of a hair-splitting exercise when the scope of those norms is studied against other important norms of the system. One eloquent manifestation of this was the ambiguity that characterized proceedings of the International Law Commission on its article 50—the article that eventually became article 53. At its 683rd meeting, for instance, the confusion was clear from Mike Taibi's observation: "no State could ignore certain rules of international law when concluding bilateral, regional and international treaties. Those rules, which had the character of jus cogens, included the provisions of the United Nations Charter and the Conventions on slavery, piracy and genocide."[28] The main difficulty with this observation is that not only is there a sharp disagreement about whether all the provisions of the U.N. Charter are of the character of *jus cogens*, but writers have diverse opinions on whether the U.N. Charter is a "peremptory norm" or a norm that has to give way to others when there is a conflict between them. Thus, whereas authorities, notably Verdross, deny the peremptory character of the U.N. Charter,[29] others like Tunkin disagree.[30] One cannot help but accept the following statement of Brownlie as a most apt reflection of the possible difficulties that might be entailed in the use of *jus cogens* as a test for choice of laws in the international system:

> Many problems remain: more authority exists for the category of *jus cogens* than exists for its particular content, and rules do not develop in customary law which readily correspond to the new categories. However, certain portions of *jus cogens* are the subject of general agreement, including the rules relating to the use of force by states, self-determination, and genocide. Yet even here many problems of application remain, particularly in regard to the effect of self-determination on the transfer of territory. If a state uses force to implement the principle of self-determination, is it possible to assume that one aspect of *jus cogens* is more significant than another?[31]

The Charter of the United Nations

Intimately related to the issue of *jus cogens* is whether the U.N. Charter can be used as a test for determining the priority between norms in the international system. It is not entirely inappropriate to conceive of the Charter as a "higher norm," at least on the basis that it is the most important document for the highest politico-legal organization of the international community.[32] Indeed, article 103 of the U.N. Charter states: "In the event of a conflict between the obligations of the Members of the United Nations under the present Charter and their obligations under any other international agreement, their obligations under the present Charter shall prevail."

However, the use of the Charter as a "higher norm" to test priorities among other norms needs further analysis. The article's specific elevation of obligations assumed under the Charter over "obligations under any other international agreement," for instance, has triggered debate about whether the Charter's supposed supremacy does not apply solely to conflicts between the provisions of the Charter and those of a treaty and, thus, is inapplicable to conflicts between provisions of the Charter and obligations assumed by means other than treaties.[33] Nor is this construction entirely without foundation. Apart from the clear meaning of the article, we have supportive information from the San Francisco proceedings. Not only was the article inserted to supersede a relatively broader formulation—"any other international obligations to which they are subject"—but it was adopted in spite of strong opposition.[34]

Yet it is doubtful whether this construction is compatible with the principle of effective interpretation. The obligation of the United Nations to maintain international peace and security is of a universal character—a fact amply borne out by article 2(6).[35] It would be illogical to suggest that the Charter regulates things on which states agree but leaves every state with absolute freedom to determine what it wants to do about things on which it does not agree with the other members of the international community. Since the basis of international law is agreement between states, and since agreement can be reached through a treaty or custom, any construction that seeks to restrict the relevance of the Charter's "supremacy clause" to formal agreements seems inadequate at best.

What makes the broader construction even more irresistible is that although the San Francisco debates on article 2(6) raised eyebrows as to whether it would not be offensive to the maxim *res inter alios acta nec nocere prodest*, it was finally agreed that the obligation was binding on members and nonmembers alike. Thus, it was observed in Committee IV/2:

> The Committee has considered that in the event of an actual conflict between such obligations and the obligations of Members under the Charter, particularly in matters affecting peace and security, the latter may have to prevail. The Committee is fully aware that as a matter of international law it is not ordinarily possible to provide in any convention for rules binding upon third parties. On the other hand, it is of the highest importance for the Organization that the performance of the Member's obligations under the Charter in specific

cases should not be hindered by obligations which they may have assumed to non-Member States. The Committee has had these considerations in view when drafting the text. The suggested text is accordingly not limited to pre-existing obligations between Members.[36]

Simple as it may therefore seem to use the Charter as a test for priority between norms in the international system, in practice the value of this formula is very slight. How, for instance, is the choice to be made between norms or "obligations," which, though relevant to a particular issue, might have no corresponding provision in the Charter? Significantly, neither the supremacy clause nor the Charter makes any statement on this. Nor is there much information in the *travaux preparatoires* as to how the issue is to be dealt with. It may be argued, however, that by the principle of effective construction, it may be possible to find a solution by matching the various norms against the principles of the Charter to see which of them is more compatible with the letter and spirit of that august document. This argument is not entirely new in the international legal literature. One interesting expression of it is Benjamin Cohen's, who, in extrapolating from the established canons of interpretation of statutes, observed:

> The Charter, like our Constitution, sets forth a few basic principles and leaves to those who would live under it the responsibility of finding suitable means of carrying out those principles. *Some means are specified in the Charter. But these are not necessarily exclusive.* . . . I know of no better canon of construction to be used in determining Charter power than that laid by Chief Justice Marshall in McCulloch v. Maryland. . . . "Let the end be legitimate, let it be within the scope of the Constitution, and all means which are appropriate, which are plainly adapted to that end, which are not prohibited, but consist with the letter and spirit of the Constitution. . . ." *Member States have the right and responsibility to find means which are appropriate, which are not prohibited but consist with the letter and spirit of the Charter.*[37]

But the crucial question is what meaning is to be attributed to this suggested test—the "letter and spirit" of the Charter. Although the author does not define it, it is apparent from the decision from which he borrowed it—the *McCulloch* case—that he means the broad goals of the United Nations and, a fortiori, the Charter. In other words, the test urges that in cases where the relevant norms have no direct expression within the framework of the Charter, an investigation should be made to determine which are more closely in tune with the objectives of the United Nations and to give priority to those norms.

This brings the inquiry back to whether the Charter has any defined objectives, and if so, what those objectives are. Considering the circumstances in which the United Nations was created, particularly its mission as expressed in the preamble of the Charter, one cannot escape from the conclusion that the maintenance of peace is one of the main objectives, if not the main objective, of the organization.[38] In chapter 1, entitled "Purposes and Principles," the maintenance of peace is listed along with other values that seem to be indispensable to realizing that objective. Following the statement of purposes of the organization in article 1, article 2 goes further to urge that "the Organization . . . in pursuit of the Purposes stated in Article 1, shall act in accordance with the following Principles."

To determine the scope of the objectives of the organization, one must first ask what the relationship between the "Purposes" and "Principles" is—whether they carry equal importance. The Charter makes no direct statement on this issue, but because they are presented in the same chapter as indispensable to one another, it is reasonable to conclude that they are meant to be *pari passu* and mutually constitutive of the objectives of the organization. Since this suggestion is premised on implication rather than the plain provisions of the Charter, we need to examine the subsidiary means of interpreting treaties—the preparatory work—to see whether it is sustainable.

To be sure, the *travaux preparatoires* do not say exactly whether the "Principles" have priority over the "Purposes." Nevertheless, the proceedings are not entirely silent on the issue. In dealing with the chapter on purposes and principles, the Technical Committee urged:

> The "Purposes" constitute the *raison d'etre* of the Organization. They are the aggregation of the common ends on which our minds met; hence, the cause and object of the Charter to which Member States collectively and severally subscribe. The Chapter on "Principles" sets in the same order of ideas the methods and regulating norms according to which the Organization and its Members shall do their duty and endeavor to achieve the common ends. Their understandings should serve as actual standards of international conduct.[39]

The statement refers to the purposes as the raison d'etre of the organization, but like the Charter itself, it also indicates that the raison d'etre cannot be achieved. The purposes are meaningless unless the principles are followed. When one looks at the issue in this light, particularly in view of the expression that immediately follows the description of the purposes, it is difficult to attribute different weights to the "Principles" and "Purposes." Their mutual indispensability is obvious from the fact that one is the end while the other is the means to that end.

But to construe the "Principles" and "Purposes" as an aggregation of the "letter and spirit" of the U.N. Charter is not to establish the practical significance of the Charter as a reliable tool for choice of law in the international system. The principles and purposes are sometimes irreconcilable. Nor do the norms constituting the principles or purposes agree *inter se*. How, for instance, does one reconcile the diverse means for maintaining peace with one another? Should the principles of territorial integrity, sovereignty, and friendly relations have priority over those on human rights and self-determination? What about a situation where a state employs force in violation of the human rights and the rights of self-determination of its people? Is it consistent with the undertaking to *"fulfill in good faith the obligations"*[40] to act in accordance with the Charter, if states remain unconcerned about, or pay lip service to, human rights violation in other states? Needless to say, there are no answers for these in either the Charter or its preparatory work. Likewise, the practice of the United Nations is mixed. In consequence, what states do is invoke the principles and purposes that favor their opposing positions.[41]

If even the provisions of the Charter are not consistent with one another, how can that document serve as a test for the determination of priority between norms outside the Charter? To answer that question, we need to examine more closely the modes of applying the norms of the system.[42]

THE APPLICATION OF THE NORMS IN THE INTERNATIONAL SYSTEM

One or a combination of several methods can be employed in the interpretation of the norms of the international legal system. In his commentary on how treaties are interpreted, Sir Gerald Fitzmaurice, for instance, lists three methods: the "intention of the parties" or "founding fathers" method, the "textual" or "natural meaning of the words" method, and the "teleological" or "aims and objectives" method.[43] The "intention of the parties" test favors the use of the *travaux preparatoires* of the document to be interpreted, the "textual" method employs the ordinary meaning of the words as construed within the context in which they were used at the adoption of the particular document, and the "teleological" formula interprets the words depending on the way they are used or understood in the subsequent practice of the parties to the treaty. The interpretations of the same text resulting from the use of these methods often differ.[44] Considering that the meaning given to a particular provision is the main means for determining the legality of an act, it is self-evident that even without the problem of choice of law or consistency of rules with one another, the existence of a variety of methods for interpreting norms raises difficulties. How can one use the solution offered by any one in cases where any of the others can apply?

It is suggested in some quarters that, regardless of their inherent differences, each of the methods carries the same weight as the others. Fitzmaurice says:

> The ideas of these three schools are not necessarily exclusive of one another, and theories of treaty interpretation can be construed (and are indeed normally held) compounded of all three. However, each tends to confer primacy of one particular aspect of treaty interpretation, if not to the exclusion, certainly to the subordination of the others. Each in any case employs a different approach.[45]

But not all authorities agree with this view. Between the school that supports the use of the *travaux preparatoires* and that which supports the use of the text of the document to be construed, the weight of evidence seems to favor the textual school. Thus, endorsing the I.C.J.'s opinions in the case of the *Competence of the General Assembly Regarding Admission to the United Nations* and that concerning the *Polish Postal Service in Danzig,* Judge Sir Percy Spender issued the following statement as part of his separate opinion in the *Certain Expenses* case:

> The cardinal rule of interpretation that this Court and its predecessor has stated should be applied is that words are to be read if they may so be read, in their ordinary and natural sense. If so read they make sense, that is the end of the matter. *If, however, so read they are ambiguous or lead to an unreasonable result, then and then only must the Court, by resort to other methods of interpretation, seek to ascertain what the parties really meant* when they used the words under consideration.[46]

Recently this logical position has received international imprimatur from the Vienna Convention on the Law of Treaties, which lists the *travaux preparatoires* as a "subsidiary means of interpretation."[47]

Wright cautioned that the *travaux preparatoires* could be treated only as evidence of the sense of the text, not as modifications of or exceptions to it, or even as conclusive interpretations.[48] Indeed, the significance of the *travaux preparatoires* is diminished further by the fact that the acceding parties to the U.N. Charter so outnumber the parties that brought the organization into being that an undue emphasis on what transpired in earlier negotiations is likely to run afoul of the principle of sovereign equality of states. This, needless to say, puts one in a dilemma about what purpose the *travaux preparatoires* should serve in the construction of a treaty like the Charter. Should it be discounted altogether? Should it apply to only those who participated in the negotiations? Or should it be applied with equal force to all parties to the treaty—old and new alike?

In the case *Concerning the Aerial Incident of July 27th, 1955*, judges Sir Hirsh Lauterpacht, Wellington Koo, and Spender urged in their joint dissenting opinion that even though new members would be admitted in due course, it cannot be suggested that "a treaty of that character was used as an instrument for embodying private agreements of limited scope and duration between a limited number of the Members of the U.N."[49] Though it is the dissenting opinion, it cannot be discarded because a state that applied for admission into an organization can be presumed to have accepted the organization with all the obligations and considerations that brought it into being. Pollux speaks directly to the point: "it is hard to see how a State on being elected to membership of the United Nations, could claim to disregard the preparatory work which was fully accessible to it before it applied for membership."[50]

In the context of a multilateral organization like the United Nations it would be one thing to agree to be bound by its Charter and yet another to say that in being bound one must accept all the observations in the preparatory work of that document. Given the characteristic problems of negotiations, particularly the expression of varying views, it would be difficult to say which opinions in the *travaux preparatoires* should be considered binding on all the members of the organization. It might be impossible to reach a consensus on the full implications of the views in the preparatory work; authorities are understandably skeptical about its value as a tool for interpretation. There may even be doubts about the usefulness of the *travaux preparatoires* as a supplementary means of interpretation. If the text itself cannot provide an unambiguous picture on its issue, it would be highly unlikely that, with all its characteristic ambiguities and discordancies, the *travaux preparatoires* can.

The "textual" and "aims and objects" schools focus on different criteria: the ordinary meaning of the words as understood within the context in which they were used at the time the document was adopted, and the possible meanings that the words in the text attain as a result of the way the parties conduct themselves as they face new challenges and problems over time. Here, the issue seems to defy normative solution. In the Vienna Convention, for instance, both the "textual" and the "aims and objectives" schools are presented in a way that suggests that one is as important as the other. In distinguishing between the "General Rule" and the "Supplementary Means of Interpretation," article 31 reads in part: "A treaty shall be interpreted in good faith in accordance with *the ordinary meaning to be given to the terms of the treaty in their context and in the light of its object and purpose.*"[51]

But long before the adoption of the law on treaties, authorities have argued as to which, the textual or the aims-and-objectives school, should have priority. Favoring the textual school, Judge Spender noted in the *Certain Expenses* case:

The stated purposes of the Charter should be the prime consideration in inter-preting its text. Despite current tendencies to the contrary the first task of the Court is to look, not at the *travaux preparatoires* or the practice which hitherto has been followed within the Organization, but at the terms of the Charter itself. What does it provide to carry out its purposes?
If the meaning of any particular provision read in its context is sufficiently clear . . . there is neither legal justification nor logical reason to have re-course to either the travaux preparatoires or the practice followed within the United Nations.[52]

On the other hand, Judge Alvarez places so much emphasis on the aims-and-objectives test that he considers it necessary to examine the subsequent practice even where the text is unambiguous:

The text must not be slavishly followed. . . . *When the wording of a text seems clear, that is not sufficient reason for following it literally, without taking into account the consequences of its application.* Multilateral treaties are not drafted with the help of a dictionary, and their wording is often the result of a compromise which influences the terms used in the text.[53]

Judged strictly by these observations, it may be tempting to give preference to the textual method, especially considering that the opinion of Judge Alvarez was merely dissenting and thus bereft of the weight generally carried by the majority. Again, because the acceding parties far outnumber the original mem-bers of the United Nations, undue emphasis on subsequent practice might un-dermine the Charter. Moreover, because the Charter stipulates how it should be amended *expressis verbis*,[54] any practice that is not pro forma incorporated into the document by the amending process cannot supersede any of its texts. In-deed, these arguments were emphasized by Judge Spender in his separate opin-ion in the *Certain Expenses* case:

However the Charter is otherwise described, the essential fact is that it is a multilateral treaty. It cannot be altered at the will of the majority of the Mem-ber States, no matter how that will is expressed or asserted against a protesting minority and no matter how large the majority of Member States which assert its will in this manner or how small the minority.[55]

But these arguments are not without flaw. Take Judge Spender's opinion, for instance: By flatly rejecting any kind of alteration of the Charter by what-ever means and no matter how sizable the support for the change of the mem-bers might be, the learned judge not only errs insofar as his statement negates the express provision of article 108 of the Charter according to which an amendment can be effected by a certain number of votes, but he also shows gross disregard of the fact that a constant practice can bring about a new law, as customary international law.

Nor is the argument that the aims-and-objectives test would undermine the importance of the Charter flawless. Although a reckless eradication of the collective security system by abolishing the use of the veto by the permanent members might affect the credibility of the Charter, it is equally true that the failure to accept a majority practice that consistently diverges from certain provisions would create a gap between the realities of international life and the theoretical provisions of the Charter and, hence, would diminish if not vitiate its credibility. Perhaps the best manifestations of this paradox is the failure of the majority to do away with the veto and the many new meanings that have been given to certain provisions, notably: the liberal construction of the domestic-jurisdiction clause of article 2(7); the assumption that an abstention by a permanent member from voting in the Security Council should not be taken as a veto; the increasingly new meaning given to the principle of self-determination; and the practices under the Uniting for Peace Resolution. Most of these new meanings are neither expressly supported in the Charter nor incorporated into it by amendment. The obvious question here is: What is the legal significance of these inroads?

To those whose thinking is like Judge G. Morelli's, the legality of such changes would not be in doubt, even if they had been adopted *ultra vires*. He states: "The failure of an organ to conform to the rules concerning competence has no influence on the validity of the act, which amounts to saying that each organ of the United Nations is the judge of its own competence."[56] Judge P. Spender, on the other hand, seems to have a different answer; he vehemently insists:

> I find difficulty in accepting the proposition that a practice pursued by an organ of the United Nations may be equated with the subsequent conduct of parties to a bilateral agreement and thus afford evidence of intention of the parties to the Charter (who have constantly been added to since it came into force) and in that way or otherwise provide a criterion of interpretation. Nor can I agree with a view sometimes advanced that a common practice pursued by an organ of the United Nations, though ultra vires and in point of fact having the result of amending the Charter, may nonetheless be effective as a criterion of interpretation.[57]

Of the two views, Judge Morelli's seems more persuasive because Judge Spender's runs into many difficulties, particularly when it is considered that

each of the organs of the U.N. is the master of its jurisdiction and of its interpretation of the Charter—a fact that suggests that these changes in meanings
might have been reached by bona fide construction of the relevant texts.

Although it is clear that the textual technique cannot enjoy preference over
the subsequent-practice test, the latter is so overwhelmingly favored in the literature and the case law that it might not be wrong to give it priority. Apparently,
the crucial factor is how to choose between two conflicting standards: Should
preference be given to a position that, though very persuasive at the time a
treaty was adopted, has proven to be obsolete and so unresponsive to contemporary issues as to make it almost nonexistent? Or should the preference be
given to the position which by adjustment is able to face both new challenges
and old problems expressed straightforwardly in new forms? The majority position accords with the principle of contemporaneity, expressed by Judge Alvarez: "A treaty or a text that has once been established acquires a life of its
own. Consequently, in interpreting it we must have regard to the exigencies of
contemporary life, rather than the intentions of those who framed it."[58] Likewise, Judge Azevedo states:

> The interpretation of the San Francisco instruments will always have to present
> a teleological character if they are to meet the requirements of world peace,
> co-operation between men, individual freedom and social progress. The Char-
> ter is a means not an end. To comply with its aims one must seek the methods
> of interpretation most likely to serve the natural evolution of the needs of
> mankind. Even more than in the application in municipal law, the meaning
> and scope of international texts must continually be perfected, even if the
> terms remain unchanged.[59]

Among the other supporters of the aims-and-objectives test are Brierly,[60]
McDougal, and Schachter. According to McDougal, "the major purpose of
Charter interpretation is to find out what the contemporary expectations of its
goals are, and not what some may think the words say literally or what the
founders may have initially intended."[61]

Moreover, this position has been endorsed by the I.C.J. in the case of the
*Legal Consequences for States of the Continued Presence of South Africa in
Namibia (South West Africa) Notwithstanding the Security Council Resolution
276*, where though the court found it compelling to take into account the fact
that the provisions embodying the original intentions of the parties were not
static but evolutionary, the judges added:

> The parties to the Covenant must consequently be deemed to have accepted
> them as such. That is why viewing the institution of 1919, the Court must take
> into consideration the changes which have occurred in the supervening half-

century, and its interpretation cannot remain unaffected by the subsequent development of law, through the Charter of the United Nations and by way of
customary law.[62]

Finally, the subsequent-practice test is supported by the maxim *clausula
rebus sic stantibus*, according to which a treaty is binding only so long as there
is no fundamental change in the circumstances that existed at the time of its
adoption.

But the problem does not end here. It affects as well the question of who is
authorized to interpret a legal document. Thus, after rejecting a suggestion to
confer on the I.C.J. the power of authoritative interpretation of the Charter, the
Legal Committee, Committee IV/2, considered it appropriate for any organ to
interpret the Charter but added that interpretational issues can be referred to the
court if an organ so desires.[63] Since a position that would designate the I.C.J. as
the sole interpreter of the Charter might flood the Court with insignificant issues and thereby lead to chaos, the wisdom in this principle is indisputable. But
how does one determine the priority between two conflicting interpretations by
different organs that fail to agree on any issue? Obviously, inasmuch as the
different tools of interpretation can lead to conflicting results, the permission
for any organ to interpret the Charter as it likes cannot bring uniformity to the
system. Nor is the problem alleviated merely by bringing interpretational issues
before the experts. Apart from the fact that different results may be produced
by the different experts, or sometimes even by the same body of experts, the
expert interpretations are generally not considered binding on the requesting
organ. The law was stated in the case of the *Interpretation of Peace Treaties
between Bulgaria, Hungary, and Romania*, where expert opinions were held to
be merely advisory and, hence, nonbinding.[64] In so broadly generalizing about
expert opinions, the court took its cue from the San Francisco proceedings,
which urged

> that if an interpretation made by any organ of the Organization or by a com-
> mittee of jurists is not generally acceptable it will be without binding force. In
> such circumstances, or in cases where it is desired to establish an authoritative
> interpretation for the future, it may be necessary to embody the interpretation
> in an amendment to the Charter.[65]

Although the court's position is thus technically right, its validity is doubtful inasmuch as by placing more emphasis on the *travaux preparatoires*, it
disregards the need to uphold the credibility of the court. Again, since the mere
request for expert opinion not only suggests that the requesting body is unable
to find solution for the particular issue but also presupposes that it has faith in

the experts, it is difficult to agree with this position of the law. The only occasion where the law is defensible is when the experts patently violate any of the principles of natural justice, notably the *nemo judex* rule or the duty to act in good faith.

The Relevance of International Arbitration and Adjudication

Despite the problem with the nonbinding status of expert opinion, the role the court and ad hoc committees can play in making the method of resolving conflicts more certain should not be underestimated. The court and arbitral bodies are among the mechanisms used by the international community to insure that international disputes are settled pacifically. The importance of these mechanisms is that, like all judicial systems, they are manned by experts on the law and capable of producing binding decisions on parties who use them. With these attributes, it may not be wrong to consider these avenues as important means by which the international legal system can enjoy some certainty and uniformity in its conflict resolution. Yet this optimism is qualified by a number of factors.

First, it should be realized that regardless of the court's expertise and traditional neutrality, the same ambiguous and inconsistent rules that characterize the international legal system provide the basis for the court's ultimate decisions. Thus, depending on the composition of the court or any ad hoc judicial body, decisions on similar issues may differ. Perhaps the discrepancy between the 1962 and 1966 decisions in the South-West African cases are a sufficient reminder of this real predicament. But the best way to elucidate the problem is to examine the practice of the International Court in detail.[66]

According to article 34, paragraph 1 of the I.C.J. Statute, "only states may be parties in cases before the Court." Although the court can presumably exercise jurisdiction over any interstate conflict, the question is whether it can adjudicate intrastate conflicts. For instance, in a typical liberation movement between a state and a nonstate entity, difficulties would arise as to who can be the contestants before the court. Since the issues in most of these cases center on human rights and self-determination and thus concern the whole international community, it may be tempting to expect the international community to represent the nonstate entity. But what would constitute the international community in this instance—is it any of the U.N. organs or its members? Since the United Nations is neither a state nor listed as a possible party to contentious cases, the question about the U.N. organs may be rejected *in limine*. In respect to the individual U.N. members, however, it is necessary to examine in depth the South-West African cases.

The South-West African Cases and the Requirement for Statehood in Contentious Cases Before the I.C.J.

To understand fully the relevance of the South-West African cases to the issue of conclusive solution of legal problems under international law, we must review briefly the South-West African history.

South-West Africa was formerly a German colony. After the Germans' defeat in World War I, it was placed under the League of Nations mandate system, which sought to insure that the former colonies of the vanquished were administered as a sacred trust for civilization. Because of the colony's peculiarities and contiguity to South Africa, it was categorized as a Class C mandate and placed under South Africa. Like all the other mandatory territories—those of the classes A, B, and other C types—South-West Africa was to be administered in accordance with certain regulations. For example, its "trust" instrument not only entrusted the League Council with supervision over South Africa's administration of the territory, but it conferred the individual members of the organization with the right to go before the P.C.I.J. to redress irregularities in the operation of the mandate: "If any dispute whatever should arise between the Mandatory and another Member of the League of Nations relating to the interpretation or application of the provisions of the Mandate, such dispute, if it cannot be settled by negotiation, shall be submitted to the Permanent Court of International Justice."[67]

At the terminal meeting of the League, although South Africa challenged the arrangement for orderly transition of the mandate to the succeeding U.N. regime, it failed to prevent the United Nations from assuming control over the mandate system. Thus, in acknowledging its continuing responsibilities under the mandate, South Africa agreed to "continue to administer the territory scrupulously in accordance with the obligations of the Mandate, for the advancement and promotion of the interests of the inhabitants." Again, while acknowledging that it might face technical difficulties in "compliance with the letter of the Mandate" because of the "disappearance of those organs of the League concerned with the supervision of mandates," South Africa reaffirmed its determination to comply in spirit by assuring that "the Union Government will nevertheless regard the dissolution of the League as in no way diminishing its obligations under the Mandate, which it will continue to discharge with the full and proper appreciation of its responsibilities"[68]

Quite contrary to these avowals, however, South Africa never observed its obligations under the mandate, and although numerous efforts were made by the supervisory organs of the United Nations through resolutions, negotiations by ad hoc committees, and a Committee for Good Offices, and, sometimes, even by advisory opinions of the International Court, nothing could move the South African government to comply with the terms of the mandate.[69] As a result of the ever-increasing frustration caused many states by South Africa's stubbornness, and with the U.N. General Assembly's support,[70] Ethiopia and Liberia in 1960 brought the matter to the court. South Africa filed a number of preliminary objections seeking the dismissal of the application on the grounds that the applicants, Ethiopia and Liberia, had "no *locus standi* in the contentious proceedings," and that the court consequently lacked "jurisdiction to hear, or adjudicate upon, the questions of law and fact raised in the memorials."[71]

Ethiopia's and Liberia's contentious case against South Africa was not the first occasion in which the I.C.J. had sought to settle this issue. In its 1950 advisory opinion on the *International Status of South West Africa*, the court held in part:

> According to Article 7 of the Mandate, disputes between the mandatory State and another Member of the League of Nations relating to interpretation or the application of the provisions of the Mandate, if not settled by negotiation, should be submitted to the Permanent Court of International Justice. Having regard to Article 37 of the Statute of the International Court of Justice, and Article 80, paragraph 1, of the Charter, *the Court is of opinion that this clause in the Mandate is still in force and that, therefore, the Union of South Africa is under an obligation to accept the compulsory jurisdiction of the Court* according to those proceedings.[72]

Since there is a general presumption that advisory opinions of the court are not automatically binding, it is surely doubtful how much weight could be given to this decision in an effort to determine the sustainability of South Africa's preliminary objections to the contentious case. However, the General Assembly did not have any difficulty in accepting the court's opinion as valid.[73] Considering that the presumption against the bindingness of advisory opinions may be rebutted if the opinion is generally accepted, the General Assembly's endorsement of the court's opinion would favor the determination of the procedural issue in favor of the applicants. However, there is so much controversy about the significance of resolutions of the General Assembly that one faces difficulty as to whether the General Assembly's endorsement of the 1950 advisory opinion can conclusively determine the issue under investigation. But the court was not deterred by this technicality. It affirmed its 1950 advisory opinion by holding that the applicants had *locus standi*. It reads:

> [Though] the League of Nations and the Permanent Court of International Justice have both ceased to exist, the obligation of the Respondent to submit to the compulsory jurisdiction of that Court was effectively transferred to this Court before the dissolution of the League of Nations. . . .

> The only effective recourse for protection of the sacred trust would be
> for a Member or Members of the League to invoke Article 7 and bring the dis-
> pute as also one between them and the Mandatory to the Permanent Court
> for adjudication. It was for this all-important purpose that the provision was
> couched in broad terms embracing "any dispute whatever . . . between the
> Mandatory and another Member of the League of Nations relating to the inter-
> pretation or the application of the provisions of the Mandate . . . if it cannot
> be settled by negotiation." It is thus seen what an essential part Article 7 was
> intended to play as one of the securities in the Mandates System for the obser-
> vance of the obligations by the Mandatory.[74]

However, insightful though this survey is, it must be seen merely as a tiny
part of a larger problem. For, if it is considered that the court's decision was
based mainly on article 7 of the mandate, the question immediately becomes
whether a different result could have been reached if the issue had been considered in a broader context. For example, outside the League mandate system,
can any state espouse the rights of stateless people before the I.C.J; or even
within the context of article 7 of the Covenant, can a nonmember of the League
file an action before the I.C.J. to enforce the "sacred trust" enunciated by the
Covenant?

Obviously, this question may pose some difficulties. However, with the rise
of international concepts like sovereignty, self-determination, and human
rights, it may not be entirely out of line for any state at all—whether a former
member of the League or otherwise—to contemplate litigation on behalf of
nonstates who might be faced with oppression.

Progressive and plausible as this conception might seem, it suffered a severe jolt from the I.C.J. 1966 decision. Here—a ruling supposed to dispose of
the case on the merits—the court retracted the 1962 holding, rejecting the case
on the grounds that the applicants lacked the "legal right or interest regarding
the subject matter of their claim." It is interesting that in arriving at this conclusion, the court, which was evenly split on the issue before its president, Judge
Spender, cast his veto to arrive at the so-called majority opinion,[75] apparently
readdressed the procedural issue, which had already been disposed of in 1962:

> In the course of the proceedings on the merits, comprising the exchange of
> written pleadings, the oral arguments of the Parties and the hearing of a con-
> siderable number of witnesses, the Parties put forward various contentions.
> . . . In this connection, there was one matter that appertained to the merits of
> the case but which had an antecedent character, namely the question of the
> Applicants' standing in the present phase of the proceedings,—not, that is to
> say, of their standing before the Court itself which was the subject of the

Court's decision in 1962, but the question, as a matter of the merits of the case, of their legal right or interest regarding the subject-matter of their claim, as set out in their final submissions.[76]

To the extent that this decision not only negated the court's own opinion on the same issue but made the whole proceedings between 1962 and 1966 useless, one is likely to be skeptical as to its soundness. Indeed, apart from the confusion surrounding the prevention of Judge Zafrullah Kahn of Pakistan from participating in the ruling,[77] the decision was further undermined by its digression from article 60 of the I.C.J. Statute, according to which any judgment issued by the court is final. Besides, it failed to comply with articles 61 and 78 of the I.C.J. Statute and Rules, which respectively delineate the circumstances and means by which a decision could be reviewed. Naturally, the decision outraged some members of the international community. Judge Jessup, for instance, described it in his dissenting opinion as one "*completely unfounded in law.*"

The judgment of the Court rests upon the assertion that even though—as the Court decided in 1962—the Applicants had *locus standi* to institute the actions in this case, this does not mean that they have the legal interest which would entitle them to a judgment on the merits. No authority is produced in support of this assertion which suggests a procedure of utter futility. Why should any state institute any proceeding if it lacked standing to have judgment rendered in its favor if it succeeded in establishing its legal or factual contentions on the merits? Why would the Court tolerate a situation in which the parties would be put to great trouble and expense to explore all of the details of the merits, and only thereafter be told that the Court would pay no heed to all their arguments and evidence because the case was dismissed on a preliminary ground which precluded any investigation of the merits?[78]

Likewise, the chairman of the Special Committee of 24 said sternly:

Since the last meeting of the Special Committee, the World has received with shock and dismay the judgment of the International Court of Justice on the South West Africa case. This was particularly so because by that judgment the International Court evaded every substantive legal issue placed before it for decision. . . .

One might well ask, as indeed Judge Jessup of the United States in his dissenting opinion asked, why the Court would "tolerate a situation in which the parties would be put to great trouble and expense to explore all the details of the merits, only to be told"—and that after six long years of litigation—"that the Court would pay no heed to all their arguments. . . ." Indeed, the

Court had led public opinion to believe, by its 8 to 7 majority judgment of
1962, that the issue of the parties to the dispute had already been resolved and
that it would investigate the merits of the dispute. By an accident of fate, what
was the minority of 1962 became a majority of 1966 by virtue of the casting of
the vote of Judge Spender of Australia, a circumstance allowing the 1962
minority to interpret, and, in effect, to reverse the judgment reached by a
majority of the Court in 1962.

For these reasons, it was not surprising that large sections of international
opinion believed that the judgment had diminished the prestige of the Court as
a means of settling international disputes, and raised serious doubt about its
integrity and usefulness.[79]

If it is conceded that the South African activities in South-West Africa
violate international law and the mandate alike, and if it is also understood that
all the pacific efforts for settling disputes were exhausted before the matter was
brought to the court for settlement, the issue arising from the startling 1966
decision is whether the disappointment of the international community would
not open the floodgates to an increasing use of force, as "liberation fighters"
resort to force in the belief that it is now the sole instrument by which they can
improve their circumstances. But the fact that merits special attention for our
purpose is the discrepancy between the two decisions: it is a clear manifestation
of the problem as to whether there can be any conclusive determination of the
legal significance of issues arising under the international system.

Unfortunately, the I.C.J. Statute has a provision that makes it possible for
similar cases to be treated differently.[80] It is, of course, necessary to draw a
distinction between the discrepancy between the two South-West African decisions and the implications of the article in question—article 59—lest one might
erroneously attribute the court's inconsistency to it. For whereas, by implication, the article authorizes digression only where the cases are different,[81] the
parties and the jurisdictional issues in the two South-West African cases were
the same and thus beyond the reach of that provision.

Article 59 and the Place of Judicial Precedence in
International Law

The South-West African case raises certain interesting questions about article 59. For instance, it has triggered a controversy as to whether the article's
theoretical stipulations are observed in practice. In his critique of the article,
Judge Fitzmaurice, for example, argues that although technically an international judicial decision need not be followed in other cases, in reality such
decisions often have the impact of legal precedent. He adds that some kinds
of decision are almost certain, or intrinsically likely, to be followed, and
that they may be followed even by a tribunal that, had it been the one origi-

nally called upon to decide the point involved, might have decided it differently.[82]

Since the essence of adjudication is to administer justice, and since the dispensation of justice necessitates compliance with the law, it is difficult to disagree with the distinguished judge. His conclusion seems even more irresistible if it is considered that the decisions of the court are not made in a legal vacuum, but mostly on the basis of preexisting norms that would not necessarily apply to certain parties alone. Yet it might not be sound to premise the argument solely on these attributes of adjudication. By nature, the circumstances of international disputes are so peculiar in each situation that one may question whether the use of the precedents established in one case to resolve the issues in another may be justifiable at all. These complexities of international disputes are clearly delineated in one commentary:

> The principle of *stare decisis* . . . does not apply to the International Court of Justice. . . . *A deeper reason for the inapplicability of any strict doctrine of precedent to international legal decisions is, however, the far more individual character of international judicial decisions which adjudicate disputes between states. To a far greater extent than in municipal law . . . each dispute between states tends to have an individual character.* Historical and political peculiarities and diplomatic actions often prevail over generality of a legal principle. Any strict rule of *stare decisis* would therefore be largely theoretical since the weight and variety of individual circumstances would tend to multiply the possibilities of distinguishing the case before the court from any precedent. Moreover, the balance between various national outlooks and approaches is hardly ever the same in any two cases before the I.C.J. which has 15 judges of as many different nationalities. How strongly these factors militate against even the implementation of the *res judicata* principle laid down in article 59, is evident from the contrast between the two judgments given by the International Court in the South West African Cases.[83]

That the individual character of international disputes greatly influences the outcome of cases is indisputable. If one is to cite this to suggest that "any strict rule of *stare decisis* would therefore be largely theoretical," one crucial point must be mentioned lest one be tempted to ignore a very important principle of judicial decision making. In reaching their decisions, judges employ two main tools of reasoning—*ratio decidendi* and *obiter dictum*. The former, the more important of the two, is the linchpin or legal principle on which the decision is based, whereas the latter, though often important for finding the *ratio decidendi* of the particular case, is more of an extralegal nature—the nonlegal commentary that the court uses in explaining the *ratio decidendi*. The relevance of these techniques in determining the place of *stare decisis* in international adjudication is that precedents per se are not dispensed with merely because of the peculiarities of a given situation. The factual circumstances of one case may differ from those of another, but the subject matter and issues involved in them might be so closely related that it may not be easy to distinguish between them on the basis of the legal principles involved therein.

Certain considerations might make this conclusion more complicated than it may seem at first sight. Juxtapose, for instance, international adjudication with its counterpart in municipal legal systems. Whereas the contentious parties in the latter context cannot have a say about the applicable law and, a fortiori, the decision that might be given by the court, those in any international adjudication—whether in arbitral tribunals or the I.C.J.—can influence the court's decision by expressly indicating what law is to be used.[84]

Again, one can talk about the basis of jurisdiction in international adjudication: the court cannot assume jurisdiction over any contentious case except with the consent of the contentious parties.[85] This consent may be expressed in many different ways. It may be by a *compromis* like the declaration accepting the I.C.J. compulsory jurisdiction under article 36 of the Statute. It may be by an ad hoc treaty between two or more states, or by what is commonly known as "prorogated jurisdiction," that is, an unqualified appearance before the court to contest the case on the merits. The situation is illustrated by the I.C.J. practice. Evidently, in accepting the jurisdiction of the Court as compulsory, the individual declarations do so in differing terms. Some, notably the original U.S. declaration (now abandoned), contain reservations that the court's jurisdiction cannot extend to "disputes with regard to matters which are essentially within the domestic jurisdiction of" the issuing state "*as determined by*" that state itself.[86] Others accord jurisdiction only insofar as the court cannot exercise jurisdiction "over disputes with regard to questions *which by international law* fall exclusively within the domestic jurisdiction" of their countries,[87] and still others reserve to their issuers the right to vary the terms of their acceptance by a simple notice to the secretary general.[88]

It is important to note the full implications of these reservations. With the United States' former type—what is commonly called the "Connally Reservation"—there was the tendency to nullify the court's jurisdiction whenever it was invoked. With the British type in which the domestic-jurisdiction reservation is to be applied in accordance with the principles of international law, it is obvious that with the inroads into the domestic-jurisdiction concept as expressed by the *Tunis Morocco Nationality Decree* case, the *Russian Wives* case, and the case *Concerning the Violation of Human Rights in Bulgaria, Romania and Hungary*, the final determinant would be the court. Though the Portuguese type has a nullifying effect that resembles that of the United States, the court in a somewhat restrictive interpretation insists that a notice to terminate or vary a declaration is effective to avoid jurisdiction only if that notice is given before the plaintiff state files its application, no matter how short the space of time between the application and the revocation notice.

These peculiarities of the jurisdictional circumstances of each case cannot be ignored in any study of the place of precedents in international adjudication. For instance, in a case between two states having a reservation similar to the British type, it would be impossible to apply the result of a case that had the Connally type of reservation, no matter how closely related the two cases might be in their substantive facts. This principle is bolstered by the fact that international law subjects jurisdiction to the principle of reciprocity. Thus, a reservation in a state's declaration may be used even by a state that has no analogous reservation, for, as aptly pointed out in the *Certain Norwegian Loans* case, it is only by using the greater limitations in one reservation as a common denominator for two states with different jurisdictional circumstances that the "common will of the parties, the basis of the Court's jurisdiction," can be realized.[89]

It is evident, then, that although the factual circumstances might differ from case to case, the legal principles involved are not radically different. If the governing norm is consent, it is applied in all the cases with almost the same force. Thus, although it may be right to distinguish the outcome of a case in which the consent is lacking from that in which it is found to exist, it may be possible to acknowledge the relevance of precedence inasmuch as the same legal principles apply.

The modus operandi of the international legal system cannot be fully understood without considering also the implications of compromissary clauses sometimes accompanying the grant of jurisdiction. Inasmuch as these clauses have the tendency to nullify the court's jurisdiction, a question arises as to the validity of those documents and whether the court would be right in upholding them. In the two cases wherein the court had the opportunity to pronounce on these issues, it is unfortunate that the judges declined to do so.[90] But the question cannot be ignored. Thus, in his individual opinion in the *Norwegian Loans* case and his opinion together with those of Judges Spender, Klaestad, and Armand-Ugon in the *Interhandel* case, Judge Lauterpacht did not fail to express misgivings about these self-judging reservations. He cautioned: "an instrument in which a party is entitled to determine the existence of his obligation is not a valid instrument of which a court of law can take cognizance" but "a declaration of a political principle and purpose."[91]

Considering the place of the court in any legal system—the most equitable institution for the dispensation of justice—it may be easy to agree with this critical view and, consequently, expect the court to expeditiously dispense with any reservation to achieve its noble duty of rendering justice. One comfortable way of doing this is by applying the well-established principle of interpretation—the presumption against the construction that would suggest that the parties to a treaty meant to nullify it by making its objectives unattainable. But, of course, one can also cite article 36(6) of the court's statute—the provision that empowers the court to be the judge of its own jurisdiction.

Yet it is doubtful whether the International Court would be attracted by these arguments. First, it might feel that by going outside the scope of the permission given to it, it might be offending the consensual basis of jurisdiction and, consequently, encouraging states to disregard its jurisdiction. Second, although unlike the Model Rules of Arbitration the I.C.J. Statute does not expressly permit parties to repudiate the court's decisions on grounds of noncompliance with the terms of a reservation, it is conceivable, particularly from the record of the International Court, that the court would be mindful of its integrity and prestige and, hence, comply with a compromise in order to avoid the undermining of its integrity by repealed noncompliance with its decisions. Whatever doubt might be entertained about this prediction would be dispelled if one were to look merely at the circumstances under which France revoked its acceptance of the court's jurisdiction after the *Nuclear Test* case. One can also appreciate the situation better by studying the practical and insightful commentary by Sohn in the article "Step-by-Step Acceptance of the Jurisdiction of the International Court of Justice"[92] and this reminder by Schachter:

> The fact that there has been statistically a good record of compliance must be assessed in the light of the relatively unimportant disputes that have been submitted to arbitration or judicial settlement. Should there be a wider acceptance of compulsory jurisdiction—as through compromissary clauses—the chances of non-performance would almost certainly increase; for it is evident that a state would not then be prepared to accept an adverse decision as where it had agreed to the submission of a particular dispute. Obviously, any extension of international adjudication into the area of more vital questions would also increase the risk of non-compliance.[93]

Conflict Resolution by the Political Organs of the United Nations

If even the judicial process cannot provide conclusive solution for legal questions, how useful can an exploration of the ability of the other organs of the United Nations to provide a better solution be? The General Assembly and the Security Council have certain unique attributes that would render this investigation incomplete if it were limited to the judicial process.

First, almost all the procedural limitations characterizing international adjudication are nonexistent in the operation of the political organs. For instance, neither the requirement for statehood nor that for consent is a sine qua non for the assumption of jurisdiction in any of them. The natural corollary of these, particularly the requirement for consent, is that the tendency to negate jurisdiction by extensive caveats in the declarations accepting the compulsory jurisdiction of the court is not a problem for any of these proceedings. Among the provisions that elucidate these procedural advantages are articles 10 to 14 of the U.N. Charter, according to which the General Assembly is authorized to discuss and resolve any case arising under the Charter,[94] and chapter VI of the Charter, which empowers the Security Council to investigate any situation that is likely to cause international friction, dispute, or threats to the peace. The simple inference is that, at least in theory, any case at all involving liberation movements—whether intrastate or not—can be resolved by any of the political organs.

Yet this is not to say that the political organs can offer conclusive answers for legal issues arising under the system. As international institutions, the political organs do not use any other rules than those available to all the other devices. Thus, to the extent that the rules are not only ambiguous but also lack precise means for interpretation, it is obvious that the determinations of the political organs would be inconclusive, inasmuch as different rules or methods of interpretation can always be employed to challenge the accuracy of any determination rendered.

But there are many other reasons why the political organs cannot provide a more conclusive solution for international legal issues. Because these are political organs of the organization, authorities are generally skeptical about the legal significance of resolutions issued by any of them.[95] One group insists that resolutions, particularly those issued by the General Assembly, are not only devoid of any legal significance but are also without any binding efficacy. Conversely, the other group contends that at least some of the resolutions have or are capable of having legal significance and of being binding.

The thesis that denies any legal and binding character for resolutions of the political organs is premised on, inter alia: (1) the fact that the political organs are not listed under the Charter as adjudicatory bodies; (2) that their determinations are made through political considerations; (3) that a suggestion made at the San Francisco conference to confer the General Assembly with legislative powers was overwhelmingly rejected; (4) that resolutions of the political organs are not listed under article 38 of the I.C.J. Statute as one of the sources of law to be applied by the court; and (5) that most of the provisions on the General Assembly suggest that the assembly's resolutions are recommendatory.

Although each of these points can draw support from provisions in the I.C.J. Statute, the U.N. Charter, or the *travaux preparatoires* of the United Nations, in practice none of them is beyond reproach. First, as to the argument

that the political organs are not listed as legislative organs: Admittedly, a specific suggestion to make the General Assembly a legislative organ was rejected.[96]
However, considering the general principle that the application of a rule involves an interpretation of it, one begins to wonder whether the political organs
really lack legislative powers. What makes this argument even stronger is that,
apart from the freedom for all the political organs to decide for themselves the
appropriate provisions for any issue, the General Assembly is specifically entrusted with initiating studies for the progressive development of the law.[97]
Since recommendations from these studies—either by the International Law
Commission or any ad hoc committee that might be established by the General
Assembly—becomes part of the laws of the United Nations if adopted, it
should be easy to see the role of the initiating organ (the General Assembly) as
a legislative body. It is, of course, possible to challenge the legislative nature
of the resolutions achieved by this process by arguing that the resolutions of the
political organs are not listed as a source of law under article 38 of the I.C.J.
Statute. But this argument is not sustainable, because not only can the power to
initiate studies for the development or codification of the law be exercised
through a variety of means, including conventions, but conventions are listed
under article 38 as a source of law.

But even assuming the powers of the General Assembly do not extend to
convention processes, and assuming conventions are not listed in the statute as
a source of law, the question is whether the list can suggest that the resolutions
of the political organs are devoid of legal significance. Suffice it to say that,
apart from the fact that the U.N. resolutions are not made in legal vacuum but
in the context of governing laws—a fact that arguably confers the resolutions
with legal character—it is common knowledge from the way most of the resolutions are couched that they are considered at least by the issuing bodies as
declaratory of the existing law. Surely, if this is matched against the principle
that empowers each organ to interpret the law, the legal nature of U.N. resolutions would be apparent.

Although the foregoing analysis can raise questions about why article 38
failed to include resolutions in its list, it may be easy to avoid the question if it
is considered that the provisions of the statute are not meant to be exhaustive of
the sources of law in contemporary international relations. Consider the following by Schreuer:

> At the beginning of our century, this catalogue could still claim to be an
> exhaustive description of the sources of international law. Today such a view
> of the sources of law can hardly cope with the new realities of organized
> international cooperation and communication. Even as an account of legal

sources to be applied by the International Court of Justice, Article 38/1 does not appear to be complete. The International Court of Justice, especially when giving advisory opinions, has relied on decisions of international organizations . . . to an extent and in a way which would make any attempt to explain this practice by reference to Article 38/1 hardly plausible. The United Nations general Assembly has not been oblivious of this development. In Resolution 3232 (XXIX) of 22 November 1970 it found that: "The development of international law may be reflected inter alia, by declarations and resolutions of the General Assembly which may to that extent be taken into consideration by the International Court of Justice."[98]

It is not right to deny the legal or even binding character of U.N. resolutions merely because the organs that issue them are not listed as adjudicatory bodies. Not only are some interpretations made by the political organs binding, but some of the determinations (for instance, those issued after the parties to a dispute have been given hearing by committees of inquiry established by the political organs) are issued after the exercise of judicial functions in a quasi-judicial capacity—a fact that suggests clearly that the process of adjudication cannot nullify the legal and binding character of resolutions of the General Assembly. This point is buttressed further by the rule whereby advisory opinions given by the International Court are considered to be binding only when adopted by the political body that requested it.

But perhaps the weakest argument against the legal nature of U.N. resolutions is the notion that General Assembly's resolutions are merely recommendatory. A comprehensive study on this subject elucidates the cause of this misunderstanding:

The authority expressly granted does not go beyond that of recommendation. It is assumed by most authorities that the competence of the General Assembly is limited by the "normal" "natural" or "obvious" meaning of recommendation, and that it is thereby prevented from making decisions which are legally binding upon Members.[99]

Consider also a memorandum issued by the General Assembly Legal Office:

In the United Nations practice, a declaration is a formal and solemn instrument, suitable for rare occasions when principles of great and lasting importance are being enunciated. . . . A recommendation is less formal. . . . A *"declaration" or "recommendation" is adopted by resolution of a United Nations organ. As such it cannot be binding to the parties to it.*[100]

And, based on how the term "recommendation" has traditionally been used in international organizations, it has been pointed out that the term as used with reference to the practice of the political organs is a matter of form rather than substance.[101]

Since the text of a legal document is one of its means of construction, the thesis that denies any binding efficacy for General Assembly resolutions is not without foundation. But the question is whether it is right to rely on the non-binding character of a resolution to claim that that resolution is void of legal effect. A resolution taken under a legal instrument by the appropriate authority is of a legal character by the mere fact that it is adopted under the said instrument. It should therefore be obvious that simply because a General Assembly resolution may not be binding on all the members of the international community or even the issuing organ does not necessarily make it void of legal significance. Consequently, it is submitted that the "recommendatory" nature of General Assembly resolutions cannot support the argument that the resolutions of the political organs of the organization are without legal significance.

But even aside from this issue, there are many provisions about the responsibilities of the General Assembly that cannot be construed within the ordinary meaning of the word "recommendation"—as meaning nonbinding. Examples of these are articles 22, 63 and 96 of the Charter, which respectively authorize the General Assembly to make resolutions to establish subsidiary organs, approve agreements, and seek advisory opinions.

Yet to the extent that the complexities of the system—ambiguities of the rules, lack of ultimate determining body, and lack of unanimity on the most reliable means of interpretation—may raise problems of inconsistency with their resolutions, any attempt to use them to determine issues must be cautious. Thus, the following criteria may be useful as guidelines on the amount of weight to be given to each resolution: Was the resolution adopted by a unanimous vote? If not, did it have the support of all the major powers, notably, the permanent members of the Security Council? How familiar is the issue on which the resolution was passed to the world at large, and how frequently has that particular resolution been cited? If the resolution was unanimously adopted, its weight can be presumed, especially if the unanimity includes affirmative votes of a superpower. If it was not unanimously adopted, its weight might be difficult to determine with precision, but it is important to realize that a resolution that was not unanimously adopted but has been recited frequently might carry a lot of weight. Again, a resolution that, though issued on a new subject, was adopted on the basis of a report by experts on the particular area might also carry great weight.

Although none of the various mechanisms for settling legal questions is foolproof, it may be inadequate to use one mechanism or a combination of some to the exclusion of the others. It may thus be necessary to employ all the different means in this book, but it needs to be borne in mind that inasmuch as a variety of means for settling issues only leads to different conclusions, the observations in this study may not always be definitive.

4

The History and Validity of Anticolonial Struggles

AN OVERVIEW OF THE COLONIAL PAST

The history of colonialism is too extensive to be covered in a single work. As the present enquiry concerns contemporary international law, it excludes pre-eighteenth-century colonies such as those in Carthage and Syracuse in the Mediterranean area and those along the coastlines of Egypt and Asia Minor, which developed into centers of settlement and shipping and, at times, even surpassed their own founders in many respects. Even though post-eighteenth-century colonial history encompasses territories around the globe, it is necessary for our purposes to concentrate on Africa.

One of the pressing legal questions raised about colonialism is, Which of the two—colonialism or the anticolonial movements—is justified under international law? This overview focuses on the arguments as they relate to the period before 1918, the interwar years (1918–1939), and the years since 1945.

The Legal Implications of Colonialism before 1918

One way to study the legal implications of colonialism is to examine the way colonies were acquired and administered. Colonies were acquired by a variety of means, including outright use of force and deceptive treaties backed by force when the colonized sought to protect their interests.[1] According to one account, the British, soon after being allowed to establish a base in Lagos, asked the African King Dosunmu of Lagos, to surrender the whole territory to them; when he resisted, the British engaged him in a war, forcing him to sign a cession treaty that stated:

> I Docemo, do, with the consent and advice of my Council, give, transfer, and by these presents grant and confirm unto the Queen of Great Britain, her heirs and successors for ever, the Port and Island of Lagos, with all the rights,

profits, territories and appurtenances whatsoever thereunto belonging, and as well as the profits and revenue and the direct, full and absolute dominion and sovereignty royalties thereof, freely, fully, entirely, and absolutely.[2]

As to the way colonies were administered, the best account is probably the one about South-West Africa, whose colonial experience has been referred to as "one of the blackest pages of the smudged history of European conquest of the African continent."[3] Of the Hereros, one commentary reads: "Their rebellion against the German rule precipitated four years of bitter warfare, from which the Herero emerged shattered. Germany's reprisals against subjects who dared challenge her were savage: if ever there was a case of genocide, this was it, for the 80,000 strong Herero tribe was reduced to a mere wandering 15,000."[4]

A similar picture emerges from accounts of the Belgian administration of the Congo. According to one observation:

The Congo . . . witnessed some of the worst excesses of economic and human exploitation. The Congolese were reduced to semi-slavery status in the service of King Leopold II. The major objective of the royal administration was the collection of wild rubber in the thick tropical jungle. . . . Refractionary villages were visited by punitive expeditions and natives were often killed casually.[5]

What were the legal ramifications of colonialism during this time?

On the basis of the force used to acquire the colonies, some scholars, statesmen, and liberation movements maintain that colonialism has been illegitimate from its inception. Considering that the use of force was a legitimate instrument in international relations at the time in question, it is difficult to support this position.[6]

Umorzurike has, however, advanced a different view, putting the emphasis on the fraudulent nature of the treaties by which the colonies were acquired:

A treaty is an agreement between entities having international personality. The early Europeans regarded African Kings as sovereigns and so used the nomenclature "treaty" to describe an agreement with them. The preamble to the Vienna Convention of the Law of Treaties, 1969 sets out the principles that treaties must respect. . . . The Convention did not create but merely reaffirmed these principles for they were in existence when the treaties were concluded with the African Kings. *The treaties with the African Kings, however, ignored some or all of these principles. They were obtained by the use of force or threat of force, deceit, or ignorance.* The Europeans were as ignorant of African languages as the Africans were of Europeans, nevertheless the treaties were usually written in the language (sometimes technical) of the European.[7]

Certainly, if the colonial activities were judged by contemporary standards, not only would they be illegal under the Vienna Convention on the Law of Treaties, but they would violate several U.N. resolutions, too. But the learned scholar's view is unsupportable, for he does not base his thesis directly on the provisions of the Vienna Law of Treaties. Instead, he rationalizes it by what he considers to have been *reaffirmed* by the recent law. Apart from his failure to look at the so-called preexisting law or to ascertain when that law was established and over whom, simple logic suggests that any act of force—whether or not it was effected by deception—cannot be declared illegal in a period when the use of force was a legitimate instrument of policy. What makes Umorzurike's argument even more untenable is that the colonialists—the so-called civilized nations—were the sole subjects of international law at the period in question. The colonies were considered merely "primitive" and beyond the reach of the regulation of "civilized" relationships. Thus, even if the alleged preexisting law could be proven, it would still be difficult to imagine how that could be used to challenge the legality of the transactions between the colonizers and the colonized.[8] Indeed, the author was not entirely oblivious of this fact when he made his statement:

> In general international law provided little or no protection for the Africans against European exploitation and expansionism. There were no restraints on colonial administration which was geared towards maximum economic benefit for the European State. International Law, intervened only to regulate relations among the colonizers in order to avoid the risk of wars.[9]

If the author himself concedes that international law was inapplicable to the colonies at the time in question, what then is his basis for saying that the Vienna Law of Treaties "did not create but merely reaffirmed these principles [which] were in existence when the treaties were concluded with the African Kings"? Perhaps he would have avoided the error if he had paid more attention to the results of the Berlin conference at which Africa was apportioned among the colonizers, wantonly removing people from their natural settings and placing them in unfamiliar situations with which they had grave problems in coping.[10] Nor is it of any use to say that the law between the colonial powers could not bind the colonized, for, even in their "primitive" systems, force was an acknowledged instrument of interaction.

Even if the author had rationalized his condemnation of the colonial adventures directly under the Vienna Law of Treaties, however, it would still be doubtful whether he could be right because, under articles 4 and 28, the convention cannot be applied retroactively.

The Legal Implications of Colonialism in the Interwar Period

The law between 1939 and 1945 had nothing to suggest that colonialism was illegal. Nor was there any change in the general view that international law was inapplicable to the colonies. Although essentially the legality of colonialism was thus intact, dramatic changes had endowed colonialism with an entirely different significance from its traditional meaning. The most important embodiment of these changes was the League of National Covenant. It is, possible, however, to find aspects of the change reflected in documents like the Paris Pact, also called the Kellogg-Briand Pact.

The Kellogg-Briand Pact and the Law Relating to Colonialism

The Kellogg-Briand Pact outlawed war as an instrument of national policy and forbade settlement of international disputes by nonpeaceful means.[11] Considering the view that colonies were outside the purview of international law, it is questionable whether these novel provisions could have any relevance to colonialism. Nor could the doubt be mitigated by the rule that parties to a treaty can create rights for nonparties. Given the nature of colonialism at the time of the pact, however, to use the above arguments to insulate colonialism completely from the scope of the pact is to approach the bounds of credibility. In the aftermath of the Berlin conference, almost all territories in Africa fell under one colonial master or another. Since colonies were then viewed as overseas adjuncts to the national territories of the colonizers and any further acquisition of colonies consequently would have affected another colonial master, it is arguable that the pact's proscription of the use of force—the most important tool for the acquisition of colonies—was an important change in the laws relating to colonialism.

However plausible the argument may seem that the pact theoretically outlawed the use of force to acquire colonies, it is doubtful whether practice supported the theory. A case in point is the Italian invasion and acquisition of Ethiopia in 1935. Although Ethiopia and Italy were both sovereigns as well as parties to the pact, its provision against the use of force could not deter Italy from its aggression on Ethiopia. Nor did the pact or League members do anything to prevent the impending aggression or to censure Italy after the attack. Indeed, although they pretended to reprimand Italy, they failed to do anything constructive to uphold their commitments under the terms of the Covenant and the pact; indeed, they endorsed the fait accompli. Moreover, when they purported to impose sanctions on Italy, they dropped any measures that could have affected the Italian plans. It is instructive to note how the British Liberal leader, Lloyd George, described the sanctions:

> First of all there was a great pretense that they were going to take strong action against Italy—I was taken in myself for twenty-four hours. . . . Then there were elaborate arrangements to deprive Italy of those things she could do without and then arrangements were made to sell her all those things indispensable for her to carry on the war. . . . We are even selling oil for their bombing aeroplanes. Ineffective sanctions are like sending a policeman to face gunmen with a birch rod.[12]

When Ethiopia drew the attention of the United States to Italy's threats to breach the pact, the United States asked Ethiopia to evacuate its inhabitants from the threatened area.[13] Similarly, while pretending to decry the threat of war and to dissuade Italy from its aggressive plans, the British noted: "We are not unsympathetic to the Italian need for expansion, and our actions since the War show that our sympathy is more than a sympathy of idle words."[14]

But the case that topped all these questionable applications of the pact and the covenant was *Haile Selassie v. Cable and Wireless Ltd.* Briefly, this case arose from a contract between Ethiopia and the defendant corporation at the time when Emperor Haile Selassie was the head of state of Ethiopia. Judge Bennett held—a ruling issued at the time when Italy's acquisition of Ethiopia had not fully matured—that the emperor was entitled to recover whatever was due him from the defendant. He based this ruling on the legal theory that the emperor was recognized by the British as both the de jure and de facto leader of Ethiopia. The case went on appeal, and before its final determination the British accorded a recognition to Italy as the de jure sovereign over Ethiopia, causing the court to overturn the previous decision.[15]

Technically this ruling is supportable in law. It is absolutely in accord with one bankrupt but yet to be effectively stifled principle of international law—the principle that recognition is a discretionary act on the part of the recognizing authority. Thus, as soon as the British recognized the Italians as both the de facto and de jure authority over the beleaguered territory, the "former" emperor ceased to represent Ethiopia and therefore lost the requisite *locus standi* to be a party to the case. But there is one reason why the international legal significance of the case cannot be left unchallenged. The crucial point here is the recognition of Italy as the de jure sovereign over Ethiopia. Since the recognizing state—Britain—was a party to treaties forbidding any acquisition of territory by the means used by the so-called *de jure* authority, the case not only manifests lack of faith in international diplomacy but negates the principle that a person cannot benefit from his own wrong—*ex injuria non oritur jus.*

The League of Nations Covenant: The Mandate System

As a creation of the League, the mandate system started after World War I. Its basic provisions were embodied in article 22 of the Covenant and the individual mandate arrangements between the mandatory powers and the League of Nations. The significance of these provisions for this study lies in their impact on the view that international law was inapplicable to colonialism.

The objective of the mandate system was to place the colonies of those defeated in the war—Germany and Turkey—under international tutelage as a "sacred trust of civilization." Essentially, this obligated the international community to insure the promotion and the development of the welfare of the colonies.[16] Although the commitment was to apply equally to all the colonies in question, the Covenant placed them in different categories depending on their individual needs, as determined by their respective levels of development.[17] Thus, colonies that had "reached the stage of development where their existence as independent nations can be provisionally recognized" were categorized as Class A mandates. These comprised the Turkish territories in the Middle East, notably Iraq, Palestine, Syria, and Lebanon, and were put under the British and the French mandateship. The only obligation for their mandatory powers was to render them aid and advice on governmental affairs until they were able to become completely independent.[18]

The less advanced colonies—the German colonies in central and southeast Africa—Tanganyika, Ruandi-Urundi, the Cameroons, and Togo—were classified as Class B mandates. The responsibilities of their mandatory powers included their "administration . . . under conditions which would guarantee freedom of conscience and religion, subject only to the maintenance of public order and morals, the prohibition of abuses such as the slave trade."[19]

Finally, the least developed, that is, the German colonies in South-West Africa and those in the Island of Nauru, the Samoan archipelago, and many others in the Pacific south and north of the Equator, were classified as Class C mandates. Because of "the sparseness of their population, or their small size, or their remoteness from the centers of civilization, or their geographical contiguity to the territory of the mandatory," they were to be administered in accordance with the laws of the respective mandatory powers as integral parts of those territories on the condition that the mandatory powers upheld the sureties for the good of their local inhabitants.[20]

But there were much more significant stipulations and inferences to be drawn from the way the colonies were to be treated. For example, not only were the mandatory powers prohibited from annexing any of the territories, but their services were to be performed solely for the benefit of the colonized, who were regarded as wards of civilization. Moreover, as "trustees," the mandatory powers were to render annual reports to the League Council about their activities in their assigned territories.

In evaluating the legal significance of all these structures of the mandate system, scholars have raised questions about the legal status of the requirement to report on the mandatory activities as well as on whether the inhabitants in the colonies could appear before the Mandate Commission to testify about allegations against the mandatory powers. Moreover, scholars do not always agree on the significance of the system. For instance, one remark runs:

> The Mandatory System was conceived in sin and born in iniquity. It was a huge fraud; the culmination of four years of hypocrisy, deception and dishonesty practiced by the Allied statesman upon the toiling masses of their countries who had been led to believe that they were fighting for "democracy" "self-determination" and "war to end wars", while in truth and reality they had been used as cannon fodder by the politicians to defend the vested interests of the capitalist classes; for the war was fundamentally a struggle between two coalitions of imperialist Powers for the domination of the world.[21]

According to another critic:

> The allies contravened their declared war aims in applying the mandate principle only to former German colonies. They continued to treat their own colonies as national possessions from which the glare of international law was excluded. The only distinguishing feature between a German colony and a colony belonging to a member of the allies was that the one belonged to the vanquished and the other to the victor. In both Africans were denied their sovereign rights by the use of superior power.[22]

It is impossible to reject these criticisms as being unfounded. First, why did the system apply solely to the colonies of the vanquished status? If the "benefactors" really wanted to uplift the colonies from their "primitive" circumstances to enable them to cope with the realities of modern international life, they could have created a system to apply generally to all colonies. Also, had the victorious powers really sought to develop the colonies towards maturity in international relations, placing the territories under themselves would not have been the only or even the most reasonable option. Other alternatives could have been considered: for one, placing the territories under Africans who had been trained in Europe—an alternative that, though somewhat questionable if it is considered that the educated Africans were very few, could nevertheless have been the most credible and fair program, if supported by foreign assistance in administrative matters or supervision until the Africans became skillful enough to manage their own affairs unassisted.

But perhaps the most serious problem with the mandate system is illustrated by the Bondelswart and Rehoboth cases in South-West Africa.

The Bondelswarts, who had been herded into a reserve by the South African authorities, refused to slave for the whites without pay. To insure their complete subordination, a law was passed to impose prohibitive taxes on their hunting dogs. While the matter was in dispute, an African named Abraham Morris who had just returned home from the Cape was accused of having done so without a permit. Upon South Africa's unsuccessful attempt to arrest him, the administrator, Hoffmayer, brought out ground and air troops and bombed the whole area of refuge from 3:00 P.M until dawn, indiscriminately massacring thousands of people—men, women, and children alike. An international commission was set up to investigate the situation, but, apart from its report that the incident arose out of a misunderstanding by both sides and its blame on South Africa for yielding to fear, it did hardly anything to redress the wrong or to prevent the occurrence of similar acts in the future.[23]

The Rehoboth affair[24] also happened in South-West Africa in the early stages of its history as a mandatory territory. To the utter shock of the Rehoboths, South Africa introduced restrictive laws—some even harsher than what the South-West Africans had ever known. One such law sought to curtail the Rehoboth's traditional freedom to use branding irons on their cattle. When the Rehoboths resisted, the same officer involved in the Bondelswart massacre employed both ground and air force against them.

Surely, if the mandate system is examined in the light of criticisms and facts such as those cited here, one would be inclined to doubt whether the system legally differed at all from colonialism. But there are many reasons why the two periods cannot be considered similar. First, using the South African acts as a basis for denying the legality of the system can be misleading. Merely breaking an existing law does not vitiate its existence. Thus, in the case of these nefarious South African acts, the issue is whether the international community handled the situation well, not whether the mandate system brought the affected colonies under the purview of international law. Nor is the international community's failure to condemn South Africa a good reason to be unequivocally critical of the mandate system and the law undergirding it. The mandate system was the first serious effort of the international community as a whole to extend the application of international law to colonies. Since the law was evolving and was still in its pioneering stages at the time in question, the international community's inability to insure the effectiveness of the system can be construed merely as one of the problems that characterize the beginnings of ambitious programs.

The mandate system was an important achievement for colonial peoples. In place of the almost nonexistent international regulation, colonies became subjects of international law. Colonial masters were barred from annexing their colonial territories, and although certain irregularities could not be prevented or redressed, considerable pressure was exerted on them by the mere fact that certain international bodies, notably the League Council and the Permanent Mandate Commission, were designated to monitor developments in the colonies. It is not without significance that before the demise of the League almost all the Class A mandates—Iraq, Syria, Lebanon, and Transjordan—gained their independence, achievements that, if ever dreamt of at all, were never seriously contemplated until the inception of the Covenant and its specific injunction on the mandatory powers to train those territories for independence. Finally, it is noteworthy that under article 23 of the Covenant, not only did the members of the League undertake to "secure and maintain fair and humane conditions for all men, women, and children," but they also undertook "to secure just treatment of the native inhabitants of the territories under their control." These provisions are so general in their formulation that it might not be wrong to cite them as having introduced international regulation, however minimal, for even the colonies that did not fall under the mandate system. Indeed, "The system of Mandates was not only the point of departure for the trusteeship system of the U.N., but also the turning point for the beginning of decolonization, which began to make its appearance at the end of World War II and which is still going on today, but at a progressively faster rate."[25]

Colonialism in International Relations after 1945

In many ways, the post-1945 law on colonialism is comparable to that of the interwar years. The main difference is that whereas the pre-1945 laws were limited in their scope of application, those after 1945 were so liberal in their formulation that they make it extremely difficult, if not impossible, to insulate any colony from their application. Again, whereas there was little or no conscious effort in the previous system to eradicate colonialism itself, there is an overwhelming enthusiasm in the present system to do away with colonialism.

It may be useful to study the trend through the U.N. Charter and the practices and rules that have unfolded in efforts to give practical meaning to the provisions of that august document.

The Charter and the Law Relating to Colonialism

The Charter does not mention colonialism *expressis verbis*. However, not only do its commitments to promote the realization of self-determination by all people and to reaffirm the faith in fundamental human rights implicitly condemn the inhuman activities in some colonies, its specific provisions on non-self-governing territories and the trusteeship system can be construed only in relation to colonialism.

The Trusteeship System

The trusteeship system, covered by chapters XII and XIII and their provisions, article 75 to 91, not only departs from the League tradition whereby only the colonies of the vanquished were brought under international "tutelage,"[26] but it imposes duties on the administering powers to promote self-government or *independence*,[27] and it establishes a system of holding the administering powers accountable for what they do in the colonies. Supervised by the Trusteeship Council, these regulations were beefed up by, inter alia, provisions to receive petition from the colonial subjects, the power to send visiting missions to the trust territories to gather information, and the power to seek information on any matter in relation to a trust territory, regardless of whether the matter is of a political nature.[28]

Considering these provisions vis-à-vis other provisions of the Charter, notably, those entitled "Declaration on Non-Self-Governing Territories," the trusteeship system seems to be the most powerful means for studying the legal status of colonialism in post-1945 international relations. This is particularly so because, very often, the other provisions not only lack clarity on the supervisory mechanisms by which the provisions on the trusteeship system can be rendered meaningful, but they are also replete with contradictions, raising questions as to whether they have any legal significance.[29] Yet a more careful comparison of the sections in the Charter entitled "Trusteeship System" and "Declaration on Non-Self-Governing Territories" shows that the coverage of the latter colonial matters is more extensive.

Consider, for instance, the range of territories regulated by the trusteeship system. Admittedly, the provisions are so liberal as to suggest that the system is authorized to deal with all colonies. But in practice this is not absolutely true. In the case *Concerning the Status of South-West Africa*, the I.C.J., for instance, held that South Africa had no obligation to place South-West Africa under the trusteeship system.[30] Nor is this holding easily assailable, for under the Charter it is only by an agreement that a territory can be brought under the trusteeship system, and it is categorically stated that unless there is such an agreement, nothing shall be construed in the Charter as placing a territory or state under the system.[31] Obviously, one can only conclude that the law relating to the trusteeship system cannot apply to colonies that are not brought under it by "trust" agreements, no matter whether the colonies had once belonged to the vanquished in any of the world wars.

And yet, the international community has not shirked its responsibilities

toward colonial territories that have not been placed under the trusteeship system. The record of South-West Africa manifests the trend. Thus, although the
I.C.J. considered South Africa to have no obligation to put that territory under
the trusteeship system, it rejected the notion that South Africa could annex it.
Nor has it absolved South Africa from accountability for the way the colony is
administered. Indeed, on the question of whether the replacement of the
League's unanimity rule by the two-thirds majority voting rule of the U.N.
system would not violate the principle that the U.N. supervision should not
exceed the powers exercised under the League, the Court upheld the revolutionary U.N. system.[32] If the provisions of the trusteeship system do not apply to
colonies that are not placed under the system, one would definitely be confronted with the problem of rationalizing these holdings, particularly since the
original trust arrangement on South-West Africa lapsed with the demise of the
League. Obviously, unless there are different provisions than those of the trusteeship system, it would be difficult to identify the grounds for these courageous
and progressive decisions.

The Provisions on Non-Self-Governing Territories

Called a "Declaration on Non-Self-Governing Territories," these provisions, which appear under chapter XI, articles 73 and 74, essentially reproduce
the ideals embodied in article 22 of the League Covenant. It reads in part:

> Members of the United Nations which have or assume responsibilities for the
> administration of territories whose people have not yet attained a full measure
> of self-government recognize the principle that the interests of the inhabitants
> of these territories are paramount, and accept as a sacred trust the obligation to
> promote to the utmost, within the system of international peace and Security
> established by the present Charter, the well-being of the inhabitants of these
> territories, and to this end:
>
> b. to develop self-government to take due account of the political aspirations
> of the peoples, and to assist them in the progressive development of their free
> political institutions, according to the particular circumstances of each territory
> and its people and their varying stages of advancement; . . .
> e. to transmit regularly to the Secretary General for information purposes,
> subject to such limitation as Security and constitutional considerations may
> require, statistical and other information of a technical nature relating to eco-
> nomic, social, and educational conditions in the territories for which they are
> respectively responsible.[33]

The Significance of the Declaration

The significance of the declaration has been the bone of contention between
two groups. One group, focusing on the term "Declaration" and where it ap-

pears in the Charter, denies that the provision has any legal effect. The position of this group is articulated thus:

> The Chapter containing this and the following article is we must note, entitled: "Declaration regarding non-self-governing Territories." Why this title "Declaration," a word which is not used elsewhere in the Charter? It clearly implies that no contractual undertaking is entered into. A declaration is unilateral."[34]

Another adherent of this position urges:

> As regards Chapter XI, I would remind you that this Chapter is not in the same form as the other provisions of the Charter. It is entitled: "Declaration." It contains a unilateral declaration by a certain number of states and the Charter merely confines itself to recording it. This is absolutely clear; there can be no argument on this point.[35]

In opposition, the other group argues:

> Chapter XI contains . . . a Declaration of duties in connection with the exercise of national trusteeship, a Declaration—this title is somewhat misleading—which forms an integral part of the whole Charter, as accepted by all the members of the United Nations. . . . It is therefore incorrect to assume that Chapter XI is a unilateral declaration by the 1945 colonial powers only.[36]

The interpretation that denies the legal efficacy of the declaration does not seem to accord with the canons of treaty interpretation. For apart from the rule that the juridical effect of a treaty does not depend on the nomenclature adopted for that instrument,[37] that position leads to the absurd conclusion that the Charter contains some provisions that are of juridical importance and some that are not.

Having determined that chapter XI entails as much legal force as any other provision of the Charter, it follows logically that the cases to which the chapter applies are now governed by international law. The questions that remain are, What are the situations to which chapter XI applies? And what really are the obligations of the administering states?

The Ambit of Chapter XI

The scope of chapter XI is stated in its first paragraph: "territories whose peoples have not yet attained a full measure of self-government." Since the chapter is not restricted to any class of colonies, as the provisions on the mandate system were, not only can it be said to have wider coverage than any preceding document, but it provides strong evidence that its provisions could apply to all colonies. Of course, there can be difficulties with this conclusion. The phrase "not yet attained a full measure of self-government," for instance, suggests a caveat that "territories whose peoples might have attained a full measure of self-government" should be excluded. But this argument is tenuous at best, because a territory that has attained a full measure of self-government would be fully independent and arguably would be beyond the range of situations covered by the definition of colonialism.

To determine the scope of the chapter with some precision, it is necessary to find out the meaning of "self-government" and, a fortiori, that of "full measure of self-government." This question is relevant to more than the theoretical stipulations of the chapter alone. The practice, particularly that about territories that are not characterized by the "salt and water" definition of colonialism (territories that though ruled by people within, are treated as part of the same constitutional system of their colonial masters, notably Rhodesia and the Portuguese colonies), has raised practical problems about the reach of the obligations under the chapter.

The first possible understanding of the scope of chapter XI is to consider the "supplementary means" of interpretation to see whether they can shed any light on the meaning of "self-government" and its relationship with "full measure of self-government" within the context of article 73.

The Dumbarton Oaks proposals did not have anything on chapter XI. The first time the chapter was contemplated was at the San Francisco conference, at the insistence of Britain and Australia.[38] But these proposals did not mention non-self-governing territories, nor did they mention colonies *expressis verbis*. Instead, they used the term "dependent territories." In the debates that ensued, however, the term "dependent territories" was used interchangeably with "colonies,"[39] providing a prima facie argument that the subject of colonialism was in contemplation when the chapter was deliberated. The Working Papers on Dependent Territories reveal that a concern was expressed about how the chapter should be construed. It was suggested that the phrase "territories inhabited by peoples not yet able to stand by themselves under the strenuous conditions of the modern world" should be inserted in place of "dependent territories."[40] This phrasing, an exact replica of article 22 of the League Covenant, was not acceptable to some members of the United Nations, notably, those that had just attained their independence. Iraq, for example, preferred the expression "peoples who are not developed." For, as it argued, the term "dependent peoples" includes both those who had not yet developed and peoples with a past civilization and history who had made a contribution to the world, whereas the phrase "peoples not yet able to stand by themselves" does not include those with developed civilizations.[41] While the issue was being considered, another intriguing question arose as to whether the term "peoples not yet able to stand by themselves" includes peoples within metropolitan areas. This issue, which eventually led to the insertion of article 74 and was probably lethal to what became known as the "Belgian thesis," was summarized in the discussion as follows:

> In connection with this phrase the question was raised whether the intention was to include among "peoples not yet able to stand by themselves" peoples within metropolitan areas. Some delegates felt that the wording of paragraph A, 2, made it clear that such was not the intention. The difficulties which would result if the principle of self-government were applied to minority groups in metropolitan areas were pointed out.[42]

The next phase of the debate was before the drafting committee, which, pursuant to the instruction that it interpret the issue on the basis of the understanding from the preceding debates, inserted the expression "territories whose peoples have not yet attained a full measure of self-government." Upon approval by Commission II/4 and Commission II, this is the wording that was used in chapter XII.

It is doubtful whether the *travaux preparatoires* provide much help for scholars interested in determining the scope of Chapter XI because the adopted version cannot be construed as an endorsement of any of the opposing positions taken in the debates. Nor is the subsequent practice of the United Nations and its member states very coherent, either. Yet it is possible to find some answers from practice, at least for the purposes of this study.

Some insight, for example, can be gained from the replies by states to a letter from the secretary general requesting them to specify their position on the meaning of "non-self-governing territories" and the factors by which that term could be defined.[43] Seventy-four territories being administered by eight states were listed as "non-self-governing territories" and, hence, entities to which the chapter applied,[44] but the information on the factors to be taken into consideration did everything but provide a working formula for the definition. In the U.S. profile, for example, the emphasis was on whether the territories enjoyed the same amount of self-government as the metropolitan areas of the member states.[45] But how does one define a "metropolitan area" or even "non-self-governing territory" for purposes of finding out whether the way a territory is administered would put it within or without the scope of chapter XI? Since this question was left open, it is difficult to see how helpful the suggestion could be in determining the status of territories that were not included in the list of seventy-four territories.

The suggestion of Egypt and India were noteworthy. Egypt's test was whether there was ethnographic compatibility between the non-self-governing territories and the administering authority.[46] India's was whether the particular territory was being administered by its own political and economic institutions.[47] Doubtless, with virtually no conclusive formula for defining territories as "non-self-governing," speculation reigned, leading to, inter alia, the enunciation of the famous "Belgian thesis."[48]

But it would be a gross misstatement to suggest that practice was entirely mute on the criteria for defining the non-self-governing territories. One precedent is provided by the resolution in relation to the Portuguese territories. Portugal had a unitary constitution, whereby all its territories were treated as a single unit. Upon its admission together with Spain into the United Nations, the question arose in the General Assembly and in the Fourth Committee as to whether their territories could be treated as non-self-governing territories for the purposes of the obligations under article 73e. Spain eventually gave in to the prevailing view that its territories were non-self-governing, but Portugal was steadfast, claiming that its territories were not "non-self-governing."[49] The ensuing confusion caused the General Assembly to pass Resolution 1467 in 1959, putting the issue before a committee of six members to determine the principles that should apply in determining whether or not a state had an obligation to transmit information under article 73. And on the basis of the recommendations of the committee, the General Assembly adopted another resolution, Resolution 1541(XV), which, though not fully disposing all the factors to be considered in determining whether a territory is self-governing, was very illuminating. According to principle IV thereof, "*Prima facie* there is an obligation to transmit information in respect of a territory *which is geographically separate and is distinct ethnically and/or culturally from the country administering it.*" The resolution then went on to say in its principle V:

> Once it has been established that such a *prima facie* case of geographical and ethnical or cultural distinctness of a territory exists, other elements may then be *inter alia*, of an administrative, political, juridical, economic or historical nature. If they affect the relationship between the metropolitan State and the territory concerned in a manner which arbitrarily places the latter in a position or status of subordination, they support the presumption that there is an obligation to transmit information under Article 73 e. of the Chapter.[50]

With this understanding, Resolution 1542 was passed, finally disposing of the issue about the Portuguese territories by compiling a list wherein the Portuguese territories were expressly brought under the ambit of the chapter.[51]

Another precedent was the Rhodesian case. Although Rhodesia was essentially autonomous, being ruled by its own political and economic institutions, the virtual exclusion of the majority—blacks—from its political process caused the United Nations to brand it as a non-self-governing territory. This position—taken by General Assembly Resolution 1747 (XVI)—was vehemently disputed by the British, who, in refusing to render information about the territory as required under article 73e, called it *ultra vires*. The ensuing confusion was eventually settled when, under pressure from the General Assembly and the Fourth Committee, the British passed the Southern Rhodesia Act of 1965, claiming "responsibilities for the administration" of the territory—a development that indicated that Rhodesia had, at least, been reverted to a non-self-governing status.

It should be obvious, then, that inadequate and checkered though international practice sometimes seems, it has, nevertheless, improved the plight of the colonies considerably. At least some (if not all) the obligations under chapter XI now apply to all territories regardless of whether they had traditionally been treated as colonial or as self-governing or as adjuncts of their metropolitan powers. The chapter can be counted as one of the provisions by which the law on colonialism has been markedly improved.

THE OBLIGATIONS ASSUMED UNDER CHAPTER XI AND THEIR ENFORCEMENT. The obligations are listed in article 73 as "a sacred trust." Essentially, their purpose is to promote to the "utmost" the "well-being" of the non-self-governing territories: (1) by protecting the inhabitants of the territories from abuse and ensuring that their culture is not only respected but advanced jointly with their sociopolitical and educational circumstances; (2) by mandating that they should be developed toward self-government; (3) by postulating that their development is to be made with the view to furthering international peace and security; and (4) by imposing a duty on the administering powers to render regular information on certain aspects of their lives to the secretary general.

How has the requirement for information and the duty to develop the territories toward self-government been handled in U.N. practice?

THE OBLIGATION TO DEVELOP TOWARD SELF-GOVERNMENT. Since the term "self-government" is not precisely defined in the charter and its *travaux preparatoires*, it is not surprising that intense disagreement has been expressed in the literature as well as between the administering powers and nonadministering powers as to what is entailed in the obligation to promote the self-government of territories. This discord has been intensified by the fact that, unlike article 76—a provision of the trusteeship system that mentioned "self-government" as well as "independence" as the goals—the Declaration on Non-Self-Governing Territories listed only "self-government" as the ultimate goal of the system. The main question about the obligation under article 73(b) is thus whether that obligation can be limited to advancement for self-government or is to include development toward independence as well.

On the face of it, the argument excluding independence from the obligation to develop toward self-government seems persuasive. It is bolstered by the maxim *expressio unius est exclusio alterius* as well as by the fact that whereas article 73(b) merely requires members to develop their territories toward self-government, the broad provisions of chapter XI, article 73, specifically, is that the territories over which the obligation to develop self-government is imposed are those that "have not yet attained a *full measure of self-government.*"

Yet this conclusion does not seem to accord with either the *travaux preparatoires* or the teleological method of interpreting treaties. Granted, a suggestion to include "independence" in article 73(b) failed to pass at the San Francisco conference.[52] But that apparent fiasco was mainly because the Chinese proponent was convinced that the word "independence" was included in the goals of the trusteeship. Thus, the omission of the term "independence" in the article is not so much because of its irrelevance as it is in relation to the fact that it is included in article 76 of the Charter. Indeed, this position is reinforced by the statement of the United Kingdom—cosponsors of article 73—which urged that the provision did not rule out independence as a possible goal for dependent territories.[53]

The practice also supports the inclusion of "independence" in the goals stated under article 73(b), for as India observes with reference to the current decolonization spree:

> The progressive development is to take place as indicated in Article 73 itself with "due account of the political aspirations of the peoples" and recognizing the principle that the "interests of the inhabitants of the territories are paramount." Who can say today that the aspirations of any peoples, whether under trusteeship or under colonial administration as a non-self-governing territory, are or can be anything short of independence?[54]

Though one can also cite article 5 of the 1960 Declaration on the Granting of Independence to enhance the scope of article 73(b) teleologically,[55] it would be stretching the point to suggest that independence is the sole objective cherished for the non-self-governing territories. There are many instances where territories too small to establish independent states have been merged with others. Also, as is expressly indicated in Resolution 1541 (IX) and, indeed, confirmed by the I.C.J. in the *Western Saharan* case,[56] a non-self-governing territory can be said to have reached a full measure of self-government by (1) emergence as a sovereign independent state; (2) free association with an independent state; or (3) integration with an independent state.

It is important to note, though, that there is some skepticism about association and integration, which is why the law subjects any such arrangements to meticulous standards. Thus on the issue of free association, principle VI of Resolution 1541 (XV) reads:

(a) Free association should be the result of a free and voluntary choice by the peoples of the territory concerned expressed through informed and democratic processes. It should be one which respects the individuality and the cultural characteristics of the territory and its peoples, and retains for the peoples of the territory which is associated with an independent State the freedom to modify the status of that territory though the expression of their will by democratic means and through constitutional processes.
(b) The associated territory should have the right to determine the internal constitution without outside interference, in accordance with due constitutional processes and the freely expressed wishes of the people.[57]

THE OBLIGATION TO TRANSMIT INFORMATION ON THE TERRITORIES. The obligation to transmit information on administered territories has raised questions about how to define non-self-governing territories; how information on those territories should be transmitted; when and under what conditions an administering power may cease to transmit information; whether the United Nations can take any action at all on the information it receives; whether any organ at all can discuss, appraise, or criticize the policies of the colonial powers in regard to their territories; and myriad others, which, together with the foregoing, can be subsumed under one heading—the legitimacy of U.N. supervision over the administration of non-self-governing territories. Here, it suffices to consider only the issue of whether there is a limit on the range of subjects on which information should be given, or whether the obligation requires information on any subject, regardless of whether that subject is political.

The relevant article reads in part: "subject to such limitations as security and constitutional considerations may require," the administering powers should render "statistical" information and information of a "technical nature relating to economic, social, and educational conditions over the territories for which they are respectively responsible other than those territories to which Chapter XII and XIII apply."[58]

Using the textual method of construction, the administering powers claim that the obligation does not include political information. Conversely, the non-administering states use the aims-and-objectives method to include political matters.

In listing the subjects to which the obligations apply, article 73(e) apparently excludes "security" and "constitutional" matters—subjects that arguably

fall within "political" information, thus making the contention of the administering powers somehow plausible. This position is further supported by the fact
that the article also excludes subjects that fall under chapters XII and XIII since
article 88—a chapter XIII article—expressly covers political questions:

> The Trusteeship Council *shall formulate a questionnaire on the political* eco-
> nomic, social, and educational advancement of the inhabitants of each trust
> territory, and the administering authority within the competence of the General
> Assembly shall make an annual report to the General Assembly upon the basis
> of such questionnaire.[59]

But it is doubtful whether these considerations are conclusive on the issue
of whether political information is excluded from article 73(e). Consider, for
instance, chapters XII and XIII—the provisions on the trusteeship system. Admittedly, its inclusion of political matters in the list on which information can
be given would, by the implications of article 73(e), be excluded from the
obligations for information as required by chapter XI. But this conclusion is
unsustainable, because if adopted it would nullify most of the obligations under
article 73(e) since the list under article 88 includes other subjects that are expressly covered by article 73(e), notably, information of a technical nature relating to economic, social, and educational advancement in the territories.
Moreover, it is obvious that the caveat in article 73(e) concerns territories covered by chapters XII and XIII, rather than subjects thereunder. Since the subject
of colonialism transcends the territories covered by the trusteeship system, the
limitation is apparent: the provisions on the trusteeship system would be inapplicable to territories that might not be placed under that system. Thus, even
assuming that political information cannot be requested in relation to the trust
territories, the argument would still fall short, considering the great number of
colonies that might not be placed under the trusteeship system.

There may even be questions about the extent to which the exclusion of
information on security and constitutional matters can be used as a basis to
preclude information on political matters affecting the territories under chapters
XII and XIII. By the terms of the article itself, the caveat does not seem to be
absolute. It says "subject to such limitations," thus indicating that, even if the
security and constitutional matters were equated to political matters, not all
political matters would be excluded from the range of subjects on which the
administering powers are required to render information. Naturally, this conclusion has not been supported by the administering states, the administering states
have acquiesced to the notion that such information can be given but only if the
administering powers want to do so voluntarily. This position is not entirely
wrong. It accords with many U.N. resolutions, notably Resolutions 144 (XX) of

November 1947, 327 (IV) of December 1949, 551 (VI) of December 1951, 848 (IX) of November 1954, and 1468 (XIV) of December 1959, wherein the General Assembly declared that the voluntary transmission of information was entirely within "the spirit of Article 73 of the Charter." Moreover, the administering powers are not only entitled to interpret their own obligations but, by being the states closely acquainted with the developments in the territories, they are also in a better position to know whether the information-transmission stage has been reached.

The question is whether a text is to be construed literally, even if such construction would negate the objectives of the document containing the text. Indeed, this was the point stressed by the nonadministering states, for, as they argued, the endorsement of the administering powers' attempt to treat the question of which matters fall within their security and constitutional considerations as domestic issues would nullify the obligation pursuant to which article 73(e) was adopted and is, therefore, unacceptable. Some nonadministering powers— Czechoslovakia and Poland—went even further to argue that if the administering powers were honest and really meant to treat the territories as a "sacred trust" as required by article 73, they would not be opposed to the construction that requires them to be open and unreserved as to the information given.

If one looks at the arguments closely, the position of the nonadministering powers seems to be more supportable than that of the administering powers. Starting from the P.C.I.J. ruling in the *Tunis Morocco Nationality* case, the world courts have held repeatedly against unilateral interpretation of multilateral treaties. It is, of course, conceded that the principle that suggests that every application of a rule implies an interpretation thereof would make it appropriate for the individual members and, a fortiori, the administering powers to interpret their obligations by themselves. But it is also clear that the rule immediately gives way to an international body if an issue arises as to whether a particular interpretation is right. For it would obviously be absurd for a state to claim that a certain international matter is one on which it is given the sole responsibility by a multilateral treaty, and at the same time argue that in each case, it and it alone should decide which matters are left to its exclusive jurisdiction by that treaty. From this it should be obvious that the question as to what falls within the security and constitutional considerations of the administering powers cannot be determined conclusively by those powers.

Intimately related to the question of the nature of information required from the administering powers under Article 73(e) is the question of who determines whether the obligations over a particular territory have been fulfilled, and what consequences flow from that determination. The instances where the United Nations has frequently dealt with these issues are (1) when a state ceases to transmit information on territories on which information had hitherto been rendered, and (2) when upon admission to the United Nations a state that had never rendered information on its territories is brought under the information-transmission scheme.

THE LEGALITY OF COLONIALISM

The U.N. Charter and the Legality of Colonialism

The international community has had to contend not only with the question of international accountability over colonies but also with the legality of colonialism itself. Although the Charter does not mention "colonialism" *expressis verbis*, that document has been the focus of this controversy. And interestingly enough, the protagonists often cite the same provision to make their opposing points.

What is the provision in question, and how has it been advanced to anchor the different positions in this controversy? The position of the group that considers colonialism to be legal under the U.N. Charter has been asserted by Kunz: "The Charter of the United Nations not only fails to permit the use of force to eradicate colonialism, but it expressly recognizes the legitimacy of colonialism in Chapter XI."[60] Similarly, in his response to the anticolonialists, Dugard urges: "Such a view [the view that colonialism has been outlawed by the Charter] is untenable, for Chapter XI in imposing the duty of accountability to the United Nations for the administration of colonies, recognizes the legitimacy of colonialism."[61] On the other hand, the Brazilian delegate urged in the Security Council debate on the Portuguese colonies that "no one doubts that the Charter in Chapter I puts an end to the so-called legitimacy of colonialism."[62]

Because neither the Charter as a whole nor the provision in question mentions colonialism, it is possible to brand both positions as unfounded. Yet the theory that colonialism is legitimate is not entirely indefensible. First, it should be recalled that regardless of the Charter's failure to mention colonialism expressly, the relevance of that document, particularly its chapters XI–XIII, to the institution of colonialism is unquestionable. As colonialism was legitimate in the period immediately preceding the Charter, it is not at all unreasonable to construe the Charter's failure to outlaw it as an endorsement and perpetuation of its previous legitimacy.

Another way to look at the issue is to examine Dugard's statement more closely. As he aptly observed, the Charter in its chapters XI, XII, and XIII merely stipulated how colonies are to be administered. Since the regulation of a thing can obviously not be the same as outlawing that thing, it should be easy to detect the fallacy in the argument that chapter XI outlaws colonialism. Nor can that position be salvaged by the provisions that required the administering powers to prepare the colonies for self-government and independence.[63] By failing to condemn colonialism outright or even to set up a time-table for its immediate demise, the injunction on the administering powers to develop the colonies toward independence or self-government *can arguably* be construed as a recognition of the legality of colonialism.

Yet this position does not seem to be supported by international practice. Considering that the text of a treaty is not conclusively determinative of its provisions, especially when the provisions are not very precise, it is necessary to study how the issue has been handled in practice to see whether or not this position is sustainable.

The O.A.U. and the Legality of Colonialism

Unlike the U.N. Charter, the O.A.U. Charter not only mentions colonialism expressly but calls for its total eradication from Africa.[64] Since the U.N. Charter does not expressly call for eradication of colonialism, it is questionable whether, as a commitment assumed outside of the U.N. Charter, the African provision against colonialism can have any significance.[65] Many scholars, in their critique of the O.A.U.'s anticolonial posture, have certainly invoked the supremacy clause of the U.N. Charter to impugn the validity of the O.A.U. Charter. But these criticisms are not very persuasive.

First, it should be realized that the supremacy clause of the U.N. Charter does not preempt the provisions of any other instrument unless there is a conflict between that instrument and the Charter. Inasmuch as the U.N. Charter does not have express information on whether or not the eradication of colonialism is illegal, it would be inappropriate to invoke its supremacy clause against the O.A.U. commitment to eradicate colonialism. Nor is it impossible to reconcile the O.A.U. position with the provisions of the U.N. Charter. By the terms of its charter, the O.A.U. is so deferential to the U.N. Charter that it is difficult to imagine how a provision on a subject that is not mentioned in the U.N. Charter can be said to be contradictory of that document. For instance, the O.A.U. affirms the U.N. Charter and the Universal Declaration of Human Rights and expresses the conviction that those documents provide "a solid foundation for peaceful and positive co-operation among states."[66] Again, the O.A.U. lists the commitment "to promote international co-operation" as one of its purposes and emphasizes further that it would pursue its goals with "due regard to the Charter of the United Nations and the Universal Declaration of Human Rights."[67] Finally, by article 26 of its charter, the O.A.U. is registered with the U.N. Secretariat as required by article 102 of the U.N. Charter.

Clearly, if the O.A.U. had meant to challenge any provision of the U.N. Charter, it would not have made any of these deferential references, let alone succeeded in registering its charter under the provisions of the United Nations. It is therefore not surprising that many authorities have employed the deferential references to defend the validity of the O.A.U. Charter. With reference to article 2, paragraph 1(e) Elias, for instance, has argued persuasively:

> This last reference to the Charter of the United Nations indicates not only the adherence of the Member States to the principles of the Charter, but also their awareness of the need to realize the goal of international co-operation in practical terms. One sees also in this respect a reminder that the Member States conceive of their organization as necessarily coming within the regional arrangements which paragraph 1 of Article 52 of the United Nations permits.[68]

Other interesting arguments can be used to defend the validity of the O.A.U. position. First, one must remember that a norm cannot be applied unless it is interpreted. All the members of the United Nations are obligated to apply the Charter in good faith, but the Charter has no precise tool for its authoritative construction. Accordingly, it is arguable that the O.A.U. position on colonialism is influenced by what the members of that organization understand their commitment to the U.N. Charter to be. It is, of course, conceded that an undue emphasis on this argument might lead to absurdities, inasmuch as it would suggest that any interpretation made pursuant to the U.N. objectives should be upheld as valid merely because the Charter has no authoritative means for its interpretation. Yet this conclusion would seem to be far-fetched in this particular instance. In placing emphasis on how the O.A.U. interprets the U.N. Charter, the argument does not suggest that the O.A.U.'s interpretation must be conclusive. It is not conclusive, but it cannot be branded as inappropriate unless it is so declared by the international community through any of the competent organs of the United Nations. Nor is there much reason to question the soundness of the O.A.U. position. Indeed, apart from the U.N. Charter's provisions on self-determination, human rights, and the commitment to maintain international peace and security—all of which arguably support the O.A.U. stand against colonialism—it is very clear from article 52 of the U.N. Charter that, as a regional organization, the O.A.U. has the responsibility to insure that there is peace in its region. Since by its gross violation of human rights and the peoples' right to self-determination colonialism is apt to cause threats to or breaches of international peace, it is possible to take the O.A.U. anticolonial stance as a way of fulfilling its obligations under the U.N. Charter. The U.N. practice is not at variance with this anticolonial posture. Indeed, not only do most U.N. resolutions condemn colonialism, but at times they even confirm and complement the O.A.U. position. The General Assembly Resolution 35/227 of 1981, for instance, reads:

The General Assembly . . . Taking into consideration the resolution in Namibia adopted by the Council of Ministers of the Organization of African Unity at its thirty-fifth ordinary session . . . and endorsed by the Assembly of Heads of State and Government of the Organization of African Unity . . . , especially its decision reaffirming the unequivocal support of member States for the just armed struggle of liberation waged by the people of Namibia . . . , strongly condemns South Africa's continued illegal occupation of Namibia . . . as well as its attempts to destroy the national unity and territorial integrity of Namibia.[69]

Likewise, in the 1979 resolution on the Implementation of the Declaration on the Granting of Independence to Colonial Countries and Peoples, the General Assembly emphasizes

the urgent need to take all necessary measures to eliminate forthwith the remaining vestiges of colonialism . . .

2. Affirms once again that the continuation of colonialism in all its forms and manifestations—including racism, apartheid, the exploitation by foreign and other interests of economic and human resources . . . is incompatible with the Charter of the United Nations, the Universal Declaration of Human Rights and the Declaration on the Granting of Independence to Colonial Countries and peoples and poses a serious threat to international peace and security . . .
11. *Urges all States, directly and through their action in the specialized agencies and other organizations within the United Nations system, to provide all moral and material assistance to the oppressed peoples of Namibia and Zimbabwe and, with respect to the other Territories.*[70]

U.N. Resolutions on Colonialism

The U.N. resolutions on colonialism have been often reiterated in the General Assembly, the Security Council, and the Economic and Social Council (ECOSOC), and sometimes in subsidiary organs or independent agencies like the United Nations Commission on Human Rights and the United Nations Educational, Scientific and Cultural Organization (UNESCO). The general theme and tone of resolutions by all these bodies has been consistent.

General Assembly Resolution 1514: The Declaration on the Granting of Independence to Colonial Countries and Peoples

Resolution 1514, which has been applauded as the "Magna Carta of colonial peoples,"[71] has been described by scholars as epitomizing the current international position on colonialism. Moore considers it as evidence of "a strong community consensus against colonialism."[72] Schwelb sees it as an assertion about the present state of international law on colonialism,[73] and Higgins calls it an illustration of a "trend towards acknowledging self-determination as a legal right" for all.[74]

Adopted in 1960 by a vote of 89–0 with 9 abstentions,[75] the preamble of the declaration decried colonialism not only by sounding all its negative features but also by observing the universal position against perpetuation of colonialism and expressing belief in liberation from anything that is colonial. It must be quoted *at length*:

> The General Assembly,
> Aware of the increasing conflicts resulting from the denial of or impediments in the way of the freedom of such peoples, which constitutes a serious threat to world peace . . .
> Recognizing that the peoples of the world ardently desire the end of colonialism in all its manifestations . . . Convinced that all peoples have an inalienable right to complete freedom, the exercise of their sovereignty and the integrity of their national territory,
> *Solemnly proclaims the necessity of bringing a speedy and unconditional end to colonialism in all its forms and manifestations.*[76]

Like the U.N. Charter, the declaration does not set up a time-table for demolition of colonialism. However, the preamble leaves no doubt that the general attitude is against colonialism.

Nor could the fact that the last paragraph of the provision called for a "speedy" end to colonialism provide a basis for argument that until a territory is liberated, its colonial status is irreproachable. Admittedly, expressions like that were employed to satisfy the political interests of the colonial powers and, consequently, to pose impediments to the efforts to eradicate colonialism immediately. Yet they are not totally without legal significance in the anticolonial drive. Colonialism is considered by most members of the international community to be an anathema. Indeed, the international community assumed a commitment to promote the well-being and protect the interests of the colonies to the utmost long before the adoption of Resolution 1514. However, there is also an awareness that because of the varying circumstances of the colonies, some might be unable to manage their own affairs if decolonized immediately. Besides, even if all were to be liberated at the same time, it is axiomatic that such liberation cannot be done simply by the stroke of the pen. The liberation from colonialism is to be effected through the principle of self-determination, but the right cherished by this principle can be realized only through free and open decision made by adequately informed people. Therefore, it is reasonable to rationalize the declaration's failure to terminate colonialism immediately as necessary—not only to avoid the chaos that might set in if liberation was brought about haphazardly, but to allow time for the colonial peoples to freely express their will. In adopting this position—the position that is arguably not only the most practical but also the least imperfect of several positions—the declaration does not fail to caution about the United Nations' uncompromising position on the issue of colonialism. It proclaimed loud and clear in article 3: the inadequacy of economic, political, social, or educational preparedness of a colony should not be used as an excuse for delaying independence.

Articles 1 and 2, among others, also made clear the anticolonial position of the declaration:

1. The subjection of peoples to alien subjugation, domination and exploitation constitutes a denial of fundamental human rights, is contrary to the Charter of the United Nations and is an impediment to the promotion of world peace and co-operation.

2. All peoples have the right to self-determination; by virtue of that right they freely determine their political status and freely pursue their economic, social and cultural development.[77]

The U.N. Declaration on Friendly Relations

The U.N. Declaration on Principles of International Law Concerning Friendly Relations and Co-Operation Among States in Accordance with the Charter of the United Nations[78] has been referred to as "one of the most complex documents in international law."[79] Nevertheless, its stance on the status of colonialism is not hard to discern. The main theme of the preamble is the maintenance of international peace and security; the basis for the realization of peace is freedom, equality, justice, and respect for fundamental human rights. The preamble further expresses conviction that "the subjection of peoples to alien subjugation, domination, and exploitation constitutes a major obstacle to the promotion of international peace and security"; that "the principle of self-determination of peoples constitutes a significant contribution to contemporary international law"; and—most importantly—that "its effective application is of paramount importance for the promotion of friendly relations among States, based on respect for the principle of sovereign equality." In the substantive provisions the declaration not only enjoins states from actions that would impede people from realizing their "right of self-determination and freedom and independence," but it also notes in the section titled "The principle of equal rights and self-determination" that by virtue of the principle of equal rights and self-determination of peoples enshrined in the Charter of the United Nations, *all peoples have the right freely to determine, without external interference, their political status and . . . every State has the duty to respect this right . . .*

To bring a speedy end of colonialism, having due regard to the freely expressed will of the peoples concerned; and bearing in mind that subjection of peoples to alien subjugation, domination and exploitation constitutes a violation of the principle, as well as a denial of fundamental human rights, and is contrary to the Charter.[80]

Even though the declaration emphasizes the objective of achieving peace and friendly relations among states by prohibiting any intervention by a state in the affairs of another, it excuses states from that obligation in cases where the peoples' right of self-determination is being violated. It continues:

Every State has the duty to refrain from any forcible action which deprives peoples . . . of their right to self-determination and freedom and independence. In their action against, and resistance to, such forcible action in pursuit of the exercise of their right to self-determination, such peoples are entitled to seek and receive support in accordance with the purposes and principles of the Charter.

However, there are many curiosities about the declaration. The paragraph that calls for eradication of colonialism, "with due regard to the freely expressed will of the peoples concerned," for instance, is apt to suggest that if the inhabitants of the colony decide to continue with their colonial situation, that decision would automatically legalize the situation. Another conceivable difficulty with the declaration is the reference to the Charter as its main basis of support. Since the declaration's tenets are obviously more radical than those of the Charter, the question is how to reconcile the two? This question can be asked about virtually all the U.N. resolutions on colonialism. In fact, this has been one of the grounds for challenging the resolutions.

FACTORS AFFECTING THE LEGAL STATUS OF THE ANTICOLONIAL RESOLUTIONS

The Originating Agency

The fact that Resolutions 1514 and 2625 emanated from the General Assembly is used by critics to deny them any legal significance. In a commentary on Resolution 1514 one writer, for instance, asserts: "The Members of the General Assembly passed Resolution 1514 with relative ease. But it is far more difficult to gauge its effects. The traditionalist position that General Assembly resolutions are merely recommendations would relegate Resolution 1514 to the realm of hortatory."[81]

It already has been shown that merely because a resolution is passed by the General Assembly or couched as a "recommendation" does not make it a less legal instrument than the U.N. Charter. But even if we ignore this point, it is still difficult to use the traditional argument against General Assembly resolutions to nullify the provisions on colonialism, for not only are such resolutions passed repeatedly by the General Assembly but other organs and sometimes even agencies of the organization issue similar documents. Moreover, this chorus of anticolonial sentiment is so vindicated by the record of the anticolonial movements that it can be taken as representing customary international law. The following excerpts are representative of the resolutions sounding the anticolonial note.

Security Council Resolutions

Among the many resolutions issuing from the Security Council that expressly support the eradication of colonialism and, a fortiori, the view that colonialism is an anathema are these: Resolution 473 of 1980 in which the council reaffirmed

> its recognition of the legitimacy of the struggles of the South African people for the elimination of apartheid and the establishment of a democratic society in accordance with their inalienable human and political rights as set forth in the Charter of the United Nations and the Universal Declaration of Human Rights;[82]

Resolutions 532 and 539 of 1983 in which the council condemned South Africa for its continued illegal occupation of Namibia; Resolution 445 of March 1979 in which the council reaffirmed

> the inalienable right of the people of Southern Rhodesia (Zimbabwe) to self-determination and independence in accordance with General Assembly resolution 1514 of December 1960 and the legitimacy of their struggle to secure the enjoyment of such rights as set forth in the Charter of the United Nations;[83]

Resolution 311 of 1972, which recognized "the legitimacy of the struggle of the oppressed people of South Africa in pursuance of their human and political rights, as set forth in the Charter and the Universal Declaration of Human Rights;"[84] and Resolution 312, which recognized the legitimacy of the movements in Angola, Mozambique, and Guinea Bissau.

Resolutions of ECOSOC

The Economic and Social Council of the United Nations[85] not only supports liberation movements against colonialism but has expressly decried colonialism in many of its recent resolutions. Among the most notable are Resolutions 1450,[86] 1543,[87] and 1892.[88]

Subsidiary Organs and Other Agencies

By Resolution 19 of 1973 the Human Rights Commission recommended that "moral and material assistance to liberation movements and the liberated territories and their population should be extended on a full scale."[89] Taking essentially the same position, other agencies, notably UNESCO, the U.N. Development Program, the Food and Agricultural Organization, the International Children's Fund, the World Health Organization, and the International Labor Organization, have all expressed their support by providing health care, food, educational resources, and the like to the afflicted areas.

The Compatibility of the Resolutions with the Provisions of the U.N. Charter

Another set of arguments advanced against the anticolonial resolutions questions their validity. In his attack on Resolution 1514, Dugard, for instance, has noted:

> But is there a legal right to decolonization? The main argument in support of such a right is based on the view that Resolution 1514 (XV) is a valid interpretation of the Charter and as such binding upon member States. This proposition is based on the rule that the General Assembly may interpret the provisions of its own Charter. But the General Assembly is not an international legislature and may alter the provisions of the Charter only in accordance with the procedure provided for amendment. It may not legislate under the mantle of interpretation. *Not only is the interpretation of the Charter in support of a legal right of decolonization unacceptable to a substantial number of States, but the provisions of Resolution 1514 (XV) exceed the bounds of legitimate interpretation.* . . . The Declaration on the Granting of Independence to Colonial Countries and Peoples, *in so far as it purports to create a new legal right to decolonization seeks to amend the Charter*. To be effective, such an innovation must comply with the correct procedure for amendment: dynamic methods of interpretation cannot create a new right.[90]

According to Tyner

> Article 5 extends the reach of the Resolution to "Trust and Non-Self-Governing Territories or all other territories which have not yet attained indepen-

dence. This extension is almost certainly ultra vires. The General Assembly under Article 16 of the U.N. Charter has jurisdiction only over those Trust Territories which fall under the definition contained in Article 77. This definition establishes only three categories—"territories now held under mandate; territories which may be detached from enemy states as a result of the Second World War; and territories voluntarily placed under the system by states responsible for their administration." Two of the territories in the special subset are mandate territories (Namibia and Palestine). But the others clearly are not mandate territories. Nor have they been detached from enemy states. Certainly they have not been voluntarily placed under the trusteeship system. Nor can the General Assembly seek to base its authority on Chapter XI—the "Declaration Regarding Non-Self-Governing Territories."[91]

At first sight it may be difficult to reject these arguments. The fact that the Charter neither mentions "colonialism" *expressis verbis* nor labels it as illegal is one possible support for this position. On a more careful study of the arguments vis-à-vis the relevant provisions of the Charter and the circumstances in which the resolutions were made, however, it is clear that the arguments are deficient and flawed.

Take, for instance, the view that brands the anticolonial provisions as "illegitimate interpretation" and goes further to suggest that the "interpretation of the Charter in support of a legal right of decolonization is unacceptable to a substantial number of States."[92]

That the Charter fails to mention colonialism is indisputable. But the mere fact that a principal document does not mention a subject *expressis verbis* is not a good reason to deny the validity or even relevance of that subject to every instrument created under the principal document. The Charter simply delineates the goals for which the United Nations was established. As a dynamic instrument created to address familiar as well as unforeseen problems, it does not pretend to cover exhaustively all the purposes or the means by which the stated goals are to be realized. Instead, it merely sets up guidelines under which the organs are to operate. One scholar pointed out:

One may say of the Charter, as Chief Justice Marshall said of the Constitution of the United States, that "it was intended to endure for ages to come and to be adapted to various crises of human affairs". That it did not "attempt to provide, by immutable rules, for exigencies, which if foreseen at all, must have been seen dimly, and which can best be provided as they occur". Like our Constitution, the Charter was made flexible enough to be adapted to exigencies, which, in the words of Justice Holmes, "could not have been completely foreseen by the most gifted of its begetters."[93]

Although the Charter's silence on colonialism can thus not be argued to preclude the express mention of colonialism in the resolutions, there are even more formidable points that vindicate the resolutions' express mention of colonialism and justify their branding colonialism as illegal. Among these points are the Charter's provisions on self-determination and on human rights, the trusteeship system, and its specific mention of non-self-governing territories. Who can claim that the provisions of self-determination and human rights or even those on non-self-governing territories do not apply to all colonies? Since the Charter considers the protection of fundamental human rights and promotion of self-determination as principles through which the U.N. objective of maintaining international peace and security can be realized, it follows that anything that violates or impedes the realization of any of these principles is unwarranted. Considering that colonialism has always been offensive to these values, it is self-evident that the resolutions' anticolonial provisions are a reflection or application of what the Charter has stated.

It is conceded that like Judges Spender's and Winiarski's[94] argument that the General Assembly cannot legislate under the mantle of interpretation, Dugard's observation that the General Assembly cannot legislate is an argument well made. But the question is: who decides whether or not an interpretation has overstepped its bounds and become legislation? This issue is obviously academic; both the General Assembly's authority to interpret the Charter and the Charter's broad generalization on concepts relating to the subject of colonialism leave little room to doubt the validity of the resolutions under the Charter.

The contention that decolonization is "unacceptable to a substantial number of states" is even more ludicrous. It is an argument that, to say the least, flies in face of all evidence. To limit oneself to the particular document in relation to which this argument was made is to ignore the countless other U.N. resolutions against colonialism—notably, the Declaration on Friendly Relations and the Definition of Aggression, wherein the international consensus against colonialism is unequivocally expressed. Resolution 1514 was adopted by 89 votes, with no opposition and but 9 abstentions. What, then, are the "substantial number of states" that do not accept its stipulations? The nine abstentions? If that is what the author meant, then his claim obviously cannot be right. The issue of the significance of an abstention in the General Assembly has not arisen, although it has, in the Security Council.[95] By the principle that each organ of the United Nations should be in charge of its own jurisdiction, it may be questionable whether the precedence established on the issue in the the Security Council can be applied to the General Assembly. Yet, there are good reasons why that issue can be considered irrelevant in this instance. First, the voting procedure in the Security Council is entirely different from that in the General Assembly: whereas the permanent members of the Security Council can block the passage of an otherwise popular resolution by vetoing, no members of the General Assembly have such power; all its resolutions are passed by a vote of the majority. Moreover, even if an abstention in the General Assembly were to have the same significance as one in the Security Council, the argument would still be unsalvageable, given the 89–0 vote. The measure had no votes against it, and as has been settled by the practice in the Security Council, even an abstention by a permanent member cannot prevent a resolution from being passed.[96]

A more plausible argument about the effect of abstention is that suggested in Dugard's later statement:

> Undoubtedly the organs of the United Nations play an important role in the development of customary international law, *but consent remains the basic requirement in the creation of customary law.* Portugal, the United Kingdom and South Africa not only abstained from voting on Resolution 1514 (XV), but have consistently refused to apply the principles contained in this resolution to their territories in Southern Africa. Consequently it seems impossible to accept that these States have consented to a new customary rule of decolonization applicable to their territories in Africa.[97]

Considering the presumption against erosion of sovereignty,[98] particularly the view expressed in the *Lotus* and *Fisheries* cases, that a state which refuses to participate in the formation of, or to accede to, a custom cannot be bound thereby, this argument addresses a question that is surely controversial: can the abstainers be bound by the resolutions?[99] With three of the permanent members of the United Nations (Britain, France, and the United States) participating in the abstention, it is even possible to raise doubts about the general significance of the resolution in the international community.

Yet this is as far as the argument can go. It cannot be sustained within the context in which the issue arose. The law or the so-called custom in question is expressed by U.N. resolution. It was passed under a multilateral document that binds all the members. Since the U.N. Charter enjoins all members of the United Nations to accept the obligations assumed thereunder, and since the organization also requires of its members to interpret and apply the Charter in good faith, it should be obvious that a resolution adopted by the authorized organ and by the stipulated procedures should have a legal force for every member. This argument has even greater force in connection with the issue being considered, for not only is abstention too equivocal to support the argument that the abstainers were opposed to the resolution, but it is possible to argue that the abstainers would not be exhibiting good faith if after participating in all the debates and proceedings leading to the adoption of the resolution, they were to turn their back on what the overwhelming majority decide. What would be the case if their position, for instance, had prevailed in the voting? Would they have been willing to accept the notion that the resulting resolution should have no legal consequence on those who voted negatively? If it is conceded that the vote of the majority should be the crucial test by which the legality of a situation should be determined, then the argument that seeks to shield a minority of abstainers from the effects of a resolution is an application of a double standard.

But even if it is still maintained that the abstention by the former colonial powers from the 1960 resolution undercuts the legal force of the anticolonial position at the time of its passage, it would be difficult to argue that it still does, because virtually all the abstainers took a different position less than a decade after the passage of Resolution 1514. For instance, Britain not only applauded the principle of self-determination and urged that self-determination should be the basis for the dismantling of its colonial citadels in Southern Africa but it was unequivocally opposed to colonialism during the debates on the Portuguese colonies, declaring at one point that colonialism was "dead and that the current policy of the Portuguese government was wrong."[100] In his address before the special Committee on Friendly Relations, the British representative drew attention to his country's continuing fulfillment, in good faith, of the Charter's obligations in respect to non-self-governing territories "with a view to enabling all the peoples of those territories to exercise their right to self-determination."[101] Britain emphasized its anticolonial posture at a meeting of the Security Council, saying that it "agrees . . . that the peoples of the Portuguese Territories should, if it is their wish, be enabled to exercise their inalienable right to self-determination, and that the Government of Portugal, in accordance with Chapter XI, has the responsibility to lead its dependent peoples toward that goal."[102] France, also an abstainer from Resolution 1514, has likewise abandoned its former position to join the the anticolonial forces. Taking a strong stand on the Portuguese territories, it acknowledged "*the inalienable right* of the peoples of Angola, Mozambique, and Guinea Bissau freely to choose their own destiny" and their right to independence.[103] Belgium and the United States have repeatedly also expressed similar opinions, though often even more forcefully stated.[104] The positions taken by these nations have more than theoretical significance. With the support of the international community, many territories have been decolonized either by becoming independent or by being associated with or integrated into other states. In Africa the trend is especially obvious when one compares the number of independent countries with the decreasing number of territories that have yet to attain their independence.

Another point advanced by the critics to challenge Resolution 1514 concerns the scope of article 16. According to the critics, because the General Assembly was authorized by the Charter to deal solely with the trust territories, the Assembly exceeded its authority when it used Resolution 1514 to regulate all colonies, trust and nontrust alike. Since article 16—the provision that authorized the General Assembly to deal with the trusteeship system—mentions only the trust territories, and since these encompass only the territories captured from the vanquished in the world wars and such other territories as may voluntarily be added by the administering powers, this position may not be entirely indefensible. But the duties of the General Assembly are not confined to the provisions of article 16; they transcend it. Take, for example, the provisions on the non-self-governing territories. Since the governing provisions on this subject, chapter XI, authorize the General Assembly to deal with any dependent territory, it is obvious that the assembly has grounds for passing resolutions that apply to all colonies. In other words, even if under article 16 the assembly lacks the power to pass resolutions concerning some territories, that would not bar it from passing resolutions under chapter XI.

Even if it is contended that the assembly's powers under chapter XI do not extend to supervision, it would still be difficult to deny the validity of Resolution 1514. The responsibilities of the General Assembly far transcend the limits of the provisions in article 16, chapters XII, XIII, and even chapter XI combined. Under article 10, for instance, the assembly has the duty to discuss and make recommendations on any issue within the scope of the Charter or relating to the powers and functions of any organ of the United Nations. Since the United Nation's responsibilities include the protection of human rights, promotion of self-determination, and preservation of international peace and security, and since colonialism—whether under chapters XI–XIII or otherwise—affects any of these matters, it is a foregone conclusion that what the General Assembly cannot discuss under chapters XII–XIII can be discussed under article 10. Nor did the assembly in passing Resolution 1514 suggest that it was acting under chapters XII–XIII. But even if it is argued that discussion and recommendation are different from binding resolutions, General Assembly Resolution 1514 still cannot be disregarded merely because it was passed under article 10. Apart from the notion that the term "recommendation" is not to be construed literally, it is crystal clear that a resolution like the one under investigation is not without legal force.

The fact that the assembly did not pass Resolution 1514 through the amendment process cannot be of much service to the critics. Apart from the fact that the assembly clearly acted within its powers, there is the question of who is the right person to determine whether or not an amendment is called for. Since the assembly has the responsibility to interpret the Charter, no single act of the assembly can be impugned simply for not having been accomplished by an amendment of the Charter. Clearly, in passing the resolution, the assembly found nothing wrong with the Charter, and thus saw no reason to amend it. The resolution does not suggest, even implicitly, that the soundness of the Charter's provisions are questionable or outmoded, or even unreasonable. On the contrary, the assembly cited the Charter as the basis for the resolution.

The record leaves no room to doubt the authenticity of the law against

TABLE 1
AFRICAN STATES DECOLONIZED BEFORE AND AFTER 1965

State	Date of independence
Before 1965	
Algeria	7/1/62
Benin	8/1/60
Botswana	9/30/60
Burundi	7/1/62
Cameroon	1/1/60
Central African Republic	8/13/60
Chad	8/11/60
Congo	8/15/60
Egypt	2/28/22
Gabon	8/17/60
Gambia	2/18/65
Ghana	3/6/57
Guinea	10/2/58
Ivory Coast	8/7/60
Kenya	12/12/63
Lesotho	10/4/66
Liberia	7/26/47
Libya	12/24/51
Madagascar	6/26/60
Malawi	7/6/64
Mali	7/20/60
Mauritania	10/28/60
Morocco	3/2/56
Niger	8/3/60
Nigeria	10/1/60
Rhodesia[a]	11/11/75
Rwanda	7/11/63
Senegal	8/25/60
Sierra Leone	4/27/61
Somalia	7/1/60
South Africa[b]	3/31/10
Sudan	1/1/65
Tanzania	12/9/62
Togoland	4/27/60
Tunisia	3/20/56
Uganda	10/9/62
Upper Volta	8/5/60
Zaire	6/30/60
Zambia	10/24/64

TABLE 1 *(Continued)*

State	Date of independence
After 1965	
Angola	11/11/75
Bophuthatswana[c]	12/6/77
Cape Verde	7/5/75
Comoro Islands	1/1/76
Ciskei[c]	12/4/81
Djibouti	6/27/77
Equatorial Guinea	10/12/74
Guinea Bissau	9/10/74
Mauritius	3/1/68
Mozambique	6/25/75
Namibia	3/21/90
Sao Tome and Principe	7/12/75
Seychelles	6/28/76
Swaziland	1/6/76
Transkei[c]	10/26/76
Venda[c]	9/13/79

Source: Derived with minor modifications from F. R. METROWICH, AFRICAN FREEDOM ANNUAL 2–6 (1977); *id.* at 7–11 (1979).
[a]In the eyes of international law Rhodesia never attained independence until 1981, when independence was granted to the black majority through a free election. It is significant that the so-called 1965 revolution was a unilateral declaration that consequently failed to receive recognition of the international community and the colonial master of the time. Legal issues arising out of this case have been treated at length in Chapter 10, infra.
[b]With the on-going apartheid policy and its colonial features, it is doubtful whether this country is really independent. For the legal significance of the apartheid policy, see the next chapter.
[c]These territories are not recognized as independent by the international community because not only are they offsprings of the apartheid system, but they are regulated by apartheid-related institutions.

colonialism. The years 1960 to 1965 witnessed the greatest sweep of decolonization (see Table 1). The decline after 1965 seems to suggest a reversal of the trend; but a careful study of the entire colonial record shows the "reversal" to be no decline at all; it is merely because the anticolonial war is nearly over. After the great sweep in the early sixties, the number of territories left for decolonization were far less numerous. But although the rate of decolonization has slowed, the intensity of the anticolonial movement has not declined. The international community remains united in its fight to liberate the remaining territories—the two apartheid territories in Southern Africa, and others like Spanish Sahara and East-Timor, whose independence is yet to be rendered meaningful.

Chapter

5

Decolonization Movements Against Apartheid

Aᴘᴀʀᴛʜᴇɪᴅ ʜᴀs ʙᴇᴇɴ described as an anathema, an "evil" system posing serious threats to international peace and security, and its eradication has been proclaimed imperative.[1] In fact, because of apartheid, the United Nations has terminated the South African mandate over Namibia (South-West Africa) and has designated a caretaker government—the U.N. Council for Namibia—to administer the territory till the Namibians exercise their right of self-determination.[2] Regrettably, however, none of these actions has moved South Africa to abandon its apartheid policy.[3]

Given the extensive powers of the United Nations to execute the commitments of the Charter, particularly those relating to human rights and the maintenance of the peace, one difficulty about the continuing survival of apartheid is whether the United Nations has been doing the right thing. As the highest peace-keeping institution, the United Nations has occasionally used its extensive powers to bring recalcitrant protagonists into line; its apparent inability to eradicate apartheid thus is not without serious implications. The survival of apartheid vitiates confidence in the world organization, raising doubts as to whether that world body is capable of meeting the challenges for which it was created. Interesting and revealing as a discussion of these shortcomings of the United Nations might be, they fall outside the scope of this study. Our focus regrettably cannot do much to illuminate the capabilities of the United Nations to fulfill its obligations under the Charter. Nor does it provide much information on the political undercurrents that make the United Nations seem unequal to some of its challenges. Yet the central theme of this book is very important to the issue of liberty within the framework of contemporary international law. Essentially, it involves certain developments in the apartheid systems—the creation of new states and nationalities—which revive traditional questions regarding, for example, the laws relating to nationality—whether a state can denationalize some of its nationals—and whether recognition is a sine qua non for the creation of states.

124

WHAT IS APARTHEID?

"Apartheid" simply means "separateness" or "separate development." It is a policy uniquely used by the South African government to insure the hegemony of a white minority over a vast majority of blacks in South Africa and South-West Africa.[4] As a policy, it did not come into vogue until the Nationalist party of South Africa assumed power in the late 1940s, but aspects of it have been known and in operation in South Africa since the advent of Europeans in that country.[5] Although explanations by the South African government are for the justification, rather than the illumination, of what apartheid entails, it is appropriate to use some of those rationalizations to evaluate the tenets of the apartheid system.

Dr. H. F. Verwoerd, one of the leading exponents of apartheid, describes its goals:

> *We want each of our population groups to control and govern themselves, as in the case of other nations.* They can co-operate as in a commonwealth—in an economic association with the Republic. . . . This is our policy of separate development. South Africa will proceed in all honesty and fairness to secure peace, prosperity and justice for all, by means of political independence coupled with economic interdependence.[6]

Similarly, according to Mudler: "If our policy is taken to its full logical conclusion . . . there will be not one black man with South African citizenship. . . . Every black man in South Africa will eventually be accommodated in some independent new state in this honorable way."[7] Again a 1980 declaration urged:

> Whites and non-whites are so dissimilar in their culture that they can never live together as a community. If they were to try, the numerically stronger non-whites would swamp the whites politically, culturally, and economically. The only solution therefore is to partition the country into areas where whites alone will have full rights and privileges.[8]

Considering that the whites have wielded power in South Africa for a long time, and that by the acute racial imbalance in the apartheid territories a reversal of the power structure might destroy the white hegemony, the concern that motivates supporters of the policy is not unnatural. Yet, even if the policy was taken to be as "honest" or "honorable" as its architects suggest it is, it is evidently so at odds with all sanity and contemporary thinking that it defies rationalization, legal or political.

The political rationale for one race's lording it over another merely because it has done so in the past has been exploded. With the notable exception of the apartheid regimes, virtually all colonialists who used longevity to rationalize their hegemony—Britain over the United States; France over Algeria; Spain over Spanish Sahara; and Portugal over East Timor, Angola, Mozambique, Guinea Bissau, and Goa, to mention only a few—have been proved wrong by history. Nor is it possible to rely on the supposition that one race will be swamped by the other if apartheid is dismantled. Apart from the axiom that all races are equal,[9] and consequently that the principle of one man, one vote should be the basis for determining who should rule a country, it has been demonstrated in almost all the former settler colonies that the rule of the majority does not erode the socioeconomic and political rights of a minority race. In Zimbabwe, Angola, Mozambique, and Zambia the fear that the black majority would overrun the whites was among the principal considerations behind the whites' reluctance to give in to the blacks. Yet the postindependence politics of all these countries has demonstrated that people of diverse races—whether black, "colored," or white—are of equal importance in the determination of the destiny of a country. Thus their political systems provide equal opportunity to their different races, and issues of who should rule are resolved by political campaigns premised on capabilities and conscience rather than the color of people's skin. This is the test recognized in virtually all civilized countries. The collusion by members of a minority race to rule a majority merely because the minority might be discriminated against is not only dishonest and prejudicial against the majority, but equivalent to acting according to a double standard and committing wanton discrimination.

Recently, political arguments and propaganda have been advanced in pro-apartheid circles to downplay the monstrosity of apartheid. One such argument concerns the regrettable human rights situation in most third world countries, notably, in Africa. It claims that if the anti-apartheid movements were to overthrow the racist regime in Southern Africa, the champions of those movements would disregard all democratic principles and become tyrants like the leaders in some African countries.

That democracy is at its lowest ebb in most parts of Africa is beyond question.[10] Likewise, the human rights situation in that continent is bad. But what does the misuse of power in one state have to do with the fate of the inhabitants of another state? The violation of the law by any person does not warrant infraction by others. The inhabitants of the apartheid territories should be free to establish their own systems in their own ways and by their own rights; they are entitled to develop through their own experiences and mistakes. If they abuse their inherent right to rule themselves, of course, they would be subject to criticism and the application of the law, just like any other infractor. But to rely on other people's misuse of their rights as a basis for predicting how the victims of apartheid may use theirs and, consequently, to deny them the right to rule themselves is unwarranted prejudice, at variance with all civilized standards.

Another pro-apartheid argument is anticommunist propaganda. Pointing to the revolutions in Angola, Mozambique, and Rhodesia, the argument postulates that if the struggles against apartheid were to succeed, South Africa—a strong and perhaps the only true Anglo-American ally in Africa—would go communist and be lost to the Western camp. Like the others, this argument suffers from several fatal flaws. First, the fear of communism: the question is whether Western support for the apartheid system can forestall a procommunist stance by the anti-apartheid leaders, particularly in the present international system, where there is near unanimity as well as a strong pressure against apartheid. Paying lip service to apartheid rather than taking an objective position in the conflict would do more harm than good to the South African–Western alliance if the apartheid system were to lose in favor of a majority rule—a possibility that from all indications is only a matter of time. Obviously regardless of how well founded the Western fear is, its pro-apartheid stance is not only a misdirection, but it also fails to exhibit any rational relationship between the professed objectives of the West and its acts. It suffices to note that in virtually all the cases where the "liberated" leaders have gone communist, it is the Anglo-American negative attitude against the legitimate struggles of the majority that caused the enstrangement and, consequently, the alliance between the majority and the communists.

An even stronger argument against anticommunist support of apartheid is that—unlike apartheid, which has suffered severe condemnation from the international community—communism is a recognized form of government. In favoring apartheid over communism, the Western position suggests that mere political or ideological incompatibility is reason enough to prefer an illegal system over a system that is not necessarily illegal under international law. Obviously, apart from being dangerous to international peace and security,[11] this position contradicts all the values established by such landmark documents as the Magna Carta of 1215 and the Bill of Rights of 1688. Not only does it undo the achievements of historic movements like the French and American revolutions, but it negates the honorable values and images fostered by heroes like Presidents Thomas Jefferson, George Washington, Franklin Roosevelt, and Woodrow Wilson, and thus undermines the confidence in the position of the West as the citadel of liberty.

Another dubious pro-apartheid stance links the Namibian problem with withdrawal of Cuban troops from Angola. This equation is embodied in the master plan proposed by the Contact Group as the basis for peaceful settlement of the Namibian problem. As will be recalled, the Contact Group comprises five Western countries—Britain, the United States, Canada, France, and West

Germany—which unilaterally assumed the responsibility for negotiation with South Africa over the implemention of major international policies regarding Namibia.

The South African presence in Namibia has been illegal from the time the mandate was terminated in 1966 by U.N. Resolution 276, and South Africa's continuing intransigence was not abated even by Security Council Resolution 385 with its six-month ultimatum, failing which, the United Nations threatened to apply sanctions against South Africa. There have therefore been questions as to whether the belated formation of the Contact Group is legal within the framework of the United Nations. Apart from the fact that the group's doubtful record on anti-apartheid issues raises questions about the intentions of its members, there are serious issues about its legal authority, particularly because its purposes virtually revise the preexisting U.N. policy.[12]

The thrust of the propaganda is that South Africa should not withdraw from Namibia until the Cuban troops are removed from Angola.[13] Its deficiencies are evident. First, is there any correlation between the Angolan and Namibian cases? Namibia and Angola are separate territories that, but for the colonial presence of South Africa in Namibia, would be independent sovereign states. Neither the U.N. Charter's general provisions on self-determination nor the specific U.N. resolutions on the Namibian situation link problems in other territories to any particular case involving the struggle for self-determination, and the United Nations has never linked the situation in Angola to the solution of the Namibian problem, but it has incessantly called upon states to help Angola defend itself against South Africa's aggression. Questions, of course, may arise about whether the occasional use of Angola as a base by the South-West Africa People's Organization (S.W.A.P.O.), the Namibian liberation movement, does not create a link between the two territories and hence justify the proposed trade-off. However, upon the termination of South Africa's mandate over Namibia, South Africa ceased to have anything to do with Namibia. Its continuing presence there is thus not only an affront to the international community and its terminal resolution, but it illegally interferes with the Namibians' right to self-determination. Since international law encourages all states to give any kind of assistance to people struggling for self-determination, the permission for the Namibian freedom fighters to use Angolan territory to wage their war of liberation is warranted and hence cannot provide any rational relationship between the Namibian case and the presence of Cuban troops in Angola.

The irrelevance of the Angola-Cuban relationship is even more evident from the circumstances surrounding the Cuban presence in Angola. Long before Angola's independence, South Africa had been launching attacks against the most widely supported and internationally recognized liberation movement in Angola, the M.P.L.A. Toward the end of 1975 when Angola was fast approaching independence, for instance, South Africa launched an invasion by a force of 6,000 South African troops and foreign mercenaries in an attempt to prevent the M.P.L.A. from assuming power as the country's first independent government. Thereafter, South Africa has been using its illegally occupied territory of Namibia as its military springboard for continued attacks on Angola. According to some sources, these attacks had caused damages amounting to US$10 billion to Angola by the year ending 1982.[14] One of the reasons, if not the main reason, why the Cubans are in Angola is to help that country combat these attacks and those perpetrated by the South African–supported U.N.I.T.A. Consequently, not only is the legal sanctity of the Cuban presence in Angola unassailable, but the linking of it with the Namibian case is misplaced. It is no wonder, then, that the United Nations condemns South Africa for its activities and calls on any state to assist Angola. Thus, according to Resolution 36/172, the General Assembly commends

> all States which have provided assistance to Angola and other front-line States in accordance with the relevant resolutions of the United Nations . . .

> 5. Calls upon all States and intergovernmental and non-governmental organizations to provide moral and material support to the Government and people of Angola and other independent African States subjected to acts of aggression, subversion and terrorism by the apartheid regime.[15]

But there is another ground for separating the Cuban issue from the Namibian case. Angola is an independent country. It thus is entitled to enter into a defense pact with any country for assistance against aggression. Since the Cuban troops did not go to Angola without invitation, and since the invitation has not been revoked by the Angolan government, it is unimaginable why that perfectly legal arrangement should be intertwined with the movement to rid Namibia of South Africa's oppression. Even if the Cuban troops had gone to Angola illegally, the Namibian movement is so independent of the South Africa–Angolan situation that it would be wrong to make the solution of one a precondition of the other.

As to its legal justifiability, the only conceivable defense for the South African government is the principle of sovereignty as reinforced by the domestic-jurisdiction clause of the U.N. Charter. The question is whether it is anybody's business to tell South Africa, a sovereign nation pursuing what it considers best for its country, what to do with its subjects.[16] South Africa has indeed pursued this argument. It articulated it forcefully in the South-West Africa case and in the case involving discrimination against Indians in South Africa. As a member of the United Nations—which requires that every state observe the principle of self-determination for all its subjects, insure that the fundamental human rights of its subjects are not compromised, and promote friendly relations among states—the South African argument could not prevail even under the domestic-jurisdiction concept. All these cases branded the human rights issues as international rather than domestic subjects.

The Features of Apartheid

There has been much discussion of apartheid in the international literature; passages from the most descriptive works provide the best introduction to the subject. Thompson, for instance, says:

> The whites have monopoly of political power. . . . Economic power, too, is vested to an overwhelming extent in the hands of Whites who also own most of the land and control all the major industries and businesses. But every appreciable enterprise in the country employs non-whites who do the unskilled work at low wages. . . . Thus, although members of all the racial groups participate in the modern sector of the economy, and are dependent on it, their opportunities and rewards are determined by race.[17]

He continues:

> South Africans rarely meet members of racial groups other than their own, except as white employers and non-white employees. . . . Members of racial groups live in different areas; they attend different schools and churches; they sit in different parts of buses, trains and aircraft . . . and when they die they are carried in different hearses to different cemeteries. *Most of this separation is embodied in laws enacted by sovereign all white cabinet applied by all white courts and enforced by police under all white officers.*[18]

The components of apartheid are also powerfully described in a statement by one Namibian in a recent terrorist trial:[19]

> You my Lord, decided that you had the right to try us. . . . We are Namibians and not South Africans. . . . Those who have brought us to trial . . . do not even do us the courtesy of calling us by our surnames. . . . Many of our people, through no fault of their own have had no education. . . . A man does not have to be formally educated to know that he wants to live with his family where he wants to live; and not where an official chooses to tell him to live; to move about freely and not require a pass; to earn a decent wage; to be free to work for the person of his choice as long as he wants, and finally, to be ruled by people that he wants to be ruled by, and not those who rule him because they have more guns than he has. . . . We believe that South Africa has

abused that trust [the mandate] because of its belief in racial supremacy. . . . Where are our trained men? The wealth of our country has been used to train your people . . . and the sacred duty of preparing the indigenous people to take their place among the nations of the world has been ignored. . . . *Separation is said to be a natural process. But why, then is it imposed by force?*[20]

The racial separation dictated by apartheid is not premised on the free will of the different races but is imposed and enforced by the state. In its transgression of the generally accepted principles of freedom of movement, expression, and nondiscrimination it violates contemporary international law and makes any condoning of the policy indefensible. This is especially true in light of the fact that all the members of the international community have pledged themselves to insure that the precious values of humanity are not compromised anywhere. Yet the descriptions quoted are mild; the full inhumanity of the apartheid system is exposed by the instruments used in operating it.

The Legal and Institutional Framework of Apartheid

Whether in South Africa or Namibia, apartheid is operated through a "reserve system," or the "Bantustan" or "Homelands" scheme, as it is otherwise called. Essentially, this scheme insures the division of the apartheid territories in the ratio of approximately 8 to 2. The larger portion, which comprises almost all the fertile landmass and which has all the wealth—minerals, industries, and good schools, is given to the whites, who constitute less than 15 percent of the population (see Table 2) The remaining 20 percent (13.7 percent by some estimates) of the land—the portion that is barren and bereft of minerals and industries—is earmarked for blacks, who constitute more than 80 percent of the population.[21] Whereas the system treats the whites as a single nation with scarcely any regard to their different national origins, the blacks are artificially divided into many small "nations" according to their "tribal" backgrounds. Again, whereas the whites are not restricted in their movements—neither within the compass of their territorial zone nor to other countries—the blacks are regulated by what is known as the "pass system." To move even from one reserve to another, a black must obtain a pass from the authorities, and this pass must be carried at all times and be produced on demand by any police officer. Nor is there any guarantee that the blacks will live in their "reserves" forever, for under the Group Area Act, Act No. 14 of 1950, which caused the relocation of millions of blacks from their traditional homes, the minister of community development may designate an exclusive area for any group of blacks and move them forcibly from where they live onto that designated area. In 1959 the government attempted to apply this act to some 30,000

TABLE 2

ESTIMATES OF THE RACIAL COMPOSITION OF SOUTH AFRICA AND NAMIBIA

Race	Number	Percentage of population
South Africa by Mid-1984[a]		
Total population	32,642,730	100
White	4,818,679	14.8
Nonwhite	27,824,051	85.2
Colored	2,830,301	
Asian	890,292	
Black	24,103,458	
South Africa and Namibia by 1980[b]		
South Africa		
Total population	24,091,000	100
White	4,446,000	18.5
Nonwhite	19,645,000	81.5
Colored	2,533,000	
Asian	792,000	
Black	16,320,000	
Namibia		
Total population	969,100	100
White	112,700	11.6
Nonwhite		
(Colored, Asian, and Black)	856,400	88.4

Figures compiled with little variation from estimates provided by
[a]C. COOPER, J. SCHINDLER, C. MCCAUL, F. PORTER, M. CULLUM, RACE RELATIONS SURVEY 1984, at 184–85 (1984). This source includes the estimated populations living in the "independent" homelands.
[b]AFRICA SOUTH OF THE SAHARA 1981–1982, at 732, 937f (1980). This source excludes the inhabitants of the "independent homelands." For earlier information, see U.N. Dept. of Political and Security Affairs Unit in a study titled "Facts and Figures on South Africa," No. 16/72 (1972), and U.N. DEP'T OF PUBLIC INFORMATION, A TRUST BETRAYED: NAMIBIA at 6–7, U.N. Sales No. E.74/1.19 (1974).

Namibians. When the Namibians opposed the order to move to the new area named "Katutura," arguing that the order treated them as inanimate chattels and threatened them with harsher living conditions because they would have to pay more for transportation to work than they had been paying, the government promptly dispatched armed troops, killing and wounding many people, flattening houses with bulldozers, and eventually effecting the relocation.[22]

The only way a black can go to the white zone is to go there as a worker. But even then, the black worker is not free to go anywhere within that zone; nor can just any black go to the white areas. In 1922 the purpose of this policy, otherwise known as the migrant labor system, was clearly spelled out by a government commission: "Natives should only be allowed to enter the urban areas to muster the needs of the white man and should depart therefrom when he ceases so to minister."[23] In 1975 a government spokesperson also stated tellingly: "These people are here, as far as we are concerned, for all time on a casual basis, they are here because they come here to work, but without land ownership and without political rights."[24] Still yet another statement released by M. C. Botha, then a government minister, ran: "The basis on which the Bantu is present in the white areas is to sell their labor here and for nothing else."[25]

To qualify as a passholder for work in the white areas, a black must undergo a humiliating medical examination[26] and be tagged as a potential worker by a labor bureau specifically set up to select potential black workers. Even the candidate who passes the examination is not free to look for an employer; under the law candidates can be hired only through an employment agency and have no choice about the type of work; moreover, the length of time candidates may work for an alloted employer is stipulated. Blacks have no right to stop working for an employer unless the latter agrees in writing. Under the Master and Servants Proclamation a black worker is severely penalized for: (1) failing to begin work at the stipulated time; (2) being absent from work without "lawful cause"; (3) becoming unfit for work because of intoxication; (4) neglecting one's duty or failing to perform it properly; (5) making use of the master's horse, vehicle, or other property without permission; (6) refusing to obey any order given by the master; (7) damaging property willfully or through neglect or drunkenness; and (8) using abusive language to the master, the master's wife, or any other person of authority. Blacks can be prosecuted and imprisoned or fined for insubordination. They can be flogged by an employer at will. If a black is no longer of any use to an employer—which often occurs because of sickness or age—the black has only a few hours within which to leave the area or risk becoming a vagrant under the Vagrancy Act and, consequently, being punished, sometimes by long-term imprisonment or, if the black is lucky, by being forced to work without pay.

Jobs are classified as skilled and nonskilled, and the ones for which blacks generally qualify are those in the latter category. Even blacks who are qualified for a skilled job are not classified as such, and no matter what a black does, remuneration is just a tiny fraction of what a white in the same category is paid. Where there is no white in South Africa or Namibia to cover a skilled position, whites are lured from Europe to emigrate and fill the job. It is only when no white can be obtained that a black is considered to fill the position, and even if a black is hired for the job, remuneration is not commensurate with what normally is paid for that post. The black is designated as semi-skilled and paid accordingly.

In the isolated area where the black migrant laborers lodge to work for the whites, the living conditions are deplorable. The workers cannot be visited by their wives and children, and one recent study reveals that under this system an average black man is compelled to spend more than two-thirds of his married life away from his family. This, the study indicates, is the main cause of the frequent breakup of black families and marriages. Apartheid's tragic catalogue of social disruption and unhappiness includes turning blacks into drunkards, forcing children to grow up virtually fatherless, and creating abandoned mothers who cannot cope with the myriad responsibilities for their children's upbringing.[27] To appreciate the gross indignity and indecency to which blacks are subjected, consider the following:

> The majority of contract workers . . . live in bleak concrete compounds housing in many cases several thousand workers. . . . The conditions in the compounds, no less than their appearance, invite comparison with prisons. The main white English-language newspaper in the territory, The Windhoek Advertiser, has described Katutura's strife-torn compound as "little less than a filthy ghetto." This compound is surrounded by barricades so that the police can readily check the passes of inmates going in and out, and its walls are crowned with broken glass and barbed wire. The interior has been reported to be cold and dank and men sleep twenty to a room on wooden lidded concrete boxes that contain all their possessions. Each man receives a piece of felt one centimeter thick as a mattress. Sanitary conditions are disgusting, with many flies and an all-pervading stench of urine and unappetizing food, cooked in bulk, is ladled out with shovels. . . . Walvis Bay compound, the biggest, is not as dirty and the workers say the food is edible, but the lavatories are communal without any partitions for privacy. No women are allowed into any of these compounds and the men must live in a soul-destroying all-male environment.[28]

Although trade unions are not outlawed, whites are forbidden to recognize any black trade unions. Indeed, industrial acts, such as strikes, "go-slows," boycotts, and noncooperation are outlawed for black workers and punishable in serious terms. The observation of one union representative before an investigative panel of the U.N. Commission on Human Rights is revealing:

> In South West Africa, where our union (the South African Food and Canning Workers Union) had a branch in Ludentzborg, we negotiated an agreement for the workers—the conditions and the wages were terribly bad there—and as

soon as we had made an agreement for the workers with the employers, then the Government police and detectives came to the union meeting and closed it. I was present there and they ordered me out of the place and terrorized the workers, our committee members and shop stewards, and forced us to break up the branch in South West Africa in this way.[29]

If blacks are treated with such gross indignity, why don't they just stay in their reserves and work for themselves? The answer is simple. Traditionally, most South African blacks were agricultural; they depended heavily on their land for grazing and farming. With the seizure of almost all their land, they have been reduced by overgrazing to the point where their only chance for survival is to diversify from their traditional calling. But not only are there no opportunities for diversification in their allotted areas—no minerals, no industries, and so forth—they are barred from acquiring valuable skills. One report about the plight of the migrant workers before a U.N. expert group points out:

When he [the migrant laborer] comes there [meaning the "Homeland"] he will not have any food; there will be no provisions for him to make a living, because there will be no work for him. And if a person . . . does not have means of getting food, he has to die; and I think there is a tendency to starve our people . . . and if these people do not starve, they will forever remain dependents of South Africa.[30]

Another account makes the same point:

In 1975 only three per cent of the country's total Gross Domestic Product was produced inside the bantustans. The income of the bantustans . . . is almost all generated outside these areas. In 1976 for example, over 70 per cent of the Gross National Product of the Bantustans came from "commuters" and migrant workers . . . only 13 per cent of the income of the bantustans was generated within their boundaries in 1980.
   The fact that so little economic activity takes place in the bantustans is a reflection of their role in the economy, as suppliers of labor and depositories for the unemployed, the aged and the sick.[31]

Often, blacks do not even have the right to decide whether or not they want to work for the whites, because the powers exercised under the vagrancy laws are so broad that blacks who do not want to work for whites can be put into forced labor for no pay:

An additional spur is the need to pay poll-tax to the tribal authorities. If this were not enough, "Native Reserve Regulation 27bis" of 1922, allows the superintendent of a reserve to order any male resident who is living an "idle" existence to take up employment in essential public works. Further, under the "Vagrancy Proclamation" of 1920, Africans can be convicted for vagrancy and be "sentenced" to work in essential public works or even for a private individual.[32]

The discrimination against blacks in the workforce is a reflection of the way the educational system and training facilities have been planned. Although the educational system had been disadvantageous to blacks ever since the dawn of colonialism,[33] the situation has been even worse since the South African Nationalist government assumed power. This deplorable trend was initiated by the Bantu Education Act of 1953, and its purpose is discernible from the recommendations by the Eiselen Commission. According to it, the teaching of Africans should be done

> in such a way that the Bantu child will be able to find his way in European communities, to follow oral or written instructions, and to carry on a simple conversation with Europeans about his work and other subjects of common interest. . . . Handiwork in the first four years of school should aim at the establishment of the habit of doing manual work.[34]

Upon the passage of the act, considerably more emphasis was placed on the instruction of blacks in their mother tongue and religion;[35] the minimum standards for teachers of African schools were lowered;[36] government grants for African education were reduced substantially (by 1958, the subsidies had been reduced from 100 percent of salaries and allowances to teachers to no subsidy at all);[37] and a new system of registering schools was introduced, closing many mission schools, especially the best ones. To fill in any loopholes, the act made it illegal to operate any unregistered school.[38] One cannot but accept the report given by the U.N. Special Commission on the Racial Situation in Africa as an accurate appraisal of the South African educational system: "It is clear that the aim of the Act is to give the African an inferior kind of education so as to keep him permanently as a hewer of wood and a drawer of water."[39] Another observation describes the situation thus:

> There can be little doubt that it is the intention of the framers of the Act that the education of the African child shall be different from that of the European and, further, that *this difference shall establish and perpetuate an inferior status in the African in relation to the European.* The education of the child is therefore not intended to stimulate the development of its intellect and character, but to prepare it for a certain service to the state; a service which is

primarily that of servant of the Europeans and secondarily one which carries with it no promise of advancement towards the eventual social and political status which he covets in order to benefit to the full under western democracy.[40]

But the rigors of apartheid are not felt solely in the socioeconomic and educational lives of the blacks in South Africa and Namibia; they are suffered in the political and criminal justice systems as well.

By law not only are blacks prohibited from standing as candidates for government posts, but they cannot be elected into the South African or Namibian parliaments. Nor do they have the franchise to play any role in the selection of candidates. This clearly is government without representation. But perhaps the most regrettable attribute of the system is its categorical prohibition of blacks' working in the South African civil service.

Blacks cannot freely express themselves, associate with people (whether of their color or otherwise), or move from one place to another. The legislative weapons (which the system classifies as "security laws") include the Suppression of Communism Act, the Unlawful Organizations Act, the Terrorism Act, the Riotous Assemblies Act, and the General Law Amendment Act. The scope of these laws is so wide that the regime is able to use them against any conceivable opposition.

The Suppression of Communism Act,[41] for instance, commences with long, complex definitions of "communism" and "communist."[42] The term "communist" applies not only to people who though once communists no longer support that political persuasion, but as well to any person who, though not communist, is tagged as one by the governor general.

Under the Riotous Assemblies Act,[43] any magistrate is empowered to prohibit any public gathering if he feels that the public peace would be endangered, and he may prohibit specified public gatherings, or any person from attending specified gatherings, during a specified period or in a specified area if he perceives the engendering of hostile feelings between Europeans and "any one section of the inhabitants of the Union." Any person who convenes, addresses, or prints notices of a prohibited meeting or attends that meeting after having been prohibited from doing so is subject to criminal penalties. In *Sachs v. Minister of Justice* the accused petitioned the Supreme Court to enjoin the minister of justice from prohibiting him from certain areas until the minister had specified the grounds on which the notice was given. Applying the Riotous Assemblies Act of 1914, the court ruled in part: "Parliament may make any encroachment it chooses upon the life, liberty, or property of any individual subject to its sway, and . . . it is the function of the courts of law to enforce its will."[44]

Under the Union Regulation Act of 1955 the government has complete control over the possession of South African passports;[45] it can refuse to grant a passport or visa to anybody or even revoke any passport at any time without accountability to anyone. Thanks to this act, several people have been prevented from appearing to testify against apartheid in the United Nations and other human rights organizations.

The offense of "terrorism" carries penalties for treason, namely, sentences that may include the death penalty. Under the Terrorism Act, this offense is defined as an act of violence committed with the intent to "overthrow or endanger the State authority"; to bring about "any constitutional, political, industrial, social or economic aim of change"; to "induce the Government . . . to do or abstain from doing any act or to adopt or abandon a particular standpoint" or to "put in fear or demoralize the General Public" or a particular group of inhabitants. Anyone who encourages, aids, or advises another person, or conspires with another, to commit a violent act to bring about any of these objects is also guilty of terrorism.

To streamline the apartheid policy, most of these "security laws" have been changed over the years. Often, the change is effected by amendment or the incorporation of an old security law into other laws. One of these changes is embodied in the Internal Security Act of 1982. In addition to covering much of the preexisting security legislation, this new act created new offenses, including the offense of "subversion," which is defined broadly to include actions that are aimed at "causing or promoting general dislocation or disorder"; "prejudicing the production and distribution of commodities or the supply and distribution of essential services or the free movement of traffic"; causing "feelings of hostility between the different population groups"; and encouraging or aiding any other person to commit any of the acts listed. Another new offense introduced by the 1982 Internal Security Act is the offense of "incitement," which encompasses any act that encourages or aids another to protest against any law or in support of any campaign for the repeal or modification of any law or for the change in the administration of any law.

Generally, the police are authorized to search premises, vehicles, and persons without warrant. These searches, which can result in indefinite detention for interrogation, have led to the torture and death for many people. One former detainee describes his experience:

They would come in the middle of the night. The last key in the succession of prison doors belongs to security police—all other doors can be opened by prison staff. So they would come at night. . . . You just heard someone interfering with your neck, they came with a wire. He says, "I am going to strangle you, because you don't want to tell the truth or tell me about other people. I will tell the whole world that you've committed suicide." Then he'd walk out. Some days I'd feel cold steel next to my temple. He would say "I am going to shoot you and nobody will ever know about you because, I have the power, the privilege and the protection as a policeman. . . ." Some days they would come in and beat me up in the cells.[46]

Another description is provided by a Johannesburg lawyer:

You have accused persons who have been in detention incommunicado—without access to anyone—for lengthy periods. They all make statements at one stage or another. You have witnesses in solitary confinement, incommunicado, held away from everyone. They all make statements. And what you then do is put the accused in the dock and you bring up the witness—straight out of solitary confinement—totally disoriented, not knowing what his rights are, usually not knowing what the charges are and sometimes not knowing who the accused are. And you say to him: "speak, and tell us the truth" (which he may have learnt in solitary confinement).[47]

Unlike most civilized legal systems, notably those of Anglo-American orientation wherein an accused is innocent until proven otherwise, the criminal justice system under apartheid is very peculiar; a person is presumed guilty, and unless the accused can conclusively rebut this presumption—an almost impossible task in a system where there is strong prejudice against anybody brought for trial—that person's guilt and punishment is assured. Because there is no legal aid, innocent people who are unable to afford legal representation or to survive the intimidation and/or the technicalities of the law often fall prey to the omnibus provisions of the laws. As for the arbitrariness of the whole process, one need only observe the status of evidence brought against the accused. By Amendments to the Criminal Procedure Act and the pre-1982 Internal Security Act, statements made by defendants during detention are presumed to be voluntary confessions, and even where defendants had been tortured, put into solitary confinement, and deprived of the right to legal advice before the so-called confession is made, it forms the cornerstone of the state's case and often the basis for conviction and punishment.

Perhaps the most graphic illustration of the outrageous nature of the apartheid judicial process is the "terrorist trial" of Namibians who were indicted for conspiracy to overthrow law and order in Namibia. In this trial—which, to say the least, is the most blatant manifestation of travesty of justice in our times—not only was the evidence incoherent and patently ludicrous, but it was also bereft of any substance to sustain it. Yet the accused were convicted and punished in disregard of opposition from the United Nations and the international community at large. Falk, a renowned international lawyer who attended the trial as an observer for the International Commission of Jurists, observed with regret:

> During the trial, the prisoners were referred to by numbers pinned to their shirts or jackets. . . . This impersonal mode of reference would not have been used if the prisoners had been white people. The use of numbers rather than names is consistent with the general depersonalization and dehumanization of Africans that pervade every aspect of apartheid. . . .
>
> Each day the prisoners were taken back and forth from the Pretoria jail in a large van. This van delivered the defendants to a cage that had been placed in a small enclosed courtyard. . . . Outside the cage were a large number of uniformed policemen carrying sten-guns or holding onto aggressive police dogs. These dogs were trained to bark furiously at the smell or sight of Africans. The prisoners were led through a gauntlet of police and barking dogs from their cage to the courtroom. . . . The lawyers for the defense told me that many (if not all) of the defendants were terrified by this daily experience. I stood in the yard and was very frightened by the generally menacing quality of the scene.[48]

In another account, another observer, Arthur Larson, who with Falk had expressed his serious regret about the torturing of prisoners, reported:

> Much of the evidence presented at the trial had been procured by the arrest of 180 witnesses and the holding of them in solitary confinement for unlimited periods. There was a considerable amount of torture of prisoners and witnesses. Some of the police testimony was so obviously perjured as to be ludicrous, as in the case of one officer's testimony that each of the accused he caught voluntarily blurted out a full confession, after having been assured of his legal right to remain silent, each confession being practically identical to every other confession. When asked what happened to the written statments of confession he said these prisoners had signed, the response was that it was raining very hard and all the written confessions got soaked and disintegrated. . . . Given the background and procedure in this affair, one simply cannot assume that anything in the record is reliable, whether purported confessions or anything else.[49]

Of course, as broad as the laws are, one might question whether it is right to view them solely in racial terms. But this objection cannot be entertained for long. The crucial point is the purpose of the apartheid system. It unquestionably seeks to entrench a racist minority rule by suppressing all opposition, and the application of the laws to whites is intended to discourage liberal whites from sympathizing with the victims of apartheid. The U.N. Special Commis-

TABLE 3
PEOPLE KILLED AND INJURED BY THE POLICE "IN THE
EXECUTION OF THEIR DUTIES"

	KILLED			WOUNDED		
Year	*Blacks*	*Colored*	*Total*	*Blacks*	*Colored*	*Total*
1974	88	11	102	288	57	354
1975	106	25	134	299	79	382
1976	165	28	195	345	53	410
1977	128	20	149	321	76	403
1978	173	28	203	373	126	514
1979	133	28	163	398	87	495
Totals 1974–79	793	140	946	2,024	478	2,558

Note: Excludes people who died while in detention or who were killed by police during the protests of 1976–1977.
Source: Drawn with minor variation from South Africa Institute of Race Relations citing official figures, cited in APARTHEID THE FACTS (Publication of International Defense Aid for Southern Africa, in cooperation with the U.N. Center Against Apartheid) at 63 (1983).
*It is significant that the chart does not show any white casualties and that the totals are not mathematically correct. For example, the reported accumulative figures amount to 13 fewer killed and 56 fewer wounded than do the figures, added down, from the individual years. However, even if the differences were taken as white casualties, these figures are just a tiny fraction (1.4% for deaths and 2.2% for wounded) of the total.

sion on the Racial Situation in South Africa was thus by no means exaggerating when it said of the security laws that they "certainly . . . make it more difficult than before for non-White organizers to launch any concerted campaign of resistance against the laws, and even to prevent non-European leaders stating their opposition to a bill introduced by the Government or criticizing it."[50] According to the regulations, anybody, including whites, who gives audience to, associates with, or sympathizes with an anti-apartheid activist who vents any view in support of any anti-apartheid values is culpable. However, the record provides evidence to suggest that white and black "offenders" are treated differently (see Table 3).

THE CENSURE OF APARTHEID

Since it has been observed that the apartheid system is indistinguishable from colonialism, the conclusion that colonialism is illegal makes any further inquiry into the legality of apartheid superfluous. However, because of the continuing survival and intransigence of the apartheid regime, the U.N. position on apartheid has become so transparently hortatory that it is imperative to study the issue more carefully, at least to see whether the apartheid system can be rationalized teleologically.[51] Before we embark on this inquiry, a brief overview of the status of the two apartheid territories is in order.

As apartheid exists in two entirely different entities—one a sovereign state, the other a nonsovereign being administered as a "sacred trust" on behalf of the international community—its legal significance in each entity might be unique under the domestic-jurisdiction concept. It should, however, be clear that with the development of concepts like self-determination and human rights and the international community's commitment to maintain the peace and security of the world, such a distinction is tenuous. Yet, no matter how closely the two apartheid territories may have related to one another at any time, it is inappropriate to treat them similarly now. After the termination of the mandate under which apartheid was introduced in Namibia, anything done by South Africa in Namibia—whether pursuant to apartheid or otherwise—is a nullity, including any right acquired or obligation incurred by any state under a transaction with South Africa. This conclusion may not apply to the apartheid regime in South Africa. Because it is a sovereign state whose sovereignty is upheld by virtually the whole international community, any act properly entered into with South Africa in relation to South African territory or citizens may not be void; at worst, it would be voidable at the option of the other party.

The Significance of Apartheid under the U.N. Charter

One basic principle, indeed the most fundamental under the U.N. Charter,[52] is that human beings are endowed with certain inalienable rights that constitute the cornerstone of the maintenance of international peace and security. In the preamble this idea is repeatedly pronounced by such expressions as "fundamental human rights," "the equal rights of men and women," "the dignity and worth of the human person," "justice," "social and economic advancement of all peoples," "social progress and better standards of life in larger freedom," "tolerance" and many others. These notions are elaborated in several of the main provisions of that august document. In stating the purposes of the United Nations, article 1, for instance, mentions "the principle of equal rights and self-determination of peoples"; "problems of an economic, social, cultural, or humanitarian character"; and "respect for all without distinction as to race, sex, language, or religion."

In delineating the functions of the General Assembly, article 13 empowers and requires the assembly, among other things, to initiate studies and make recommendations for the purpose of "promoting international co-operation in the economic, social, cultural, educational, and health fields, and for assisting in the realization of human rights and fundamental freedoms for all without distinction as to race, sex, language, or religion."[53] Again, in article 55 the observance of equal rights and self-determination is listed as one of the means by which the commitment to maintain the peace and stability of the international community can be realized. And in article 56, all members of the United Nations, including South Africa, *"pledge"* themselves to take joint and separate action in cooperation with the organization for the achievement of these goals.

Considering the principle that, unless otherwise stated, all parts of a treaty should carry the same weight, and considering also the rule that a treaty should not be construed in a manner that would suggest that the drafters intended to make it ineffective, the only inference to draw from the Charter's commitment to insure the promotion of human rights is that it is a binding commitment, the violation of which is unquestionably illegal. Other factors by which this conclusion can be reinforced are the numerous reiterations of the commitment in several parts of the document and the institutional machineries established to effect the commitments. Since, as a member of the United Nations, South Africa is bound by the maxim *pacta sunt servanda* to abide by all commitments assumed under the Charter, it is proper to brand the inhuman nature of its apartheid system as a violation of its treaty obligations and, hence, as illegal acts.

Apartheid under the Universal Declaration of Human Rights

The Universal Declaration of Human Rights[54] proceeds on the premise that "all human beings are born free and equal in dignity and rights."[55] It postulates certain "rights and freedoms" to which "everyone is entitled." These include the right to life, liberty, and security of person; freedom from slavery, servitude, or inhuman treatment; the right to nondiscrimination and equal protection under the law; freedom from arbitrary arrest; freedom of movement, speech, thought, association, conscience, religion, and assembly; the right to equal pay for equal work; and the right to take part in the government of one's country, either directly or through freely chosen representatives.

The tenets of apartheid—its labor system, social system, political system, and educational system, to mention only a few—obviously defy these standards, but a number of questions have to be resolved before the full legal significance and implications of apartheid can be determined under the document.

First, how binding is the document on South Africa? Since South Africa abstained from the vote adopting the declaration as a resolution of the United Nations, the effect of the document on that country, and a fortiori the few other abstainers, may be at issue. But the deficiency of this argument is not hard to find, for neither abstention nor a negative vote in the General Assembly can block a resolution from being passed.

Another possible question about the significance of the resolution is whether it has any legal efficacy. According to one view, the declaration merely stipulates "oughtness" of international behavior and is consequently bereft of legal significance.[56] But this perception cannot be sustained, either. One merely need recall the unanimity with which the document was adopted and its reiteration of the principles of the U.N. Charter and those of the Nuremberg Tribunal, not to mention the document's endorsement by countless other landmark instruments of international law, notably the International Covenant on Civil and Political Rights; the Optional Protocol to the International Covenant on Civil and Political Rights; the International Covenant on Economic, Social and Cultural Rights; the International Convention on the Elimination of All Forms of Racial Discrimination; and the European Convention on Human Rights[57]—which elevates the declaration's anti-apartheid stance to at least the status of customary international law.

Apartheid and the Genocide Convention

The apartheid system offends the laws against genocide, too. The Genocide Convention of 1948[58] reads:

> Genocide means any of the following acts committed with intent to destroy, in whole or in part, a national, ethical, racial, or religious groups as such:
>
> (a) Killing members of the group;
> (b) Causing serious bodily or mental harm to members of the group;
> (c) Deliberately inflicting on the group conditions of life calculated to bring about its physical destruction in whole or in part;
> (d) Imposing measures intended to prevent births within the group;
> (e) Forcibly transferring children of the group to another group.[59]

To expose the illegality of apartheid under this regime one merely need show that apartheid is a system having the specific purpose of establishing and maintaining control over people of a specific race. It inflicts serious bodily and mental harm on the members of that racial group by subjecting them to such inhuman treatments as torture, arbitrary arrest, and illegal imprisonment. And it imposes living conditions calculated to interfere with, or deny their enjoyment of, certain basic human rights. It kills people wantonly, taking measures designed to prevent the improvement of the people of a rival racial group, and forcibly moves them from their traditional places of habitation to areas that are unsuitable for their living conditions and with which they have had little or no contact in the past. Because the convention does not apply solely to the destruction of a whole race, it is immaterial that the architects of apartheid have turned some members of the beleaguered race, notably the traditional rulers, into stooges for implementing the policy. It is significant that under article 3 of the convention (the provision that is arguably reminiscent of the the Nuremberg principles),[60] not only is action pursuant to a superior's orders no defense for any actor under the apartheid system, but it is also clear that any person who contributes in any way—whether by conspiracy, instigation, or collaboration in the implementation of apartheid, or whether a superior, a state, or a private individual—would be culpable under the convention. Finally, in addition to providing adequate machinery for apprehending and punishing culprits under articles 4 through 8, the convention provides categorically that the principle that protects political criminals from extradition would be of no avail to anyone charged under the convention.[61]

Our overview of the apartheid system makes clear why it is often equated with Nazism,[62] but it also offers a sound basis for the view that apartheid violates the laws against slavery and the exploitation of workers. Similarly, to the extent that the apartheid system thrives on the branding and punishing of all opponents, including internationally recognized liberation movments, as criminals, it can be condemned under the laws of war, which require activists in liberation movments to be treated as prisoners of war.

RECENT DEVELOPMENTS IN THE APARTHEID SYSTEM

Starting in the early sixties, South Africa embarked on a new set of "Bantustan" policies that, in its view, were tantamount to recognizing and granting the right of self-determination to the victims of apartheid.[63] Beginning with the Transkei Constitution Act of 1963,[64] which purportedly accorded "self-government" to Transkei, South Africa dished out "independence" to Transkei under the South African Status of Transkei Act of 1976[65] and subsequently to such others as Venda, Bophuthatswana, and Ciskei—all of whose alleged "independence" drew from the Transkei Act as their masterpiece document. Pursuant to this act, local "Independence Constitutions" were passed for all the "Homelands," and cumulatively they vested formal independence in the respective authorities: their legislative assemblies were conferred with plenary authority to make legislation whose validity cannot be impugned in any court; and they were given full powers to change any law, including their constitutions, if they wished.

Interestingly, these packages have failed to have the impact that South Africa expected them to have on the international community. For not only have they been condemned worldwide,[66] but the United Nations has, by resolutions 31/6A and 402 of the General Assembly and Security Council, respectively, called upon all states to withhold recognition from Transkei and a fortiori, from any of the others.

Though it is not surprising that the "independent" homelands have been denied recognition by all states, a number of questions must be asked. For instance, one may like to know why, after all the entreaties that the South African government stop violating the African's right of self-determination, the United Nations and the international community failed to welcome the independence of the "homelands." Moreover, there are issues about the legal effect of the nonrecognition. To put these issues in their proper perspective, it is useful to explore the factors that might have caused South Africa to decide to give independence to the "homelands."

Why South Africa "Changed" Its Policy

International Pressure

Some scholars suggest that the pressure from the international community is a potent force behind South Africa's decision to embark on the "homelands independence" scheme.[67] Ironically, South Africa uses this same argument to bolster its so-called "independence" policy. Dr. Verwoerd urged in a 1961 House of Assembly Debate:

> This is not what we would have liked to see. It is a form of fragmentation which we would not have liked if we were able to avoid it. In the light of the pressure being exerted on South Africa there is, however, no doubt that eventually this will have to be done, thereby buying for the white man his freedom and his right to retain domination in what is his country. . . . If the Whites could have continued to rule over everybody, with no danger to themselves, they would certainly have chosen to do so. However, we have to bear in mind the new views in regard to human rights, . . . the power of the world and world opinion and our desire to preserve ourselves.[68]

Since the observation does not specify which types of international pressure might have triggered this development in the apartheid system, it may be right to attribute the change to all the different forms by which the international pressure has been expressed. This position is unlikely to survive an empirical test. Accordingly, we will examine the issue through two of the most important forms of pressure—that brought to bear by U.N. resolutions and that by the liberation movements.

The U.N. Resolutions

One of the first U.N. resolutions on South Africa's racial policy was Resolution 395 (V) of 1950, which, after holding that "a policy of 'racial segregation' is necessarily based on the doctrines of racial discrimination" and hence violates the U.N. Charter, called for a round-the-table discussion of the situation for an amicable settlement of the conflict.[69] In subsequent resolutions of that decade the assembly "called on" and "appealed to" South Africa to observe the human rights obligations contained in the Charter[70] and expressed its "regret and concern" that "the Government of the Union of South Africa has not yet responded to appeals . . . that it reconsider governmental policies which impair the right of all racial groups to enjoy the same rights and fundamental freedoms."[71] With the swelling of the U.N. membership in the 1960s, the apparently moderate skirmishes against the apartheid system became more vigorous onslaughts. In 1962 the assembly passed one of its most far-reaching resolutions, calling upon the Security Council to take effective measures, including sanctions, to secure South Africa's compliance with prior resolutions and, if necessary, to consider possible action under article 6 of the Charter.[72] Pursuant to another resolution adopted shortly thereafter, the secretary general, per the council's authorization, established a group of experts

> to examine methods of resolving the present situation in South Africa through full, peaceful, and orderly application of human rights and fundamental freedoms to all inhabitants of the territory as a whole, regardless of race, color or creed, and to consider what part the United Nations might play in the achievement of that end.[73]

In their report, these experts urged that "all people of South Africa should be brought into consultation to decide the future of their country at the national level," and that the council should invite the government of South Africa to participate in discussions to convene a representative national convention under the United Nations' auspices. It then concluded that if the South African government refused to comply with the request or invitation, the council should henceforth consider itself as left with no other peaceful means for settling the conflict except to apply economic sanctions.[74] The council accepted these recommendations and appealed to the South African government to do the same and to cooperate with the secretary general by submitting its views on the issue of the national convention.[75]

South Africa, however, rejected all these exhortations. The arrogance with which South Africa has responded to these entreaties of the international community casts great doubt on the question of whether international pressure had any influence on its decision to grant "independence" to the homelands.

As a member of the United Nations, South Africa would have responded appropriately had it been influenced by U.N. resolutions. However, those who deny that U.N. resolutions are binding except when taken under chapter VII of the Charter consider the described resolutions as having no force over South Africa. Thus, according to one view:

> Resolutions of the General Assembly which are directed at the regulation of the international affairs of the U.N. are legally binding. . . . On the other hand, resolutions addressed to member states in terms of articles 10–14 (Chapter IV) . . . are recommendatory. . . . Unlike the General Assembly resolutions, the Security Council is competent to adopt legally binding resolutions on matters relating to international peace and security. But like the Assembly, the Council also has the lesser power of recommendation. . . . Chapter VI of the Charter grants the Council competence in the field of the "Pacific Settlement of Disputes". Resolutions made under this head are generally accepted as not being legally binding. . . . Chapter VII of the Charter gives the Council competence to take action in the event of breaches of the peace. . . . Decisions taken under these articles . . . are obligatory. . . . In order that Chapter VII apply, a determination in terms of article 39 that apartheid constitutes "a threat to the peace, breach of peace, or act of aggression" is a conditions precedent. No such determination has been made. . . ." These cautiously phrased findings . . . leads [*sic*] to the conclusion that *resolutions of the Security Council calling upon South Africa to alter her racial policies are not legally binding and that South Africa is not bound to comply with them.*[76]

No matter how plausible this argument may be, it does not apply to those cases wherein a state decides to be bound by a resolution or "recommendation," as people may call it.[77] Thus, where South Africa has expressly stated that its decision was influenced by international pressure, which for the present discussion is construed as pressure exerted by the U.N. resolutions, it remains valid to conclude that it was indeed the U.N. pressure that occasioned the decision, even though that pressure took the form of "recommendations."

Nevertheless, it is difficult to sustain the notion that the resolutions and the South African Bantustan policy are correlated. The weakness of the U.N. pressure is evident: there were no enforcement measures, there were the occasional abstentions of the only members whose voices matter to South Africa (Britain, the U.S., and France). Besides, there is a gross disparity between what the United Nations enjoined South Africa to do and what South Africa actually did in its "independence" deals. In the United Nations' entreaties, South Africa is called upon to recognize and promote the black South Africans' fundamental human rights and rights to self-determination by restoring their sociopolitical rights in their country. This was to be done inter alia by letting them participate freely in the political process, possibly under U.N. suprevision. The South African "independence" scheme, on the other hand, took entirely the opposite direction: it was formulated and pronounced unilaterally without any regard to the views of the black majority and was a perpetuation of the apartheid socio-economic and political systems.

If the alleged "independence" program was at such cross-purposes with the U.N. exhortations on South Africa, it would obviously be misleading, if not wholly impossible, to find any correlation between the two. The claim that South Africa's decision to hand out the "independence" packages was influenced by U.N. pressure is therefore untenable.

The United Nations has been mindful of the gross discrepancy between its pronouncements and the course taken by South Africa in its so-called progressive Bantustan policy. The organization cited the incompatibility of the policy with the values cherished by the international community as the basis for withholding recognition of any of the "independent homelands," and virtually all its recent resolutions on South Africa portray the policy as outrageous. In Resolution 35/206 of 1981, for instance, the General Assembly,

> Recognizing that the so-called constitutional and other reforms by the racist minority regime are no more than mere adjustments within the framework of apartheid, *Again denounces the establishment of bantustans as designed to consolidate the inhuman policy of apartheid, to destroy the territorial integrity and to deprive the African people of South Africa of their inalienable rights*, and calls upon all Governments to continue to deny any form of recognition to the so-called "independent" bantustans and to refrain from any dealings with such entities as have been declared null and void.[78]

Similarly, the Security Council resolution declares:

> The Council does not recognize the so-called "independent homelands" in South Africa. It condemns the purported proclamation of the "independence" of the Ciskei and declares it totally invalid. . . . It seeks to create a class of foreign people in their own country. . . .
> The Council calls upon all Governments to deny any form of recognition to the so-called "independent" bantustans, to refrain from any dealings with them, to reject travel documents issued by them.[79]

Pressure from the Liberation Movements

The struggles against South Africa are launched by the freedom fighters in Namibia and South Africa who, on occasion, get assistance from the O.A.U.

and countries from many parts of the world. But it is doubtful whether such assistance could have had any impact on South Africa in its decision to grant "independence" to the "homelands." First, South Africa has always firmly refused to recognize any of the liberation movements as legitimate, labeling them "terrorist" movements. It has consequently been an implacable opponent of any member of the movements. If the movements are recognized by South Africa only as "terrorist," it is ludicrous to suggest that the government would have given in to pressure from them when even the most powerful world organization—the United Nations—was unable to make it repudiate the policy.

Nor could the liberation movements have had much impact on South Africa at all. Notwithstanding the numerical advantage of the strugglers over the South African white population, the South African government's armed superiority is so overwhelming that it is difficult to substantiate any presumption that the new policy could have resulted from the pressure of the liberation movements. Not only is international assistance to the liberation movements marginal, but virtually all the neighboring African countries that are committed, either individually or through the O.A.U., to help the liberation fighters are so riddled by their own socioeconomic and political problems that they sometimes play a double game when it comes to fulfilling their commitment to fight South Africa.

If international pressure cannot account for the South African "homeland" policy, what then could have influenced South Africa in its decision to adopt that deceptive policy?

The "Independent Homeland" Packages:
The Next Step of Apartheid

A close look at apartheid and the "homeland" packages confirms the U.N. position as expressed in its resolutions A/31/62, A/35/206, and S/402: the "homeland" policy is nothing but a logical next step in the evolution of the apartheid system.

First, apartheid is a discriminatory system in which personal, economic, political, social, and educational resources of a country are distributed unequally on the basis of race. Second, apartheid is a system in which whites want to have nothing in common with blacks, except to reduce them to subhuman beings whose value is measured solely in terms of master-servant relations. Finally, apartheid seeks to guarantee its survival by putting blacks into small political enclaves that, because they are economically unviable, would constitute labor pools from which South Africa could derive its migrant workers, and which, because of their rivalry and mutual animosity, would be unable to create a formidable political force against apartheid.

How different is the "homeland" policy from these? By transforming the "homelands" into small independent states whose inhabitants are thereby denationalized as South African citizens,[80] not only does the apartheid system achieve its objective of permanently separating blacks from whites, but it also fulfills its basic aspiration of turning blacks into a labor pool from which the frustrated could be pulled to work in South Africa as alien guest laborers. In competing with each other for favorable treatment from South Africa, the "homelands" would not be able to unite in opposition to the formidable South African system.

It may be difficult to pinpoint the time when the "independence" notion was conceived and introduced, but the records leave no doubt that the apartheid authorities never contemplated any movement away from the basic tenets of apartheid. Territorial autonomy for the reserves first appeared in 1951 when the Bantu Authorities Act[81] was passed. Then came the Transkei Constitution Act of 1963, whose dramatic granting of self-government to Transkei revealed what might have been playing in the minds of the architects of apartheid—the development toward autonomy and eventual independence for the reserves. Interestingly, the underlying theme of the "homeland" policy is not concealed in statements made by South African politicians. Here it may be useful to reiterate what has been quoted from Dr. C. P. Mudler:

> If our policy is taken to its full logical conclusion as far as the black people are concerned, there will be not one black man with South African citizenship. . . . Every black man in South Africa will eventually be accommodated in some independent new state in this honorable way and there will no longer be a moral obligation on this Parliament to accommodate these people politically.[82]

Likewise, according to H. J. D. van der Walt:

> The stated policy and priorities of the Government are to develop the various national States. . . . The National party has a specific policy, a policy which amounts to a division of power. . . . We cannot share power in a unitary State in South Africa. Therefore the National Party's policy of the division of power gives rise to black national states.[83]

THE INTERNATIONAL COMMUNITY'S CHILLY RESPONSE TO THE "HOMELANDS' INDEPENDENCE" SCHEME

It is the sole prerogative of a state to decide whether or not to accord recognition to a newly created state. The decision to withhold recognition of the "independent" homelands was officiated by the United Nations; one wonders therefore whether the United Nations did not overstep its powers in bypassing this established principle of international law. But this question cannot be of much significance in the evaluation of the failure to recognize, for the law on recognition does not question the background in which an entity is refused recognition, and it is obvious from the the the domestic-jurisdiction concept that the right of states to exercise their discretion is not absolute in international law. Even if it were, it would still be difficult to say that the U.N. resolution against the recognition of the homelands encroached upon the sovereign rights of states, because the decision was neither imposed nor adopted in a vacuum. It was taken on the basis of a full U.N. deliberation on the issue, and only after the requisite votes had been cast. Since the voting in the United Nations is unquestionably an exercise of the rights of the member states, the U.N. resolution forbidding its members to recognize the "independent" homelands cannot be construed as an invasion of the sovereignty of any state.

But there are other grounds on which to base the decision not to recognize. Of these, three require special study.

Territorial Integrity

One principle by which the international community is maintained is the respect for territorial integrity of states. Thus, in the League of Nations era when Japan sought to carve a puppet state out of Manchuria, the League refused to recognize it.[84] But the issues in this precedent are distinguishable from the issues raised in the "independence" packages. First, in the Manchuria case, the League's injunction on states to withhold recognition was occasioned by the Japanese aggression. Article 10 of the Covenant was the basis of its action:

> The High Contracting Parties undertake to respect and preserve as against external aggression the territorial integrity and existing political independence of all States members of the League. In case of any such aggression or in case of any threat or danger of such aggression the Executive Council shall advise upon the means by which this obligation shall be fulfilled.[85]

The League's resolution on Manchuria addressed this principle: "It is incumbent upon the Members of the League of Nations not to recognize any situation, treaty or agreement which may be brought about by means contrary to the Covenant of the League of Nations or to the Pact of Paris."[86]

Since the South African independence scheme was not preceded by aggression, and since the U.N. Charter does not specifically require the United Nations to take an action against any act except those that breach, or pose threats to, international peace and security, the Manchuria case might be a doubtful precedent for the "homelands" situation. As a sovereign whose ownership of the "homelands"—those in South Africa but not Namibia—was unencumbered by the rights of any other state, South Africa had the freedom to cede any part of its territory in any way it deemed fit.[87] According to some writers, this freedom can be exercised without any regard to the will of the affected inhabitants. Thus, in the words of Oppenheim, "It is doubtful whether the Law of Nations will ever make it a condition of every cession that it must be ratified by plebiscite."[88] Drawing from this observation, it can be argued that the "homelands" independence policy is in accordance with the established principles of international law. Yet it does not seem possible to uphold this view in the present system, since with the United Nations' development of human rights and self-determination for all people, any cession of territory is not only required to be done in good faith but to conform to the principles of self-determination and human rights as well. Numerous writers have expressed disagreement with the traditional view. One critic, for instance, has pointed out: "The doctrine of self-determination and the prohibition of the use of force for territorial changes [have] transformed the component acquiescence of the indigenous people into a peremptory aspect, and a virtual requirement of lawful transfers of title."[89] Even if this inexceptionable opinion could be refuted, it would still be obvious that, by its perpetuation of apartheid, the "independence" policy has all the "evil" associated with the South African system; hence, there are no grounds for assailing the U.N. resolution against its recognition.

The Principle of Self-Determination

Although the principle of self-determination is almost absolute when it comes to settling colonial issues, there is strong disagreement on whether it can apply to independent countries, too. The 1970 U.N. Declaration on Friendly Relations, however, has provided a valuable answer that is accepted widely as authoritative. It postulates that if an entity within a state is discriminated against or unrepresented by its government, then the principle of inviolability of states cannot bar that entity from fighting for its right of self-determination. When we apply this to the apartheid scheme, a number of questions arise. For instance, can the fear of the South African whites that they may be discriminated against, and overrun, if they live together with the blacks in a single state where the democratic principle of one man, one vote is observed be advanced to rationalize the "homeland" policy as a legitimate exercise of the white South Africans' right of self-determination?

This question can easily be dispelled. First, the law cannot apply to speculations as to what the possible victims of oppression fear might happen to them in the (unforeseeable) future. It applies to tangible situations in which victims are actually oppressed or on the verge of being oppressed. The white

South Africans have been oppressing those whom they claim might oppress them. If the principle of the declaration should apply, it would be rather in favor of the blacks. But the blacks have never called for secession. White South Africans are the oppressors in South Africa, and the endorsement of their "homeland" policy would only compromise the maxim *ex injuria non oritur jus*. The chronology of the proceedings leading to the passage of the Independence Act helps to clarify:

1. 1963—Transkei was granted self-governing status and a legislative assembly. This decision was made unilaterally by the South African government, which included no Transkeian, let alone black, representation. Nor was the assembly composed by any meaningful democratic process. It was constituted mainly of chiefs who had been hand picked by the South African government and were subject to replacement if they failed to see eye to eye with it on any issue.
2. 1966—A discussion regarding the independence of Transkei was tabled in the newly formed Transkei Legislative Assembly, but a motion on this question failed to pass.
3. 1974—A proposal to conduct a referendum to determine whether or not independence should be granted succeeded in the Legislative Assembly, but the South African chief minister for Bantustans unilaterally rejected it.
4. A constitutional committee was then formed, comprising appointees from the Transkei Legislative Assembly and South African civil servants.
5. 1975—The Transkeian Constitution Act confirmed the position of the Constitutional Committee and granted independence to Transkei.

Considering the fact that the proceedings violate all the tenets of self-determination—that is, a free decision made by all those affected after having been fully informed of the possible consequences of their choice—it seems impossible to criticize the international community's decision to withhold recognition to the "states" created by the encroachment upon the "homelanders'" inherent right to self-determination.

THE LEGAL CONSEQUENCES OF THE "HOMELANDS" NATIONALITY LAWS AND HUMAN RIGHTS

If the "homelands" policy is a perpetuation of apartheid, and if apartheid lends itself to being called genocide, slavery, and discriminatory, the U.N.

refusal to recognize the "independent homelands" is surely bolstered by the human rights principles, too. The full ramifications of these principles vis-à-vis apartheid have been demonstrated in several parts of this study. Yet there is one aspect of the "homeland" policy—its nationalization law—whose violation of the human rights law has not been explored properly and therefore calls for special examination.

The "homelands" nationality laws are enshrined in section 6 of the independence-conferring statutes; essentially, they all take the same form as the Transkei's, which read in part: "Every person falling in any of the categories of persons defined in Schedule B shall be a citizen of Transkei [Bophuthatswana, Venda, or Ciskei] *and shall cease to be a South African citizen.*"

The provisions of schedule B vary according to the ethnic composition of each homeland, but the Transkei's is representative:

Categories of persons who in terms of section 6 are citizens of the Transkei and cease to be South African citizens:

(a) every person who was a citizen of Transkei in terms of any law at the commencement of this Act . . .

(d) every person born out of wedlock (according to custom or otherwise) and outside the Transkei whose mother was a citizen of the Transkei at the time of his birth . . .

(f) every South African citizen who is not a citizen of a territory within the Republic of South Africa, is not a citizen of Transkei in terms of (a), (b), (c), (d), or (e), and speaks a language used by Xhosa or Sotho speaking section of the population of the Transkei, including any dialect of any such language;

(g) every South African citizen who is not a citizen of a territory within the Republic of South Africa, and is not a citizen of the Transkei in terms of paragraph (a), (b), (c), (d), (e), or (f), and who is related to any member of the population contemplated in paragraph (f) *or has identified himself with any part of such population or is culturally or otherwise associated with any member or part of such population.*[90]

Although the law is presumed to affect only the inhabitants of the "homelands," in actuality it denationalizes all black South Africans. By referring to the Sotho and the Xhosa languages—languages spoken by almost every black South African—the law is made extremely broad; it entraps people who have only the faintest connection with any of the independent "homelands," replacing their South African nationality with the nationality of that "homeland." Bishop Tutu was by no means exaggerating when he lamented:

Overnight they will become foreigners in what for many of them has been the land of their birth and be forced to adopt the citizenship of a country that many do not know at all and in whose creation they have played no part at all. They

have contributed in their various ways to the prosperity of this beloved South
Africa and now it seems at the stroke of a pen they will forfeit a cherished
birthright.[91]

One notable problem with the "homeland" nationality law is that although
South Africa would have everybody believe that it is a law that was passed by a
sovereign state, the role of its government in the passage of the act and the
status of the so-called independent homelands make it more plausible to see it
as a South African-made law. This entails legal consequences that are not necessarily the same as those that would arise if the law was treated as having been
made by the "homelands."

Viewing the Law as South Africa's Enactment

International law generally considers matters relating to nationality as issues
falling within the domestic jurisdiction of states, and, consequently, it requires
states to respect each other's nationality laws. In the *Nottebohm* case, the general view was stated as follows:

> It is for Liechtenstein as it is for every sovereign State to settle by its own
> legislation the rules relating to the acquisition of its nationality by naturaliza-
> tion granted by its own organs in accordance with that legislation. It is not
> necessary to determine whether international law imposes any limitation on its
> freedom of decision in this domain.[92]

Since South Africa is a sovereign, it seems perfectly legitimate for it to
make nationality laws in relation to its subjects. On a more careful study of the
"homelands" law vis-à-vis this general rule, however, serious questions arise
about whether the law really permits South Africa to do what it did. Although
the extract from the *Nottebohm* case suggests that a sovereign can make law to
confer nationality, it says nothing about denationalization, thus indicating that
the "homelands" nationality law may not necessarily be defensible under this
rule.

In the *Tunis Morocco Nationality Decrees* case, the right of states to make
nationality laws was also asserted and upheld. It was, however, qualified in a
way suggesting that the principle in the *Nottebohm* case is only an aspect of the
general law on nationality. The qualification in the *Nationality Decree* case has
some relevance to the South African "homeland" independence statute. It reads:

> Thus, in the present state of international law, questions of nationality are, in
> the opinion of the Court, in principle within this reserved domain. . . . It is
> enough to observe that it may well happen that, in a matter which, like that of

nationality, is not in principle regulated by international law, *the right of a State to use its discretion is nevertheless restricted by obligations which it may have undertaken towards other States.* In such a case, jurisdiction which, in principle, belongs solely to the State, is limited by rules of international law.[93]

Obviously, this suggests that the scope of the right of a sovereign to make a nationality law depends on whether or not it has made international commitments to circumscribe its rights. Or to put it more clearly, a state's right to enjoy international recognition for its nationality law is qualified by the extent to which international law has developed at the time the issue arose. Now, the question is whether at the time of the "homelands" policy, international law had developed in a way that impinges upon South Africa's freedom to make certain types of nationality law.

Article 15 of the Universal Declaration on Human Rights states that "no one shall be arbitrarily deprived of his nationality." Article 5(d)(iii) of the International Convention on the Elimination of All Forms of Racial Discrimination guarantees the right of everyone, without distinction as to race, equality before the law, "notably in enjoyment of the right to nationality."[94] And the Convention on the Reduction of Statelessness[95] postulates that a "Contracting State may not deprive any person or group of persons of their nationality on racial, ethnic, religious or political grounds." Obviously, any of these instruments can provide a basis to fault the South African-sponsored "homelands" nationality laws. Even on the doubtful assumption that there can be any technical flaws against using these provisions to challenge the nationality laws, the widespread international abhorrence and opposition to the 1941 Nazi decree that denationalized German Jews[96] provide ample ground for treating the anti-denationalization concept as having attained the status of customary international law.

Perhaps the most reprehensible consequence of the "homelands" nationality laws is their creation of statelessness. As has been noted already, no other member of the international community besides South Africa has extended its recognition to any of the "homelands." Nor has any state any meaningful diplomatic relations with any of them. One important attribute of nationality under international law is that it is the sole medium by which interstate conflicts ensuing from infracted rights of individuals are redressed. According to the established law, if the rights of an individual are violated in a foreign country, only the state of that person's nationality can espouse his or her rights in an international adjudicatory forum. Thus, individuals whose rights are violated and who are not adequately redressed after exhausting the available domestic remedies in the country in which they are victimized would be helpless if they do not have their own state to espouse their claim through diplomatic channels or international forums. It is obvious that many problems would be encountered

by any of the supposed "nationals" of the "homelands" if they run into difficulties with foreign countries. It is, of course, arguable that with the nonrecognition of the "homelands" and therefore of the nationality of their inhabitants,
the South African "homelands" nationality law can be treated as *void ab initio*,
and, a fortiori, that the preexisting South African nationality would still attach
to the individuals and, consequently, entitle them to South Africa's protection
and defense on the international plane. In practice, this argument is untenable;
it regrettably overlooks the essential fact that the right of individuals to be
protected diplomatically by their own government is a prerogative of the state.
Thus, no one, not even the international community, can compel a state to
espouse a claim on behalf of its national. If a state cannot be made to pursue a
claim for a person whom it agrees to be its national, it would certainly be
optimistic, if not totally ludicrous, to say that South Africa would espouse a
claim for any of the "homelanders"—people who in its eyes are not South
Africans.

Granted that the "homelanders" theoretical right to South Africa's protection is meaningless, it is obvious that South Africa's denationalization of these
people has made them stateless. International law, however, frowns upon statelessness. Thus documents such as the Convention on the Reduction of Statelessness, the Convention Relating to the Status of Stateless Persons,[97] the Convention Relating to the Status of Refugees,[98] and the Protocol Relating to the
Status of Refugees[99]—all render the "homeland" policy illegal.[100] South Africa
is, of course, not entirely defenseless in the face of the censure of its creation
of statelessness by its "homelands" policy. One possible argument to defend it
may be derived from article 10 of the Convention on the Reduction of Statelessness, which reads:

> (1) Every treaty between contracting states providing for the transfer of terri-
> tory shall include provisions designed to secure that no person shall become
> stateless as a result of the transfer. . . . (2) In the absence of such provisions
> the contracting state to which territory is transferred or which otherwise ac-
> quires territory shall confer its nationality on such persons as would otherwise
> become stateless as a result of the transfer or acquisition.[101]

Since South Africa considers the "homelands" as states, the pertinence of
this provision to the issue under discussion cannot be ignored outright. Yet the
convention cannot apply to the "homelands" because they are neither contracting parties nor designated as intended beneficiaries. It is also questionable
whether any of the statutes conferring "homelands" independence can be likened to a treaty between states. Considering that the statutes were meant to

create statehood for the "homelands" and that they were illegal for being racially motivated and hence *void ab initio*, it is obviously not possible to defend the South African scheme thereunder; any such defense would violate the maxim *ex injuria non oritur jus*.

Viewing the Laws as the "Homelanders'" Enactment

If the creation of states out of the "homelands" is a nullity, then anything done by the "homelands" in their capacity as "states" would be void of any effect. Accordingly, there is no point in making further inquiry into whether the nationality laws would have legal force if they had been enacted by the "homelands." But this does not entirely resolve the issue. The main reason cited for the "homelands'" failure to attain statehood is the fact that they obtained no recognition from any state except South Africa, whose complicity was too tainted to give that recognition legal significance. The problem with recognition on the issue of statehood, however, is that it is surrounded by two diametrically opposed theories. One—the declarationist theory—denies that recognition has any significance in the attainment of statehood;[102] the other—the constitutivist theory—considers recognition to be a necessary condition for the existence of statehood.[103] Obviously, although the nonrecognition of the "homelands" conclusively leads to the inference that they are not states by the constitutivist theory, the same may not be true with the declarationist theory. Thus, by the declaratory principle the "homelands" can qualify for, if not actually attain, statehood if they satisfy all the traditional requirements for statehood, to wit, if they have a territory, a population, a government, and the capacity to enter into international relations with other states.[104]

Regrettably, neither the traditional law nor contemporary practice has any precise criterion for measuring whether the prerequisites for statehood are satisfied in any given situation. Nor is there any indication as to how sizable the population and territory should be. Yet there is considerable agreement that a territory does not need to have defined borders with precise population to qualify for statehood. In the case of *Deutsche Continental Gas Gesellscraft v. Polish State* this flexibility was articulated by the judges:

> In order to say that a State exists and can be recognized as such . . . it is enough that the territory has a sufficient consistency, even though its boundaries have not yet been accurately delimited, and that the State actually exercises independent public authority over that territory. There are numerous examples of cases in which States have existed without their statehood being called into doubt . . . at the time when the frontier between them was not accurately traced.[105]

Evidently, the same flexibility was exhibited in the *North Sea Continental Shelf* case; the International Court ruled:

> The appurtenance of a given area, considered as an entity, in no way governs the precise delimitation of its boundaries, any more than uncertainty as to boundaries can affect territorial rights. There is for instance no rule that the land frontiers of a state must be fully delimited and defined, and often in various places and for long periods they are not, as is shown by the case of the entry of Albania into the League of Nations.[106]

Other interesting examples were the recognition of Albania by a number of states in 1913 and the admission of Israel into the United Nations notwithstanding the fact that their boundaries were undefined.[107] To the extent that a territory without precise borders satisfies the condition for statehood, it should be obvious that the population test can equally be met even if the size of a given population is inexact. Since most of the "homelands" have territories and populations larger than the territories and populations of some members of the international community, for instance, Gambia, it is difficult to fault them under the territorial and population tests. It is, of course, possible to argue that the statutes' use of the Sotho and Xhosa cultures to determine the population of a "homeland" is too fluid to accord that criterion any significance in law. However, because the population test does not need to be precise, this is not a serious setback, especially if it is considered that each of the "homelands" is inhabited by a sizable population even without counting those included because of their Sotho and Xhosa backgrounds.

Two other criteria, having a government and the capacity to enter into international relations, pose difficult problems. Although they are regarded as "central" to the issue of statehood,[108] it is not clear how strong a government or its capacity to have international relations should be to meet those conditions. Evidently, the ideal test is for the entity to have a stable political community supporting a legal order with a centralized administrative, legislative, and judicial systems with plenary powers as well as the ability to control external relations without dictation from any other state.[109] The practice shows, however, that this test is not followed closely in any situation,[110] and that an entity can meet the test even where its internal government may be supported by another state and some aspects of its international relations are handled on its behalf by other states. Thus, in *Duff Development Co. v. the Government of Kelantan*,[111] the fact that the government of Kelantan was to look up to the British government on several international matters as well as for advice on virtually all its internal matters except those touching upon religion was held not to have impaired its independence or statehood:

The question put was as to the status of the ruler of Kelantan. It is obvious that for sovereignty there must be a certain amount of independence, but it is not in the least necessary that for sovereignty there should be complete independence. It is quite consistent with sovereignty that the sovereign may in certain respects be dependent upon another power; the control, for instance, of foreign affairs may be completely in the hands of a protecting power, and there may be agreements or treaties which limit the powers of the sovereign even in internal affairs without entailing a loss of the position of a sovereign power.[112]

But perhaps the best illustration is the case of the Congo, which, in spite of its chaotic circumstances and the fact that it was dependent on its former sovereign, Belgium, for much of its internal and external affairs, was considered a state[113] in its early years of "independence" in the 1960s. One can also cite the case of Liechtenstein, which, though denied admission to the League of Nations because it had contracted with other states to conduct some of its internal and external affairs, was admitted as a party to the Statute of the I.C.J. on the theory that its customs union and arrangements for diplomatic protection by other states did not compromise its independence and sovereignty.[114] It is, of course, questionable whether the admission or failure to admit an entity into an international organization is a conclusive test for statehood, especially since the attributes and responsibilities of the two are not the same. But it is equally true that in an organization like the United Nations, particularly the I.C.J., whose membership is open solely to states,[115] the admission of an entity as a member can bolster the inference that that entity is a state. This having been said, the question is whether the "homelands" meet the requirements for government and capacity to enter into international relations. Each of the "homelands" has its own constitution, legislature, executive, and judiciary. Besides, although the "homelands" are still bound by preexisting treaties between South Africa and other countries, they are entitled to terminate or alter any such pact in any way they like.[116] Finally, there is no dispute between any of them and any other country over title to their territories. Admittedly, there are some ostensible limitations on their sovereignty. For instance, they all lack a judiciary with plenary powers. Thus, the South African Supreme Court is empowered to entertain appeals from cases decided by the supreme courts of the "independent homelands." But this does not seem to pose any serious impediment to statehood, because apart from the theory that an entity does not need to be absolutely independent to attain statehood, there are states whose statehood is not lost merely because they lack judiciaries with plenary powers. Clear examples of these are the relationships of the Australian Supreme Court and, until recently, Canada's with the Privy Council of Great Britain, which had appellate jurisdiction over their cases.

Although at first glance this analysis may suggest that the "homelands" satisfy the conditions for statehood, a more critical study proves this to be unsustainable. Among the most important questions here is whether any of the "homelands" has the economic strength to support itself as a state. Even Transkei—the one with the brightest economic prospects—is so dependent on South Africa that more than 80 percent of its $140 million budget is contributed from South Africa.[117] What would happen if South Africa terminated this relationship?

Conceivably, though, a number of counterarguments can be put forward. For example, one could cite several other countries that depend economically on countries that are relatively better off. Moreover, the very nature of the South African economy vis-à-vis its neighbors makes it unthinkable that South Africa would cut the economic apron-strings of the homelands. However, since these economic relations are nothing but a projection of the apartheid policy and all the inhumanity and exploitation attendant thereto, giving them any positive force as meeting the requirements for statehood would be tantamount to disregarding their patent illegality; moreover, it would contradict the principle that one should not be allowed to benefit from one's own wrongfulness.

While the fact that the "homelands'" heavy dependence on South Africa would provide Pretoria with undue leverage to manipulate them and their foreign activities to its advantage is also relevant to the question about the "homelands" statehood, it is even more important that, with the exception of South Africa, no member of the international community has any diplomatic relations with or even accords any validity to passports from any of them. If the capacity to enter into international relations is a sine qua non for statehood and, a fortiori, independence, then the "homelands" fail to satisfy statehood under even the declarationist principle.

If the "homelands" are not states, one must ask how injuries inflicted on any of their inhabitants in a foreign country are to be redressed, especially where the countries concerned do not provide adequate remedy for foreigners or observe international minimum standards. Since states are the sole entities that can appear before an international body like the I.C.J., obviously the only effect of the "homelands" nationality policy is that it deprives those people of their right of representation before an international adjudicatory body.

But even assuming the "homelands" have all the necessary attributes of statehood, the problem remains: Can they make any type of nationality laws they want? In other words, is a state free to make nationality laws of overreaching consequences like those purportedly made by the "homelands"? The point at stake is that the criteria used—the Xhosa and the Sotho cultures—to confer "homelands" nationality on anyone with Xhosa or Sotho background entraps people who might have little or no connection with the "homelands," because the Xhosa and Sotho languages are used throughout southern Africa, including states like Botswana and Lesotho. Since South Africa serves as a host country for guest workers from all over southern Africa, and since some of these guest workers might have attained all the traditional prerequisites for South African nationality, for example, birth and substantial connection, the grant of the "homelands" nationality raises conflicts not only as to which "homelands" the new nationals really belong to, but also about whether the nationality laws are not too broad to "steal" the nationals of other countries. The seriousness of these issues are self-evident, and doubtless state practice and juristic opinion respond to them with one voice wherever they occur. At the Hague Codification Conference of 1930, which culminated in the Convention on Certain Questions Relating to the Conflict of Nationality Laws, the German government, for instance, urged:

The general principle that all questions relating to the acquisition or loss of . . . nationality shall be governed by the laws of the State whose nationality is claimed or contested should be admitted. *The application of this principle, however, should not go beyond the limits at which the legislation of one state encroaches on the sovereignty of another.* For example, a state has no power, by means of a law or administrative act, to confer its nationality on all inhabitants of another state or on all foreigners entering its . . . territory. Further, if the state confers its nationality on the subjects of other states without their request, when the persons in question are not attached to it by any particular bond, as for instance, origin, domicile, or birth, the states concerned will not be bound to recognize such nationalization.[118]

At the same instance, the United States stated its official position thus:

No state is free to extend the application of its laws of nationality in such a way as to reach out and claim the allegiance of whomsoever it pleases. The scope of municipal laws governing nationality must be regarded as limited by consideration of the rights and obligations of individuals and of other States.[119]

When the Peruvian Constitution of 1939 sought to confer Peruvian nationality on any foreigner who had either resided in Peru for four years and married a Peruvian, or who had acquired real property in Peru, the international opposition was very clear. The British, for instance, responded: it is "an incontrovertible principle of the law of nations" that the "consent of a foreigner is necessary to legalise his naturalization in another state whatever may be the provisions of the civil law of that state on the subject."[120] In registering its unequivocal oppostion to Peru, and to Mexico, which had a similar law, the United States expressed nearly the same position. According to de Visscher, it is "contrary to law" for a state to impose compulsory nationality on aliens by reason either of their acquisition of real property or their residence in that country.[121] Again, the Harvard Research in International Law has pointed out that it is to be "generally recognized" that a state may not acquire the allegiance of natural persons without their consent.[122]

Since the "homelands" nationality laws are arbitrary in the sense that they automatically give people certain nationalities without their consent, it follows from the established law that they cannot enjoy automatic validity beyond the borders within which they were enunciated. But perhaps the most interesting issue raised by the nationality laws can be illustrated by the hypothetical question of the plight of a Xhosa or Sotho who, except for the language or cultural criteria, may have no connection whatsoever with any of the "homelands," but who by the same criteria and residence in one of the two "homelands" would automatically be tagged as a national of one of those two "countries." This brings the discussion back to the other aspect of the *Nottebohm* case, which may be referred to as the restrictive view on the nationality law. To put the issue in its proper perspective, it is useful to mention, briefly, the facts of *Nottebohm*.

Nottebohm was a German national who went to Guatemala and took up residence and established a headquarters there for his flourishing business. He headed the firm and made Guatemala his fixed place of abode but, occasionally, visited his relatives in Germany. In the 1930s he underwent a cursory procedure for Liechtensteiner nationality. Pursuant to certain political upheavals, Guatemala nationalized all the assets of Nottebohm's firm. Liechtenstein then instituted an action in the I.C.J. seeking redress for Nottebohm on the basis of his acquired Liechtensteiner nationality. Although the court upheld the general rule of the domestic nature of nationality laws, it not only upheld the restrictive view that the consent of a foreigner is a sine qua non for acquisition of foreign nationality but further pronounced the principle that has come to be known as the "substantial link test." It ruled:

> According to the practice of states, to arbitral and judicial decisions, and to the opinions of writers, nationality is a legal bond having as its basis a social fact of attachment, a genuine connection of existence, interests and sentiments, together with the existence of reciprocal rights and duties. . . . The Court must ascertain whether the nationality granted to Nottebohm . . . is of this character . . . whether the factual connection between Nottebohm and Liechtenstein in the period preceding, contemporaneous with, and following his naturalization appears to be sufficiently close, so preponderant in relation to any connection which may have existed between him and any other state, that it is possible to regard the nationality conferred upon him as real and effective, as the exact

juridical expression of a social fact of a connection which existed previously or came into existence thereafter. . . . Nationalization is not a matter to be taken lightly.[123]

It then concluded that the connection between Nottebohm and Liechtenstein was so "extremely tenuous" and so "lacking in the genuineness requisite to such an act of importance, if it is to be respected by a state in the position of Guatemala," that Guatemala was under no obligation to recognize it.

To the extent that the nationals of the newly created "independent" states— the "homelands"—might have had nationalities other than those purportedly created by the "homelands," the *Nottebohm* principle suggests that the relationship between the new "nationals" and the "homelands" would be too tenuous to carry any effect. It is arguable, of course, that if the "homelands" nationality laws were null and void, the people on whom the new nationalities were purportedly conferred would continue to be nationals of the states to which they belonged before the new system was launched. But consider the plight of people who had South African nationality before the so-called new nationality law was introduced. Since South Africa no longer considers them as South African nationals, it is obvious that the only practical consequence of the policy is to convert them into denationalized or stateless people—a status that, as previously noted, is illegal under contemporary international law.

Chapter 6

Cases Not Related to Apartheid

THE APARTHEID TERRITORIES are not the only cases that pose impediments to the international community's anti-colonial crusade and its cherished values. There are a few other territories that, though not exposed to the odious socioeconomic and political policies of apartheid, have found it impossible to extricate themselves from unwelcome circumstances. Although, by virtue of their size and demographic composition, these territories may seem insignificant when compared with the territories liberated in the great decolonization era, they evoke questions that are as important as and at times reveal the challenges facing the international legal system even more clearly than those raised by the liberated territories.

Some of the unliberated territories are small enough in size and population that whether their right of self-determination can include the right to independence is questionable.[1]

Because of the vicissitudes of war, many people in the territories are refugees, and they plus the immigrants brought into the territories as refugees pose problems as to who is entitled to vote for legitimate self-determination and who is not.[2] A related dilemma is whether self-determination is a right for people or territories.[3]

Cumulatively, all the difficulties, including the survival of those who have faced the brunt of the anticolonial drive to "liberate" these remaining few territories, undermine the claim to legitimacy of most states. Indeed, they raise questions about whether some of the values cherished by the anticolonialists—especially self-determination—need to be rewritten.

The cases examined in this chapter fall in two categories: the simple cases and cases with uncertain and deep-seated questions about historical connections. The simple cases include such traditional colonies as Djibouti (formerly French Somaliland), Belize (formerly British Honduras), Gibraltar, and the Falkland Islands (the Malvinas). The complex cases include the struggles over

Western Sahara, East Timor, and occasionally some cases intertwined with those in the first list, notably those involving Somalia and Ethiopia vis-à-vis their respective connections with the Issas and Afars in Djibouti, Guatemala over Belize, and Spain over Gibraltar. Since a discussion of the cases in the first group would merely repeat material already covered in the chapter on colonialism, I concentrate here on the territories whose struggles involve the issue of revindication—those based on historical connections. The focus is on the Saharan and Timorese cases.

SELF-DETERMINATION AND REVINDICATION: THE SAHARAN AND TIMORESE CASES

Background

One of the negative consequences of colonialism was the separation of people from their natural kinsmen and territories and traditional settings. Unjust, unpalatable, and unfair as these consequences are, the international community has realistically accepted them as facts with which all members of the world have to live. The rationale for this apparent paradox is that not only is it impossible to redress the situation but any attempt to revise present international boundaries to accommodate traditional connections would produce chaos.[4]

In legal parlance the concern has been expressed through concepts like *uti possedetis* and the territorial integrity of states.[5] Reasonable as this concern is, it has suffered serious attacks in recent practice. In some cases—those wherein the attacks have been directed by states against established states, notably those conflicts between Somalia and Ethiopia, Somalia and Kenya, Uganda (under Idi Amin) and Kenya, and more recently Iraq against Kuwait—the wisdom of applying the *uti possedetis* concept seems indisputable, especially if there is nothing to prove that people of a particular ethnic background are being maltreated or discriminated against.[6] Conversely, in the cases involving entities that are yet to become states—for example, the Spanish Sahara, East Timor, Gibraltar, and Belize—the fact that the status of statehood is yet to be attained by the coveted entities poses thorny questions as to whether the concept of *uti possedetis* can be of any avail. But the covetous states do not take this factor seriously. They argue that if the nonstate entities are not integrated into them, their own territorial integrity would be impaired. Sometimes they go even further, to use the famous Declaration on Colonialism to urge that the principle of self-determination cannot be pursued if the consequence would be the violation of the territorial integrity of states. Interestingly, after advancing this argument in the Belizean situation, Guatemala went on to threaten: "If our Belizean com-

patriots . . . led by their secessionist enthusiasm, should pretend to adopt unilateral initiatives which could seriously affect our territorial integrity and offend
Guatemalan dignity . . . in that case they would force us to show them, very
much against our will, that law is more important than peace."[7]

But the crux of the matter is whether the law permits the use of territorial
integrity or historical ties as an excuse for states to force other states to integrate with them. The lack of statehood is no excuse to perpetrate aggression
against a nonstate. Moreover, the entities in question were not part of the covetous states at the time the latter attained their independence, and by the longevity of their separation from one another, both the independent states and the
nonstate entities have separately developed their own identities and conscious-
ness. Thus to force a merger on them in disregard to their individual circumstances is not only to betray the very principles the covetous states claim to
pursue but would also introduce a new brand of colonialism, activating volatile
though currently dormant situations, and thereby undermining the peace and
security of the international community. Yet one U.N. resolution—Resolution
2353 on Gibraltar—has endorsed one claim based on historical ties. Since this
resolution was taken in disregard to the wishes of the overwhelming majority of
Gibraltarians[8] and thus contradicted the formidable U.N. precedents on the exercise of self-determination, it was wrong and consequently failed to establish
any precedent worth following. The British secretary of state for Commonwealth affairs came directly to the point when he said, "I frankly regard the
adoption of Resolution 2353 as little short of disgraceful. . . . It does great
damage to the reputation of the General Assembly as the guardian of the rights
of colonial peoples."[9]

The Decolonization of Western Sahara

Western Sahara, known also as Spanish Sahara, epitomizes almost all the
issues addressed so far. It was formerly a Spanish colony, and it has been an
object of dismemberment by neighboring states, which, on the pretext of restoring historical connections, have been striving to appropriate it for themselves.

The decolonization history of Western Sahara has been a rather sad affair.
Pursuant to the entreaties by the Declaration on Colonialism, Resolution 1514,
several resolutions were passed in the United Nations urging Spain to release
the Sahara from the throes of colonialism.[10] Yet apart from Spain's repudiation
of its initial policy against giving information on the Sahara,[11] nothing significant happened to suggest that it had been moved by any of the resolutions.
Owing to what might be called a twist of fate—the debility and demise of
General Franco and the consequent accession of Prince Juan Carlos to the

Spanish throne—a more progressive policy was later enunciated toward the decolonization of Western Sahara.[12]

Ironically, what was to be the best news ever for the colony marked the beginning of the second stage of its arduous struggle toward decolonization. This time, the struggle was between the Sahraouis and their neighbors—the Moroccans and Mauritanians. Citing their so-called historical ties with the colony, the Sahara's two neighbors designated themselves as the lawful "heirs" to the outgoing colonial masters.

The claim was not a new one in Western Saharan history. In the early 1960s Morocco made similar overtures against the Sahara and others, like Mauritania and Algeria. But not only were those claims very casual, they were never pursued; and, indeed, until its recent reincarnation in the Sahara situation, Morocco had abandoned its claim and joined in the anticolonial crusade against Spain. Why did Morocco decide to revive its claim against the Sahara? According to reliable sources, the recent discoveries of the Sahara's wealth in easily extractable minerals and petroleum were the main factors motivating Morocco.[13]

The legal question centers on the conflict between historical claims and the exercise of the peoples' right of self-determination. Since the claim by the Moroccans was aimed at achieving integration of the Sahara into Morocco, it would be useful to consider the issue under any of the following U.N. resolutions: the General Assembly Resolution 1541 (XV),[14] the famous Declaration on Colonialism, Resolution 1514, and the Declaration on Friendly Relations, Resolution 2625.

At first sight, Resolution 1541 might seem to support the Moroccan position, since in its list of the forms through which the right of self-determination can be exercised, "association" with another state and "integration" into an independent state are bracketed together with the emergence into an "independent" nation. But there is one attribute of the resolution that undermines the apparent plausibility of Morocco's position. In stipulating how the options for the "association" or "integration" should be made, the resolution cautions emphatically that the association must come about as the "result of free and voluntary choice by the people of the territory concerned expressed through informed and democratic processes" and, similarly, that

the integration should be the result of the freely expressed wishes of the territory's peoples acting with full knowledge of the change in their status, their wishes having been expressed through informed and democratic processes, impartially conducted and based on universal adult suffrage.[15]

Likewise, after listing the possible goals of self-determination, Resolution 2625 reiterates the fundamental necessity of taking the wishes of the people concerned into consideration.[16]

U.N. practice follows the principles enunciated in these declarations. Whenever there was a question about the relationship between historical claims and self-determination, the United Nations showed no hesitation in making the people decide for themselves. The evidence is a long list of cases, including the U.N.-administered plebiscite culminating in the merger of British Togoland with the Gold Coast just before the latter became the independent state of Ghana; the referendum leading to the merger of the North and South Cameroons with Nigeria and the Republic of Cameroon, respectively; the referendum that led to the partition of the Belgian-administered Ruanda-Urundi; and that by which Western Samoa decided to join New Zealand in free association. Recent U.N. deliberations confirm its long-held position.

With this record, it is not surprising that the United Nations sought to organize a referendum for the Sahraouis to determine what they wanted their right over their territory to be.[17] Realizing what the outcome of a referendum would be, particularly as evidenced by the program of the newly formed independence-poised Sahraoui group called the POLISARIO (Frente Popular para la Liberacion de Saguia el Hamra y Rio de Oro), Morocco cleverly sought to delay the referendum. Initially, Spain was made the object of this ploy:

> You, the Spanish Government, claim that the Sahara was *res nullius.* You claim that it was a territory or property left uninherited, you claim that no power and no administration had been established over the Sahara: Morocco claims the contrary. Let us request the arbitration of the International Court of Justice. . . . It will state the law on the basis of the titles submitted.[18]

Spain, however, failed to take the bait, whereupon Morocco directed its tactics toward the General Assembly, which fell prey by adopting Resolution 3292 (XXIX): (1) requesting an I.C.J. advisory opinion; (2) setting up a commission to investigate all relevant information on the disputed territory; and (3) suspending the referendum until after the I.C.J. had given its opinion.[19]

Since the law is certain that the free will of the inhabitants of a territory is the test for exercising the right of self-determination, one might wonder if the U.N. concession to request for the advisory opinion was sound, especially in light of the way the questions were framed:

> 1. Was the Western Sahara . . . at the time of colonization by Spain a territory belonging to no one (terra nullius)? If the answer to the question is in the negative,

2. What were the legal ties between this territory and the kingdom of Morocco and the Mauritania entity?[20]

By its failure to address the main issue in the case—the principle of self-determination—the General Assembly posed questions that were not only ambiguous but also irrelevant to the conflict. Yet the approach is not entirely devoid of practical significance, at least in the development of the law on self-determination. It not only provided the court with the opportunity to clarify the law by judicial opinion but also demonstrated the capabilities of the court to go beyond its ostensible limits in pursuit of equity and justice. A brief study of some of these developments is in order.

Western Sahara before the World Court

Jurisdictional Problems for the Court

To assume jurisdiction over the case, the court was faced with two procedural hurdles: (1) whether the case was of political nature and was presented to it in conformity with the jurisdictional provisions of the U.N. Charter and the I.C.J. Statute, and (2) whether the decision in the *Eastern Carelia* case that there could be no jurisdiction except with the consent of both parties to the suit could be ignored in this instance.

WERE THE QUESTIONS PRESENTED TO THE COURT LEGAL OR POLITICAL? The first set of questions involved the construction of articles 96 and 65 of the U.N. Charter and the I.C.J. Statute, respectively. The former reads: "The General Assembly or the Security Council may request the International Court of Justice to give an advisory opinion on *any legal question.*"[21] And with almost the same voice, article 65 of the statute states:

1. The Court may give an advisory opinion on *any legal question* at the request of whatever body may be authorized by or in accordance with the Charter of the United Nations to make such a request.
2. Questions upon which the advisory opinion of the Court is asked shall be laid before the Court by means of a written request *containing an exact statement of the question upon which an opinion is required, and accompanied by all documents likely to throw light upon the question.*[22]

Most significantly, the question of whether the issue was political or legal did not receive a unanimous response. Judge Gross of France, for instance, was of the opinion that inasmuch as the questions were of a historical nature and about specific facts, they were political because "economics, sociology, and human geography are not law."[23] In his opinion, the court could not lawfully assume jurisdiction. Similarly, Judge Ignacio-Pinto of Dahomey contended that the questions were "loaded" and necessarily would lead to an arbitrary concession to the claims by Morocco and Mauritania.[24] Since there is no hard-and-fast rule about how law and politics should be distinguished from one another, and since the provisions in question do not contain any criteria for the determination of whether a question is legal or political, it is doubtful what weight is to be given to these objections. But this is not to say that the court had an automatic right to assume jurisdiction over the case. On the contrary, it has been urged in the *Certain Expenses* case that the court does not have discretionary powers to hear nonlegal questions.[25] Though this ruling may be relevant in determining whether the court can exercise jurisdiction over the case, it suffers from the same fatal deficiency as the provision in the court's Statute, because it sheds no light on how legal and nonlegal questions can be distinguished.

Nevertheless, given the circumstances under which the resolution requesting the advisory opinion was adopted and the irrelevance to the main issue of the questions posed,[26] Judge Ignacio-Pinto may have been right: the request was too "loaded" to be legal. To follow this fully, it is enough to observe that Resolution 3292 was fraught with such inherent contradictions and ambiguities as to compromise whatever legal substance it might have. As has been demonstrated consistently in U.N. practice, the main means for exercising the right of self-determination is simply to let the people decide for themselves. Although Resolution 3292 did not in any way suggest that there was anything wrong with this procedure, it nevertheless went on to call for the postponement of the exercise of that basic right until the court had given its decision on the question of historical connections. What purpose was the court's opinion to serve? And what was to be done if the Court had found the existence of historical ties and given its opinion accordingly without making any further observations on the case? Inasmuch as the questions left no room for the consideration of the main issue in the case and thus could have led to an unfair conclusion in disregard of the numerous precedents, obviously the resolution was filled with contradictions. Accordingly, the only course open to the court was to reject the request, at least on grounds of nonjusticiability.

Yet, no matter how difficult the situation, the court could assume jurisdiction. Conceivably, it could marshal support from article 36, paragraph 6, of its statute, according to which "in the event of a dispute as to whether the Court has jurisdiction, the matter shall be settled by the decision of the Court." No doubt, once the court declared the questions legal by holding that they were "scarcely susceptible of a reply otherwise than on the basis of law,"[27] nothing could bar it from proceeding with the case.

But apart from the twin questions of whether an issue is legal or political in nature and whether the court could assume jurisdiction over some political matters, there is an entirely different ground on which the court's jurisdiction over the Saharan case can be disputed—at least for the sake of academic curiosity. It should be recalled that even as the question was put before the court, a fact-finding commission was sent onto the beleaguered territory to gather information on the opinions of the inhabitants on the issues arising from the case. It is not certain whether the *sub judice* rule of municipal legal systems can apply to advisory opinions of the court, nor can one hazard a guess about the impact the rule could have had on the case if it was relevant. It is certain, though, that inasmuch as the sending of the fact-finding mission to the area of the conflict suggests that the General Assembly was not prepared with all the relevant information for bringing an issue for the court's advisory opinion, the requirement of article 65, paragraph 2 of the I.C.J. Statute was not satisfied; and this constitutes a crucial basis on which the court's jurisdiction can be impugned.

IS CONSENT A SINE QUA NON FOR ADVISORY OPINION OF THE COURT? Since request for advisory opinion is essentially a matter between the requesting body and the court, and considering further that the opinion rendered in response to the request is not binding on anyone unless it is adopted by the requesting body, it is inconceivable that the refusal of Spain to be a party to Morocco's proposed contentious case could have any effect on the court's jurisdiction. Yet there are two previous rulings that are apparently so confusing and conflicting as to necessitate a more detailed discussion of the issue. These rulings were on the *Eastern Carelia*[28] and the *Peace Treaties*[29] cases.

Whereas the *Eastern Carelia* case was rejected for lack of consent of one of the parties,[30] the *Peace Treaties* case was sustained. Although the latter ruling was technically a departure from *Carelia*, it would have been difficult to consider it as an overthrow of the precedent if the *Carelia* case had been rejected merely on the basis of nonjusticiability for lack of adequate information on the issue or even on the theory of the court's inherent power to determine its jurisdiction. However, since the court in *Carelia* used the lack of consent as a reason for rejecting the case, the *Peace Treaties* case could easily have overturned the *Carelia* opinion, at least on the issue of consent. Yet the *Peace Treaties* court ignored this eminently defensible course and forged an ambiguous reconciliation[31] between the two diametrically opposed opinions, thereby causing confusion about the relevance of consent to jurisdiction in advisory opinions cases. Judge Hudson lamented: "One may wish that the Court had dealt more completely with the Eastern Carelia case, in order that it may not plague the Court in its exercise of advisory jurisdiction in the future."[32] From these, and in concordance with Janis, it is submitted that the I.C.J. address and rejection of the *Carelia* case can be cited as a manifestation of a progressive clarification and disposition of the confusion caused by the *Carelia* and *Peace Treaties* cases.[33]

Disposition of the Substantive Issues

In its solution of the substantive issues, the court went through all the relevant information, including evidence on how the Sahara had paid allegiance to the sultan of Morocco before it became a Spanish territory,[34] and the court faced the questions posed in Resolution 3292 squarely by holding that Western Sahara was not an unowned territory at the time of its colonization by Spain and that the materials and information presented bore evidence of existence, at the time the Sahara was colonized by Spain, "of legal ties of allegiance between the Sultan of Morocco and some of the tribes living in the territory of Western Sahara. They equally show the existence of rights, including some rights relating to the land, which constituted legal ties between the Mauritanian entity, as understood by the Court, and the territory of Western Sahara."[35] Yet it did not stop there. In spite of the restrictive formulation of the questions— which could have seriously affected the plight of the colony[36]—the court went on to address the main issues of decolonization and self-determination and to use them as a warrant for invoking and applying the principles in Resolutions 1514 and 2625. Thus, after endorsing the principle of self-determination as having become a norm over the past fifty years and reiterating the aforementioned tenets of its realization,[37] it concluded that

> the materials and information presented to it do not establish any tie of territorial sovereignty between the territory of Western Sahara and the Kingdom of Morocco or the Mauritanian entity. Thus the Court has not found legal ties of such a nature as might affect the application of Resolution 1514 (XV) in the decolonization of Western Sahara and, in particular, of the principle of self-determination through the free and genuine expression of the will of the peoples of the territory.[38]

This ruling is irreproachable. To appreciate this conclusion fully, one merely has to consider the sociopolitical aspects of the lifestyles of most of the inhabitants of the region in question—northwestern Africa, particularly Morocco, Mauritania, Algeria, and the Sahara. One scholar's description of the nomadic use of territory is to the point:

> A population consisting almost entirely of nomads . . . traversing the desert in all directions like an ocean leaving little or no trace, is not a good starting point for territorial considerations. . . . Thus, the tribal routes inside the Western Sahara and across the artificial colonial frontiers overlapped without coin-

ciding, totally irrespective of any territorial delimitation, simply following climatic changes and being dictated by sparse grazing grounds and waterholes.
. . . The arguments by Morocco and Mauritania in this connection were simply a foreboding of their future action, i.e dividing the territory amongst themselves.[39]

The court's bold gesture is not entirely without problems; insofar as it went beyond the bounds of the questions in Resolution 3292, there may be doubts as to whether it acted properly. However, given its place as the highest court of justice for the international community and considering also that justice cannot be fully rendered if the whole context of its dispensation is not taken into account, the court's approach is not unfounded. The court's position is even more difficult to challenge if one considers that not only is the I.C.J. the master of its jurisdiction but that the law of international relations requires the liberal construction of legal questions.[40]

The Legal Significance of the Court's Opinion

As the Court's action was advisory, the case could have limited impact on the contestants in the Saharan dispute. Morocco and Mauritania could thus have prima facie arguments against its being binding on them, but their position could be deflated by a number of counterarguments.

First, it should be recalled that not only were they among the interested parties in the case, but they were also the main architects of the resolution to present the matter to the court for advisory opinion. Since these suggest that they had confidence in the court's ability to dispense with the case judiciously, it would be unconscionable on their part to repudiate the ruling after it has been given. Perhaps this was why Morocco pretended that the court's finding of the existence of legal ties between it and the disputed territory was an endorsement of its claim.

Second, the organ that requested the opinion adopted it as sound—a fact that, considered in the light of the opinion's consistency with the huge edifice of the law on self-determination, would upgrade the opinion to the status of customary international law.

Finally, the finding of the observation team that investigated the position of the Sahraouis on the subject is significant:

Owing to the large measure of co-operation which it received from the Spanish authorities, the mission was able, despite the shortness of its stay in the territory, to visit virtually all the main population centers and ascertain the views of the overwhelming majority of the inhabitants. At every place visited, the mission was met by mass political demonstrations and had numerous private meetings with representatives of every section of the community. From all of these, it became evident to the mission that *there was an overwhelming consensus among the Saharans within the territory in favor of independence and opposing integration with any neighboring country.*[41]

Western Saharan Decolonization after the I.C.J. Action

"The Green March"

Bent on consummating its plan to integrate Western Sahara into itself, Morocco ignored the common view that the issue should be resolved by an uncoerced decision by the territory's inhabitants. No sooner had the court's opinion been issued than Morocco, on the pretext of what it fraudulently construed as the court's endorsement of its claim, announced an impending march by an "unarmed" enthusiastic 350,000 Moroccans to the Sahara to effect a "reintegration" of the two territories with one another.[42] Naturally, not only did many states express revulsion,[43] but the Security Council promptly assumed an emergency session and requested Morocco "to put an end forthwith to the declared march into Western Sahara."[44]

The Tripartite Agreement between Morocco, Mauritania, and Spain

Realizing the virtual impossibility of preventing Morocco from moving ahead with its plan—evident from the lukewarm attitude of the international community and the overt support of such important countries as France and the United States—Spain changed its position from opposition to participation. Thus, after a secret meeting of Spain, Morocco, and Mauritania[45] in Madrid, an accord was made wherein the Sahara and its resources were divided among the three countries. Spain was to have fishing rights in the Saharan coast and 35 percent interest in FusBucraa, the multimillion-dollar phosphate company; Morocco and Mauritania were assured participation in an interim three-power government in the Sahara, pending the final handing over by Spain in February 1976, and were apportioned the Saharan territory in the ratio of two-thirds to one-third.[46] The crucial question here is that if Morocco really had the interest of the Sahraouis at heart, and if it genuinely wanted to pursue the territory as a matter of its own right based on historical claims, why did it share the spoils with Mauritania and Spain? Obviously, the share of the spoils not only makes one wonder if Morocco's intentions were suspect but creates an instance warranting the application of the celebrated test of King Solomon for settling disputes between two self-interested parties.

The Proclamation of the POLISARIO State—The Sahraoui Democratic Arab Republic (S.A.D.R.)

The opposition triggered by the plan to "steal the Sahara,"[47] particularly the joint opposition put up by Algeria and the POLISARIO, could not be silenced

even after the Sahara was "stolen." Yet Morocco and Mauritania were unde-
terred by the opposition. They embarked on the consolidation of the spoils by
dispatching troops to the Sahara and, after intimidating and causing tens of
thousands of the Sahraouis, including 61 of their 122 tribal leaders, to flee the
territory, secured the approval of their takeover from the remaining 61 tribal
leaders. At this point, with virtually no room left for diplomacy, the POL-
ISARIO, with the support of Algeria, took up arms to wage a "guerrilla warfare
against neocolonialist Morocco and Mauritania." The POLISARIO also proclaimed an independent "state" of "Sahraoui Democratic Arab Republic,"
which the Algerians and the POLISARIO administer from Algeria.

The Response of the United Nations

On the whole, the U.N. response was anything but encouraging. It was
reflected in two conflicting General Assembly resolutions, which have been
described aptly as a combination of a "maximum of hypocrisy with a minimum
of . . . practical effect" on the "battered self-determination norm."[48] These were
Resolutions 3458A (XXX) and 3458B (XXX).[49] Whereas the former was at
least consistent with the formidable precedents on self-determination in affirm-
ing the "inalienable rights of the people of the Spanish Sahara to self-determination" and reiterating the call on Spain to hold a referendum to implement
that right, the other approvingly took note of the "shameful" Madrid Accord,
recognized the "interim administration" established by the three countries, and
called upon the administration to permit free consultation with the people.

It is difficult to understand why Resolution 3458B was passed. Not only
does international law unequivocally oppose the use of force by states to settle
international conflicts, but it also enjoins members of the international community from recognizing any territorial acquisition that is brought about by the use
of force. Considering the entire history of the Saharan case, especially with the
announcement of the "Green March," undoubtedly a threat of force, as well as
the dispatch of troops into the coveted territory, the only inference about Resolution 3458B vis-à-vis the principle of self-determination is that it was unfaith-
ful to a principle that the rest of the world is expected to honor.

East Timorese Decolonization

In several ways, the East Timorese case is a mirror reflection of the Spanish
Sahara case. In this instance, a colonial power that had proven intransigent to
numerous entreaties from the United Nations to dismantle its colonial system
eventually decided to decolonize; this situation involves the covetousness of a
powerful state that, having secured its independence through the principle of
self-determination, seeks to deny that right to neighboring people with whom it
claims to have historical, ethnic, cultural, and geographical ties; it is contem-

poraneous with the Saharan case; and it depicts how, by the United Nations' failure to translate its normative prescriptions into action, aggressors are able to accomplish their illegal plans.

East Timor was for more than four hundred years a colony of Portugal. As with Western Sahara, all efforts of the United Nations to achieve independence for East Timor were to no avail because its colonial master treated it as an integral possession and, consequently, as a territory not subject to the thrust of the Declaration on Colonialism, Resolution 1514. Yet like the Saharan situation, and at almost the same time, a new government that assumed power in Portugal[50] amended its constitution to provide for a policy of decolonization through the exercise of the colony's right of self-determination. A time-table was set up in the referendum, delineating how the supposed right of self-determination was to be exercised, and numerous political parties started to emerge. Of these, three are noteworthy: Unao Democratica de Timor (U.D.T.), Frente Revolucionaria de Timor Leste Independente (FRETILIN), and Associacao Popular Democratica de Timor (APODETI), which respectively favored the continuation of the Portuguese presence, complete independence of East Timor, and integration with Indonesia.

Portugal's announcement of the change in its colonial policy was initially received with ecstasy by Indonesia. In welcoming that long-awaited news, Indonesia not only gave the assurance that it would not interfere with the implementation of the independence plan but it also agreed that the future of the Timor was an internal matter for Timorese to decide alone.[51] But Indonesia did not maintain this posture for long. It soon released a statement that restricted the Timorese rights to only two—integration with Indonesia or association with Portugal[52]—leaving out independence, the third and obviously the option most favored by the majority of the Timorese. After this, reports started pouring in about an impending invasion by Indonesia. The FRETILIN and U.D.T.—for independence and for association with Portugal, respectively—formed a coalition to combat any possible threats that might come from Indonesia and its ally, the APODETI. The coalition did not last long, though, and soon after its demise, the U.D.T., in a move to exploit the confusion endemic in the territory at the time, launched an unsuccessful coup against the debilitated administration. The FRETILIN then launched a countercoup, took control over almost the whole territory, and issued a proclamation of independence, establishing the Democratic Republic of Eastern Timor.

The conflict escalated with fierce intervention by Indonesia, which, in collusion with the U.D.T. and APODETI, not only denounced the FRETILIN-proclaimed independence but endorsed the counterproclamation by the U.D.T.–APODETI coalition to integrate East Timor into Indonesia. It sent in troops "to maintain law and order." Following a heavy bombardment of the

FRETILIN stronghold, Dilli, and months of ground fighting in which more than 60,000 people—about 10 percent of the Timorese population—perished, Indonesia took over East Timor. It then embarked on a number of measures to consolidate the fait accompli.[53] For instance, in the immediate aftermath of the intervention, not only was a provisional government established for East Timor but a People's Assembly was constituted to formally authenticate the integration.

Naturally, the FRETILIN denounced the People's Assembly as unrepresentative and branded the process of integration as a sham. Claiming to be the most authentic representative of the majority of the East Timorese,[54] it then renewed its struggle to "liberate" East Timor from Indonesia's grip.

But Indonesia stuck to its position, claiming that Timor is a small, poor, and sparsely populated territory whose inhabitants are too backward to stand on their own feet as an independent state. While the claim about the poverty, size, and population of Timor can easily be refuted, especially considering that Timor is not only larger and more heavily populated than many other countries but is also believed to be rich in natural resources, it may be sufficient for the present purposes to evaluate the claim in relation to the choices offered for Timorese self-determination. Thus, granted that Timor is so small, so sparsely populated, and so backward that it cannot stand on its feet as a state, the question is whether, with such a background, it can integrate with Indonesia under Resolution 1541.

As can be recalled from the discussion on colonialism, one of the tenets of the Declaration on Colonialism, Resolution 1514, is that "unpreparedness" should never impede the dismantling of any colony. Admittedly, as Indonesia was not the colonial master of Timor, it may be questionable whether this inhibition can have any relevance to the Indonesian-Timorese conflict. Yet, on the other hand, by its complicity in the affair and its obvious intention to annex the territory, not only is Indonesia's plan to take over the Timorese colonial overlordship patently treacherous, but it is also illegal, inasmuch as it uses its own standards to preempt the right of the Timorese to determine their political future. But even if one were to ignore the caution in the Declaration on Colonialism and evaluate Indonesia's position *proprio vigore* under Resolution 1541, it still would be doubtful whether its argument can hold water. It need only be noted that under Resolution 1541 some amount of preparation is required before the exercise of self-determination by integration or association can be legitimate. Thus, in principle IX: the "integrating territory should have attained an advanced stage of self-government with free political institutions, so that its people would have the capacity to make a responsible choice through informed and democratic processes." If Resolution 1541 is the professed basis of Indonesia's action in Timor, and if Indonesia uses the backwardness of

Timor as the reason to favor integration with it, then principle IX of the resolution exposes the argument as contradictory, and consequently as one that cannot stand.

Indonesia also uses the concept of self-defense to bolster its cause. According to it, the situation had produced "tens of thousands of refugees," gravely destroying the national stability and endangering the security of Indonesia.[55] Obviously, this echoes one of the arguments used in the West Pakistani case. But the two situations are distinguishable, because whereas India did nothing to foment the Bengali situation, it was the Indonesian interference with the Portuguese program to make the Timorese decide for themselves that triggered the Timorese conflict. Moreover, at the time of the intervention, the FRETILIN had, for all intents and purposes, won the war and was thus, arguably, the ruling government. Therefore, not only does Indonesia's complicity make its self-defense argument untenable under the principle that prevents a state from benefiting from its own wrongful acts, but it can also be condemned as violating the principle of nonintervention—whether construed under the U.N. Declaration on Inadmissibility of Intervention, Resolution 2131 (XX), or the traditional principle of effective control. Nor can it be defended by the numerous U.N. resolutions that favor assistance to liberation movements, since, in this instance, the most widely recognized liberation movement was that against which Indonesia's attack was directed.

Finally, Indonesia cites the security of the Indonesian hemisphere as one of its defenses. But not only does its complicity in the conflict make it an interested party and thus render its argument too political to stand, but as ably stated by Judge Dillard in the *Spanish Saharan* case, territorial claim cannot by itself stand as a reason to dispense with the people's right of self-determination.

The U.N. response was not surprising. Consistent with the time-honored principles of self-determination and the inadmissibility of aggression, the United Nations condemned Indonesia and called upon it to withdraw its forces in order for the Timorese to exercise their inherent right of self-determination. The main resolutions on the issue were General Assembly Resolutions 3485 (XXX)[56] and 31/51 of 1975 and 1976, respectively, and Security Council Resolution 384[57] and Resolution 389[58] of 1975 and 1976, respectively.

Indonesia failed to comply with any of these entreaties, but regrettably the United Nations did nothing to force it to comply. Franck lamented:

On December 22, a divided Council unanimously adopted a resolution which, in addition to reiterating the General Assembly's call on Indonesia to withdraw "without delay" from the territory and recognizing Portugal's continuing status "as administering power with the obligation to co-operate with the United Nations so as to enable the people of East Timor to exercise freely their right to self-determination", requested the Secretary General "to send urgently a special representative to east Timor for the purpose of making an on-the spot assessment of the existing situation and of establishing contact with all the parties . . . in order to insure the implementation of the present resolution. . . ." The Security Council notably did not dust off even its low level diplomatic sanctions under Chapter VII of the Charter, let alone economic or military collective measures on behalf of the right of the more than half a million Timor people to enjoy the same right accorded in the past two decades to more than half the membership of the U.N.[59]

Since effectiveness of a resolution is not a sine qua non to its legality, it is, of course, unquestionable that Indonesia's steadfastness in its activities in East Timor is illegal, for as a member of the United Nations it is bound under article 25 of the Charter to comply with Security Council resolutions.

CONCLUSION

Although a few of the U.N. resolutions on these cases, particularly Resolution 3458 on the Saharan situation, are so ambiguously couched as to raise questions about the United Nations' commitment to the principle of self-determination, in most of its resolutions the United Nations still clings to the principle of self-determination and the established modes for its implementation. Yet there is one basic problem with the U.N. attitude: Although it does not hesitate to apply the values underlying its resolutions and, indeed, is willing to condemn violators in harsh terms, it does not seem to favor the use of its enforcement measures—not even economic sanctions—to produce what it and the international community strongly believe to be the right thing. Considering that the organization is the strongest peace-keeping institution in the world and that its failure to give practical meaning to some of its behests is likely to undermine its credibility, one wonders whether the organization is not headed toward the same fate as that which befell its predecessor, the League of Nations.

Since the ethnographic base on which the world community is built is very weak, and since, without strong dogmas like *uti possedetis*, that structure can easily crumple and break up the international community, one finds it difficult to understand why the United Nations does not do the only thing needed to maintain the system, at least in its present form. With threats from Gibraltar, Argentina, Ethiopia, Iraq, and what was Idi Amin's Uganda over territories they covet, it is obvious that if the international community does not do anything to prevent the covetous annexation of other people's territory, any state at all, and especially those that consider themselves stronger than their neighbors, would be tempted to make claims. Such actions could prompt intervention by other states, causing the escalation of minor conflicts into more serious ones, threatening international peace and security.

This process has already begun to unfold; look at the Iraqi invasion of Kuwait and the tension created by its skirmishes over the other Persian Gulf states, for instance. But perhaps the destructive effect of the Saharan conflict on the African regional body, the O.A.U., is the best example to date. The United Nations relies strongly on regional organizations as the primary bodies for the maintenance of the peace. And, indeed, the O.A.U. has proven to be useful in this way. Not only has it solved many intraregional conflicts before they could escalate, but its abhorrence of revindication has been one of the most effective mechanisms sustaining the African continent. With the double game played in the Saharan case by the United Nations and the consequent inflammation of the Moroccan appetite, states in the region have been so split that not only has the organization been brought to the brink of collapse, but there has been so much enmity between the factions that one cannot be sure whether the amity which is required for the U.N. pacific mission in the region can be mustered any longer.

Finally, one might look at the effects of the conflicts in the Sahara and Timor vis-à-vis the principle of self-determination to see if the principle is fully operable. One of the important corollaries is that the inhabitants of the territory in question are the only people entitled to vote in the exercise of their right. Yet, as is evident in the cases of Djibouti, the Sahara, and East Timor, or even Kuwait, the mere mobilization of forces by one territory against another is a sure way to create refugees by intimidation. If the international community does not step in promptly to undo the damage caused by such actions, they may become increasingly common, for they are effective. Not only can the intimidating territory bring in more people to swell the number of people who would support its cause and thereby make any purported exercise of self-determination a sham, but, by the refugee situation created, it can make it impossible to know who can be a legitimate participant in the exercise of the right to decide. If the international community really bases international peace and security on freedom and faith in human rights, then it must make its presence felt in any conflict by deeds rather than by mere words. In a world where the distinction between politics and law is blurred, there may be questions as to whose standards should be used in meting out this all-important justice. But, so long as the international community is fortunate enough to have an overwhelming majority of its members supporting the principle of self-determination and its corollary measures, there should be little problem with the soundness of any action undertaken against a state that is found by the majority to be violating the rights of another.

Chapter 7

The Noncolonial Cases and the Law

NONCOLONIAL CASES AS "LIBERATION STRUGGLES": THE RATIONALE

Many contemporary writers exclude the noncolonial cases from the rubric "liberation struggles."[1] Their views are very important in the ascertainment of rules of law, particularly those rules and subjects on which existing prescriptions are anything but clear. In delivering the opinion of the court in the case of *Paquete Habana*, Justice Gray said as much:

> International law is part of our law, and must be ascertained and administered by the Courts of justice of appropriate jurisdiction as often as questions of right depending upon it are duly presented for their determination. For this purpose, where there is no treaty, and no controlling executive or legislative act or judicial decision, resort must be had to the customs and usages of civilized nations; and as evidence of these, to the works of jurists and commentators, who by years of labor, research and experience, have made themselves peculiarly well acquainted with the subjects of which they treat. . . .
> Wheaton places, among the principal sources of international law, "Text writers of authority, showing what is the approved usage of nations, or the general opinion respecting their mutual conduct, with the definitions and modifications introduced by general consent."[2]

But perhaps the most authoritative support for the consideration of opinions of writers on issues pertaining to any subject of international law is the Statute of the I.C.J.:

> The Court, whose function is to decide in accordance with international law such disputes as are submitted to it, shall apply: . . .
>
> (d) subject to the provisions of Article 59, judicial decisions and the teachings

of the most highly qualified publicists of the various nations, as a subsidiary means for the determination of rules of law.[3]

It is possible, of course, to use the caveat "subject to the provision of Article 59" and the expression "as a subsidiary means" to minimize the weight of writers' opinions. Considering the scope of the caveat—it apparently applies only in situations where the I.C.J. is deciding a case[4]—and considering also the paucity of information in the law, particularly laws specifically dealing with the liberation movements, the relevance of article 59 in determining the weight of writers' opinions is inexceptionable. But even on the doubtful assumption that designating the views of writers as a subsidiary means reduces their signifi-cance, one still finds some support from the provision of paragraph (c) of the article, wherein "the general principles of law recognized by civilized nations" has been categorized with the so-called primary sources. To appreciate this point, one need only realize that the development of the laws in civilized na-tions are often influenced, if not determined, by opinions of distinguished writers.

The Definition of "Liberation Movement" in Relation to Noncolonial Cases

The Authorities

One notable definition of liberation struggles is that offered by Abi-Saab: "Wars of national liberation constitute a category of conflicts which though not previously unknown, has gained great importance since the Second World War. *These are conflicts which arise from the struggles of peoples under colonial and foreign rule for liberation and self determination.*"[5] This definition restricts the subject to colonial cases. However, because the author did not suggest that his was a conclusive definition one may question whether it would be correct, to use his definition as a basis for excluding the noncolonial cases from libera-tion struggles.

Natalino Ronzitti's work also highlights the problem of defining "liberation movements":

> War of national liberation means the armed struggle waged by a people through its liberation movement against the established government to reach self-determination. The definition is primarily intended to cover (i) the strug-gles of the people under colonial rule. . . . The definition may also be applied to (iii) the struggles of the people against a government which though not colonial or racist, is nevertheless not conducting itself according to the princi-ple of equal rights and self-determination as embodied in the U.N. Declaration on Friendly Relations. The Biafran, Bangladesh and Palestinian conflicts char-acterize a type (iii) situation.[6]

This definition is of particular interest because, by including the Biafran and Bengali cases, it suggests that some noncolonial cases—those involving the issue of secession—can be treated as liberation struggles. The main difficulty with this definition, though, is that it does not shed much light on the status of the struggles against existing governments. Although the writer's statement that the definition "is primarily intended to cover" only the cases mentioned therein may suggest that the definition is not exhaustive, that caveat cannot be used to include the struggles against existing governments because in another of his works—a work to which he alluded in the definition being presently investigated—he emphatically excludes the struggles against existing governments:

> Also to be excluded from wars of national liberation are those civil wars (like the Communist guerilla struggle in Cambodia) regarded by one of the parties (the insurgent party, naturally) as pertaining to national liberation. At issue are struggles that take place within the context of an independent state; their cause does not lie in realizing the principle of self-determination in the same way as a community which has not yet reached its own state of identity. The claim to qualify them as wars of national liberation essentially resided in ideological motivations to which the insurgents make frequent reference so as to weaken and discredit the regime in power.[7]

When an author addresses an issue in one work but leaves it out in another, unless there is a strong reason to the contrary, a cumulative reading of the two is appropriate. Thus viewed, Ronzitti, we conclude, does not favor the inclusion of struggles against existing governments in the definition of liberation struggles. But is his stance sound? Although he offers no empirical analysis, he apparently bases his definition on two attributes of the struggles against existing governments: (1) that they occur within independent states, and (2) that they are motivated by ideological considerations.[8]

That the struggles against existing governments are intrastate conflicts is indisputable. It is doubtful, however, whether that fact can sustain the exclusion of those cases from liberation struggles. Recall that the "type (iii) situations," which the author included in the definition, are also conflicts within independent states.

Most people do not categorize the noncolonial cases as liberation struggles because most of the documents containing provisions on self-determination fail to mention any such cases.[9] Among the documents often cited in support of this are the Hostages Convention and Protocol I to the Geneva Convention.[10] Since these documents expressly mentioned the colonial cases as struggles for self-determination, obviously there is nothing wrong with using them as a basis for equating the anticolonial struggles with liberation movements. But it is unsound to exclude the noncolonial cases merely because they are not mentioned in those instruments. One must appreciate the circumstances in which the documents were adopted. They, particularly the Hostages Convention,[11] were adopted in response to the issue of whether, regardless of its nature, anything done pursuant to anticolonial movements or struggles against racist regimes or alien occupation could be entitled to the special status given to liberation struggles. Though this obviously suggests that the colonial cases were mentioned because they were within the conventions' terms of reference, it is arguable that the failure to mention the noncolonial cases was probably because those cases were not within the convention's terms of reference.

The Definition and the Realities of the Noncolonial Cases

Since the definitions do not show whether the noncolonial cases are liberation struggles, it is necessary to assess the individual situations. Here, our inquiry will focus on the struggles against existing governments.

These struggles fall in two categories, those that are transient and those that take a more protracted course. The struggle between the forces of Hissen Habré and Goukouni Oueddi in Chad is illustrative of the latter; examples of the former category are the numerous coups and countercoups that have characterized the politics of most African countries. For our purposes, it may be useful to concentrate on the coups. Again, although coups have been common elsewhere,[12] our focus is on African cases.

The Struggles for Overthrow of Existing Governments

Although there are no prescriptions as to who could lead or participate in a coup, the common pattern in virtually all the cases is that coups are based in and led by the military.[13] Indeed, the circumstances that foster coups are so rampant in Africa that one writer declared: "Another African coup had taken place. Since the beginning of this decade, the decade of African independence, there have been more than twenty coups in African nations. *The next one may occur tomorrow. Just where would be impossible to say.*"[14] Even Liberia, the African country that has enjoyed the longest and perhaps the most stable political system, has recently experienced a coup. The trend is evident in the data (see Table 4). Many authorities, and most notably William Gutteridge, have found it appropriate to refer to military intervention as "a norm rather than aberration."[15]

The Military as "Liberators" in Africa

According to writers[16] on African politics, coups are launched (1) in response to such debilitating ills in African societies as corruption, mismanage-

TABLE 4
THE INCIDENCE OF COUPS IN SUB-SAHARAN AFRICA

Country	Year of independence	No. of coups	Dates of coups (to 1975)
Botswana	1966	0	
Burundi	1962	1	11/28/66
Cameroon*	1960	0	
Central African Republic	1960	1	1/1/66
Chad	1960	1	4/14/75
Congo (Brazaville)	1960	2	7/15/63; 7/4/68
Dahomey	1960	6	10/23/63; 11/29/65; 12/22/65; 12/17/67; 12/10/69; 10/26/72
Equatorial Guinea*	1968	0	
Ethiopia	—	1	9/12/74
Gabon*	1960	0	
Gambia*	1965	0	
Ghana	1957	2	2/24/66; 1/3/72
Guinea*	1958	0	
Ivory Coast*	1960	0	
Kenya*	1963	0	
Lesotho	1966	1	1970
Liberia*	1847	0	
Madagascar	1960	1	5/18/72
Malawi	1964	0	
Mali	1960	1	11/19/68
Mauritania*	1960	0	
Niger	1960	1	4/15/74
Nigeria	1960	3	1/15/66; 7/29/75; 7/5/73
Rwanda	1962	1	7/5/73
Senegal*	1960	0	
Sierra Leone	1961	3	3/21/67; 3/23/67; 4/18/73
Somalia	1960	1	10/21/69
Swaziland	1968	0	
Tanzania	1961	0	
Togo	1960	2	1/13/63; 1/13/67
Uganda	1962	2	1966; 1/25/71
Upper Volta	1960	2	1/3/66; 2/8/74
Zaire	1960	2	9/14/60; 11/25/65
Zambia	1964	0	

Sources: B. O. NWABUEZE, CONSTITUTIONALISM IN THE EMERGENT STATES 219 (1973); R. FIRST, THE BARREL OF THE GUN: POLITICAL POWER IN AFRICA AND THE COUP D'ETAT 12–13 (1970); F. R. METROWICH, AFRICAN FREEDOM ANNUAL 1–70 (1977); William Gutteridge, "African Military Rulers: An Assessment" 62 CONFLICT STUDIES 11 (Oct. 1975).

*The asterisked countries have either experienced coups or abortive coups between 1975 and mid-1984. It is also significant that most of the countries in which there had been coups before 1975 experienced more coups or attempted coups during the next decade.

ment of national economies, chaos resulting from incompetence of governments, the inability of civilian leaders to respond efficiently to interethnic and
related strife, the oppressiveness of governments, and gross disregard for the
plight of the masses; and (2) by the military, because they possess certain
special qualities that are lacking in the civilian leaders, which thus impel them
to intervene to correct the mess caused by inept civilians.

The so-called special qualities of the military have been described by Levy:
the military "is the most efficient type of organization for combining maximum
rates of modernization with maximum levels of stability and control."[17] Likewise, Lucian Pye observes:

> Above all else . . . the revolution in military technology has caused the army
> leaders of the newly emergent countries to be extremely sensitive to the extent
> to which their countries are economically and technologically backward.
> Called upon to perform roles basic to advanced societies, the more politically
> conscious officers can hardly avoid being aware of the need for substantial
> change in their own societies.[18]

Although Samuel Decallo apparently does not support this general view
about the spate of military intervention in government in Africa, it is instructive
to note how he described that view:

> African armies and officer corps are seen to have certain characteristics related
> to their special skills. . . . They are supposed to be molded into cohesive,
> nontribal, disciplined and national units; as a result of their command of so-
> phisticated weaponry and their membership in a complex hierarchical struc-
> ture, African armies are viewed as the most modern, Westernized, and effi-
> cient organizations in their societies and the repositories of bureaucratic and
> managerial skills. . . . Allegiance to these values is then severely tested on
> their return home, where they see corruption, mismanagement . . . and inter-
> elite strife. Eventually unable to tolerate abuses of power, the army intervenes
> to "tidy up the mess" and to create a new political order.[19]

The political scientists are not alone; the military leaders themselves express
this same view in their choice of names for the regimes established by coups, in
the maiden speeches of the coup leaders, as well as in policy statements made
occasionally after coups. The military leaders consider themselves to be the
sole vehicles for the liberation or modernization of their societies. The regimes
established by the first two coups in Ghana adopted the titles "National Liberation Council" (N.L.C.) and "National Redemption Council" (N.R.C.), respectively. The Sierra Leonean coup against Brigadier David Lansana used the title
"National Reformation Council," and the coup against General Sangoulé Lami-

zana of Upper Volta was called the "Council for National Redress." Other synonyms include "National Salvation" and "National Defense" committee.[20] Using typical wording in their first statement, the leaders of the first coup in Mali declared *"the hour of liberation has come . . .* the regime of Modibo Keita and his lackeys has fallen."[21]

One may legitimately ask whether the name adopted by a government is an appropriate criterion for ascertaining its objectives. The use of the word "liberation" in their maiden speeches, however, suggests that coup leaders indeed have the liberation of their countries as one of their main objectives. This argument is given greater weight by the fact that in virtually all cases, the alleged vices of the overthrown regime not only prevailed before intervention but also made life very difficult, if not unbearable, for the masses. Yet the names and the speeches of coup leaders are unilateral statements of people who have subverted existing political systems, and we may wonder whether they are merely self-serving political rhetoric. Indeed, the performance of the military is often at such variance with the rhetoric that the statements seem implausible. Nwabueze points out that

> discontent is widespread in the society, and is shared alike by the civilian population and the military. Yet discontent with the discreditable performance of the ruling politicians provides only a superficial explanation of the recurrent phenomenon of coups. . . . When the deeper motivations are probed, most of the coups would be found to be the product of the ambition for political power among the different elements in the society. Coup makers . . . have their own ambitions for power, independently of the failure of the ruling politicians.[22]

Likewise, William Gutteridge observes:

> If economic stagnation and a depressed standard of living were of themselves actually the generators of military coups, then such events would be even more frequent than they are. In the precarious economic circumstances of the majority of African States the army seems more likely to act in defense of its own, at officer level, privileged living standards than as a champion anxious to close the gap between the rich and poor.[23]

According to Ruth First, "Whatever their declarations of noble interest, [the coup leaders] generally act for Army reasons."[24] Commenting on the theories attributing African coups to the debilitating vices of African countries, Dennis Austin notes that the charge of corruption usually is made ex post facto to justify the intervention, and that the coup leaders are neither truly aggravated by it nor untainted themselves.[25] To assess the motives of military leaders of coups, one must consider that the term "liberation" is susceptible to exploitation by opposing factions in any conflict and, further, that motive and intention are not always reliable indicators of the objectives of revolutionary leaders.

One practical way to evaluate the rationalizations for military intervention in politics in Africa is to study the type of people involved in the upheavals. The struggles occur not only between the military and civilian leaders, but between the military and the military governments as well. Three of the Nigerian coups—those that respectively toppled Generals Aguiyi Ironsi, Yakubu Gowon, and M. Buhari—were launched by the military against non-civilian leaders. Similarly, the coups that ousted General Lamizana, Colonel Saye Zerbo, and T. Sankara of Upper Volta, as well as those ridding Ghana of Generals I. Acheampong and F. Akuffo, and Dahomey of at least three leaders have all been led by the military against their own colleagues in power.

If the theory that African coups occur in response to vices in the afflicted societies and are led by the military because they have the special skills for administration is really true, there must certainly be different rationalizations for the coups by the military against the military. The rationalizations normally advanced in the maiden speeches of the leaders of the coups against military regimes, however, do not appear to be different from those given in the coups against the civilian leaders. In the coup that ousted General Gowon of Nigeria, for instance, General Murtala Muhammed recited the excuses used in the speech of the leader of the first Nigerian coup: "Nigeria has been left to drift. The nation was being plunged inexorably into chaos. Allegations of graft, misuse of public funds and nepotism gave the impression that the states were being run as private estates.[26] Likewise, Captain Sankara, later to be toppled and executed by his own military cronies, stated in his coup against Saye Zerbo: "We have to deal with a small circle of professional politicians who lived in great luxury at the expense of the impoverished masses. Why the peoples' revolutionary courts? To avoid the traps of the laws of the bourgeoisie, who can afford to pay talented—and expensive lawyers with the money they have stolen."[27]

Thus, contrary to what the theories suggest, it seems that the coup leaders are equally culpable for the vices that allegedly characterize the civilian regimes. Wherein, then, one may ask, lie the so-called special skills and concerns that cause these military takeovers from the civilian leaders? It is arguable, of course, that the military leaders who have so far survived coups might have done so because they provide better services for their countries. But this argument is fraught with many contradictions; it crumples the fabric upon which the theories are founded, because by its logic, one can conclude that the civilian regimes that have not been overthrown have survived because they are better administrators than the military leaders that have been ousted.

The fact that certain countries have been free of coups is not because the leaders in those countries have been more concerned about the plights of their countrymen. The living conditions in Tanzania, Kenya, Ivory Coast, and Zambia—countries that have so far avoided coups—are not remarkably different from those in coup-afflicted countries like Ghana, Nigeria, Togo, and Liberia. Nor is it empirically sound to ascribe better living standards to the countries with stable military regimes than to those characterized by a multiplicity of coups. One only has to compare the plights of the masses in Zaire and Somalia (under Sese Seko Mobutu and Said Barre, respectively) with those in Acheampong's Ghana, Jean-Bedel Bokassa's Central African Republic, and Y. Gowon's Nigeria to appreciate the correlation fully.[28]

Indeed, the living conditions in most African countries are, in a large measure, determined by circumstances that have little, if anything, to do with the regimes in power. Most African economies are weak: they are not only impermeable to diversification but also economically based on primary commodity production. Consequently, in addition to their poor prospects for development to improve the circumstances of the masses, they are normally incapable of providing the necessary facilities for better living conditions. The natural consequence of this is that the subjects and leaders alike scramble for the existing few amenities. But since one has to be more than ordinary to survive the scramble, every effort—even if such effort aggravates the countries' ailments—is resorted to by all, regardless of who is in power. Decallo describes the typical situation most tellingly:

> If not already present, corruption tends to seep into military regimes as if to prove that greed and avarice know no distinction between soldier and civilian. Contrary to pseudotheoretical literature about its austerity and puritan tastes, the officer corps does not differ markedly in its bourgeois tastes from other elites; traditional African cultural values do not place high premium on ascetic lifestyles. *There are apparently few saints in situations of acute economic scarcity*, especially in cultural systems where the rise to eminence of one individual triggers an obligation to provide for the welfare of an entire kinship group.[29]

Of course, there are African countries where economies have shown improvement under military regimes. The relatively better handling of the Ghanaian balance-of-payment deficits in the early years of the N.L.C. and the N.R.C. regimes, the Togolese under Gnassingbe Eyadema, the Nigerians under Y. Gowon, and the Zairian and Congolese under Sese Seko Mobutu and Marien Ngouabi, respectively, are cases in point.[30] Indeed, a superficial study of these economies might tempt one to give some credit to the regimes in question, but the factors that led to the so-called improvements were absolutely unrelated to the people in power. The Ghanaian and Ivorian situations were mainly due to the rise in the price of cocoa on the world market. The Congolese situation was due to the quadrupling of oil prices. Similarly, the Zairian, Nigerian, and Togolese cases were in response to the discovery and demand for their copper, oil, and phosphate, respectively. Since any of these developments could have occurred under civilian regimes as well, it is difficult to attribute them to the administrative prowess of the military.

In all the so-called successful cases there was no transformation of the economies from the primary commodity-producing type to a manufacturing one—the crucial and, perhaps, the most essential antidote to African economic ailments. No doubt, when the demands and prices for the primary goods declined, the economies of the countries switched back to the same, if not worse, levels than they were before the so-called improvements. The pattern underscores the statement of Eric Nordlinger—that if the economy improves, it is often in spite of the military regime in power.[31]

Nor did any of the military regimes use the proceeds of their "successes" to create the infrastructure from which the masses in their countries could benefit. The facts suggest that the military has neither the alleged qualities for better administration nor the deep concern for the improvement of conditions for their people, a conclusion confirmed by the acts and policies pursued by the military regimes.

Socioeconomic Unrest and Coups in Africa

Judged by the living conditions typical of African societies, it is tempting to say that the coups have been launched to "liberate" the afflicted people from their harsh conditions. A more careful study, however, indicates that most coups are caused by factors that have little, if any, relevance to preexisting socioeconomic conditions. One indication is the timing of the coups. In virtually all cases, the problems that purportedly led to the coups had existed long before the coups were staged. Why did the "redeemers" not intervene earlier? Evidently, the factors that provoked the coups were unrelated to the failings of the ousted regimes.

The issue of corruption may provide a good starting point. Corruption is prevalent in many an African society. Yet, that vice seems not to have been a cause of coups. Indeed, not only do the military leaders remain unconcerned about the pervasiveness of corruption in their societies; they also participate in it and, sometimes, even fight relentlessly to maintain corrupt leaders in power. In Ghana, General Joseph Ankrah, one of the leading architects of the 1966 coup, had been implicated in deals prior to the coup. Indeed, even after assuming the office, his corrupt habits continued and eventually led to his removal from office by his fellow members of the N.L.C.[32] The many commissions of inquiry that were set up by the Acheampong regime to investigate the great riches of the other members of the N.L.C. furnish strong testimony of the prevalence of corruption and, hence, how little the other 1966 coup leaders in Ghana were motivated by the corrupt practices in that country. The Nigerian coup of 1966 and those that followed the first military intervention in Ghana were similar.

Before the coup that brought Gowon into power, for instance, corruption was pervasive in the Nigerian society.[33] And, no doubt, the military was an active participant in that corruption. After the coup, the vice became even more deeply entrenched. One Nigerian professor observed that the government paid lip service to combating the vice and disregarded the numerous petitions calling for the investigation of the assets of some military officers who had acquired monumental riches overnight.[34] The "gold and ivory" case of Uganda is even more illustrative of the corrupt tendencies of the African military.[35] At issue was an attempt by some members of the Obote government to impeach or overthrow President Milton Obote for his involvement in the smuggling of valuable commodities.[36] Notwithstanding the notoriety of the case in the Ugandan society, Idi Amin not only fought relentlessly to keep the president in power but served as the instrument by which the president purged his critics. Nor was Amin innocent. Indeed, besides being a party to the "gold and ivory affair," there were reports from the Ugandan auditor general's department that Amin had embezzled funds earmarked for military hardware.

Although the complicity of the military in corruption may dispel the suggestion that the coups are staged in response to the vices in the afflicted African societies, it is possible to explain the frequency of coups by other factors, notably, personality differences, competing ambitions, and the corporate security of the members of the army.

The 1966 coup in Ghana is an example. General Emmanuel Kotoka and virtually all the other participants in the coup had personal grievances against the Nkrumah regime. Kotoka, for instance, was known not to get on well with Major General Charles Barwah, and like several other officers in the army, he was doubtful of the latter's professional advancement under Nkrumah's government.[37] Similarly, there were resentments throughout the officer corps over the "political" promotions of some officers, the retirements of Generals Joseph Ankrah and S.J. Otu, cutbacks in amenities and services for the armed forces, rumors regarding the possible dispatch of the army to fight in Rhodesia,[38] attempts to indoctrinate the army with Nkrumaist philosophy, and the direct threat to the military's professional autonomy and self-image from the increasingly powerful, better equipped, and more trusted units of the President's Own Guard Regiment (P.O.G.R.).[39]

In the 1972 coup against Kofi Busia, General I. K. Acheampong complained specifically about Busia's cutbacks in defense spending, officers' salaries and fringe benefits—which he referred to as "the few amenities." He also resented the "discrimination" in favor of the officers who had helped Busia to come into power and lamented that the promotion scramble that followed the 1966 coup virtually froze his and his colleagues' chances for rapid professional advancement.[40]

The Togolese coups of 1963 and 1967 against Presidents Sylvanus Olympio and Nicholas Grunitzky, respectively; the Ugandan coup of 1971 as well as those of Dahomey (1965) and Sierra Leone (1967); and the coups against Modibo Keita, Jean-Bedel Bokassa, and Ngarta Tombalbaye of Mali, Central African Republic, and Chad, respectively, are all cases that can be explained more cogently by the competing ambition, personality differences, and corporate security of the army than by the socioeconomic problems of these countries.

The Togolese upheavals of 1963 and 1967 occurred in these contexts: After the demobilization of the French colonial forces in 1963, men who had served in the colonial armies, including those from Togo, were faced with functional unemployment. They therefore petitioned the president to incorporate them into the Togolese army. It was soon after the president turned down the request that the coup was staged and, indeed, by the same people who were about to be cashiered from the army. Obviously, facts such as these, or the fact that the threatened colonial officers became part of the Togolese army and immediately promoted themselves to captains and lieutenants,[41] make it extremely difficult to explain the upheaval in any other terms than the job security and the personal ambitions of the former noncommissioned officers of the disbanded colonial force.

It may be possible to explain the 1967 coup against President Grunitzky in terms of the impending chaos resulting from the serious rift between the president and his vice-president, Antoine Meatchi. This argument, however, has to be matched against the imminent threat to coup leader Eyadema's security.[42] Evidently, the only people with the prospects of assuming power after the fall of the Grunitzky government were the Ewes in the south. These people had vowed to prosecute and punish Eyadema and all the accomplices in the assassination of President Olympio. Thus, it is highly conceivable that the foreclosure of that threat was a significant, if not the main, incitement to the coup.

The Amin coup against President Obote of Uganda is another case in point. It has already been shown how firmly Amin clung to President Obote when the president's shortcomings brought his regime to the brink of collapse.[43] This warm relationship, however, soured shortly before the coup. Among the many factors cited to explain this hostility are Amin's embezzlement of funds, his complicity in the assassination of an army friend of Obote's, and his tribalistic tendencies, particularly his gross discrimination against people from tribes other than his own.[44] Signs of his loss of favor from Obote were reportedly expressed in governmental acts, including the creation of rival posts to the one held by him.[45] Indeed, according to one report,[46] the president had just issued an order for Amin's arrest and trial when the coup erupted. Surely, the only inference to be drawn from all these developments is that it was Amin's personal security, not the ineptitude of President Obote, that led the general to oust the civilian government.

If the causes of the coups cannot be explained by the ailments in African countries, what about the performance of the military? Is it an accurate rationalization for the spate of military takeovers?

How Military Regimes Have Handled Corruption

One common attribute of all the military regimes in Africa is that the sociopolitical institutions in which corruption thrived under the preceding regimes are not only maintained but also heavily relied on for all governmental purposes.[47] This, needless to say, accounts for the perpetuation of corruption under military rule. The military leaders do not make serious efforts to eradicate the vice. Very often the civilian leaders whose venality had allegedly caused the coup are treated with magnanimity that contradicts the impassioned accusations previously leveled against them. In Ghana, notwithstanding the numerous complaints and massive demonstrations by workers and students against the intense corruption under the Acheampong regime, the succeeding military government did nothing to make the ousted leader accountable for the problems for which he was allegedly ousted. All it did was to retire Acheampong peacefully to his village, where he could enjoy the proceeds of his "corruption business." In the Dahomeyan coup of 1963, General Christophe Soglo did not even consider detaining the ex-president and some of his more corrupt ministers. Indeed, not even Chabi Mama (the power broker behind the president) was arrested for trial. It was only after he started to foment opposition from his northern fiefdom that the government went after him.[48]

The 1966 upheaval in Ghana did not do much to sustain the argument that the military assumed power to redress debilitating corruption, either. Evidently, the ostensible sweeping probes into the affairs of the Convention Peoples' Party (C.P.P.) government were merely peripheral. They left intact the civil service, the army, and the police—the most corrupt structures in the country.[49] In Upper Volta, a trial of President Maurice Yameogo was never considered by the government. It was only after a strong pressure was exerted from the Upper Voltan professionals and trade unionists that the government tried him.[50] Finally, Liberia—at the start of his regime, Master Sergeant Samuel K. Doe earned strong support from his compatriots because of his intention to confiscate the assets of, and possibly to execute, people found to be corrupt.[51] However, in 1982 when some police officers were convicted and sentenced for corruption, the master sergeant suspended the sentences and exculpated the convicts on the flimsy excuse that there was no honest person to carry out the execution.[52] Surely, although this portrays how the leader himself acknowledges the heights of corruption in Liberia, it is an act inconsistent with the goal of stamping out corruption.

Another incident equally difficult to explain was Doe's confrontation with his foreign minister, H. Boima Fahnbulleh. At issue was Fahnbulleh's allegations that the "big cars, luxurious houses and the practice of living higher than the ordinary man are some of the corrupt values which continue to breed in our society."[53] The foreign minister's allegations echoed Master Sergeant Doe's own maiden speech in which he berated the members of the government for their ostentatious living habits. His stance is paradoxical: corruption and inequality were loathed, impermissible if pursued under any other administration, but perfectly sound and unchallengeable if practiced under his regime. He stated sarcastically:

> If he [Fahnbulleh] wants the government to sell the cars assigned to him and use the proceeds for the masses, we will be too happy to approve that. . . . If minister Fahnbulleh feels that he should remain a poor man in society, there is nothing wrong with that but he should not condemn those who want to live a better life.[54]

The Management of African Economies under Military Regimes

The policies adopted in the immediate aftermath of African coups suggest that coup leaders have assumed power to clear up the mess generated by the ousted regimes. But, on closer scrutiny of the policies of military regimes, the circumstances under which they were adopted, and subsequent programs, all raise a number of questions: (1) Were the initial policies of the military leaders introduced merely to make the regime popular with the masses? (2) Did the policies not merely reproduce programs enunciated by the preceding government? (3) Were the real intentions of the coup leaders not simply designed to "satisfy" only the people with whom they closely relate?

One reason why the N.L.C. coup was warmly welcomed by most Ghanaians was that the leaders initiated some austerity measures, indicating that the extravagant habits of the previous government were now a thing of the past.[55] Later, when people learned of the increase in the defense budget by 41 percent, which indeed absorbed more foreign exchange than any other department, most Ghanaians became skeptical about the government's intentions.[56] It is, of course, arguable that the increase in the defense expenditure might have been rendered inevitable by the ill treatment meted out to the regular army by the president, whose interest lay solely with the P.O.G.R. The problem with this reasoning, though, is that in a country where most people suffer from abject poverty and essential commodities are scarce, it is unimaginable that a government that had genuine concern for its country would have chosen to spend more of the nation's meager resources on the military. What makes one even more suspicious about the government's concern is that other privileged groups, notably, some university lecturers, medical officers, and civil servants who had strong links with those in power, were exempted from the austerity measures. Indeed, the salaries of these privileged people were increased by as much as 40 percent, while cutbacks were made in fields of industrial and agricultural development and trade and communication by as much as 70 percent.[57]

In the Acheampong regime, where the austerity measures of the Busia regime were reintroduced by heavy cuts in social and infrastructural building allocations, the military budget was given a substantial increase.[58] Likewise, in Congo (Brazaville), Upper Volta, and Dahomey under Generals Nguoabi, Lamizana, and Soglo, respectively, the austerity measures did not extend to the military.[59] In the Congolese situation there was a pay increase by 20 percent to 40 percent for the members of the army.[60] In Upper Volta, although the military regime reintroduced the austerity measures of President Maurice Yameogo, the salaries of the military were not touched.[61] In Dahomey, General Soglo went even further to exempt imported goods (private cars) for officers from custom duties.[62] Evidently, the handling of the economies in Mobutu's Zaire, Bokassa's Central African Republic, Said Barre's Somalia, and Amin's Uganda are mirror reflections of the foregoing, except that in addition to the usual biases in favor of the military and leaders' cronies, the leaders in these cases raided their national coffers as if those coffers were their personal preserves.[63]

The Management of African Economies by the Military:
Amin's Uganda in Retrospect

Like most other military regimes, Amin's started with overwhelming support from the Ugandan populace. One explanation[64] for this is Obote's radical socialist policies, which threatened to provoke massive repatriation of foreign private capital from Uganda. Amin's repudiation of those policies was welcomed as an act that would salvage the Ugandan economy from imminent collapse. Other policies that won Amin the support of the masses were his decontrol of commodities that had previously been monopolized by the state and his reduction of Ugandan governmental partnership in foreign companies from 60 to 49 percent.[65] The optimistic assumption of Ugandans was that these policies would reduce the financial load of the government and enable it to concentrate more on social services.[66] But the question is, did Uganda realize any of these expected benefits?

Evidently, except for the temporary psychological satisfaction generated by the optimism, the average Ugandan gained nothing from any of Amin's policies. Even before implementation could begin, the government had spent the expected proceeds on expensive programs for the army: salaries were increased substantially, heavy artillery was procured for them, and the government made expensive contracts for the construction of new military barracks, airfields, and officers' housing.[67] Later, when the expected proceeds proved elusive, the measure became but one of the numerous ill-planned ventures that contributed to the balance-of-payment deficits that characterized the regime.

The discussion of Amin's economic policies to illustrate the egocentric disposition of some African military leaders and the recklessness with which they handle their economies cannot be complete without also mentioning his nationalization policies. Ironically, although nationalization was at variance with the notions that earned him the support of his subjects, his nationalization policies were welcomed by most Ugandans. This paradoxical response was based on the assumption that the policies would put the economy in the hands of Ugandan nationals and rid that country of the "exploiters," "extortionists," and "swindlers" who had contributed immensely to the country's economic woes.[68] And the nationalization of capital and the repatriation of business people that followed achieved something for Uganda. Indeed, the short-term consequences of the policies alleviated some of the problems that had hitherto plagued the country's economy.

However, a more critical examination, especially of the long-term consequences of the policies, raises many difficult questions, most particularly whether a well-advised leader would have instituted any of them. The situation was precarious because of the indispensability of the Asians and other affected expatriates to the Ugandan socioeconomic life. Suffice it to note that, not only were the expatriates the main group of people running the import-export trade in Uganda, they provided the country with almost all its trained manpower, professionals, and with most of the employment opportunities in farms, homes, firms, and shops. Thus when they were removed without anyone to fill the void, the whole socioeconomic system of Uganda went to the brink of collapse.[69] Unemployment attained alarming heights, foreign capital became unreachable, and as a natural consequence of depleted inventories, essential commodities became very scarce, factories operated below their normal capacities, and the prices of goods skyrocketed.

The government showed no wisdom in its administration of the proceeds of the nationalized businesses, either. Nor did it display any interest in improving the lot of the suffering masses. Thus, rather than employing the seized assets in ventures from which the country could benefit, the government allotted most of them to people with whom it had strong connections (mostly the military and people of the Kwakwa tribe) and under such terms as to make it difficult, if not impossible, for the treasury to collect rents and taxes from the new owners.[70]

Although the foregoing surely warrants the statement that Amin's economic policies were not enunciated with the view to making things better for the average Ugandan, it also demonstrates how the military chose to serve its own interests at the expense of the country. The inference to draw, then, is that it might be a misuse of language to apply the treasured term "liberation" to any such struggles as these. To qualify as a liberation movement, a movement or government must meet certain standards, which inter alia are:

1. Opposition to a corrupt and dictatorial government that has closed all possible avenues for change of leadership through the normal democratic process.
2. A military leadership untainted by corruption before the intervention.
3. Circumstances surrounding the coups that do not suggest that the leaders have ulterior motives.
4. Leaders' abstention after the coup from the "winner takes all" attitude, and their formulation of policies, only after objective consideration, designed to benefit society at large.
5. Creation by coup leaders of a program to hand over power to qualified citizens through normal democratic processes.

It is conceded that some of these may raise questions that have no easy answers. For instance: What is the status of an intervention until the leaders succeed in establishing a government? When should the strugglers manifest their intention to hand over power through normal democratic processes? Does the introduction of the democratic idea not conflict with the right of each state to adopt the government that it deems fit? How are we to judge the objectivity of policies? Any of these questions may necessitate many interesting analyses, but they lie beyond the scope of this study.

THE NONCOLONIAL CASES UNDER THEIR MUNICIPAL SYSTEMS

At first glance, it may be tempting to brand the noncolonial cases as illegal, not only because virtually all of them are aimed at overthrowing the established legal systems of their countries, but particularly because the supremacy clauses in nearly all the overthrown legal systems expressly forbid any extraconstitutional acts. In article 1(2) of the 1979 Constitution of Ghana, which was a verbatim repetition of the corresponding article of its 1969 counterpart, one such provision reads: "The . . . Constitution shall be the supreme law of Ghana

and any other law found to be inconsistent with any provision of this Constitution shall to the extent of the inconsistency be void and of no effect."[71] Likewise, the 1963 Constitution of Nigeria provided:

> This Constitution shall have the force of law throughout Nigeria and, subject
> to the provisions of section 4 of this Constitution, if any other law (including
> the Constitution of a region) is inconsistent with this Constitution, this Consti-
> tution shall prevail and the other law, shall to the extent of the inconsistency
> be void.[72]

In article 1(2) of the 1979 Constitution of Nigeria: "The Federal Republic of
Nigeria shall not be governed, nor shall any person or group take control of the
Government of Nigeria or any part thereof except in accordance with the provi-
sions of the Constitution."[73]

Ironically, all these constitutions have been overthrown by the military,
their so-called supremacy clauses and provisions against extraconstitutional activities notwithstanding. Do such antisubversion provisions have any legal
force? In a commentary on the 1979 Constitution of Nigeria, Billy Dudley
branded such provisions as empty and meaningless:

> The new (1979) Constitution of the Federal Republic of Nigeria makes it un-
> constitutional, and hence illegal, for the military to "take over" through coup
> d'etat the instrumentalities of government from the elected representatives of
> the people. . . . Who for example, is supposed to enforce the provision once
> the civil authority has been overthrown? For ultimately the really coercive
> power which underpins the authority of the civil regime is the military. It
> could of course be that the "force" of such a provision is in fact exhortatory, a
> "call" on the people to rise against the military in defense of the "constitu-
> tional order". But there are two difficulties with that interpretation. First the
> "people" do not just rise in revolt. . . . The second difficulty is related to the
> first. To demand that an unarmed electorate rise against the army is nothing
> short of [calling for] self-immolation on the part of the electorate. . . . Hence
> the demand itself cannot but be empty and meaningless.[74]

But this position is not shared by all writers. According to one view, the
provisions against extraconstitutional activities are enforceable against coup
leaders.[75] Since the tools of construction require a constitution to be read as a
whole, it is appropriate to brand any anti-coup provisions of any constitution as
being as enforceable as any other provisions of that document. No doubt, many
African constitutions have been used to convict several coup and secessionist
leaders as traitors.[76] But the question is: What is the status of those revolutions
that succeed in supplanting the preexisting systems? One possible answer may
be gathered from the 1979 Constitution of Ghana:

Article 1(3) All citizens of Ghana have the right to resist any person seeking to abolish the constitution should no other remedy be possible.

Article 2(1) A person who alleges—

    (a) that an enactment or anything contained in or done under the authority of that or any other enactment, or

    (b) that an act or omission of any person, is inconsistent with or in contradiction of, a provision of this constitution may at any time bring an action in the Supreme Court to that effect.[77]

Since governments established by military intervention often "save" some aspects of their preexisting judicial systems,[78] it is arguable that the citizens of a country with this kind of provision can challenge any subversive act in court. However, this can be conceived only in theoretical terms; in practice, such action would run into many difficulties. For instance, there may be questions as to whether the provision is mandatory or merely permissive. If permissive, what would happen if nobody challenges the upheaval? Conversely, if it is mandatory, would the whole society be culpable if no one challenges the matter? Again, assuming there could be courageous or patriotic citizens to mount a case in the ordinary courts, and assuming, further, that the courts may be receptive to a request to declare the government illegal, further questions may arise as to how the revolutionary government can then be replaced by a constitutional one.

Third, there may be difficulties as to whether any citizen at all can be a party to the case. In other words, there may be a procedural question of whether any individual at all can have a *locus standi* in the case. According to the law on the issue, an individual citizen cannot champion a case for the enforcement of the public law, unless that person has an interest transcending that of the general public.[79] Without that requisite special interest, the only recourse for the individual citizen is the institution of a relator action through the attorney general. In *Onyia v. Governor in Council and Others*, where the plaintiffs could neither prove special interest nor institute the action through the attorney general, the law was pronounced and applied by the court:

> I think it plain that there has been no interference with any private right of the plaintiff nor has he suffered special damage peculiar to himself. . . . He therefore should not sue without joining the Attorney General. The persons really interested were not before the court.[80]

Since the office of the attorney general changes with the government in power, it is easy to see the possible contradictions into which one would fall if one were to seek to employ the services of the attorney general to challenge the government on which the attorney general's authority is founded.

It is, of course, possible to discount the potential hurdles, because any member of the ousted regime can argue that he or she has a special interest in the ousted regime. But even that is a very doubtful hypothesis, especially under a military that has just overthrown the government under which the minister served. The Judicial Committee of the Privy Council articulated the true position in the case of *Vajesingji Joravarsingji v. Secretary of State for India*, when it described the effect of a revolutionary change: "Any inhabitant of the territory can make good in the municipal courts established by the new sovereign only such rights as that sovereign has, through his officers, recognized. *Such rights as he had under the rule of the predecessors avail him nothing.*"[81]

Kelsen elaborates:

> From a juristic point of view, the decisive criterion of a revolution is that the order in force is overthrown and replaced by a new legal order in a way which the former had not itself anticipated. Usually the new men whom a revolution brings into power annul not only the constitution and certain laws of paramount political significance, putting other norms in their place. A great part of the old legal order "remains" valid also within the frame of the new order. But the phrase "they remain valid" does not give an adequate description of the phenomenon. It is only the contents of these norms that remain the same, not the reason of their validity. . . . That constitution is no longer in force; it is replaced by a new constitution which is not the result of a constitutional alteration of the former. If laws which were introduced under the old constitution continue to be "valid" under the new constitution, this is possible only because validity has expressly or "tacitly" been vested in them by the new constitution.[82]

The point has been confirmed in many judicial decisions, including the Pakistani case of *The State v. Dosso*[83] and the Ugandan case of *Uganda v. Commissioner for Prisons, Ex parte Matovu*.[84] The Ugandan case was an offshoot of the prime minister's substitution of the Ugandan 1963 Constitution with one that made him the executive president of the country. Since none of these acts had been contemplated by the Ugandan Constitution, their constitutionality was challenged. And the court spelled out the operative law by citing and approving the *Dosso* case:

> The President's proclamation of October 7th 1958, by which the Constitution of 1956 was annulled and martial law was proclaimed, constituted an "abrupt" political change not within the contemplation of the said constitution, i.e., a revolution. A victorious revolution is an internationally recognized legal method of changing a Constitution. Such a revolution constitutes a new law creating fact. *Laws which derive from the "old order" may remain valid under the "new order" only because validity has expressly been vested in the same, not the reason of validity.*[85]

Noncolonial Cases and the Law

Although the foregoing survey amply elucidates the legal effect of revolutions on preexisting legal systems, it may be of interest to explore how courts in other countries have treated the issue. Our focus is on the Ghanaian case of *Sallah v. Attorney General* and the Nigerian *Lakanmi* decision.

Sallah v. Attorney General

Sallah v. Attorney General[86] involved the interpretation of a provision of the 1969 Constitution of Ghana, which dealt with the continuance in office of a certain group of staff in the new regime. The provision in question is found in section 9(1) of the Transitional Provisions contained in the first schedule of the constitution. It reads:

> Subject to the provisions of this section, and save as otherwise provided in this Constitution, *every person who immediately before the coming into force of this Constitution held or was acting in any office established*
>
> a. by or in pursuance of the proclamation for the Constitution of the National Liberation Council . . . dated the twenty-sixth day of February, 1966, or
> b. in pursuance of a Decree of the National Liberation Council, or
> c. by or under the authority of that Council, shall, as far as is consistent with the provisions of this Constitution, be deemed to have been appointed . . . to hold or act in the equivalent office under this Constitution for a period of six months from the date of such commencement, unless before or on the expiration of that date, any such person shall have been appointed . . . to hold or act in that office or some other office.

In 1967 Mr. Sallah became a manager of the Ghana National Trading Corporation (G.N.T.C.), a public corporation that had originally been established in 1961 by an executive instrument issued pursuant to the Statutory Corporations Act of 1961.[87] In 1964 a new Statutory Corporations Act and a legislative instrument[88] continued the existence of the G.N.T.C. as a body corporate. The office of Sallah was thus in existence before the N.L.C. coup. On February 21, 1970, six months after the 1969 Constitution came into force, Sallah and some 567 other public officers were terminated under the Transitional Provisions. Sallah and others then challenged their termination in the Court of Appeal (then the highest court in the country). The attorney general invoked the Kelsen theory on revolutions, urging that the preexisting legal system had been supplanted by the coup, and that any aspect thereof survived only to the extent the new system allowed it to continue. He contended that the word "established," in the Transitional Provisions, should be given the technical meaning of "deriving validity from." The court rejected the relevance of the jurisprudential argument to the case[89] and held that the explanation of the word "establish" by its technical meaning as suggested by the attorney general would be tantamount to an abuse of language.[90] It then concluded that insofar as the office of the applicants preexisted the N.L.C. government, the latter did not create it, and so the purported dismissals were invalid.

On a careful study of the case, one may be impressed by the court, not only for the interest shown in the need to preserve the continuity of the legal system, but also for its concern for human rights, which were apparently the main pillars on which the decision was anchored. However, there were some problems with the jurisprudential ramifications of that judgment. First, it is significant that even though the majority overruled the relevance of jurisprudential analysis to the issues at stake, there was nothing in the judgment to suggest whether the analysis was wrong. Perhaps this posture was taken as a logical inference from the ruling that the analysis was irrelevant to the case. But the problem is that, as the main point on which the respondent's arguments were founded, it is puzzling why the court did not evaluate it. It is suggested that the only way the analysis could have been rejected without affecting the significance of the decision would have been if the arguments had been addressed but rejected on the merits. Evidently, the only ruling that alluded to the jurisprudential analysis was that of the dissenting judge. But as it is the minority position, it is difficult to give it a conclusive weight on the jurisprudential issue. It is not surprising then that Date-Bah felt constrained to say:

> It cannot really be said of any of the judgments in the case that it provided "manna for jurisprudes," [and that] Jurisprudes who might have hoped to find in these judgments profound analytical discourses on the legal effect of a *coup d'etat on a country's pre-existing legal system are likely to be somewhat disappointed.*[91]

The second reason why the *Sallah* ruling provides a dubious basis for a meaningful discussion of the effect of revolutions is that although the court found the dismissals to be invalid, the ruling was unable to overturn the position of the government—the dismissals were implemented.[92]

Third, it is significant that Justice Apalloo, who was very outspoken about the need to insure protection of human rights by judicial review of administrative action, had in a previous decision manifested a position that was conspicuously at variance with the position taken in the *Sallah* case; in *Awoornor Williams v. Gbedemah*,[93] the distinguished justice not only paid lip service to a controversial provision of the 1969 Constitution but went further to uphold a decree that violated the respondent's constitutional right of access to the ordinary courts of the land:

Although paragraph 1(2) of the Courts Decree, 1966 (N.L.C.D.84) . . . conferred the judicial power of the State on the courts in a familiar terminology, it was accurate to say that judicial power was exercised by the courts during the era of the National Liberation Council at sufferance. To say this is not to accuse the National Liberation Council even obliquely of totalitarianism or cast anything like a posthumous reflection on a regime which was in many respects a liberal one. But we think this is the true constitutional position. *No Decree which was passed by the National Liberation Council could have been struck by the courts as unconstitutional.*[94]

One interesting thing about the *Gbedemah* and *Sallah* cases is that they were products of the constitution adopted under the "omnipotent," albeit "undictatorial," N.L.C. Thus the question is why one was upheld but the other failed to receive the judicial imprimatur. Conceivably, a critical study of the two cases would suggest that the *Gbedemah* case rather deserved the fury of the court. For, whereas that case involved an encroachment on judicial power by an administrative body and thus warranted a strong challenge from a sensitive judiciary,[95] the *Sallah* case involved more of an administrative act on an administrative issue where the acceptance of the dismissal was more easily defensible.

The problem with the significance of the effect of revolutions on preexisting legal systems is exemplified in the *Lakanmi* case also.[96] Before we set out to discuss this celebrated case, however, it may be pertinent to mention the cases of *Ogunlesi v. Attorney General*[97] and *Adamolekun v. The Council of the University of Ibadan.*[98]

Ogunlesi was a case in which the salaries of a group of staff in the public corporations of Nigeria were reduced under decrees of the federal government. Naturally, the affected individuals challenged the validity of these decrees, claiming that they were *ultra vires* of the federal military government and that, insofar as the latter had taken over from the government under the 1963 Constitution, it could not exercise legislative powers in excess of what the constitution prescribed. The High Court of Lagos upheld the decrees, noting further that the federal military government had the power to issue decrees that could override the provisions of the constitution. Again, in the *Adamolekun* case the court refused to question the authority of the federal military government "in making a decree or an edict on the ground that there is no legislative authority to make one."[99]

The Lakanmi Case

Like *Ogunlesi* and *Adamolekun*, the *Lakanmi* case was an offshoot of decrees passed under the federal military government of General Gowon of

Nigeria. Unlike the other two, however, *Lakanmi* struck out decrees that had sought to deprive some individuals of their properties and right of access to the ordinary courts of Nigeria.

Although the court may be applauded for its courage in rejecting the decrees, there are a number of reasons why the decision cannot be an authoritative pronouncement on the effect of coups on preexisting legal systems. First, the events that immediately followed the decision eroded any possible effect that the judgment could have had on the issue under discussion. Second, its premise of the judgment was so fallacious that it can be discarded for having been rendered with gross disregard to the essential facts of the case.[100]

Studying the case within the constitutional contexts in which it arose is essential to a full understanding of its legal ramifications. Nigeria became independent in 1960. On January 15, 1966, some members of the Nigerian military attempted a coup, resulting in the assassination of the prime minister and some members of his government. On January 16 the surviving members of the government tried to resuscitate the cabinet by appointing an acting prime minister under section 92 of the 1963 Constitution. However, their efforts were foiled by the commander of the Nigerian army, General Aguiyi Ironsi, who, on the pretext of the "serious military situation," urged that an immediate military takeover was inevitable. Naturally, with scarcely any other choice than to submit to what the people with the machine guns had dictated, the civilians surrendered. General Ironsi then promulgated the decree entitled "The Constitution (Suspension and Modification) Decree No. 1, 1966," schedule 3 of which reads:

> This Constitution shall have the force of law throughout Nigeria and if any other law (including the Constitution of a region) is inconsistent with this Constitution, this Constitution shall prevail and the other law shall, to the extent of the inconsistency be void.
>
> Provided that this Constitution shall not prevail over a decree, and nothing in this constitution shall render any provision of a decree void to any extent whatsoever.[101]

Under section 6 of the decree, no court of law could entertain any question as to the validity of any decree or edict. By the Decree No. 34 of May 1966 the federation was dissolved and a unitary system was instituted in its stead. On July 29 another coup was launched, making General Gowon the head of the Nigerian government. Significantly, this second upheaval not only restored the Federation[102] but it reinstated Decree No. 1, which had been abrogated soon after the transformation of the country into a unitary state.

Pursuant to a decree under the Gowon administration, a tribunal issued an order confiscating assets of the appellants. Lakanmi and others challenged the order in court, arguing that as an interim constitutional government, the military regime was bound to abide by the provisions of the 1963 Constitution, and that inasmuch as the decree under which their assets were confiscated was *ultra vires* the Constitution, that decree was invalid, and therefore, anything done thereunder was ipso facto void of any effect. The court rejected these arguments, and the appellants reappealed. While the suit was pending the federal military government promulgated three successive decrees that cumulatively validated all acts done by the tribunals that gave rise to the *Lakanmi* case, applied solely to the people specifically mentioned in the schedule to the Decree No. 45, and precluded the courts from exercising jurisdiction over any matter relating to the case. These decrees were upheld by the court, and Lakanmi and others brought the matter to the Nigerian Supreme Court, whose ruling has been summarized by one Nigerian author as follows:

> The Supreme Court declared Decree No. 45 invalid as contrary to the Constitution, thereby allowing the appeal of the appellants. For the sake of clarity, we would set out what we conceive to be the *rationes decidendi* of the judgment of the Supreme Court.
>
> (1) The event of January 15, 1966, did not amount to a revolution but a mere offer of invitation to the Armed Forces to form an interim military Government, making it clear that only certain sections of the 1963 Constitution were to be suspended, and the offer was duly accepted by the Armed Forces. . . .
> (2) The Constitutional interim government which came into being by the wishes of the representatives of the people, and whose object is to uphold the Constitution, could only derogate from the Constitution if the derogation is justified under the "doctrine of necessity". . . .
> (4) Since Decree No. 45 of 1968, which sought to validate the order made by the tribunal under Edict No. 5 of 1967 (and this implied that it was otherwise invalid), was a legislative act which impinged upon the sphere of the judiciary (by specifically naming the appellants and some other persons in its schedule) it was an unnecessary intrusion into the sphere of the judiciary and it is therefore void.[103]

The lesson from the *Lakanmi* case is that decrees of military regimes are reviewable and may be dismissed if they encroach upon the powers of the judiciary. Obviously, this necessitates inquiries into whether the *Lakanmi* case can be reconciled with *Ogunlesi* and *Adamolekun* cases.

It may be argued that as a decision of the Supreme Court of Nigeria, the *Lakanmi* case cannot be reproached by the High Court decision on Ogunlesi's. While the case of Adamolekun defies this argument, particularly since it was also a Supreme Court decision, the decision in *Lakanmi* can enjoy priority over it, for whereas the decision in *Lakanmi* was mentioned as the *rationes de-cidendi*, the decision in *Adamolekun* has been described as a mere *obiter dictum*.[104]

Persuasive though the *Lakanmi* decision may thus be, the assumptions on which it was founded were so fallacious that it cannot be accorded the significance generally given to decisions of the Supreme Court.[105] Before we get into these crucial problems with the case, it is pertinent to address one attribute that evidently contradicts the conclusion that the *Lakanmi* case was unsupportive of the decisions in *Ogunlesi* and the rest. It is sufficient to note that the court in *Lakanmi* approved of the decisions rendered in the *Dosso* and *Ex parte Matovu* cases, that the revolutions in those situations absolutely supplanted the preexisting legal systems. The court's difficulty with issuing a similar ruling in the *Lakanmi* case was because it found the Nigerian coup to be anything but revolutionary.[106] This, needless to say, necessitates a definition of the words "revolution" and "coup" to find out whether they can be used to distinguish between the two sets of cases.

Evidently, the factor that influenced the court's distinction between the coups leading to the *Dosso* and *Lakanmi* cases was the pre-takeover communication between the surviving members of the civilian government and General Ironsi.[107] Admittedly, after that confrontation, the spokesman of the battered government handed over authority to the military in a peaceful way. But the fact remains that the transfer was effected in a way that had not been contemplated by the Constitution.[108] Thus, even if the handing over had been as voluntary as the court suggested, the validity of that exercise still would be questionable. On this issue, one writer has revealingly invoked the *nemo dat* rule:

> As is thus seen, the court accepted the theory of the "handing over" of government to the military in 1966. This theory is open to the following objections. First, it is contrary to the principle *nemo dat quod non habet*. The 1963 Constitution contained no provisions for any kind of handing over and the "rump" of the Council of Ministers who purported to hand over the reins of government to the Army in law handed over nothing: they had no Constitutional power to do so.[109]

It is, of course, possible to use the doctrine of necessity to argue that certain acts that were unforeseeable at the framing of a constitution may be undertaken when contingencies so require, and further that the transfer of power to the military was a delegation from the members of government who had been impelled by events to delegate their constitutional authority to the people who could handle the situation more effectively. This argument, however, is unsustainable because the transfer in question offended all principles of delegation.

The effect of the transfer was not in tune with the spirit of the constitution, the main document under which the transferors owed their authority. Second, inasmuch as the transfer was a total divesture of the powers of the transferors and made the acts of the transferees unreviewable, the so-called transfer violated the principle *delegatus non potest delegare.*

But even if there had been a peaceful transfer like that suggested by the court, it would still be doubtful whether that transfer would have made the change of government any less revolutionary. According to most writers, all that is required to have a revolution is that the change of government should not be within the contemplation of the existing order. Kelsen has said it well:

> A revolution . . . occurs whenever the legal order of a community is nullified and replaced by a new order in an illegitimate way, that is a way not prescribed by the first legal order itself. It is in this context irrelevant whether or not this replacement is effected through a violent uprising. . . . It is equally irrelevant whether the replacement is effected through a movement emanating from the masses of the people, or through the action from those in Government position. From a juristic point of view, the decisive criterion of a revolution is that the order in force is overthrown and replaced by a new order in a way the former had not itself anticipated.[110]

Nor are the circumstances of the *Dosso* and *Matovu* cases markedly unsuited for this reminder. It has already been observed that the Ugandan upheaval was effected peacefully by the leader in power. The circumstances of the *Dosso* case were essentially similar to that of the Ugandan case. Barely two years after the adoption of the 1955 Constitution of Pakistan, the president, Iskander Mirza, annulled it, dissolved the cabinet and national assembly, and declared martial law throughout the country. Needless to say, none of these actions had been contemplated by the constitution. Yet the Pakistani Supreme Court upheld it, stating:

> A revolution is generally associated with public tumult, mutiny, violence and bloodshed but *from a juristic point of view the method by which and the persons by whom a revolution is brought about is wholly immaterial.* The change may be effected by persons already in public positions. *Equally irrelevant in law is the motive for a revolution,* inasmuch as a destruction of the constitutional structure may be prompted by a highly patriotic impulse or by the most sordid of ends. For the purposes of the doctrine here explained *a change is, in law, a revolution if it annuls the Constitution and the annulment is effective.* If the attempt to break the Constitution fails, those who sponsor or organize it are judged by the existing Constitution as guilty of the crime of treason.[111]

Since the *Lakanmi* decision itself acknowledged that the Ugandan and Dosso upheavals were revolutions, it is impossible to see how the Supreme Court reached the conclusion that the Nigerian upheaval was anything but revolutionary.

One author has pointed out the mistake in assuming that the upheaval that brought Ironsi into power was a peaceful transfer.[112] And there is every reason to agree with him. The constitutional government had been assaulted in an upheaval, killing some prominent members of the government; the upheaval was spontaneous and led by the military—the only people in control of the national arsenal; a lot of mystery surrounded the cause and outcome of the upheaval; some members of the military had asked the panicked surviving members of the government to hand over the government to them—what would happen if they refused to comply? Would they also not have been subjected to brutality and even deprived of their lives? Since, as previously pointed out, an upheaval does not need to be violent to become a revolution, it may be unnecessary to explore this issue further. Yet it may be reassuring to quote briefly from the critique in question:

> It is not correct in fact, because those summoned were too frightened and panicky to say no to Major-General J. T. U. Aguiyi-Ironsi's firm declaration of intent to take over power immediately, and this amidst the rattle of weapons and the whirr of the military engines in and around the cabinet premises on that awesome night.[113]

But the biggest flaw in the *Lakanmi* decision is yet to be explored. As can be recalled from the constitutional context in which the case arose, both the issues in the case and the decision thereon occurred in a regime that made the whole notion of voluntary transfer of power superfluous. Gowon took over from Ironsi in a manner that had nothing to do with the "consent" of the preexisting government. He overthrew him by use of violence in circumstances that were unquestionably a coup d'état.[114] It is therefore difficult to understand why a case that had arisen from actions of a government established by such an upheaval could be said to be a continuation of the constitutional government. There is, nevertheless, one crucial factor that can explain why the "transfer" notion was brought into the case. Apparently, the whole judgment made hardly any mention of the Gowon coup. If the court had alluded to that crucial element, it might have reached a verdict that would have been less vulnerable to criticism than the one given. But to the extent that the court failed to pay attention to the most crucial factor in the case, the ruling was rendered *per incuriam* and therefore cannot be authoritative on the issue of the significance of coups on preexisting legal systems.

The weakness of the *Lakanmi* decision is exposed further by the disparity between the decision and the developments that followed. Without going through the pains of challenging the decision, the federal military government demonstrated its supremacy by passing the Federal Military Government (Supremacy and Enforcement of Powers) Decree to overturn what the court had ruled.

One question that may be posed out of curiosity is whether Dudley's observation that the constitutional provisions against coups are merely hortatory is not absolutely in accord with the practice. Certainly, it is undeniable that the provisions against extraconstitutional activities cannot be enforced against successful movements. But the same is not true with the abortive ones. It is thus sound to conclude that the question as to the legality of coups and secessionist movements can be answered only this way: they are legal if they succeed but illegal if abortive.

SECESSIONIST STRUGGLES AND COUPS: THE DIFFERENCES

First, although the legitimacy of both coups and secessionist struggles depend on whether or not they succeed, it may be unsound to say that the legal effect of one category is the same as that of the other. For whereas a successful coup may have the destruction of the preexisting legal system as one of its ultimate consequences, the effect of a successful secessionist struggle is that its destruction of the preexisting legal system extends solely to the portion of the territory that falls under the secessionists. Second, unlike the struggles against existing governments whose outcomes can be determined soon after the struggles are initiated, the secessionist struggles are often attended by a prolonged period of uncertainty, during which two governments contend for power.

Chapter

8

Self-Determination

T HE FIRST QUESTION raised by noncolonial intrastate conflicts is whether they can constitute an appropriate subject of international law. This question is inevitable, because international law considers it the sole responsibility of every sovereign state to enforce its laws on its subjects.[1] However, with the recent emergence of principles like self-determination and human rights, the gap between interstate and intrastate conflicts has virtually been bridged, so that now it is almost impossible to insulate these cases from the purview of international law. Indeed, even if we set aside the impact of these newly developed concepts, there still are several instances in which international law may be applied to events occurring essentially within borders of an independent state.[2] For example:

1. Conflicts fomented from outside, as was the case of the Soviet installation of the Karmal regime in Afghanistan.
2. Conflicts involving intervention by other states, as exemplified by the Soviet intervention in Hungary and Czechoslovakia in 1956 and 1968, respectively; the French and Senegalese reinstatement of Leon Mba and Dawda Jawara in Chad and Gambia, respectively; and the U.S. suppression of the coup that toppled the government of President Maurice Bishop of Grenada.
3. Cases that violate the rights of other nations. For example, where foreigners are taken hostage (as in Iran) or are deprived of their properties by the excesses of nationalization, notably, expropriation without prompt, adequate, and effective compensation.

Granted that international law applies to noncolonial struggles, the question now is: What are the international legal implications of the noncolonial movements? Evidently, the international legal system has no general rule directly supporting or condemning any of these struggles. This lacuna is a product of an old tradition. It is traceable to the inability of the traditional law to determine the priority between two competing values, the rights of revolution and sovereignty. What the law did, in effect, was to apply the effective-control test in much the same way as in the domestic legal systems. Thus, the legality of a coup or secession depends mainly on whether or not the movement succeeds in supplanting the preexisting authority or system. In modern times one concept that has gained prominence in relation to the issue is the principle of self-determination. In practice, however, this principle has proven so inadequate that the relevance of the effective-control principle is still an important factor in the determination of the legality of intrastate conflicts.

THE NONCOLONIAL CASES AND THE PRINCIPLE OF SELF-DETERMINATION

The Principle of Self-Determination and Its Application

Although the U.N. Charter is the most important document embodying the principle of self-determination,[3] there is little information in that document about what the principle really means. In U.N. practice, however, the concept has been associated with the notion that all people have the right to determine their own sociopolitical and economic circumstances. Among the documents reflecting this are the Universal Declaration of Human Rights;[4] the Declaration on the Granting of Independence to Colonial Countries and Peoples;[5] the two covenants on human rights—the International Covenant on Civil and Political Rights and that on Economic Social and Cultural Rights;[6] the recent Definition of Aggression;[7] and the Declaration on Principles of International Law Concerning Friendly Relations and Co-Operation Among States in Accordance with the Charter of the United Nations.[8] The latter states: "By virtue of the principle of equal rights and self-determination of peoples enshrined in the Charter of the United Nations, all peoples have the right freely to determine, without external interference, their political status and to pursue their economic, social and cultural development."[9] Likewise, the two covenants on human rights provide in their Common article 1: "All peoples have the right of self-determination. By virtue of that right they freely determine their political status and freely pursue their economic, social and cultural development."[10]

Nor is this understanding to be gathered from U.N. practice alone. Indeed, many historical achievements—from the French, American, and Russian revolutions to Woodrow Wilson's Fourteen Point Program[11] and the Atlantic Charter—all had it as their principal theme. The nations signing the Atlantic Charter asserted:

2. They desire to see no territorial changes that do not accord with the freely expressed wishes of the peoples concerned.

3. They respect the right of all peoples to choose the form of Government under which they will live; and they wish to see sovereign rights and self-government restored to those who have been forcibly deprived of them.[12]

The practice of parties to a treaty is one of the important tools for interpreting the treaty.[13] It may be useful to cite here the International Law Commission's draft on the law of treaties and its commentary, which urge that subsequent practice can even modify treaties:

> The importance of such subsequent practice in the application of the treaty, as an important element of interpretation, is obvious; for it constitutes objective evidence of the understanding of the parties as to the meaning of the treaty. . . . [A] consistent practice, establishing the common consent of the parties to the application of the treaty in a manner different from that laid down in certain of its provisions, may have the effect of modifying the treaty.[14]

Since the notion that all people are entitled to decide their own circumstances is reflected in virtually all the relevant U.N. resolutions on self-determination, this consistent practice provides the meaning for the "principle of self-determination" as embodied in the Charter.

Yet, there is no clear indication as to the scope of the principle—whether the right of self-determination can be pursued by all peoples regardless of whether they belong to an independent state. Nor is there adequate information on what constitutes the "people" or the "self," who defines them and by what means, and the exact circumstances in which the right can be said to have been denied.[15] These issues have serious implications, as the achievement of the right by one group often entails its denial to other competing "selves."

Delineating the Scope of the Principle of Self-Determination

Since 1945 in international affairs, the problem with the scope of the principle has arisen in two categories of conflict, namely, the struggles for decolonization and those with secessionist aspirations.

The Decolonization Cases

The colonial version of the problem was easily solved.[16] By the mid-1960s it was well established that the inhabitants of the colonies constituted the "selves" or "people" to whom the principle applies. It is significant, however, that this practice does not always favor the majority at the expense of minorities in the affected societies. In cases where minorities expressed opposition to becoming part of certain territories, the United Nations promoted the realization of minority aspirations by holding referendums. The practice has been confirmed in the Advisory Opinion on the Western Saharan Dispute[17] and the Declaration on Friendly Relations,[18] whose ancestry can be traced back to the General Assembly Resolution 742 (VIII) of November 27, 1953, and such others as Resolutions 334 (IV), 648 (VII), 567 (VI), 637C (VII), and 1541 (XV).[19]

Not that there are no problems with the application of the principle to the decolonization cases. Indeed, in pluralistic systems where different groups are involved in the struggles for independence, there is little information as to how the issue should be determined between many competing selves. Classical instances include the anticolonial movements in Angola, Algeria, Mozambique, Zimbabwe, Guinea Bissau, Eritrea, East Timor, and Western Sahara. In most of these cases the United Nations recognizes some of the competing groups as the legitimate or authentic representatives of the peoples' struggles for self-determination. In Angola the groups included the M.P.L.A., U.N.I.T.A., and Governo Revolucionario de Angola–Frente Nacional de Libertação de Angola (G.R.E.–F.N.L.A.). The group officially recognized by the United Nations was the M.P.L.A. Yet this recognition did not stop other countries, notably, the United States, recognizing and aiding the other factions.[20] In Guinea Bissau the United Nations' recognition went to the Revolutionary African Party for the Independence of Guinea and the Cape Verde Islands (P.A.I.G.C.) The difficulty with these cases is that in addition to the problem with the legality of the aid given to the recognized group,[21] there is the question of the criteria used in branding one group as the most legitimate representative of the people. Evidently, the most important test used is which group wields more strength than the others. Since such a test is not easily applied objectively,[22] and since it is obviously premised on the notion of the survival of the fittest, one wonders whether it does not warrant the following statement by Prakash Sinha: "Once the decision for political reorganization or redistribution of power has been made, the principle of self-determination is invoked to attain the result in a desirable fashion. The principle is thus one of political expediency which states may not use."[23]

Applying the Principle to the Secessionist Cases

Within independent states the issue is whether any group of people has the right of self-determination. The U.N. Charter commitment is to protect the "equal right and self-determination of *peoples*,"[24] and it further guarantees the "territorial integrity and sovereign equality of states"[25] without indicating what the relationship is between "peoples" and "territorial integrity." Neither authorities nor the practice of nations has provided the necessary agreement and consistency to resolve the issue. Although some visualize the right as that which can be exercised both within and without states, others see it as relevant solely to the colonial cases, and there are yet others who consider it as a right that can be enjoyed by states alone. We will examine the problem in terms of both practice and the diverse statements of respected writers, after examining first how the issue was tackled at the conferences culminating in the birth of the United Nations.

Self-Determination as Perceived from the Travaux Preparatoires of the U.N. Charter

If the preparatory history of a treaty is used as a supplementary means of interpretation, it should probably be employed only in exceptional situations. How much weight should be given to what transpired at the conferences leading to the adoption of the U.N. Charter? Since the Charter's provisions—the so-called primary means of interpretation[26]—lack the precision needed to construe the scope of the principle of self-determination, the *travaux preparatoires* may have the same, if not greater, weight. Yet the materials preceding the adoption of the Charter were so unclear on the subject of self-determination that it is doubtful whether they can shed a better light on self-determination than the ordinary meaning of the words used in the Charter's provisions on the subject. A brief excursion into the relevant materials is necessary.

Significantly, the Dumbarton Oaks Proposals did not make any reference whatsoever to self-determination. The phrase "based on respect of the principle of equal rights and self-determination of peoples" was introduced at the insistence of the Soviet Union at the San Francisco conference.[27] Although neither of these facts has any direct effect on the legal scope or significance of the principle, our understanding the circumstances under which the proposal was adopted at the San Francisco proceedings is important to our interpretation of the Charter's meaning.

In the Soviets' proposal, their foreign minister, V. M. Molotov, stated that the goal was to "draw (the) particular attention of the populations of colonies and mandated territories" and that "we must first of all" see to it that "dependent countries are enabled as soon as possible to take the path of national independence." He called upon the United Nations to expedite "the realization of the principle of self-determination of nations.[28] What does this mean? Is the principle one that applies solely to entities that are yet to be decolonized, or does it apply to "nations" within independent countries—ethnic units—as well?

The conference proceedings complicated the issues.[29] It was confessed in one committee:

Concerning the principle of self-determination it was strongly empasized on the one side that this principle corresponded closely to the will and desires of peoples everywhere and should be clearly enunciated in the Charter; on the other side, it was stated that the principle conformed to the purposes of the Charter only in so far as it implied the right of self-government of peoples and not the right of secession.[30]

Finally, although the memorandum submitted by the U.N. Secretariat to the Coordination Committee suggested that the principle could be pursued without any caveats, it actually raised confusion as to whether the principle could apply in intrastate situations:

> No difficulty appears to arise from the use of the word "peoples" which is included in the Technical Committee texts whenever the idea of all mankind or all "human beings" is to be emphasized. . . . The word "peoples" is used in connection with the phrase "self-determination of peoples." This phrase is in such common usage that no other word seems appropriate. The question was raised in the Coordination Committee as to whether the juxtaposition of "friendly relations among nations" and "self-determination of peoples" is proper. There appears to be no difficulty in this juxtaposition since "nations" is used in the sense of all political entities, states and non-states, whereas "peoples" refers to groups of human beings who may, or may not comprise states or nations.[31]

The Scope of Self-Determination as Perceived by Authoritative Writers

There is a wide spectrum of opinions about the scope of the principle of self-determination. The opinions fall under three different categories; one is championed by Kelsen and Sinha, the others by Emerson and Eagleton, on the one hand, and Chowdhury and Nayar, on the other.

Sinha states the view of the first group as follows:

> A state's obligation under international law may find its counterpart in another state's right, but not in the right of a people. . . . It is either a state or the community of states forming the United Nations which can seek performance of a state's obligation to accord self-determination to its people, not the people of that state. . . . What is involved here in terms of international law is the international obligation of a state and not the right of its people.[32]

Similarly, Kelsen observes:

> Self-determination of the people usually designates a principle of internal policy, the principle of democratic government. However, Article 1 paragraph 2,

refers to the relations among states. Therefore the term "peoples" too—in connection with "equal rights"—means probably states, since only states have "equal rights" according to general international law. . . . If the term "peoples" in Article 1 paragraph 2, means the same as the term "nations" in the preamble, then "self-determination of peoples" in Article 1 paragraph 2, can mean only "sovereignty" of states. The principle of "equal rights" that is the principle of equality of states, and the principle of self-determination, that is the principle of sovereignty of states, are two different principles. But Article 1 paragraph 2, refers to the "principle" and not the "principles" of equal right and self-determination of peoples. This seems to indicate that the formula of Article 1 paragraph 2 has the same meaning as the formula of Article 2 paragraph 1, in which the principles of sovereignty and equality are combined in the rather problematic way into one principle: that of "sovereign equality."[33]

These observations suggest that the principle of self-determination can be pursued solely by states. Yet they are too ambiguous to indicate conclusively whether that is what the writers really understood the principle to mean. If, indeed, that is what they meant, then they cannot possibly be right, because from the practice of states and the numerous U.N. resolutions on the subject of self-determination, it is abundantly clear that the object of the principle is non-states. (However, this is not meant to suggest that states cannot enjoy or participate in making others fulfill their obligation to respect the right of self-determination of their peoples.)

The positions of the other two groups are even more difficult to appreciate. One adopts a restrictive thesis evidently equating "peoples" with colonial peoples and arguing that the right ceases to exist as soon as a colony attains independence. Conversely, the other group interprets the principle with greater latitude and considers it to be enjoyable by all peoples, whether within or without states.

In outlining the thesis of the restrictive school, Emerson describes the liberal view as one that "in fact verges on being meaningless" and that "alternatively, in the highly unlikely event of its being taken at all seriously, it is a declaration of an extreme liberation or even anarchistic variety, authorizing any group which designates itself as a people to disrupt the existing polity and set up a new one which meets their desires."[34] In his opinion, self-determination has meaning only if the peoples to whom it applies are, by some form of consensus, specifically identified in advance, and that the place, the time, and the circumstances under which it is applied are all similarly pinned down.[35] In another context Emerson has stated firmly that the principle of self-determination in the contemporary system applies only to overseas colonialism, and that as soon as that course is ended, self-determination will have exhausted its mandate.[36] He postulates that "all peoples do not have the right of self-determination: they have never had it, and they never will have it."[37]

The liberal position is presented by one of its adherents thus:

The beneficiaries of the right are the people themselves, within a defined territory, not the territory to which they belong. The right to self-determination is the right of the people—not of a non-representative ruler—freely to determine their political status and to pursue their economic, social and cultural developments without discrimination. The proponents of the equation viz. peoples-nations-states, are of the view that self-determination of peoples only means sovereignty of States and it does not postulate any democratic form of government. The major premise of the theory is that States alone have equal rights and the Charter grants specific rights only to States and not individual human beings or groups of them. The basic foundation of this theory, it is submitted, is erroneous because it overlooks the preamble of the Charter, enumerating the ends to be achieved, which provides inter alia, for "the equal rights of men and women and of all nations large and small." As a matter of interpretation, the use of the word "and" is very significant. In other words, on a national plane, the nation must be based on equal rights of men and women.[38]

It may seem as if the author's specific mention of "democratic form of government" restricts his understanding of the "peoples" to those fighting against existing governments and thus excludes the right of secession. A more careful scrutiny of his position, however, shows this impression to be incorrect. For in the statement below, he is emphatic that the "peoples" could be taken literally to mean both those within states—those fighting against existing governments and those seeking secession—and those without states:

The application of the principle, however, is not confined to colonial or trust territories. It is of universal application. It would therefore also apply to territories which are technically independent but whose peoples do not enjoy full governmental powers. The fact that the principle is of universal application is further strengthened by the provisions of Principle 5 of the 1970 Declaration. . . . "It provides that the defence against secession or dismemberment of the territorial integrity or political unity is only available to those "sovereign" and independent states *conducting themselves in compliance* with the principle of equal rights and *self-determination* of peoples as described above and *thus possessed of a government representing the whole peoples* belonging to the territory without distinction as to race, creed or color." [emphasis added] *It is therefore difficult to contend that an independent State can with impunity deny representative government to its peoples and yet claim that it has in good faith implemented the principle of self-determination.*[39]

The controversy is thus between the Emerson group, which limits the application of the principle to the anticolonial cases, and Chowdhury's, which construes the principle as one that can be pursued by all peoples whether or not in colonial settings.

Conceivably, many arguments can be made for or against any of these schools of thought. The principle of territorial integrity of states, for instance, has been used repeatedly to dispute the right of secession in independent states.[40] For, as the critics contend, legitimizing secession would be opening the Pandora's box; the results would include the creation of unviable states.[41] Since the United Nations, and for that matter the international community, is founded on the principle of sovereign equality of states,[42] the argument seems persuasive, particularly considering that the unregulated right of secession may lead not only to the creation of unviable states but the fragmentation of the present international system.

During the Nigerian-Biafran conflict, Colonel Odumegu Ojukwu, the leader of the secessionist movement, urged that "a country never disintegrates because another one did. . . . one so called secession does not necessarily lead to another,"[43] thus implying that secession depends more on how people are treated than whether there has been secession elsewhere. Surely, by emphasizing how people are treated—whether their human rights are violated, whether they are discriminated against, whether their right to participate in existing political processes is respected—this view appears to be more logical and persuasive than the rather sweeping one of the restrictive school. But it does not correspond fully with practice, for difficulties arise as to how one determines whether or not people are treated fairly. It is conceded that in cases like the Nigerian-Biafran conflict, the East-West Pakistani war, and the struggle between North and South Sudan the issue of fairness may be easy to ascertain. In others, however, the issue is not so simple. For, like the concepts "liberation" and "motive," "fairness" does not always lend itself to objective assessment. Obviously, the underlying issues in most of these cases are very political. Thus, regardless of how the would-be secessionists are treated, the appetite for secession may not be diminished. This tendency was manifested in the Congo situation where the Conakat, the party representing the Katanga secessionist struggle (the organization whose membership has been described by one writer as people "with incurable secessionist gene"),[44] was able to marshal support from within and without the Katanga province even though there was no manifest discrimination against them.

Ojukwu's position is even more difficult to rationalize by the practice. In the Nigerian crisis, for instance, it is common knowledge that the Mid-Belters and the Yorubas threatened to secede from the federation if the Biafran cause was translated into reality. And in the Congo situation the Balubas issued a similar threat.[45] Since none of these threats was predicated on how the respective governments treated the would-be secessionists, those cases unquestionably support the argument that the success of one secessionist movement can indeed spark off a chain of similar movements.

Even if these practical examples were ignored, it still would be difficult to overrule the credibility of the restrictive theory completely. One only has to match the underlying concern of the adherents of the theory against the nature of the international system. The ethnographic map of the contemporary world is so topsy-turvy that few states can confidently claim sufficient homogeneity to avoid completely any secessionist tendencies. Pluralism takes many forms besides the ethnic: religious, tribal, linguistic, geographical, economic forms, among others. And most members of the international community—Spain, Australia, Iran, Cyprus, Canada, Britain, the U.S, China, Russia, India, Pakistan—share this problem. Clearly, the antisecession stance is an international policy that is basic to maintaining public order and the system as it now is.

Nevertheless, there are flaws in the arguments supporting the restrictive interpretation. First, an undue emphasis on them nullifies the word "people" in the Charter, the Declaration on Colonialism, the International Covenant on Civil and Political Rights, the recent Definition of Aggression, and the Declaration on Friendly Relations. The fact that people are the intended beneficiaries of virtually all the values cherished by the international community also raises doubt about the plausibility of the restrictive theory. Indeed, it has aptly been pointed out that the denial of the right of self-determination of people in independent countries may lead to serious violations of human rights. Nayar, for instance, has stated:

It has been observed that "if the right of secession is eliminated and the maintenance of territorial integrity of states takes priority over the claims of 'peoples' to establish their own separate political identity, the room left for self-determination in the sense of the attainment of independent statehood is very slight, with the great current exception of decolonization." But it needs to be stressed that there will still be peoples within the recognized political boundaries of Member States of the United Nations being subjugated, dominated, exploited, and denied fundamental human rights. . . . *The relevant question, therefore, is whether such people should be denied a right to self-determination because of the fortuity of their geographical location.*[46]

Again, in the words of Chowdhury:

Literally considered, such an anatomical dissection of the right to self-determination is not permissible for the simple reason that it detracts from the universality of the concept and converts a continuing, dynamic right into a static one. *If applied the result would be: Every existing independent State and*

every colonial or non-self-governing territory after attaining statehood can
with impunity disregard human rights and fundamental freedoms under the
protective garb of non-intervention.[47]

The reality of these problems has been manifested in state practice, notably the Biafran and the Bengali secessionary movements. Nor is the general literature silent or even unsupportive of the liberal view. Thus, according to most writers, human rights and self-determination issues are inextricably related to the present international commitment to maintain world peace and security. At the San Francisco conference this notion was expressed in the following words: "The principle of equal rights and that of self-determination of people are two complementary parts of one standard of conduct; that the respect of that principle is a basis for the development of friendly relations and is one of the measures to strengthen universal peace."[48] Again, after pointing out the international nature of human rights, Lauterpacht urges: "The correlation between peace and observance of fundamental human rights is now a generally recognized fact. The circumstance that the legal duty to respect fundamental human rights has become part and parcel of the new international system upon which peace depends, adds emphasis to that intimate connection."[49] Similarly, McDougal and Reisman have stated that "the intimate nexus between human rights and minimum world order is clearly articulated in article 55 of the [U.N.] Charter."[50]

Since the denial of the right to secede may lead to gross violation of human rights and, consequently, to threats or breaches of the peace, obviously the principle of public policy may equally support the liberal construction. From this, it is clear that the underlying concerns of the two schools are equally important and are hence not very helpful in finding conclusive solutions for the relevance of self-determination to secessionist movements.

Another possible criterion by which the two views can be evaluated is whether the principle of *uti possedetis* can be extended into one that mandates all parties to the independence arrangements to abide by their terms. In other words, is it possible to consider whether a contractual argument, namely, the principle of *pacta sunt servanda*, can be invoked to keep the components of each state as they were at the times of the state's independence? Relying on this theory, the antisecessionists often maintain that the right of self-determination can be exercised only before independence and that a group that fails to do so at that time loses the right altogether. But this argument is as faulty as many of the others. In the Congo situation it is common knowledge that the Katanga secessionist aspirations had been expressed even before the Congolese independence was attained.[51] The question thus arises whether the antisecessionists ever considered that point in favor of the Katangans. On the other hand, even though the Biafrans and the Bengalis never sought to separate from their respective countries until after independence, the circumstances in which their struggles broke out warrant the invocation of the maxim *rebus sic stantibus* against the so-called contractual theory. This maxim is the one according to which a treaty becomes modified when the fundamental conditions in which it was adopted change.

Secession in Practical Situations

State Practice

Constitutional provisions whereby people in certain countries are accorded the right to secede[52] are of little value for our purposes. History and the hidden caveats in some of these constitutions[53] indicate that these provisions are mere window dressing, propaganda gambits bereft of practical significance. It is equally useless to explore the significance of the mergers between states that have been dissolved by agreement between the relevant parties,[54] because by the nature of these mergers—arrangements between states with predetermined sociopolitical, economic, and territorial borders—the critical elements in the controversy about secession are virtually absent.

The most useful way to explore the issue of secession is to see how claims by people in artificially carved-out states have been handled. The attitude of individual states toward specific secessionist struggles has tended to depend on the political or strategic benefits that the state expects to derive from each case. Thus, the official policies of countries like Ethiopia, Nigeria, and Kenya, where secessionist tendencies are a fact of life, have been to oppose secession in any country. The Haile Selassie statement on the Nigerian crisis is a good illustration.[55] Indeed, even though Kenya and Ethiopia are ideologically far apart, their experience with secession has brought them together, to them, secession is a more "serious evil" than ideological incompatibility. It is very difficult to disagree with Samuel Makinda, who said:

> The Somali belligerency in the Horn has drawn Kenya and Ethiopia together. The two states signed a friendship and cooperation treaty in 1964 and, in spite of the ideological differences now existing between the pro-American Kenya and pro-Soviet Ethiopia, the two states signed a mutual desist pact in 1979. That pact was signed shortly after Saudi Arabia, an American ally that has considerable influence in Somalia, had failed to unite Kenya and Somalia with a view to isolating Ethiopia. The situation in the Horn demonstrates that although ideology plays a significant role in shaping a country's foreign policy, it has severe limitations in this region owing to the national security problems obtaining in it.[56]

Conversely, in Somalia and Togo, where there is more to gain than to lose by backing the secessionist principle, the propaganda for secession has been actively pursued right from the times those countries gained their independence. In 1976 a Togolese minister, Kwaovi Beni Johnson, for instance, challenged what he termed the "sacrosanct principle of the immutability of African frontiers" adopted by the O.A.U. Describing that principle as having been "a wise idea at the time of the O.A.U.'s inception," he stated that it is no longer so because it "does not stand up to an objective historical analysis," nor does it face "the fundamental question of human groupings separated by colonial treaties."[57]

Such varied stances in regard to secession are found the world over, and not just in African politics; in the 1950s when the issue of the former Italian colonies was being debated, the Soviets and the Americans were on the opposite sides in the struggle between Ethiopia and Eritrea—the Americans supporting the Ethiopian right of territorial integrity, which to them was not negotiable, the Soviets clinging to the notion that the Eritreans' right to independence, in the exercise of their inherent right of self-determination, could not be compromised. Interestingly enough, these hard-line attitudes of the superpowers have been reversed since 1977, when the pro-Western government of Haile Selassie was ousted by a Marxist regime: the Soviets now support the territorial integrity of Ethiopia, and the United States favors self-determination.[58] Indeed, the inconsistency of the Soviets has been demonstrated on numerous occasions, including the Congolese-Katangan, Nigerian-Biafran, and the West-East Pakistani conflicts. The Soviet Union could not sympathize with the Biafran and Katangan secessionary movements at all, but it so strongly supported the Bengalis that it even vetoed a Security Council resolution against the Bengali struggle.[59]

Finally, the attitudes of Pakistan and India. During the dispute over Kashmir, India invoked the principle of territorial integrity, urging that "the principle of self-determination cannot and must not be applied to bring about the fragmentation of a country or its people."[60] Pakistan, on the other hand, contended that the right of self-determination of the people of Kashmir must be realized by their own decision about their political future.[61] In the 1970s when the Bengali case arose, however, the two countries reversed their positions on self-determination and territorial integrity[62] in a way that suggests that the issue is to be determined by military capabilities rather than the noble notions embodied by the principle of self-determination.

The Practice of International Organizations

The O.A.U. and the Issue of Secession

The best way to understand the O.A.U. position is to look at the preamble of its charter:

Determined to safeguard and consolidate the hard-won independence as well as the sovereignty and territorial integrity of our States, and to fight against neo-colonialism in all its forms . . . the organization shall have the following purposes . . . (C) to defend their sovereignty, their territorial integrity and independence;

The Member States, in pursuit of the principles stated in Article II, solemnly affirm and declare their adherence to the following principles . . . 3. respect for the sovereignty and territorial integrity of each State and for its inalienable right to independence and existence.[63]

Clearly, the O.A.U. is committed, inter alia, to the prevention of secession in any of its member states. Yet the provisions are equally susceptible to the interpretation that the antisecessionist commitment is limited solely to cases fomented from outside, implying that secessionist struggles involving no external influences are acceptable. Among the factors bolstering this conclusion are the organization's undertaking to realize its purposes by adherence to "sovereign equality of all [its] Member States"; its inhibition of interference "in the internal affairs of States"; its commitment to respect the "sovereignty and territorial integrity of each state and for its inalienable right to independent existence"; and its "unreserved condemnation in all its forms, of political assassination as well as of subversive activities on the part of neighboring States or any other States."[64]

Doubtless, in the Nigerian crisis, the Biafran leader employed these clauses to argue that the provision on the inviolability of the borders of African states "can legitimately be invoked if one member-state attempts to enlarge its territory at the expense of another member-state, but certainly not in respect of the emergence of new states arising from the disintegration of a member-state."[65] Sound and perceptive as this argument may seem, it cannot be accepted as an accurate presentation of the O.A.U. position. It has been pointed out by one writer that the apparent equivocality of the O.A.U. Charter on the subject was occasioned by the fear that a clearer provision would have prompted a boycott by states like Morocco and Somalia.[66] Making the issue even more complicated is the prevailing position of most African countries at the conference that culminated in the birth of the O.A.U. The Mali president, Modibo Keita, was frank and to the point:

If all of us here present are truly animated by the ardent wish to achieve African unity, we must take Africa as it is, and *we must renounce any territorial claims*, if we do not wish to introduce what we might call black imperialism in Africa. . . . African unity demands of each of us complete respect for the legacy that we have received from the colonial system, that is to say: maintenance of the present frontiers of our respective states.[67]

In a similar vein, President Philibert Tsiranana of Malagasy remarked:

> It is no longer possible, nor desirable, to modify the boundaries of Nations, on
> the pretext of racial, religious or linguistic criteria. . . . Indeed, should we
> take race, religion or language as criteria for setting our boundaries, a few
> States in Africa would be blotted out from the map. Leaving demagogy aside,
> it is not conceivable that one of our individual States would readily consent to
> be among the victims.[68]

As these are statements supported by almost all the founding fathers of the
organization, their underlying principles should carry great weight in our considerations.

The position taken by the organization in specific cases is even more clear.
The resolution that enjoins members to accept existing borders as a "tangible
reality" has been mentioned already.[69] Although the organization had not been
formed by the time the Congo crisis started, ever since its formation in 1963 it
has been an important instrument in quelling the Katangan secessionist movement.[70] Other cases involving the O.A.U. were the Sudanese struggle by the
animists and Christians of the South who sought to separate from the Moslem
North, and the Biafran movement against Nigeria. In the Sudanese movement
the liberation fighters received very little support from the black Africans, notwithstanding their racial and religious affinity and the unpopularity of the leftist
Sudanese regime with many African leaders.[71] In the Nigerian case, where there
was a relatively more sustained O.A.U. involvement, there was a manifest bias
against the secessionist movement. At the O.A.U.'s Consultative Committee
meeting in Kinshasha on September 14, 1967, Chairman Emperor Haile Selassie of Ethiopia proclaimed the antisecessionist stance in the following statement:

> *The Organization of African Unity is both in word and deed committed to the*
> *principle of unity and territorial integrity of its member states.* And when this
> mission was established by our organization, its cardinal objective was none
> other than exploring and discussing ways and means . . . whereby Nigerian
> national integrity is to be preserved. . . . The national unity and territorial
> integrity of member states is not negotiable. It must be fully respected and
> preserved. It is our firm belief that the national unity of individual African
> States is an essential ingredient for the realization of the larger and greater
> objective of African Unity.[72]

At its meetings in Niamey on July 15, 1968; Addis Ababa on July 29,
1968; Algiers on September 14, 1968; Monrovia in April 1969; and at the
O.A.U. Algiers and Addis Ababa summit meetings of 1968 and 1969, respec-

tively, the position of the Consultative Committee remained unchanged.[73] But perhaps the most significant manifestation of the O.A.U.'s posture was its prevention of U.N. interference.[74]

Most African countries are antisecessionist. Because the O.A.U. is a regional organization whose members are also members of the United Nations, the legality of its position would, of course, depend on its compatibility with the U.N. law on the subject.[75]

U.N. Practice

THE CONGO-KATANGA CONFLICT. One interesting fact about the Katangan secessionist movement is that it was mainly by the instrumentality of the United Nations that the territorial integrity of the Congo was preserved. This fact can be better understood if it is considered that

1. The United Nations effectuated the removal of the Belgian troops and mercenaries that had been brought into Katanga to fight for the secessionists.[76]
2. The U.N. Force (O.N.U.C.) was authorized to use force to quell the rebellion.[77]
3. The secretary general, U Thant, imposed economic sanctions against the authorities in Katanga.[78]
4. The United Nations condemned the secessionist movement and urged all states to assist in the preservation of the territorial integrity of the Republic of Congo.

It would be instructive to quote an extract from one of its resolutions.

The Security Council . . .
Reaffirming the policies and purposes of the United Nations with respect to the Congo . . . , namely:

(a) To maintain the territorial integrity and the political independence of the Republic of the Congo;
(b) To assist the Central Government of the Congo in the restoration and maintenance of law and order . . .

1. Strongly deprecates the secessionist activities illegally carried out by the provincial administration of Katanga . . .
8. Declares that all secessionist activities against the Republic of the Congo are contrary to the Loi fondamentale and Security Council decisions and specifically demands that such activities which are now taking place in Katanga shall cease forthwith;

9. Declares full and firm support for the Central Government of the Congo, and the determination to assist that Government in accordance with the decisions of the United Nations to maintain law and order and national integrity, to provide technical assistance and to implement those decisions.[79]

The resolution clearly shows the United Nations' abhorrence of the Congolese secessionist movement. It may be useful to consider how it has been interpreted by some authorities, notably, Higgins:

It will be noted that the secession is not declared illegal because it is fomented by foreign elements (which is surely the crucial point), but rather because it is contrary to the Basic law. . . . Inevitably, the paragraph gives support to those who insist that the United Nations wants to end the Katanga secession and not merely to expel the foreign elements from influence in Katanga so that the Congolese may negotiate among themselves.[80]

The crucial question is whether it is sound to conclude from the U.N. attitude in this case that the international community is generally antisecessionist. One might at first answer this question in the affirmative. On a more careful study of the entire U.N. operation in the Congo, however, it is doubtful whether such an answer can be sustained. Although it was by the Congolese government's invitation that the United Nations intervened in the crisis,[81] it is clear from all the reports of the secretary general, Dag Hammarskjold, that the U.N. force in the Congo was not to be partisan in its operation; it was to be concerned solely with the removal of foreign forces and to resort to force only in self-defense. His first report reads:

The authority granted to the United Nations Force cannot be exercised within the Congo either in competition with the representatives of the host Government or in co-operation with them in any joint operation. . . . It follows from the rule that the United Nations units must not become parties in internal conflicts, that they cannot be used to enforce any specific political solution . . . or to influence the political balance decisive to such a solution. . . . In amplification of this Statement . . . "men engaged in the operation may never take the initiative in the use of armed force, but are entitled to respond with force to an attack with arms."[82]

Again in his Memorandum on the Implementation of the Security Council Resolution of August 9, 1960, the secretary general invoked the Lebanese precedent:

Operative paragraph 4 of the resolution of the Security Council of 9 August reads: Guidance for the interpretation of operative paragraph 4 can be found in the attitudes upheld by the Security Council in previous cases where elements of an external and elements of an internal nature have been mixed. The stand of the Security Council in those cases has been consistent. It most clearly emerges from the policy maintained in the case of Lebanon. . . . Applying the line pursued by the Security Council in the Lebanese case to the interpretation of operative paragraph 4, it follows that the United Nations Force cannot be used on behalf of the central Government to subdue or to force the provincial government to a specific line of action. . . . It further follows that the United Nations Force has no duty, or right, to protect civilian or military personnel, representing the central Government, arriving in Katanga.[83]

If the United Nations was so committed to neutrality, why then did it eventually contradict itself by taking sides against the Katangans? An explanation may be found in the leadership of the O.N.U.C. at the two different periods of the U.N. action in the case. During the first period, the O.N.U.C. was under Secretary General Hammarskjold, whereas the second period was spearheaded by U Thant. But the crucial question is whether the difference can be explained by the change of leadership, a change in the mandate, or error on the part of one of the secretary generals.

Because of the complexities of the case, any attempt to analyze the impact of the change in leaders would be utterly futile. Evidently, some explanation can be gathered from the mandate, because the tone of the U.N. resolutions changed a little after the death of Prime Minister Patrice Lumumba,[84] and even more after the death of Secretary General Hammarskjold. But again, intervening circumstances make it too complex to analyze. The most practical and perhaps the most instructive question to ask is whether any of the mandates was misconstrued.

Some critics, notably the Soviet Union, Poland, and some Afro-Asian countries, disagree with the way Secretary General Hammarskjold applied the mandate.[85] They argue that the secretary general not only erred in construing Resolution S/4382 as forbidding the O.N.U.C. to be partisan, but that he was wrong in applying the Lebanese case and other precedents to the Congolese situation, whose circumstances were, in the critics' view, different from the preceding ones.[86]

Article 2 of Resolution S/4387, for instance, is noteworthy:

The Security Council . . .
    Decides to authorize the Secretary-General to take the necessary steps, in consultation with the Government of the Republic of the Congo, to provide the

Government with such military assistance as may be necessary, until, through
the efforts of the Congolese Government with the technical assistance of the
United Nations, the national security forces may be able, in the opinion of the
Government, to meet fully their tasks.[87]

Again, in Resolution 4405, the mandate is stated thus:

The Security Council,
    Considering that the complete restoration of law and order in the Repub-
lic of the Congo would effectively contribute to the maintenance of international peace and security, . . .

2. Requests all States to refrain from any action which might tend to impede
the restoration of law and order and the exercise by the Government of Congo
of its authority and so to refrain from any action which might undermine the
territorial integrity and the political independence of the Republic of Congo.[88]

Since the United Nations came into the Congo only after it had been invited
by the Congolese government, it is arguable that the acceptance of the invitation implied that the United Nations would help the government maintain its
sovereign authority over its territory. And this impression is strongly supported
by Resolutions S/4387 and S/4405. What, for instance, did the resolutions
mean by enjoining states to abstain from doing anything that might "undermine
the territorial integrity . . . of the Republic of Congo"? And what did they
mean by the commitment to a "complete restoration of law and order" in that
troubled country? Since the "law and order" in the Congo was that embodied in
their "Loi Fondamentale," and since that Loi proclaimed that "the Congo constitutes within its present boundaries, an indivisible and democratic State,"[89] it
is obvious that the interpretation of the United Nations mandate as upholding
the fundamental law and the interest of the central government is not inappropriate.

But the secretary general's restrictive construction of the mandate is not
without foundation either. First, taking the invitation of the Congolese government, it is signficant that the request was solely for assistance in effecting the
withdrawal of the Belgian forces that had illegally intervened on the side of the
rebels.[90] Thus, the acceptance of the invitation was a prima facie evidence that
the U.N. operation would be confined to the objects for which the invitation
was given. But even if the resolution had gone further to ask for assistance to
quell the secession, the question still remains whether that necessarily meant
that the United Nations would have used force against the secessionists. Indeed, the issue is complicated by the precedents in past U.N. operations, notably that from Lebanon, which established that the peacekeeping force should
not be partisan in any of its operations.[91] The critics claim also that the circum-

stances of the cases in which the precedents were established were different from those in the Congolese situation.[92] But the mere fact that one case may have some factual differences from others does not necessarily make its precedent inapplicable. In the Congolese situation not only was the precedent relevant to the issues at stake, there was also the provision of Article 100 of the U.N. Charter, which requires the U.N. force to be nonpartisan in its operation. Besides, although the secretary general expressly stated that the principles of neutrality were the tenets to be followed in the U.N. operation in the Congo, the resolution that ensued from the statement, Resolution S/4387, did not reject the principle but endorsed it.[93] Given all the attributes of the case, it may be argued that the only way the U.N. mandate could have been effectively construed as authorizing a digression from the precedents is if it had been given under article 41 or 42, or under a "Uniting for Peace" resolution[94] expressly authorizing the use of force against the rebels—which the resolutions obviously did not do.

As to Secretary General U Thant's position, it is probably sound to agree with Buchheit that it was occasioned mainly by the complexities of the case, including the deaths of Lumumba and the secretary general.[95] It is significant that even after this so-called turning point,[96] the United Nations did not immediately resort to force. It continued to negotiate with the rebels until the new secretary general realized the ineffectiveness of negotiation.[97]

U.N. PRACTICE IN THE NIGERIAN-BIAFRAN WAR.   The Nigerian crisis was, in many ways, less complicated than the one in the Congo.[98] Yet the U.N. attitude was not crystal clear there, either. It did not take any resolution to enjoin members from recognizing the Biafran regime, nor did it go into the case at all. In his response to questions regarding the U.N. inaction, the secretary general, U Thant, observed at a press conference: "The question is that the issue must be brought to the attention of the United Nations. So far, not one single Member State out of 126 has brought the question of the civil conflict in Nigeria to the United Nations."[99]

Given the responsibilities of the secretary general under article 99 of the U.N. Charter,[100] it is doubtful whether this response was a legitimate excuse for the U.N. inaction. It is, of course, arguable that U Thant probably did not act under article 99 because he did not anticipate any threats to international peace. But to pursue this argument is to approach the limits of credibility, because the secretary general himself described the conflict as one involving gross violations of human rights:

> If I am unable to conceal my concern about developments stemming from the persistence of colonial and racial policies of Africa, even less can I refrain

from expressing my distress and dismay at the mounting toll of destruction, starvation and loss of life resulting from the tragic fratricidal strife in Nigeria over the past year. As have been verified from impartial sources a very large number of people, combatants and non-combatants alike, are either dying or undergoing acute suffering, many, particularly children, are dying from, or are on the verge of starvation.[101]

The inseparability of the U.N. commitment to the protection of human rights and the maintenance of the peace only make the secretary general's defense of U.N. inaction all the more transparent.

The U.N. posture, particularly its failure to enjoin states from recognizing the secessionists, may even pose some question as to whether its inaction was not an indirect endorsement of the movement. This argument, however, cannot stand. First, recall that the organization left the matter exclusively with the African regional organization—the O.A.U.—for, as it bluntly stated, the African regional organization was the "most appropriate instrument for the promotion of peace in Nigeria."[102] Given the unequivocal commitment of the O.A.U. to suppress secessionist tendencies in the continent, the United Nations' handing over of the case to that organization clearly provides arguments that the United Nations endorsed the antisecessionist stance against the Biafrans. In fact, in leaving the matter with that antisecession organization, the United Nations did not offer any cautions whatsoever against any partisan position. Nor did it reprimand the organization for its failure to be neutral in all the different efforts to settle the case.

Finally, when asked whether the Nigerian government's antisecessionist stance was not contradictory to the U.N. principle of self-determination, the secretary general responded at a press conference in Dakar:

> You will recall that the United Nations spent over $500 million in the Congo primarily to prevent the secession of Katanga from the Congo. So, as far as the question of secession of a particular section of a Member State is concerned, the United Nations' attitude is unequivocable [*sic*]. As an international organization, the United Nations has never accepted and does not accept and I do not believe it will ever accept the principle of secession of a part of its Member State.[103]

Similarly, when confronted with the issue at the press conference in Accra, the secretary general replied:

> Regarding the . . . question of self-determination, I think this concept is not properly understood in many parts of the world. Self-determination of the peoples does not imply self-determination of a section of population of a Member State. . . . If the principle of self-determination is applied to ten

different areas of a Member state, or five different areas of a Member State, or twenty different areas of a Member State, then I am afraid there will be no end to the problem.[104]

The weight of evidence indicates that the U.N. attitude toward the Nigerian case was antisecessionist. In drawing this conclusion, one merely has to consider the importance generally given to statements issued by any person in the capacity of the U.N. secretary general. The Nigerian and Congolese cases, however, suggest that the U.N. position in the Nigerian case cannot be taken as the general stand of the United Nations on the issue of secession. One would have difficulty reconciling the United Nations' initial neutral stance in the Congolese situation with its apparent switch to antisecessionism in the Nigerian situation.

THE EAST-WEST PAKISTANI CONFLICT. Like the Biafrans who were a part of Nigeria at the time of its independence, the Bengalis were a part of Pakistan when that country became an independent state.[105] Neither of these two secessionist movements started before or in the immediate aftermath of their countries' independence. It was only after the secessionists had been exposed to gross inhumanity and discrimination by their compatriots that they launched their movements.

Yet the two situations were dissimilar in a number of ways. One such difference is that, unlike the Biafran movement which ended in a fiasco, the Bengalis not only became an independent state but were admitted into the United Nations as a full member. What does the success of the Bengali movement mean? Was it an international endorsement of its cause, and, if so, can it be reconciled with the other cases, notably those championed by the Biafrans, the Katangans, the Somalis, the Sudanese, the Kurds, and the Nagas?

Buchheit contends that neither the success nor the failure of a secessionist movement is necessarily conclusive about its legality.[106] Likewise, Saxena remarks:

> Both situations involved certain . . . aspects of international law . . . like "recognition", "genocide", "intervention" of a humanitarian character, "internal affair" doctrine or the competence of the United Nations' plea. The collapse of Biafra had only strengthened the view that self-determination by secession was not permissible and the unity of the existing states was sacrosanct and could not be challenged. That view suffered a severe jolt after the success of the standard of self-determination set in the Pakistan/Bangla Desh situation.[107]

Nor is it possible to draw a more reliable conclusion from the way the individual members of the international community responded to the Bengali situation. Predictably, the mother country—Pakistan—refused to entertain any negotiation for a peaceful solution of the case. It considered the movement as treasonable and resorted to military force to suppress it. The United States and China, countries that were friendly to the Pakistani government and that, along with the latter, had supported certain secessionist movements elsewhere (e.g., the secessionist movements of the Kurds and the Nagas), favored the Pakistani antisecessionist stance against the Bengalis.[108] Similarly, although India's involvement could be bolstered by some principles,[109] its position on the issue of self-determination was hardly consistent with its position in other cases, notably, the movement of the Nagas for an independent status. Finally, just as the attitudes of the Soviets and the United States had all along been dictated by the convergence of their interests and those of their allies in all the afflicted regions, the Soviets were unswerving from the position of their ally in the Indian subcontinent, India.

It remains to be seen whether the United Nations ever took a stand in this case, and, if so, whether that attitude could provide a basis for rationalizing the success of the struggle and its subsequent recognition by the United Nations as an acceptance of its legitimacy.

The United Nations was deeply involved in the Bengali crisis, and indeed, it even passed the "Uniting for Peace" resolution in one of the troublesome moments of the conflict.[110] Yet, the U.N. involvement was so equivocal and evasive of the central issue—the legitimacy of secession—that it is difficult, if not absolutely impossible, to draw any conclusive answers from its actions.

It is generally agreed that the Bengali situation had no parallel in modern history. Thus, according to Nwabueze:

> First, as has been noted, their own half of the country is separated from the other half, the West, wherein is located the seat of government and public activities, by a thousand miles of Indian territory. The two are really different peoples, different in culture and language; Islam is the main unifying factor. Communication is difficult and consequently minimal. . . . Although the Bengalis number seventy million as against West Pakistan's fifty million, the number of the Bengalis in the army had been estimated at below one per cent. . . . Under the martial law administrators, East Pakistan was being ruled almost as a colony of the West, the martial law administrators in the East being invariably West Pakistani officers.[111]

Buchheit writes:

> The partition of the newly independent India in 1947, roughly along the lines of the Hindu-Muslim dominated regions, left the Muslim State of Pakistan in the curious position of being itself a divided country. The contiguous Muslim

states located in the northwestern portion of India . . . were formed into West Pakistan. More than a thousand miles away, on the other side of India, the province of East Bengal became East Pakistan. . . . . In terms of geography, climate, population, and culture, the 55,000-square-mile entity of East Pakistan was an unlikely partner for the 310,000-square-mile area of West Pakistan. . . . The Easterners, speaking the Bengali language, could not for the most part understand the major languages of the West. . . . Finally, the taller, lighter-skinned Westerners felt themselves to be racially distinct from (and superior to) the shorter, darker Bengalis.[112]

The relevance of these features of Pakistan to the determination of the scope of secessionist self-determination as reflected in U.N. practice is not hard to find. For even though the two parts of Pakistan constituted one sovereign state, the definition in U.N. Resolution 1541 of the type of entities that can pursue their rights of self-determination suggests that one such is any territory that has no geographical and ethnic compatibility with the state by which it is ruled. One writer has applied this provision to the West-East Pakistani conflict thus:

East Bengal probably qualified as a Chapter XI territory in 1971; if one applies the principles accepted by the General Assembly in 1960 as relevant in determining the matter. According to Principle IV of Resolution 1541 (XV), a territory is *prima facie* non-self-governing if it is both geographically separate and ethnically distinct from the "country administering it." East Pakistan was both geographically separate and ethnically distinct from West Pakistan.[113]

Clearly, if the U.N. commitment to its provisions on self-determination were absolute, its Resolution 1541 would have provided a sound support for the Bengali secessionist movement. Yet the ethnographic factor is only one of several by which the relevance of the principle of self-determination to the Bengali situation can be determined. Some of the other factors are evident from the following observation:

Unfortunately, these "natural" disparities between the two regions were further intensified . . . by an inequitable economic and political treatment of the East by the dominant Western wing. In the areas of education, employment, public expenditure, and promotion within the civil and military ranks, the Westerners were almost uniformly more fortunate than their Eastern compatriots. To the Easterners, these disparities amounted to a campaign of economic exploitation which, rather than giving preference to the East's more pressing needs because of its larger population and greater economic disability, set about sedulously ignoring them.[114]

In the words of Nwabueze:

> Bengalis were also smarting under a sense of exploitation from other sources. They felt neglected in the distribution of amenities and the siting of industrial projects, and this rankled particularly since the foreign exchange used to finance these projects was earned mostly through Bengal's export trade in jute and tea. This concentration of social amenities, industrial projects and other kinds of investment in the West has changed its infrastructure from a feudal to an industrial one, while leaving the East still relatively undeveloped, to serve only as a market for the West's manufactured product.[115]

Naturally, the Bengalis sought some autonomy to manage their own affairs. In their political manifesto for the 1970 elections, their party, the Awami League, put up a six-point program reflecting this aspiration. They won a landslide victory, but instead of being allowed to assume power, they faced strong retributions launched by the outgoing administration. They were killed indiscriminately, their leaders were branded as traitors, and some of them, including Mujibur Reham—the person who would have formed the new government if the democratic principles had been upheld—were incarcerated. Indeed, the savagery against the Bengalis was so outrageous that it has been likened to genocide. One report by the International Commission of Jurists said:

> The principle [sic] features of this ruthless oppression were the indiscriminate killing of civilians, including women and children and the poorest and weakest members of the community; the attempt to exterminate or drive out of the country a large part of the Hindu population; the arrest, torture and killing of Awami League activists, students, professional and business men and other potential leaders among the Bengalis; the raping of women; the destruction of villages and towns; and the looting of property. All this was done on a scale which is difficult to comprehend.[116]

The interesting thing about the Bengali situation vis-à-vis the issue of secessionist self-determination is that the Bengalis' proclamation for secession was issued after the adoption of the U.N. 1970 Declaration on Friendly Relations, which stated that the right of self-determination may be:

1. pursued by all peoples,
2. provided that it may not be permitted in states if the exercise thereof may lead to the disintegration of states whose governments represent all their subjects and do not discriminate against any of them.[117]

It is conceded, of course, that this provision would not be easy to apply in all situations. But it is surely not difficult to apply it in the Bengali situation, where the nonrepresentation and unfairness were very conspicuous. Nor is there any reason to say that the declaration is without significance because it failed to provide any formula for the determination of whether a government is representative or unfair. Indeed, there are a number of reasons why the significance of the provision cannot be overestimated. Foremost are the circumstances under which the document was adopted:

1. The provision on self-determination was a compromise between two competing but essential values for world peace, viz. the territorial integrity of states and the right of peoples to revolt against violation of their human rights.
2. The declaration was adopted unanimously by a committee that had been set up specifically to find practical meanings to some difficult provisions of the U.N. Charter, of which the principle of self-determination was one.
3. The committee was established by the General Assembly, the principal organ of the United Nations that has the duty to initiate studies for the progressive development of international law.
4. The unanimity of the committee was reached after many years of serious deliberation by its members.
5. The General Assembly adopted the propositions of the committee by acclamation.

Another obvious reason is that the declaration's via media stance on the issue of secessionist self-determination is shared by writers and jurists alike. Cobban, for instance, has this to say:

> The truth seems to be that if we take the right of sovereignty on the one hand, and the right of secession on the other, as absolute rights, no solution is possible. Further, if we build only on sovereignty, we rule out any thought of self-determination, and erect a principle of tyranny without measure and without end, and if we confine ourselves to self-determination in the form of secessionism, we introduce a principle of hopeless anarchy into the social order. *The only hope it seems, must be in a combination of the two principles, allowing each to operate within its own proper field, and recognizing neither as an absolute right, superior to the rights of individuals which are the true end of each society.*[118]

Apart from the opinion given by the Commission of Jurists in the earlier Aaland Island case,[119] it is significant that the declaration's via media position on the principle of self-determination has recently been endorsed by the International Commission of Jurists. Thus, in an inquiry into the significance of the

1970 declaration, the commission not only commended the document as "the
most authoritative statement of the principles . . . of self-determination and
territorial integrity" but went further to say:

> The free determination by a people of the form of their political status . . .
> constitutes the exercise of their right to self-determination; a decision freely
> taken automatically leads to the acquisition of a status, and it becomes an
> infringement of international law for any state to attempt to deprive them of
> that status by forcible action, and if any state does so, other states should give
> support to the people asserting their right of self-determination.[120]

The commission's statement on the relationship between the principle of
self-determination and the principle of territorial integrity of states is even more
instructive on how the provision of the 1970 declaration should be understood.
Thus, after adumbrating the "widely held view" that self-determination is a
right that can be exercised only once, it continued:

> It is submitted, however, that this principle is subject to the requirement that
> the government does comply with the principle of equal rights and does repre-
> sent the whole people without distinction. *If one of the constituent peoples of a
> state is denied equal rights and is discriminated against, it is submitted that
> their full right of self-determination will revive.*[121]

Obviously, given the gross discrimination against the Bengalis, the failure
to allow them to be ruled by people of their choice, and the brutality with
which the West responded to their overwhelming victory in the 1970 elections,
the Bengali struggle satisfied all the conditions listed in the 1970 declaration for
secessionist self-determination.

How did the United Nations respond to the case? The U.N. reaction was so
unclear and so evasive of the central issue that it is difficult to extract any direct
answers from it. First, we should recall that success resulted largely from the
Indian intervention in favor of the Bengalis.[122] This might make it seem that had
the United Nations been opposed to the Bengali movement, it would have deprived it of this decisive assistance. However, not only was the decision to
intervene made exclusively by India, but the United Nations called for a ceasefire and, moreover, urged India to pull out its troops. It would be ludicrous to
suggest that the same organization that urged India to move out favored its
support for the secessionist movement.

But on the doubtful assumption that the United Nations could have made
the Indians withdraw from the beleaguered territory, we would still have to ask
how the withdrawal could have been effected. A superficial reading of this

issue might prompt one to draw some parallels between the Bengali situation and the Congo-Katangan crisis and argue that if the United Nations had not meant to acquiesce in the Indian intervention, it would have driven them out the same way it drove the Belgians out when they intervened in favor of the Katangans. But the enormous economic and political problems with the U.N. intervention in the Congo makes it unthinkable that the United Nations would lightly follow that precedent in any subsequent case. Besides, the Indian intervention was armored with legal defenses that would have backfired on the United Nations had it intervened against India. Unlike the Belgian intervention, which violated the Treaty of Friendship between the Belgian government and the newly formed government of the Congolese,[123] the Indian intervention was supported by a 1950 treaty between India and Pakistan, which reads:

> The Governments of India and Pakistan solemnly agree that each shall ensure to the minorities throughout its territory, complete equality of citizenship, irrespective of religion, a full sense of security in respect of life, culture, property and personal honour, freedom of movement within each country and freedom of speech and worship, subject to law and morality.

It further declared that the members of the "minority" community should have equal opportunity with other citizens "to participate in public life of their country, to hold political office or other office," and both governments declared these rights to be "fundamental" and undertook "to enforce them effectively."[124] One other factor about the Indian intervention was the issue of self-defense, which, as noted previously, was warranted by inter alia the mass influx into India of Bengali refugees. A U.N. intervention against the Indians might be seen as violating the Indians' inherent right of self-defense.

The case was so politicized that the central issue—the merits of the struggle—was never considered. At several points in the deliberations of the Security Council the idea of considering the secessionist issue was sounded but discarded because of disagreement between the superpowers.[125] Moreover, despite the many instances when nonstates have been invited to present their cases before United Nations—Indonesia, Hyderabad, Guinea Bissau, the Palestine Liberation Organization (P.L.O.), and the S.W.A.P.O., to mention but a few— a suggestion that the Bengalis be invited to participate in the Security Council debates was rejected by the president of the council on the dubious ground that he did not think the necessary criteria for statehood had been established by the Bengalis.[126]

These facts, plus the fact that the United Nations welcomed the Bengalis into the community of nations as soon as India reported to it that West Pakistan had withdrawn its troops, make it very difficult to comprehend the U.N. stand on the issue of secession. One is even more baffled by the position of the secretary general, which, unlike his position in the Nigerian crisis, was so equivocal on the legitimacy of secessionist movements that one is inclined to conclude that the intervening circumstances probably caused the United Nations to abandon its hard-line antisecessionist stand. The secretary general said:

> A . . . problem which often confronts us and to which as yet no acceptable answer has been found in the provisions of the Charter, is the conflict between the principles of the integrity of sovereign states and the assertion of the right to self-determination, and even secession, by a large group within a sovereign State. Here again, as in the case of human rights, a dangerous deadlock can paralyze the ability of the United Nations to help those involved.[127]

The unavoidable conclusion is that the legitimacy of any secessionist movement depends on whether or not that movement succeeds, and, to a certain extent, without any regard to how that success is brought about.

THE STRUGGLES AGAINST EXISTING GOVERNMENTS AND SELF-DETERMINATION

Unlike the secessionist cases, which definitely impair the territorial integrity of states, the struggles considered in this section merely seek to change the governments in the countries in which they occur. They are therefore free of the attributes that exclude secessionist cases from the scope of the principle of self-determination. Obviously, the arguments used against secession may not apply here. Yet, virtually all these struggles violate some aspect of the principle of self-determination: they overthrow people chosen through the normal democratic process, they abrogate existing constitutions, and they rule by ad hoc laws that in most cases apply retroactively.

Nevertheless, these attributes do not necessarily cause them to violate the principle of self-determination. In most cases, the governments that initially came to power by the legitimate wishes of their subjects later changed from the positions that earned them popular support: they foreclose all opportunities for the people to be ruled by leaders of their choice, they transform their countries into one-party states, they rig elections, and they introduce dictatorial measures by which their opponents are either purged or incarcerated. Even in cases where the governments do not close all avenues for change by ordinary political processes, events in some countries, notably Sierra Leone and Lesotho, are horrifying. The Sierra Leonean coup of 1968 is a spectacular case in point. Following the victory of the Sierra Leonean opposition party in the 1967 elections, the civilian government, unwilling to step down, induced the army to take over in order to keep both parties out of power.[128] The Lesotho case was similar to the Sierra Leonean, except that in Lesotho the leader of the losing party, Chief Lebua Jonathan, not only seized power but also arrested the leaders of the victorious party and went on the air saying, "I have seized power and I am not ashamed of it."[129]

Obviously, regardless of how a government assumes power, the foreclosure of the right of its subjects to express their position on issues, or to determine whether or not they need a different government at periodic elections, is incompatible with the values on which the principle of self-determination is based. But the question is whether a few members of the population should have the right to redress this wrong. Ideally, it may be argued that for any military intervention to be legitimate, it must be premised on the popular wishes of the people as expressed through political processes like referendums and recall of the existing governments. But how are these processes to be initiated in a society where the government has closed all avenues for opposition? Again, who should initiate these processes where the government has forbidden them, especially since initiation of any movement against a government that has abolished the right of the people to change of government by the constitutional processes is treasonable and often results in the imposition of capital punishment on the "culprits"? Obviously, the more cautious approach, namely, striking the government by surprise, is the only safe way to bring about a change for the better. Dudley points out:

> One of the striking features of most of the African States is the high degree of structural violence which they exhibit. Political elites not only seek to monopolize leadership roles, but the machinery of the state is used to deny political opportunities to competing elites, while popular demands are, where not ignored, physically repressed. The resultant sense of deprivation only creates mounting discontent. With recognized avenues of change and reform seemingly foreclosed by the ruling elites, there is little option but for those who control the means of destruction, the military, to intervene.[130]

The reality in Africa matches Gutteridge's generalization: "a situation which cannot be changed by constitutional means invites the use of violent measures in the same way as a life president can only be removed by force or assassination."[131]

Military intervention, then, can be construed as a means to clear the way for the operation of free political systems. As such, military actions may be appropriately treated as movements by which the principle of self-determination may be pursued against dictatorial governments. Indeed, in most cases, not only are such interventions preceded by agitations, suggesting that the existing governments are not popular, but they are also accompanied with or followed by jubilation of the masses in support of the struggle. It is, of course, doubtful whether all of these shows of support are genuine manifestations of popular support for intervention. Nor is it always possible to obtain an accurate picture of popular sentiment before a coup. However, where the preceding administration has closed off all avenues for a proper assessment of the prevailing political cal position, it is appropriate to describe the intervention as at least a more progressive alternative. This, of course, is not to imply that any military intervention at all is compatible with the principle of self-determination. Only those interventions directed at systems that have destroyed all opportunity for peaceful change may be taken to be compatible with the principle. But even with those cases, an important qualification is necessary: Obviously, it would not be sound to describe a military intervention that fails to hand over power to the people as a movement that is consistent with the principle of self-determination.

Although noncolonial struggles per se are not illegitimate under the principle of self-determination, it is difficult to sustain such legitimacy, considering the international legal system as a whole. As will be seen in the next chapter, there is little information on the relevance of the principle to leaders who establish effective domination over their subjects.

Chapter

9

Effective Control

THE PRINCIPLE OF EFFICACY IN INTERNATIONAL RELATIONS

The application of the effective-control principle in international relations resembles its application in domestic legal systems.[1] In international relations, however, its application is less conclusive than it is in the domestic systems because it is fraught with ambiguities and limitations.

Statement of the Principle

Kelsen describes the international legal ramifications of the principle as follows:

> It amounts to this question: under what circumstances does a national legal order begin to be valid? The answer given by international law is that a national legal order begins to be valid as soon as it has become—on the whole—efficacious, and it ceases to be valid as soon as it loses this efficacy. . . . The Government brought into power by a revolution or coup d'état is, according to international law the legitimate Government of the state, whose identity is not affected by these events.[2]

Indeed, almost all authorities urge that the legality of an upheaval depends heavily on whether or not that upheaval is efficacious.[3] The principle is applied whenever there is the issue of recognizing

1. a new government that has been brought into power through unconstitutional means,
2. a forceful separation of a territory from an entity that had hitherto been a unified state, or

243

3. a faction as the legitimate authority in a conflict wherein there are two or more claimants.

Under traditional international law, a revolution is deemed to have succeeded if it is clear that a new system has been securely and permanently established in place of a former one.[4] Among the tests used in arriving at this conclusion are these:

1. whether the revolutionists have utterly defeated the champions of the preexisting system;
2. whether the leaders of the preexisting system have terminated all serious efforts to suppress the movements directed against them;
3. and whether, in spite of their efforts to bring the revolutionists under their sway, it is apparent that the leaders of the supplanted system are incapable of suppressing them.

When Great Britain recognized the rebellious colonies in Latin America, Chief Justice Best stated the law thus:

I take the rule to be this—, if a body of persons assemble together to protect themselves and support their own independence and make laws and have courts of justice, that is evidence of their being a state. . . . It makes no difference whether they formerly belonged to Spain, if they do not continue to acknowledge it, and are in possession of a force sufficient to support themselves in opposition to it.[5]

Likewise, Lauterpacht observes that other states may recognize a seceded colony as a new state when it is clear that the new state has been securely and permanently established. According to him, the sine qua non for the recognition is indicated

either in the fact that the revolutionary state has defeated the mother state, or that the mother state has ceased to make efforts to subdue the revolutionary state, or even, that, the mother state, in spite of its efforts, is apparently incapable of bringing the revolutionary state under its sway.[6]

Dhokalia urges:

When a new government comes into power by violating constitutional procedures, it should be recognized only when it can meet the objective test of being a de facto government. The test involves two distinct parts; (1) that the de facto government is in actual control of the governmental machinery of the state; and (b) that it is exercising its authority so effectively as to imply the acquiescence of public opinion or the absence of organized and substantial opposition.[7]

As a natural corollary of this understanding, virtually all authorities agree that a premature recognition of a revolutionary government is illegal. Thus, in the words of Oppenheim: "An untimely and precipitate recognition as a new state is more than a violation of the dignity of the mother state. It is an unlawful act and it is frequently maintained that such untimely recognition amounts to intervention."[8]

Application of the Principle in State Practice

Faced with the issue of deciding "the basis upon which recognition is granted to a group that takes over a government" by violence, the Canadian government stated in 1965: "A most important consideration is whether the new regime seems to be in control of the country, a control which is at least tacitly admitted by the country's people in so far as this can be ascertained."[9]

Likewise, the British secretary of state for foreign and Commonwealth affairs responded to a similar question:

> When there is a change of government by revolutionary action, Her Majesty's Government practice is to recognize de jure the new Government when they consider that it enjoys a reasonable prospect of permanence, the obedience of the masses of the population and the effective control of much of the greater part of the territory of the state concerned. These were the considerations we had in mind in the case of Uganda.[10]

But perhaps the best illustration of the British and Canadian practice was that manifested in the Dominican crisis of 1965.[11] The facts of the case may be stated briefly.

Within a year after Dr. Juan Bosch was elected, a coup replaced the constitutional government with a civilian triumvirate. In 1965 the latter was in turn ousted by yet another coup professing to reinstate the defunct Bosch government. Faced with difficulties in bringing Dr. Bosch back from Puerto Rico to take over the affairs of the state, the coup leaders elected Colonel Francisco Caamaño Déño as the leader for the remainder of the term of the battered "Constitutional Government." There was, however, an opposition from another faction that branded itself as a "government of national reconstruction." The leader of this faction was General Imbert. The Canadian and British governments were then faced with having to choose which group to recognize as the

leaders of the country. The British foreign secretary delineated the British position in the following terms: "I have received communication from both the self-
proclaimed Governments in the Dominican Republic. The Government previously recognized by Her Majesty's Government disintegrated and neither of the
present claimants meets with our usual criteria for recognition at this time."[12]
Similarly, the Canadian secretary stated: "Both the Caamano regime and the
Imbert regime have sought recognition from other countries, including Canada.
. . . We feel that the situation there is such that neither regime warrants recognition by Canada until the situation takes on a much more stabilized character
than the present time."[13]

SOME PROBLEMS WITH THE USE OF THE PRINCIPLE OF EFFICACY

Simple though the principle of effectiveness may seem, given the apparent
consistency in state practice, it does not provide an airtight resolution of the
legal issues. To begin with, principle does not apply until the outcome of a
conflict is known. To the extent that it thus applies solely on post hoc basis, it
is manifestly deficient as a tool for finding the legality of most movements,
particularly those whose outcomes are yet to be known.

The second and, perhaps, even more controversial problem with the principle concerns the method of its application. Although there is considerable consensus on the preconditions for its application, there is hardly any objective
standard for determining when those preconditions are satisfied. In effect, each
state serves as its own judge and uses subjective standards to resolve the issue.
Naturally, as a result of this, states bypass the principle when they find it
politically convenient to do so. Again because the principle is susceptible to
manipulation, it is sometimes difficult to tell whether its tenets are observed
even when the theory is professedly invoked and applied.

The Nigerian civil war illustrates these problems. Although for a number of
reasons the British could have withheld its recognition from Biafra even while
purportedly upholding its traditional support for the principle of efficacy,[14]
Great Britain did not exhibit the faintest inclination to invoke it, let alone apply
it. Instead, the official statements of the government suggested that its reaction
was dictated by considerations that had nothing to do with the issue of who was
in control. In a statement before the House of Commons, George Thompson,
the secretary of state for Commonwealth affairs, noted:

> Neutrality was not a possible option for Her Majesty's Government at that
> time. We might have been able to declare ourselves neutral if one independent
> country was fighting another, but this was not a possible attitude when a

Commonwealth country, with which we had long and close ties, was faced with an internal revolt. What would other Commonwealth countries have thought?[15]

The digression from the principle was even more evident in a subsequent statement, which suggests that the British reaction was dictated mainly by the fear that the Russians might gain influence over the federal government if Britain did not act quickly:

> The Russians have already secured a political foothold in Nigeria by supplying military aircraft and bombs, which we refused to supply. If we cut off our arms supplies, Russia would be only too willing to fill the gap and gain the influence which we would lose.[16]

In the Rhodesian crisis, on the other hand, not only did the British courts invoke the effective-control principle, they also used it as the basis for branding the "rebellion" as illegal. One case demonstrating this was *Madzimbamuto v. Larden Burke and Another*,[17] where the judges ruled:

> Their Lordships would not accept all the reasoning in these judgements but they see no reason to disagree with the results. The Chief Justice of Uganda (Sir Udo Udoma C.J.) said: "the Government of Uganda is well established and has no rival." The Court accepted the new Constitution and regarded itself as sitting under it. The Chief Justice of Pakistan . . . said: "Thus the essential condition to determine whether a Constitution has been annulled is the efficacy of the change. It would be very different if there had been still two rivals contending for power. If the legitimate Government had been driven out but was trying to regain control, it would be impossible to hold that the usurper who is in control is the lawful ruler, because that would mean that by striving to assert its lawful right, the ousted legitimate Government was opposing the lawful ruler." In their Lordships judgement that is the position in Southern Rhodesia.[18]

There is no doubt that the rebellion violated British law at the time it was proclaimed. Yet, in light of the traditional principle that the legality of revolutions depends on their success, it is obvious that the application of British law as the basis for branding the Rhodesian rebellion as illegal would be defensible only if the revolution lacked effective control. Perhaps it was for this reason that their lordships made their ruling. It is significant that the tenet on which they found the rebellion to be illegal was the fact that the struggle between the rebels and Britain had not abated. The depressing logic of this ruling is that if the conflict had ended in favor of the rebels, they would have considered it to be legal. Although such a conclusion would have been perfectly in tune with effective-control principles, it is seriously doubtful whether it was the position taken by their lordships. For although by the nature of the case there was no question whatsoever about the effectiveness of the revolution vis-à-vis the British, the ruling found the revolution to be incomplete for purposes of becoming legitimate. Perhaps the best way to make a sound evaluation of the case is to consider briefly the history of the revolution itself.

Rhodesia was one of the few British colonies that attained a self-governing status before the decolonization revolution of the 1960s.[19] Negotiations for its full independence, however, failed to materialize in 1965 because the minority regime in the colony would not accede to the British government's policy that independence would be granted only on the basis of majority rule.[20] By a proclamation issued that November, the Rhodesian authorities, then headed by Prime Minister Ian Smith, abrogated the preexisting constitution, dissolved parliament, and introduced a new constitution that unilaterally asserted Rhodesia's independence.[21] Naturally, the British promptly condemned the revolution. Yet, the "rebels" proceeded with their plan: they enacted their own laws without opposition from within or without; they insured that their laws enjoyed considerable compliance like those of any sovereign country; and they implemented them by the Rhodesian executives and judiciary[22] in the Rhodesian rather than the British way.[23]

On the other hand, the British government did little to reassert its authority over the breakaway territory. Thus, apart from securing resolutions and sanctions from the United Nations,[24] it did nothing to suggest that it was fighting back. Indeed, it did not even accede to a U.N. resolution to use force to quell the rebellion. And, when confronted with the issue of using force against the "rebels," it responded:

> I should tell the House that in my talks with the African Nationalist leaders . . .
> I made clear, with absolute frankness, three things. First, I regarded it as my
> duty to remove from their minds any idea or hope they might have that
> Rhodesia's Constitutional problems were going to be solved by an assertion of
> military power on our part.[25]

The United Nations' condemnation of the revolution certainly provides some basis for the statement that the revolution was illegal. Yet it is clear from the *Madzimbamuto* case that the judges' condemnation of the revolution was premised mainly on the principle of effective control. Therefore, it may be necessary to limit the discussion solely to the issue about the effective-control test.

The circumstances in which the effective-control test may be considered as satisfied is well settled. According to Hall:

A mere pretension on the part of the formerly sovereign state, or a struggle so inadequate as to offer no reasonable ground for supposing that success may ultimately be obtained, is not enough to keep alive the rights of the state, and so prevent foreign countries from obligation to recognize as a state the community claiming to have become one.[26]

Similarly, Lauterpacht observes:

The refusal of the mother country to recognize such independence is not conclusive. The legal title of the parent state is relevant to the extent that clear evidence is required showing that the latter has been definitely displaced and that the effectiveness of its authority does not exceed a mere assertion of right.[27]

In the words of Brierly: "It can only be said that so long as a real struggle is proceeding, recognition is premature, whilst, on the other hand, mere persistence by the old State in a struggle which has obviously become hopeless is not a sufficient cause for withholding it."[28]

Finally, the rule has been expressed by Chief Justice Taft in the following ruling in an international arbitration:

To speak of a revolution creating a *de facto* government, which conforms to the limitations of the old constitution, is to use contradiction in terms. . . . The issue is not whether the new government assumes power or conducts its administration under constitutional limitations established by the people during the incumbency of the government it has overthrown. The question is, has it really established itself in such a way that all within its influence recognize its control, and that there is no opposing force assuming to be a government in its place? Is it discharging its functions as a government usually does, respected within its own jurisdiction?[29]

Applying these standards to the Rhodesian situation, we could argue that Britain lacked the requisite belligerency status by which its right to regain control over the rebel territory could have been kept alive. Yet it should also be considered that the U.N. economic sanctions against Rhodesia were passed not only at the behest of Britain but specifically with the view of making things so unbearable for the rebels as to compel them to give up the revolution,[30] a factor not without great significance. Yet given the fact that the only instrument by which compliance with the sanctions could be assured—armed force—was ignored, it is difficult to determine how seriously this factor should be considered. In the case of *"Joanna V,"* the United Nations permitted the British to use force against the shipment of oil to Beira. But the limitations of the ensuing resolution[31] make it seriously doubtful whether the resolution could satisfy the requirement regarding belligerency status that would release states from recognizing a revolution. Even if force had been authorized to combat all other infractions of the U.N. injunctions against any form of interaction with Rhodesia, the fact that the mother country did not intend to use force against the rebels weakens any practical consequences that might otherwise have ensued therefrom. The Rhodesian chief justice elucidated the point brilliantly:

> The mere fact that sanctions might do great harm to the economy does not necessarily mean that they will have the political result desired. There are many examples in history of a country's economy being reduced to dire straits without this causing an internal revolution or an unconditional change in the grundnorm of the country concerned.[32]

Given these attributes of the Rhodesian crisis, the application of the effective-control test in the *Madzimbamuto* case left a lot to be desired. Yet the ruling is not surprising, for in situations like that in Rhodesia, the preexisting sovereigns are the last to accept the new trends as a matter of fact. Nevertheless, the case has international legal significance. In the international system where every member is equal, a position taken by one state, whether expressed in its executive, legislative, or judicial capacity, has no necessary consequences for any other state.[33] This does not, of course, mean that states are not free to take a position like the one taken by Britain in the Rhodesian crisis; Canada, for instance, declared that it would not recognize the rebellion.[34] The determination about what position to take is within the sovereign province of every state.

In sum, the effective-control principle may not be very helpful in finding answers for issues arising from armed conflicts. This may raise a debate as to the place of that principle in the contemporary legal system, but it is important to realize that further intricacies are entailed in the principle. For instance, how compatible is the principle with the international commitment to maintain world peace and security? Suffice it to note that insofar as each state is its own judge as to the legality of a revolution, states may recognize as the legitimate government different factions in conflicts. The natural corollary is that states may be tempted to go to the assistance of the different factions in any armed conflict to make sure that their favorites emerge victorious. In fact, such behavior is common in international relations. When states intervene, they often conceal their real intentions by invoking a more plausible principle of international law—that which suggests that assistance can be given to a battered government upon its invitation to foreign states. In the Yemeni crisis, for example, the United Arab

Republic (U.A.R.) and Saudi Arabia justified their assistance to the different factions, the republicans and the royalists, respectively, both on the basis of the Jiddha Pact and what they each claimed to be an invitation by the government for assistance.[35] Similarly, in the Lebanese crisis, the Egyptians and the United States purportedly intervened in favor of the opposing factions, each claiming to have been invited by the existing government. The Soviet interventions in Hungary and Czechoslovakia are other pertinent cases. In the former, the widely acknowledged government turned out to be different from the one cited in the Soviet justification for the intervention. In the latter, the alleged existing government could not be identified.[36] In Laos, the United States and the Soviets supplied arms to the different factions, which they respectively regarded as the legal government. Finally, and more recently, Iraq—after having invaded, annexed, and created a puppet government in Kuwait—tried to justify its actions with an argument that it had been invited by the Kuwaiti government. To be sure, there is little difficulty in branding some of these interventions as illegal or as premature, and hence illegal, since the outcomes were yet to be reached when intervention began. Yet, by virtue of the effective-control principle, the outcome of a successful intervention would purge the illegality it would otherwise have entailed. Because the law also permits counterintervention in cases where there have been illegal interventions by other states, the problem intensifies. Since the question as to who intervened first or whose intervention is legal is usually answered subjectively, it is obvious that the problem defies objective solution.[37]

Moreover, one must consider more than just the confusion about whose intervention was initially illegal and whose was merely to counter an illegal intervention. Since the success of an upheaval automatically makes an otherwise illegal situation legitimate, and given the intense rivalry among states and their ever-present desire to insure that their favorites wield power, not only does the principle make nonsense of landmark resolutions like that on inadmissibility of intervention, but it also tends to cause threats to, or breaches of, international peace.

OTHER LIMITATIONS OF THE EFFECTIVE-CONTROL TEST

The Universal Commitment of the International Community to Withhold Recognition of an Otherwise Effective Revolution

It is clear from the U.N. resolutions in the cases of Rhodesia, Transkei, Venda, and Bophuthatswana that sometimes revolutions that are largely effec-

tive may be refused recognition by the international community. Since the resolutions in question did not allude to the principle of effective control, it is
questionable whether they can be cited as an exception to the principle. This
question, however, may be insignificant if it is considered that the resolutions
forbid states to recognize revolutions that they may otherwise deem effective
and therefore recognize.

It is instructive to start by addressing some of the early U.N. resolutions on
the Rhodesian situation. By Resolution S/216 of 1965, the Security Council:

> 1. Decides to condemn the Unilateral Declaration of Independence by a racist
> minority in Southern Rhodesia:
> 2. Decides to call upon all States not to recognize this illegal racist minority
> regime in Southern Rhodesia.[38]

Likewise, Resolution S/217 of 1965 reads:

> The Security Council . . .
>
> 1. Determines that the situation resulting from the proclamation of indepen-
> dence by the illegal authorities in Southern Rhodesia is extremely grave, that
> the Government of the United Kingdom of Great Britain and Northern Ireland
> should put an end to it and that its continuance in time constitutes a threat to
> international peace and Security. . . .
> 6. Calls upon all states not to recognize this illegal authority and not to enter-
> tain any diplomatic or other relations with this illegal authority.[39]

Predictably, by arguments ranging from those on issues of procedure to
those on substance, not only have critics questioned the legality of the resolution, but they have gone further to challenge the competence of the United
Nations in handling the case.

The Substantive Arguments

On the issue of substance, the critics urge that the activities of the Rhodesian minority regime cannot appropriately be characterized as illegal within the
framework of the U.N. Charter. This position has been bolstered by the following arguments:[40]

1. That under the Charter, the determination of the existence of a "threat to
   peace" may be made only when there is an ongoing dispute between
   sovereign states and where the procedures for pacific settlement of disputes under chapter VI have been exhausted.
2. That the activities of the Rhodesian revolutionists contained no element
   of aggression.

3. That their activities were wholly lawful under generally accepted international law.
4. That regardless of the merits of any of the above, the Security Council was not justified in branding the rebellion as constituting a threat to the peace.

Although the drafters of the Charter might not have foreseen that there would be occasions when activities in entities that have not yet attained statehood would pose threats to the peace, there is absolutely nothing in the Charter to suggest that the Security Council must make a finding of a threat to the peace only when there is a conflict between two states. Instead, it is abundantly clear that the founders gave the council extensive leeway to combat threats to and breaches of the peace—whether such threats and breaches emanate from interstate conflicts or otherwise. In article 39, for example, not only is the council entrusted with the responsibility to *investigate and determine* when there is a threat to the peace, it also has extensive powers to take the necessary measures (decided upon by itself) to prevent or eliminate the threats. Since an intrastate conflict may pose threats to the peace, the contention that the Security Council could not find threats to the peace except in conflicts between states is manifestly without foundation. Indeed, in chapter VII of the Charter, the broad competence of the council to deal with conflicts within as well as between states is pronounced unequivocally. Such a conclusion is supported by the San Francisco proceedings, where in rejecting a proposition to curtail the scope of what the council can do, the founders decided "to leave to the Council the entire decision as to what constitutes a threat to the peace, breach of the peace or an act of aggression."[41]

It should not to be inferred, of course, that the Security Council's authority is limitless. Indeed, as a body constituted to be regulated by a written document, its authority can be challenged. In the *Certain Expenses* case, the I.C.J. made this position very clear:

The primary place ascribed to international peace and Security is natural, since the fulfillment of other purposes will be dependent upon the attainment of that basic condition. These purposes are broad indeed, but neither they nor the powers conferred to effectuate them are unlimited. Save as they have entrusted the Organization with the attainment of these common ends, the Member States retain their freedom of action.[42]

Thus, the sustainability of the criticisms depends on whether the resolutions have been taken *intra vires* the council. Nor is there any basis for the contention that there can be no finding of threats to the peace unless the parties have exhausted all the peaceful settlement measures listed under chapter VI. But even if the exhaustion of pacific measures were a necessary precondition for the finding of threat to the peace, one might still find it difficult to agree with the argument that the resolution on Rhodesia violated that condition; the unbending attitude with which Smith attended all the negotiations with the British strongly suggests that the two factions had no room left for further negotiation.

The argument that aggression is a constitutive element in the finding of a threat to peace cannot be defended, either. Under article 39 of the Charter, it is clear that the Security Council can take the necessary anticipatory measures to preempt the consummation of a disaster:

> The Security Council, shall determine the existence of any threat to the peace, breach of the peace, or act of aggression and shall make recommendations, or decide what measures shall be taken in accordance with Articles 41 and 42 to maintain or restore international peace and security.[43]

Finally, as far as conventional international law is concerned, the Rhodesian revolution is not legally defensible. It has repudiated several Security Council decisions which, under article 25 of the Charter, are binding on all member states and which, according to article 2(6), may be applied to nonmembers "so far as may be necessary for the maintenance of international peace and security." It has also rejected the human rights provisions of the Charter, as authoritatively interpreted by the competent U.N. organs.

The Procedural Arguments

Essentially, these arguments raise the issue of whether the resolutions on Rhodesia complied with the constitutive limitations of the United Nations, namely, those relating to domestic jurisdiction and the voting requirements in the Security Council.

The Domestic Jurisdiction Argument

Since the issue of international peace and security is a matter of international concern, it is obvious that the argument that supports the validity of the Security Council resolution against Rhodesia makes the discussion of the issue of exclusive domestic jurisdiction unnecessary. One fact that buttresses this point is that the very article that insulates domestic cases from the scrutiny of the United Nations suggests that the domestic jurisdiction argument is inapplicable where it would otherwise prejudice the enforcement measures under chapter VII. Conceivably, the formulation of the domestic jurisdiction provision may be a basis for questioning whether a case can even appear before any organ of the United Nations, particularly in view of the word "Nothing" and the fact that the term "intervention" is so ambiguous as to suggest that discussion of issues in the United Nations is included in the "intervention" that is prohibited under article 2(7).[44]

But this consideration is neither logical nor supported by the record. First, authorities are in agreement that the intervention that is forbidden is only that which is dictatorial.[45] And the literal meaning of the provision is not supported by the principle of effective interpretation. How, for instance, can the United Nations and, a fortiori, the Security Council determine whether a conflict is a relevant subject of chapter VII without a critical study of the entire situation? In virtually all the cases where the domestic jurisdiction argument has been raised, the United Nations has shown no hesitation in overruling the argument.[46]

The Voting Requirement

The Security Council voting requirement at the time of the Rhodesian crisis is embodied in article 27 of the 1963 text of the Charter.[47] It reads:

> 2. Decisions of the Security Council on procedural matters shall be made by an affirmative vote of nine members.
> 3. Decisions of the Security Council on all other matters shall be made by an affirmative vote of nine members including the concurrent vote of the permanent members.

There is no doubt that the principal issue in the Rhodesian case was substantive and, consequently, subject to the provision of paragraph 3 of article 27. The arguments of the critics, however, hinge on how that paragraph should be construed. According to them, the only way the "concurring" vote of all the permanent members of the council could be fulfilled is by an affirmative vote of all of them.[48]

Although it is not clear what the founders intended article 27(3) to mean,[49] there is information on how they wanted the rule to be applied in cases where a permanent member is obliged to abstain from voting on disputes to which it is a party. The rapporteur's report of Committee III/1 is noteworthy on this point:

> The most direct answer to the question concerning the effects of the abstention from voting of a permanent member of the Council, when it is a party to a dispute, was given by the Honorable Commander Harold E. Stassen, Delegate of the United States of America. . . . "He stated that when a permanent member of the Council was a party to a dispute, its enforced abstention would mean that the other four permanent members and three of the non-permanent members might reach a decision which involved a judgment concerning the rightness or wrongness of the dispute. . . ." The Honorable Representatives of the other four permanent members of the Council did not make any specific

statement in response to the question which the Honorable Representative of the United States of America answered in so direct a manner. However, no objection was raised by them concerning the statement of Commander Stassen. *It is to be hoped that this statement means the real interpretation which the Security Council will give in the future to the question.* In regard to the other cases of abstention from voting of a permanent member of the Council, no interpretation was given as to the effect of such an abstention.[50]

This statement has been used to suggest that a mandatory abstention of a permanent member could not be taken as a veto.[51] Since the voluntary abstention from voting was not specifically mentioned, one may wonder whether such an abstention could be treated as an affirmative vote. However, it has been suggested that if a mandatory abstention cannot apply as a veto, it would be even more difficult to treat a voluntary abstention as a veto.[52] However, under the Charter, the Security Council is the master of its own jurisdiction, including its voting procedures. Thus, the best way to answer the question is to consider how the council handles the voting issue in practical situations.

The issue about the voluntary abstention of a permanent member has been raised at various times in the history of the United Nations. The first occasion was during the Spanish Question, when the Soviet representative remarked:

> Bearing in mind . . . that my voting against the Australian draft resolution would make its adoption impossible, I shall abstain from voting. I consider it necessary to draw the attention of the Security Council to the fact that my abstention from voting on this matter may in no way be regarded as a precedent capable of influencing in any way the question on the abstention of permanent members of the Security Council.[53]

This statement clearly contains a reservation. Yet the occasion was not the only instance in which a permanent member's abstention failed to be treated as a veto. In 1947, when the U.S. representative abstained from voting on the Greek Question, the United States echoed the precedent in the Spanish case, although this time the caveat was muted:

> I wish the record to show that the United States will not exercise a veto, and that the United States has considerable regard for a practice which has grown in the Security Council, by usage to constitute a very good practical construction of Article 27 of the Charter. And in this case, although the United States is opposed to the resolution, it will abstain, but will not veto it.[54]

Similarly, in the Indonesian Question, the representatives of France and the United Kingdom invoked the precedent to preclude the treatment of their abstentions as negative votes. Note what the president of the council (Syria) said in response:

> I think it is now jurisprudence in the Security Council—and the interpretation accepted for a long time—that an abstention is not considered a veto, and the concurrent votes of the permanent members means the votes of the permanent members who participate in the voting. Those who abstain intentionally are not considered to have cast a veto.[55]

Finally, in the case of the *Legal Consequences for States of the Continued Presence of South Africa in Namibia (S.W.A.) Notwithstanding Security Council Resolution 276* (1970), the I.C.J. added its imprimatur to this formidable record by drawing from the established practice of the council:

> However, the proceedings of the Security Council extending over a long period supply abundant evidence that presidential ruling and the position taken by members of the Council have constantly and uniformly interpreted the practice of voluntary abstention by a permanent member as not constituting a bar to the adoption of resolutions. *By abstaining a member does not signify his objection to the approval of what is being proposed; in order to prevent the adoption of a resolution requiring unanimity of the permanent members, a permanent member has only to cast a negative vote.*[56]

It is abundantly clear, then, that a permanent member's abstention from voting in the Security Council cannot prevent a decision from being adopted.

One conceivable question about the established position is whether it does not vitiate the purpose of the veto, since, after the adoption of the 1963 text, the membership of the Security Council has swollen in such a way that it is possible to have nine nonpermanent members to adopt a resolution on substantive issues. It has been shown convincingly, however, that this issue does not stultify the established law.[57]

Granted that the U.N. resolution on the Rhodesian situation agrees with the provisions of the Charter, it is suggested that its departure from the effective-control principle is an exception to the rule. It is important, however, to limit this suggestion solely to the case in which it was taken.

Treaty Provisions

International practice also shows that occasionally states enter into bilateral or multilateral treaties to withhold recognition from entities arising from revolutions. A classical example is the 1907 arrangement among the five Central American countries to refuse recognition to any regime established in any of their countries through extraconstitutional means.[58] This arrangement, named after its exponent as the Tobar Doctrine, was incorporated into a subsequent treaty between the parties, the General Treaty of Peace and Amity of 1923,[59] which went further to apply the commitment for automatic nonrecognition to constitutional governments established by people who wielded important positions or had sanguinal relations with anyone who held an important position in a preceding revolutionary government. Its scope is clear:

> The governments of the contracting parties will not recognize any other government which may come into power in any of the five republics through a coup d'etat or a revolution against a recognized government, so long as the freely elected representatives of the people thereof have not constitutionally reorganized the country. And even in such a case they obligate themselves not to acknowledge the reorganization if any of the persons elected as President, Vice-President or Chief of State designate should fall under any of the following heads:
>
> (1) If he should be the leader or one of the leaders of a coup d'etat or revolution, or through blood relationship or marriage, be an ascendant or descendant or brother of such a leader or leaders.
> (2) If he should have been a Secretary of State or should have held some military command during the accomplishment of the coup d'etat, the revolution, or while the election was being carried on, or if he should have held this office or command within the six months preceding the coup d'etat, revolution or election.[60]

The doctrine paid no regard at all to the effective-control principle; clearly, it considered all revolutionary governments illegal. However, as the treaty is an arrangement between only a few members of the international community, the scope of its application depends on whether or not it coincides with general principles of international law. Admittedly, the current law on the issue was not extant at the time the Tobar Doctrine was adopted.[61] Nor could that law be applied retroactively.[62] Yet, it is necessary to ignore this technicality in the *lex lata* and apply it as if it were extant at the time the doctrine was enunciated to see how analogous commitments assumed after the adoption of the new law should be viewed.

The Scope of the Tobar Doctrine

To what extent does a particular treaty like the Tobar Doctrine apply to the international community at large? The answer depends inter alia on:

1. whether the provisions of the doctrine are generally accepted by the members of the international community;

2. whether the provisions of the doctrine merely repeat preexisting norms that apply to the international community in general;

3. whether in spite of the fact that it is not generally accepted by the international community, it essentially echoes other particular treaties between a few other members of the international community, in which case its terms may apply to the parties to those treaties even though such application would *stricto senso* depend on those treaties *ipso jure* rather than on the Tobar Doctrine specifically; and

4. whether states that were not originally parties to the treaty later accepted it by ratification or accession.

The governing law on the issue is reflected in the maxims *pacta sunt servanda* and *pacta tertiis nec nocere nec prodesse possunt*, which embody the general rule that the provisions of a treaty apply solely to its participants.[63] In the case of *Certain German Interests in Polish Upper Silesia*, the Permanent Court of International Justice stated the rule with utmost clarity: *"A treaty only creates law as between states which are parties to it*; in case of doubt, no right can be deduced from it in favor of third states."[64] It is, of course, not to be assumed that treaties cannot create rights for nonparties. Surely, a treaty can create rights and duties for nonparties—the only proviso being that a duty cannot be imposed on a state except with its consent.[65]

Measured by these standards, it is quite evident that the mere fact that a treaty like the Tobar Doctrine might not reflect a general principle of international law does not necessarily imply that no state can enjoy rights or have obligations thereunder. The crucial problem to consider is how the rights or obligations are created.

As has been stated already, the essential test here is whether the third party agrees to be bound by the treaty or whether there is a commitment by the parties to the treaty to create a right for a third party. According to article 11 of the Vienna Law of Treaties, this consent may be expressed in a variety of forms: "signature, exchange of instruments constituting a treaty, ratification, acceptance, approval or accession, or by any other means so agreed."[66] And under the definitional section of that treaty, " 'ratification', 'acceptance', 'approval' and 'accession' mean in each case the international act so named whereby a State establishes on the international plane its consent to be bound by a treaty."[67]

One difficulty occurs when a state that was a full party in the negotiations leading to the creation of a particular treaty fails to append its signature to it but makes a unilateral commitment to honor its terms. Indeed, the practical relevance of this was demonstrated by the U.S. position vis-à-vis the Tobar Doctrine. Although the United States participated in the negotiations leading to the doctrine, it failed to endorse it and yet committed itself to honor its principles.[68]

Its response to the El Salvadoran situation was quite spectacular. By a revolution in 1931, the government of Arturo Arajo was replaced by one led by General Maximiliano Hernandez Martinez. Since Martinez had been the secretary of state for war as well as the vice-president in the Arajo administration, not even a subsequent legitimization of his regime by the El Salvadoran public could qualify him for recognition. Thus in its refusal to accord recognition to that government, the U.S. Department of State noted:

> As concerns the present situation in El Salvador growing out of the recent revolution in that country, it is clear that the regime headed by General Martinez is barred from recognition by the terms of the 1923 treaty. It is clear, first, that General Martinez has come into power through a revolution and that the country has not been constitutionally reorganized by the freely elected representatives of the people, and, second, even in the event of such constitutional reorganization, General Martinez could not be recognized inasmuch as he held office as Minister of War up to a few days prior to the outbreak of the revolution.[69]

The United States showed no hesitation in recognizing the revolutionary government when the treaty ceased to apply to El Salvador. According to the State Department:

> In view of the denunciation by El Salvador of the Treaty of Peace and Amity of 1923, and the recognition on January 25 of the present regime by the Republics of Nicaragua, Honduras and Guatemala, Costa Rica having previously denounced the treaty and extended recognition to El Salvador, the American Charge' d'Affairs ad interim in San Salvador has today been instructed, under authorization of the President to extend recognition to the Government of El Salvador on behalf of the United States.[70]

If the United States' unilateral commitment to honor the treaty and the discrepancy between its attitude to the parties to the Tobar Doctrine and the nonparties is considered merely as the practice of a sovereign that has the sole discretion on its recognition policy, there would be no question as to its legality.[71] However, since it used the Tobar Doctrine instead of the traditional recognition policy to rationalize its position on the case, it is possible to question the appropriateness of its conduct under international law. It is, of course, arguable that by the rather omnibus way in which the consent to treaties is to be expressed under the Vienna Law of Treaties—a way that does not expressly require signatures for a treaty but considers it sufficient if the parties "ratify," "accept," or "approve"[72] a treaty, the only way the legality of the U.S. commitment could be impugned is if the treaty specifically required a mode that was contrary to what the United States did. Yet one might encounter difficulties as to whether the treaty could be binding on the United States merely because of its unilateral commitment. Conceivably, the answer to this question will depend on whether or not the parties to the treaty conferred a right on the United States, or whether the United States by the unilateral commitment assumed a duty vis-à-vis the contracting parties. But even if these questions are answered affirmatively, there may still be problems with how to apply them in practice. For instance, the U.S. failure to sign the treaty raises questions about the lack of mutuality and possibly the existence of *mala fide*. It is also questionable whether the whole circumstance of the treaty can establish a justiciable cause for either the parties or the United States in the event that any of them violated it, since the U.S. failure to append its signature could always be invoked as a shield in the unlikely event that any state should seek to enforce it. Moreover, considering the overall practice of the United States, which consistently displayed great intolerance to governments of "hostile political persuasions" in the American hemisphere, one finds it all the more difficult to believe that if any of the governments followed a political line that was not congenial to American interest, the United States would not have reneged on the so-called unilateral commitment to the treaty. Even if a treaty like the one in question were taken as a valid exception to the principle of efficacy, the scope of such a law would extend solely to the parties thereto and those who accede to it by ratification or any mode designated by the terms of the treaty.

The Legal Validity of the Tobar Doctrine

Viewed from the context of the municipal systems, the constitutional theory that a sovereign cannot bind its successors would make the doctrine extend solely to the governments that adopted it. But this argument is irrelevant to the present question because the undertaking was expressed in a treaty between states, thus making it a subject of international law. This being so, the discussion here will concentrate on the international ramifications of the treaty.

There is some controversy as to what law determines the validity of treaties. According to one school of thought, the legal validity of treaties is determined by international law, and a treaty is legally valid even if its signatories exceeded their constitutional authorities as provided by their legal systems.[73] The other view maintains that it is the constitutional law of the contracting states that determines the validity of treaties and the competence of the treaty-making authorities.[74] Although we will not evaluate the supporting arguments and relative merits of the two schools of thought, it suffices for the present purposes to say that the position of those who advocate international law as the appropriate criterion is more persuasive, because it is unreasonable and diplomatically counterproductive to go beyond the accredited representatives of contracting states and investigate the constitutional laws of each party to see whether or not there is any violation of authority on the part of any of the representatives. It is, however, arguable that when the parties expressly stipulate the type of law to be used in regulating the treaty, that express intention would have great significance.[75]

Granted that international law is the general criterion for determining the validity of treaties, the question is whether a treaty like the Tobar Doctrine is defensible under general international law.

One criticism of the Tobar Doctrine must be noted. According to this criticism, which was expressed in the Estrada Doctrine, the concept of automatic nonrecognition of revolutionary governments is not only an affront to the dignity of the affected states but also an intervention in the affairs of other countries.[76] Since contemporary international law forbids intervention by individual states,[77] this criticism is not entirely unfounded. But it can be rejected easily. The Tobar Doctrine, it should be recalled, was a mutual commitment of the contracting parties; it was not imposed by any of its signatories. It is therefore difficult to support the argument that the doctrine was an affront to the sovereignty of the parties. Nor is the rule against nonintervention a good argument against it. The prevailing position only forbids dictatorial intervention, that is, when one state coerces another to follow a certain political line.

Conceivably, the ills that occasioned the formation of the Tobar Doctrine may provide some support for its validity. The basic concern of the five Central American countries was to eradicate the practice of overthrowing constitutional governments by violence, then rife in the region.[78] Considering that the main purpose of the doctrine was thus to insure that constitutional governments— regimes established by the wishes of the majority of the peoples in the respective countries—should be protected from being forcibly supplanted by a small group of people, it is certainly possible to describe the doctrine as one that is in accord with the principle of self-determination. One problem with this contention, though, is that it is difficult to see how the principle of self-determination could be upheld by the doctrine when a constitutionally recognized government turns itself into a dictatorship.

Another possible difficulty with the Tobar Doctrine is that it conflicts with the effective-control principle as well as the notion that all peoples are entitled to revolt against oppressive systems. Considering that these concepts are so widely applied in the contemporary system as to suggest that they have now become a peremptory norm of international law, it is submitted that under article 53 of the Vienna Convention on the law of treaties, any international agreement that adopts the terms of the Tobar Doctrine will be legally difficult to defend.

Finally, even if it were assumed that the doctrine is valid, there may yet be questions as to its enforceability against any party that repudiates it. Under international law, the continuity of treaties is not affected by changes in government. By this principle, new governments are obliged by treaties that were assumed by their predecessors.

Yet it is the accepted practice that treaties can be terminated when there are serious changes in the circumstances of the parties, or when a party violates an essential term.[79] As to the former, which is expressed in the maxim *rebus sic stantibus*, there is some controversy about whether its unqualified application may lead to absurdities and, hence, undermine the whole notion of the law of treaties.[80] The prevailing position is that the maxim is not to be applied capriciously, but only on the basis of what the parties to the treaty can be presumed to have reasonably considered to be a vitiating factor for the agreement.[81] Although it is not exactly clear what criteria are to be used in arriving at this presumption, it seems safe to suggest that in the context of a treaty like the Tobar Doctrine, the mere change of government by revolution should be fundamental enough to warrant repudiation. It is submitted that because the parties to the treaty cannot urge nonparties to comply with the commitment to withhold recognition, this proposition would be difficult to challenge. For to hold otherwise not only would be impractical and tantamount to *brutum fulmen* but would also cause problems of instability that might, in turn, lead to threats to, or breaches of, the peace.

The events that led to the demise of the Tobar Doctrine give strong credibility to this conclusion. The El Salvadoran repudiation of it was considered enough to absolve the other parties from the obligations assumed under the treaty. It might seem at first that the treaty's provision requiring a year's notice from any party seeking to withdraw from it might have been the reason the parties terminated the treaty after the El Salvadoran withdrawal. There are, however, a number of facts that undermine this argument. First, El Salvador did not give the required notice, but even if it had, the question is whether its acceptance would not have shown how futile the treaty was. The government that rejected the treaty in El Salvador was one that had been established through a revolution—which needless to say, violated the treaty. Thus, to interpret the consequent repudiation of the treaty by the other parties' response to a notice from the transgressing state is not only to disregard the principle that the repudiation of a treaty by a party warrants its recession by the other, but also to suggest that the parties did not have any respect for the maxim *injuria propria non cadet in beneficium facientis*, which urges that people will not be allowed to derive benefit from their own wrongful act.

Conclusion

It should be obvious from our analysis that apart from the few situations where the United Nations may expressly call upon states to abstain from recognizing as legitimate those governments established by revolutions, the effective-control principle is a crucial standard for determining the legal validity of virtually all liberation movements. That is to say, a struggle that succeeds in supplanting a preexisting system is legal, except in situations where the United Nations states otherwise. Given the principle's patent contrariety to the goals of the contemporary international legal order, we might raise a number of questions about the relevance of the principle to the present system, particularly to those questions that relate to liberation struggles.

Without being too cynical, one may infer from the effective-control principle that it leaves a wide loophole in the present law, which frowns upon the use of force in international relations. Admittedly, the theory has no foundation in the most important document embodying contemporary international law, the U.N. Charter. And indeed, to the extent that its application is conspicuously inconsistent with the letter and spirit of the Charter, its place in the system may be very questionable. However, it should be realized that the system has not done much to obviate it, except, perhaps, the indirect stipulation in the Charter. Nor does it adopt any practical institutional approach to undo what is done by force. The Grenada intervention was clearly a use of force in the affairs of an independent state. And though the dubious concept of the right of states to rescue their nationals in foreign countries was cited as justification for the intervention, the United States surely did not comply with the minimum standards that are required of the rescuing state, to wit, that the intervention should be limited to the rescuing mission. The intervenors went further, to arrest the otherwise successful leaders of the revolution, thus preparing the ground for the installation of a more politically congenial government. Of course, the international community condemned the intervention in unqualified terms, but the condemnation did not change what the intervention succeeded in doing. In the Falklands crisis, the issues were muddy, but the outcome of the struggle became the determining factor for the legality of the confrontation. Chad, Gambia, Angola, Zimbabwe, and numerous other cases are no less representative of the obvious split between the principle of effectiveness and the contemporary law. The simple lesson to be learned from this is that the international community should, as a body, be a more vigilant in its search for a solution to the subjective considerations that make this split posssible.

INTERNATIONAL LEGAL REGULATION OF LIBERATION MOVEMENTS

This study has revealed several obstacles to finding conclusive answers for legal questions arising from liberation struggles. The problem with the effective-control principle is perhaps the most difficult of all. Its inherent ambiguities and tendency to favor the fait accompli nullify many of the hard-won values of the international community, notably, the rules against the use of force and intervention and others like the humanitarian laws of war. One need only note that by the logical implications of the principle, a struggle that succeeds in establishing itself is legitimate regardless of how it was pursued. And, needless to say, not only does this render the issue of the legality of the means by which the struggles are pursued superfluous, but it also puts the international system on a Machiavellian level where the ends, and only the ends, justify the means.

Since the legality of a cause does not necessarily legalize any act pursued in its name,[82] and laws are not to be interpreted or applied in ways that lead to absurdities,[83] the only way to make the effective-control principle credible in the present system is to subject it to the common values of the international community. It follows, then, that the principle can be useful only if it is invoked by the international community as a collective body. It is conceded that this approach may not be flawless, but it would be far more valuable than the one whereby states act on the basis of their unilateral assessments of issues.

The Use of Force

APART FROM INSTANCES where the United Nations may employ force to maintain the peace, force in liberation struggles is employed by the bona fide parties to the conflicts and, sometimes, in addition, by third parties that intervene to support one of the protagonists.

Until recently, the legality of the use of force—whether between or within states—was irrelevant to international lawyers. International law was germane solely to interstate conflicts and, in that context the use of force was considered a legitimate instrument of national policy.[1] The use of force became a serious issue of international law only after norms were enunciated to regulate international armed conflicts. Among the first documents to contain such norms were the League Covenant,[2] the Paris Pact,[3] and the Convention Respecting the Limitation of Employment of Force for the Recovery of Contractual Debts.[4] Laudable and ambitious as these were, they were so fraught with limitations[5] that the victorious nations in World War II felt it necessary to establish a more comprehensive system for the regulation of the use of force by states. Accordingly, they not only enjoined all states to settle their disputes by peaceful means but forbade the use of force in international relations. Specifically, article 2(4) of the U.N. Charter stated: "All Members shall refrain in their international relations from the threat or use of force against the territorial integrity or political independence of any state, or in any other manner inconsistent with the Purposes of the United Nations."[6]

Under article 2(6), the United Nations is to insure that "states which are not Members of the United Nations act in accordance with the principles so far as may be necessary for the maintenance of international peace and security." Since the use of force by one state against another may lead to threats to or breaches of the peace and, consequently, violate the commitment to maintain international peace and security, it is obvious that the prohibition of the use of force is to apply to nonmembers as well. Thus, according to the final report of Committee IV/2:

The Committee has considered that in the event of an actual conflict between such obligations [meaning obligations assumed between members and non-members of the United Nations] and the obligations of members under the Charter, particularly in matters affecting peace and security, the latter may have to prevail. The committee is fully aware that as a matter of international law it is not ordinarily possible to provide in any convention for rules binding upon third parties. On the other hand, it is of the highest importance for the Organization that the performance of the member's obligations under the Charter in specific cases should not be hindered by obligations which they may have assumed to non-Member States.[7]

However, the Charter's prohibition of the use of force is not without limitations. Under article 51, states can use force in self-defense if they are under "armed attack." Again, under chapter VII, the United Nations can use force as a collective body or authorize a number of states to use force to preserve the peace.

Simple as the present law seems, its application is difficult. There are questions as to what amounts to "force"; whether the proscription applies solely to "force" used in international relations, or also to intrastate conflicts; and whether it is restricted to armed force or applies to force that does not involve firearms.

THE MEANING AND SCOPE OF "FORCE" UNDER ARTICLE 2(4)

The Meaning of the Expression "International Relations"

Many writers maintain that the proscribed "force" is only that which is employed by one state against another. Pinkard, for example, urges: "Since this paragraph [article 2(4)] refers directly to international relations it only applies to force used by one state against another state and does not extend to the use of force by a state to suppress an internal disturbance."[8]

Similarly, in the words of Ronzitti:

One section of the doctrine purporting to demonstrate that repression by the incumbent government in the course of a war of national liberation is lawful, starts from the premise—which is correct per se—that Article 2 para. 4 is the only rule of the Charter which forbids the use of force. This rule forbids the use of force in international relations, i.e. in relations between States but sets no prohibition as far as civil war is concerned: the constituted government is therefore free to repress insurrection and commits no unlawful act when it uses force against the insurgents.[9]

According to Waldock:

> The corner stone of peace in the Charter is Article 2(4). . . . This general
> prohibition of the use of force is, however, qualified . . . by the fact that the
> word "force" in Article 2(4) undoubtedly covers only armed or physical force.
> . . . Then, Article 2(4) in terms confines the prohibition to the threat or use of
> force in international relations, thereby reserving by implication a State's right
> to resort to armed force for the suppression of an internal rebellion.[10]

This suggests that states can employ force against nonstates,[11] which is important in the context of liberation movements, where the majority of cases are struggles between states and nonstates. This construction accords with the principle of sovereign equality on which the United Nations is based, and it conforms to the rights of states to protect their territorial integrity and to use the necessary amount of force to insure that internal legal order is not subverted.

But it is difficult to insulate intrastate conflicts completely from the thrust of article 2(4). In prohibiting the use of force, the article includes the use of force that may "in any other manner" be "inconsistent with the Purposes of the United Nations." Since the use of force to quell an internal conflict may be tantamount to the denial of the right of self-determination or violation of human rights and may also lead to threats and breaches of the peace, it is easy to apply the prohibition to internal conflicts as well, and hence to all liberation movements.

Writers are not unmindful of this possible ramification of the provision. Indeed, even those who construe article 2(4) narrowly sometimes agree that their view is not absolute. Thus, according to Ronzitti:

> To admit the lawfulness of repressive action by the constituted government is
> therefore tantamount to admitting the lawfulness of action aimed at denying
> peoples' right to self-determination. . . . The proposition in question is backed
> by various arguments . . . : Article 2 para. 4 forbids the use of force not only
> against any State's territorial integrity and political independence, but also in
> any other manner which is not compatible with the objectives of the UN.
> Since one of these objectives is the principle of self-determination, the use of
> force against peoples under colonial rule is forbidden under Article 2 para. 4.[12]

Likewise, Waldock observes:

> It seems, however, from the Indonesian incident that a resort to force internally by a state, which is originally lawful under Article 2(4), may become a
> matter of international concern when seceding elements form themselves into a

new state. . . . . Again Article 2(4) speaks only of the threat or use of force against the territorial integrity or political independence of any state or in any other manner inconsistent with the purposes of the United Nations.[13]

Although the guidance of the Charter is unclear, U.N. practice suggests that the provision against the use of force applies also to intrastate conflicts. According to the Declaration on Friendly Relations, for instance, "every State has a duty to refrain from any forcible action which deprives peoples . . . of their right to self-determination and freedom and independence."[14]

Yet this cannot be interpreted to mean that states are absolutely forbidden to use force against their subjects. The issue is paradoxical, in that the same system that forbids the use of force to suppress the exercise of self-determination upholds the right of states to use force to maintain their territorial integrity and stability. One possible solution is to restrict the application of the prescription against the use of force to all interstate conflicts as well as to those intrastate ones involving the principle of self-determination. But even this does not completely solve the problem, for, as has been demonstrated throughout this study, whether a struggle is for self-determination is not always universally agreed upon.

Assuming it can be agreed that a particular movement is aimed at achieving the right of self-determination, and that the rule against the use of force also applies in favor of people struggling for their right of self-determination within their states, one may wonder whether the principle of self-defense can be invoked by states against their subjects who claim to be struggling for self-determination. Since the Charter does not forbid the use of force against liberation movements, *expressis verbis*, it is not surprising that the article on self-defense does not shed any light on this issue. Nor is the picture clear from relevant works on the subject. However, inasmuch as the principle of self-defense warrants use of force only when there has been an illegal resort to force by the other party,[15] the answer depends on whether the use of force by the liberation movements is legal. This issue is covered in later sections in this chapter.

The Definition of "Force"

Although Kelsen rightly admits that the term "force" in article 2(4) is a subject of intense debate,[16] he evades the problem of defining the term by noting that it at least includes armed force. Other writers, not so evasive, have conducted a raging controversy over the definition, debating whether to apply the article restrictively to "armed force" or to broaden it to cover any force.

Among the exponents of the restrictive construction are Goodrich and Hamboro,[17] Brierly,[18] and Waldock.[19] Their thesis is based on the wording of the preamble of the Charter: "*armed force* shall not be used, save in the common interest" and on the fact that a proposition at the San Francisco conference expressly to include economic force in the provision was rejected. Waldock points out:

> This general prohibition of the use of force is, however, qualified . . . by the fact that the word "force" in Article 2(4) undoubtedly covers only armed or physical force. This was the meaning given to it at San Francisco and the preamble to the Charter states the aim of the United Nations to be "to ensure by the acceptance of principles, and the institution of methods, that armed force shall not be used, save in the common interest."[20]

It is not difficult to spot the fallacy in this argument. Although the San Francisco conference employed the term "armed force" in the preamble of the Charter, it nevertheless failed to qualify the word "force" in article 2(4), a flaw that is used to bolster the other school of thought.[21] Thus, on the basis of the Charter's provision in the preamble to "practice tolerance and live together with one another as good neighbors" and such others as article 2(4) and 2(3), respectively, using the words "threat of force" and calling upon all members of the international community to "settle their . . . disputes by peaceful means in such a manner that international peace and security, and justice, are not endangered," the group contends that the forbidden "force" can definitely not be confined to armed force. In the deliberations of the Committee on Friendly Relations, for instance, several nonaligned nations broadly defined "force" to cover "all forms of pressure, including those of economic character, which have the effect of threatening the territorial integrity and political independence of any State."[22] Indeed, as specifically noted by the Chilean representative, "the term 'force' shall be broadly understood to cover not only armed force . . . but also all forms of political, economic or other pressure."[23] Again, it was emphasized in the draft submitted by the representatives of India, Lebanon, the United Arab Republic, Syria, and Yugoslavia that "no State may use or encourage the use of economic, political, or any other type of measures to coerce another State in order to obtain from it the subordination of the exercise of its sovereign rights or to secure from it advantages of any kind."[24]

Since any force is certainly not a "peaceful means" for settling disputes and, moreover, is likely to pose threats to international peace and security, it is easy to accept the broader interpretation. The third argument of the broader school is that the article proscribes the use or "threat of force" against the violation of the "territorial integrity" of states as well as against the impairment of their "political independence," and that the terms "territorial integrity" and "political independence" were inserted to prevent any confusion that they mean the same thing.[25] To bolster this analysis, they stress that whereas any kind of force can impair the political independence of any state, the force that violates the territorial integrity of a state can only take the form of armed force.

Evidently, international practice supports this construction. In the Inter-American Convention Concerning the Duties and Rights of States in the Event of Civil Strife of 1928, the parties were urged to "use all means at their disposal to prevent the inhabitants of their territory, nationals or aliens, from participating in gathering elements, crossing the boundary or sailing from their territory for the purpose of starting or promoting civil strife."[26]

They likewise forbade all traffic in arms and imposed further obligation to disarm rebels who cross into their territories. In the same vein, the General Assembly Declaration on Inadmissibility of Intervention groups together direct intervention and all forms of aggression as equally violating international law:

> No State may use or encourage the use of economic, political or any other type of measures to coerce another State in order to obtain from it the subordination of the exercise of its sovereign rights or to secure from it advantages of any kind. Also, no State shall organize, assist or foment subversive, terrorist or armed activities directed towards the violent overthrow of the regime of another State or interfere in civil strife in another State.[27]

Nor is it difficult to find situations in which states have overtly relied on the broader construction to rationalize their acts against other countries. Israel, for instance, employed it to justify the attack that precipitated the 1967 war against the Arabs, for, as it contended, the closing of the Gulf of Aqaba by the Arabs was the *casus belli*, to which their military action was only a defensive response. Since the United Nations did not criticize Israel for that attack, it is arguable that the Israeli contention enjoyed some credibility in that august international body. Other cases where the broader construction has been used were the French and British invasion of Egypt on the pretext that the closure of the Suez Canal was an act of force against them, the Indian citation of the refugee problem that attended the West Pakistani atrocities against the Bengalis as an act of force warranting the exercise of its right of self-defense, and the Indonesian use of the same argument in rationalizing its war against the FRETILIN.

The weight of evidence thus favors the view that the provision against the use of force is not limited to armed conflicts. Yet one must not accept this too quickly because, apart from the fact that an undue emphasis on the broader construction would nullify the article, it is a common knowledge that certain types of force may be legitimately employed by every sovereign, even in the present system. These permissible coercive measures include a state's right to impose a tariff on its imports, its right to deny fishing rights to nationals of other countries, its right to terminate diplomatic relations with other countries, and its right to impose punitive measures against its own subjects. Although the law thus has no conclusive, let alone objective, solution of this issue, any force that poses threats to international peace and security or impedes the realization of the purposes of the United Nations, namely (but not limited to) the promotion of human rights and self-determination, would fall within the proscription of article 2(4).

THE LEGALITY OF THE "FORCE" USED BY THE STRUGGLERS

The Self-Defense Argument

In some cases, particularly in the struggles against colonialism, the principle of self-defense has been invoked by the strugglers to justify the use of force against established authorities. In the Goa incident India invoked it in the Security Council:

> In the early morning hours on December 17, while the Secretary General was appealing for peace, Portuguese colonialist forces attacked Indians inside Indian territory. The measures taken by India were for the Goan people, who were in revolt against Portugal. . . . The Charter provides that force can be used in self-defense for the protection of the people of a country.[28]

Similarly, S.W.A.P.O. contended at the International Conference on Namibia and Human Rights:

> SWAPO is confident that a liberation war is not only morally but legally justified. It seems beyond doubt that self-determination is today a cardinal principle of international law. . . . It is a right which accrues in favor of a people. If it is forcibly denied them, under article 51 of the Charter of the United Nations, they have a right to defend themselves and their territory; the more so, against an illegal occupier. *A people's liberation war can be clearly identified as defensive action within the meaning of the Charter.*[29]

Except where it has been typically invoked in the decolonization cases, this argument is scarcely used by liberation movements. This section, then, relates only to the colonial cases. Significantly, the law of self-defense has gone through such confusion and attack that to appreciate its full ramifications one must know something of its traditional contours.

As in most domestic legal systems,[30] an otherwise illegal use of force was justified under the traditional international law if: (1) it was in response to an imminent attack, (2) it was employed under circumstances in which there could be no other means of repelling an imminent attack, and (3) it was proportional to the attack that occasioned it.[31] The most commonly cited authority to describe the principle is the *Caroline* case. In that case, the statement of the American secretary of state, Daniel Webster, which has been taken almost unanimously as the correct construction[32] of the law of self-defense, reads:

> While it is admitted that exceptions growing out of the great law of that self-defense do exist, those exceptions should be confined to cases in which the necessity of that self-defense is *instant, overwhelming, leaving no choice of means and no moment for deliberation*. It will be for it to show, also, that . . . even supposing the necessity of the moment authorized them . . . [to use the force, they] did nothing unreasonable or excessive; since the act justified by the necessity of self-defense, must be limited by that necessity, and kept clearly within it.[33]

Assuming the alleged attack against the Indians in the Goa incident were true, the only problem is whether the force used to repel the so-called Portuguese aggression satisfied the proportionality test. In the Security Council proceedings on the case, doubt was raised about India's allegation of attack. However, it was clear that India per se was never attacked. Although this, of course, triggers a debate about whether the invasion could be treated as an act of collective self-defense,[34] India rationalized it on the basis of its own right. Accordingly, it contended that the initial acquisition of Goa was an aggression, and, consequently, that the continuation of the Portuguese colonialism in that country was a perpetuation of that initial aggression. It then claimed that India, as the country of which Goa had been a part before the colonial onslaught, was entitled to invoke the principle of self-defense against the Portuguese.[35] This argument is reminiscent of the thesis of the S.W.A.P.O., which has been repeated by many third world countries in their support of the struggles against colonialism.[36] The problem, however, is whether the alleged aggression is the type warranting self-defense under the traditional law. First, the fact that the so-called aggression had been committed for a long time (450 years in the case of India) raises problems about whether the element of necessity was satisfied. Second, at the time the colonies were acquired not only was the use of force a legitimate instrument for the acquisition of territories[37] but there was also the established principle of prescription that a long-uninterrupted occupation of a territory was sufficient for the acquisition of title. Nor was this principle new to the Indians. Indeed, in its dispute with China over the Ladakh boundary, the Indian commissioner ruled in the ensuing arbitration: "It is unprecedented in the history of international relations that after one state has publicly exercised full administrative jurisdiction for several centuries over certain regions, another state should raise a dispute regarding their ownership."[38]

From these, it is easy to endorse Wright's critique of the Indian position; in exposing the fallacy in that argument, it spelled out the established law as follows:

> A State that neglects to defend its frontiers against hostile encroachment soon loses its right to do so and can only rely on negotiation or action by the United Nations to restore its rightful possession and thus remove a threat to international peace and security. . . . It seems clear that a concept of continuing aggression by Portugal against Goa, beginning in 1510 and giving India a right to engage in defense of the territory even though that right has not been exercised for 450 years, has no legal merit.[39]

This conclusion may be reached about all the cases in which the concept of self-defense is used to challenge the legality of their colonization. However, with the recent developments in the law, the conclusion would be inapplicable to force used against any colony. The question about the ongoing use of force by the minority regimes in South Africa to maintain their colonial overlordships may thus be answered differently.

The Self-Defense Provisions and the Force Used by Liberation Movements

The U.N. Charter's provision on the use of force in self-defense reads:

> Nothing in the present Charter shall impair the inherent right of individual or collective self-defense if an armed attack occurs against a Member of the United Nations, until the Security Council has taken measures necessary to maintain international peace and security. Measures taken by Members in the exercise of this right of self-defense shall be immediately reported to the Security Council and shall not in any way affect the authority and responsibility of the Council under the present Charter to take at any time such action as it deems necessary in order to maintain or restore international peace and security.[40]

Although this provision does not expressly state the traditional requirements for the right of self-defense, it calls the right "inherent." The crucial question thus rests on the meaning and significance of the term "inherent." Does it mean that the traditional preconditions for acts of self-defense are still extant? In other words, is it right to say that under the U.N. regime the right of self-defense is still warranted if it is exercised in response to an imminent attack, when there is no alternative means of repelling an imminent attack, and when the force used in self-defense is proportional to that which occasioned it? The phrase "if an armed attack occurs" that follows immediately after the "inherent right of . . . self-defense" makes this question even more inevitable. And like most other unclear provisions of the Charter, it has caused its share of controversy. One notable deficiency of the various views, however, is that they are all silent on the requirement for proportionality. We must examine the requirements to see whether the omission has affected its place in the *lex lata*.

The Relevance of the Proportionality Test

Under the traditional law the proportionality test was meaningful because it was possible for states to have at least some knowledge, albeit not always precise, of the magnitude of the impending danger. This knowledge was gathered from a number of factors, including the mobilization and movement of troops across borders. In the contemporary system where modern armed technology has made it possible to wage war without mobilization, let alone the use of many combat troops, it is difficult to say whether a state can reasonably be expected to respond proportionally to any force used against it. How, for instance, is the magnitude of the imminent attack to be assessed, and who makes that determination? At what time does a state determine whether or not the force it is using against an aggressor is proportional to that used by the aggressor? Is it while the aggression is merely imminent, or after it has been perpetrated, or both?

Assuming the proportionality test is an essential element in the law of self-defense, the question is whether, by underestimation of an aggressor's force, a state that applies the test religiously might not expose itself to destruction by a more powerful state which, if not preempted by an all-out incapacitating first strike, might come back with a more integrated force unmatchable by the one used in self-defense. If one acknowledges that the right of self-defense is essentially the right to existence, it is plausible to argue that inasmuch as a state would like to incapacitate the enemy forces beyond recovery, the requirement for proportionality would not be a crucial consideration for states in certain situations.

It is conceded, of course, that the total erasure of the proportionality test might make it more difficult for the international community to realize its commitment to preserve the peace and to insure respect for human rights. Yet the question whether proportionality is still an element in the principle of self-defense is one for which the theoretical answers do not always match those derived from the practice of states. Even in the *Caroline* case, where the traditional law was delineated, the contending parties—the U.S. and British governments—could not agree on whether the force used by the British to repel the alleged imminent danger was excessive.

Elusive as the proportionality test may be in contemporary international relations, it cannot cease to be part of the *lex lata*, at least theoretically. Considering that the essence of the test is to insure that people are not killed wantonly, there is no doubt that it is relevant to the laws of war—those that require that attacks be limited strictly to military targets. Thus, no matter how difficult it may be to determine how much force should be used against an aggressor, any force that is employed indiscriminately to kill or maim people, or even to destroy property beyond what is militarily necessary, would clearly be illegal for violating the proportionality test, and could even be branded as a war crime. Admittedly, it is not always possible to differentiate military and nonmilitary objects, especially in the present system where, by the irregular nature of most wars, it is difficult to determine what constitutes military necessity. Yet, emphasizing the distinction between military and nonmilitary targets would make the proportionality test more meaningful than it presently is. It also would contribute immensely to the development of world order, as it is easier to reconcile two factions who confine their attacks to military targets than those who direct their attacks indiscriminately against noncivilians and civilians alike.

Who May Exercise the Right of Self-Defense?

In the context of liberation movements an even more thorny question about the scope of the principle of self-defense is whether participants in struggles pursued in nonstate entities are entitled to exercise the right of self-defense. According to Dugard:

> The most serious objection to the proposed new right is that it has nothing to do with self-defense as it is traditionally understood or as it is described in Article 51. Self-defense is the right of one State acting individually, or the right of several States acting collectively. . . . A *sine qua non* for such a right is "an aggressor State" and a "victim State." . . . In the case of self-defense against colonial domination this necessary requirement is absent. It is possible to identify the aggressor State [the colonial power] but it is not possible to identify the victim State. . . . As there is no unlawful use of force against another State the question of self-defense does not arise.[41]

Conceivably, the expression "against a Member" of the United Nations may afford some plausibility to this line of reasoning, since only states are members, but this argument is unsustainable. If the expression were construed literally to urge that nonstates do not have the right of self-defense, would it not also mean that states that are not members of the United Nations are excluded from those forbidden to use force? Considering the commitment of the United Nations to maintain international peace by insuring that both members and non-members comply with the purposes and principles of the Charter,[42] and that the use of force, whether by or against a member, nonmember, or nonstate may pose threats to the peace, it is difficult to see any logic in the argument that nonstates are not entitled to the right of self-defense. It is significant that in the Charter itself self-defense is described as an "inherent" right. Since statehood is a status that emanates from certain conditions, it seems inconsistent to consider states to have the "inherent" right of self-defense when individuals—the elements to which the states owe their "hallowed" status—cannot exercise it. But even without the use of the term "inherent," it would still be difficult to contend that the status of statehood is a sine qua non for the exercise of the right of self-defense. What would the proponents of the argument say, for instance, about people who are victims of genocide? If they do not constitute a state, does that preclude them from fighting against acts of extermination? Since the right of self-defense is essentially a right to protect oneself, and since the promotion of human rights and self-determination for all peoples is an important objective of the United Nations, to accept the notion that the international community has assumed the commitment to maintain peace through these universal principles and yet contend that nonstates are not eligible to pursue the right of self-defense is, to say the least, contradictory.

The Scope of the Charter's Provision on Self-Defense

The controversy about the expressions "inherent right" and "if an armed attack occurs" is also crucial to the issue of whether the Charter's provision on self-defense is applicable to the cause of liberation fighters. One group adopts a narrow construction and contends that the Charter has qualified the preexisting right of self-defense, rendering "all use of force illegal except those exercised in self-defense 'if an armed attack occurs.'"[43] Evidently, the primary basis for this construction is the Charter's preamble, where "armed force" is specifically mentioned. Another consideration that appears to have influenced this construction is the fear that a carte blanche permission for states to launch preemptive attacks may be subject to abuse and could nullify the Charter's commitment to the maintenance of the peace and security, and, consequently, offend the principle of effective interpretation.[44] Pointing to the revolution in weapons technology, Friedmann has illuminated some of the apprehensions underlying the adoption of article 51:

Although, in the last world war, many of the states attacked by Germany, such as Poland, the Netherlands or Belgium, were almost instantly overwhelmed, it remained at least possible for the rest of the world to come to their assistance and virtually defeat the aggressor. With the advent of nuclear rockets and long-range missiles, this assumption no longer holds. The ability of missiles with nuclear war-heads, to paralyze and destroy the nerve centers even of the vast countries such as the U.S.S.R. or the U.S.A, and to kill or maim major parts of their populations in one blow, may make it a form of suicide for a state to wait for the actual act of aggression before responding. This situation has led to the complicated and controversial theses of modern "game theorists," such as the "first strike," "second strike," and "counter force" theories. Some of these include explicit or implicit postulate, that in certain circumstances, a nuclear Power might find it necessary to anticipate an imminent blow from the enemy by a pre-emptive strike paralyzing his striking capacity. . . . *This means, however, that an error in calculation or intelligence may lead a nuclear Power to start a war of universal extermination from a posture of self-defense. It was to avoid and eliminate the political and military dangers of letting the nations judge by themselves the vital issues of attack and defense that the relevant provisions of the United Nations Charter were formulated.*[45]

Those[46] who adopt a broader interpretation contend that article 2(4) is not restricted to "armed force," urging that the right of self-defense can therefore be exercised even if there is only an imminent attack. Their second argument is that article 51 was not considered until after the Latin American states expressed disaffection with the possible erosion of their sovereignty and, consequently, that the article is merely illustrative, rather than a limitation of the traditional principle of self-defense. The arguments of this school have been articulated by Brierly:

The precise scope of the right of self-defense under the law of the Charter is the subject of controversy. . . . This view [meaning the broad construction] derives some support from the *travaux preparatoires* of the Charter. Committee I . . . which dealt with Article 2(4), said outright that "the use of arms in legitimate self-defense remains admitted and unimpaired." Then the records show that Article 51 was introduced into the Charter in Committee III/4 primarily for the purpose of harmonizing regional organizations for the defense with the powers and responsibilities given to the Security Council . . . ; and they do not indicate any conscious intention . . . to put outside the law forcible self-defense against unlawful acts of force not amounting to an armed attack. . . . When the Article begins with the statement that nothing in the treaty shall *impair* an *inherent* ("imprescriptible" in the Russian, "natural" in the French, texts) . . . it is not easy to presume an intention in the following words drastically to impair that right. . . . First, the French text—*dans un cas ou un*

Membre des Nations Unies est l'object d'une aggression armée— is not expressed in the form of condition and suggests that the English "if" was used to express an hypothesis rather than a condition—which is, of course, one of the natural uses of "if". Secondly, if "effective interpretation" is to be applied to the words "if an armed attack occurs", so as to produce a restriction on the inherent right, is the same thing to be done to the very next words in the Article "against a Member of the United Nations"? If these words are given their full effect, the right of collective self-defense cannot be invoked to justify recourse to armed force in defense of a non-member state which is the victim of a flagrant aggression; but we know that this interpretation of the words was completely rejected by the United Nations with respect to the invasion of South Korea.[47]

It is possible to marshal some support for the broad interpretation. One such support may be gathered from the Kellogg-Briand Pact. Thus, although the pact did not mention the right of self-defense per se, it technically endorsed it by allowing states to make reservations by separate notes.[48] Notably, the U.S. reservation reads:

There is nothing in the American draft of an anti-war treaty which restricts or impairs in any way the right of self-defense. That right is inherent in every sovereign state and is implicit in every treaty. Every nation is free at all times and regardless of treaty provisions to defend its territory from attack or invasion and it alone is competent to decide where circumstances require recourse to war in self-defense. . . . Inasmuch as no treaty provision can add to the natural right of self-defense, it is not in the interest of peace that a treaty should stipulate a juristic conception of self-defense since it is far too easy for the unscrupulous to mould events with an agreed definition.[49]

Since the pact antedated the U.N. Charter, it is, of course, questionable whether its assertions can survive the provisions of the Charter, especially in case of a conflict between its tenets and any of the Charter's provisions. Moreover, the notion that a state is entitled to determine whether or not there is an attack against it has been rejected at the Nuremberg trials.[50]

Yet it may be difficult to give preference to the restrictive position. It is conceded that the fear that allegedly prompted the inclusion of article 51 is legitimate. Again, it is possible to find some correlation between the restrictive position and the United Nations' broad objective of maintaining international peace and security. But whether the mere outlawing of anticipatory self-defense is a sufficient guarantee that the commitment to maintain international peace and security will not be impaired remains unanswered. Consider, first, the revolution in weapons technology. It is common knowledge that only a few members of the international community have the ability to manufacture and use nuclear weapons. The issue therefore is whether it is reasonable to deprive states that do not have that ability of their fundamental right to exist. Besides, there is no rational relationship between the so-called weaponphobia and the prohibition of the right to use force against an imminent attack. Whether or not the prohibition is pronounced, nuclear war could be triggered by an error in judgment, a miscalculation, or even an accident. If the first strike by a nuclear power is capable of annihilating the intended object,[51] the question is whether a state that senses an imminent attack by a nuclear power would remain a "sitting duck" and await its doom. To the extent that the practical consequence of the suggested law is to ask states literally to commit suicide, it is contrary to common logic, incongruous with the basic notions of humanity, and not borne out by the principle of effective interpretation.

But there are other interesting arguments by which the restrictive construction can be rejected. Evidently, this construction is not in accord with the prevailing practice of states. The Cuban missile crisis, the United States' invasions of Cambodia and Laos, the recent downing of Libyan planes in the Mediterranean by U.S. F14s, the Soviet interventions in Hungary, Czechoslovakia, and Afghanistan, and recently the U.S. mobilization of heavy troops in the Persian Gulf to prevent Iraq's aggression on Saudi Arabia—all of which were done without any physical attacks on the supposed victims—are but a few examples of the way states currently behave in relation to the law on self-defense. Since subsequent practice is a tool for interpreting incomprehensible terms of a treaty, it seems safe to say that the law of self-defense embodied in the Charter is not different from that which preexisted the United Nations. Another strong argument for the broad construction is evident in article 51 itself. If anticipatory self-defense is impermissible, what, it may be asked, does the provision mean by the expression "until the Security Council has taken necessary measures to *maintain* international peace and security"? As has aptly been pointed out by some writers,[52] if anticipatory self-defense were meant to be outlawed, the article would have adopted the word "restore" rather than "maintain" in that particular clause.

In regard to all the circumstances of the concept as adumbrated in the Charter, particularly its equivocation in the use of both the word "inherent" and the expression "armed attack," and considering that the traditional law is generally seen as a peremptory norm, no matter how well-founded the concern for the *lex ferenda* is, that *lex ferenda* could not supersede the *lex lata*. As a provision seeking to modify a preexisting law, particularly that which is considered as peremptory, article 51 ought to be clear; it ought to be unambiguous; and it ought to be susceptible to no other interpretation than that sought to be established.

This conclusion is supported by the principle of restrictive interpretation, according to which, in case of doubt, a treaty should not be presumed to have eroded the sovereignty of states. Thus, the P.C.I.J. stated in the case of the *"Lotus"*: "The rules of law binding upon states therefore emanate from their own free will as expressed in conventions or by usages generally accepted as expressing principles of law. . . . *Restriction upon the independence of states cannot therefore be presumed.*"[53] Again, in the *Wimbledon*[54] case as well as that of the *Oder Commission*, wherein the court proclaimed the doctrine of the possibility of the self-limitation of sovereignty through treaties, the principle of restrictive construction was clearly upheld: "When . . . the intention of the parties still remains doubtful, that . . . interpretation should be adopted which is most favorable to the freedom of states."[55]

Since the analyses suggest that "armed attack" is not a sine qua non for a legitimate act of self-defense, it is unnecessary to ask whether the circumstances leading to liberation movements can be likened to situations of armed attack.

It is interesting to realize, however, that notwithstanding the apparent force of the arguments by which the struggles can be rationalized within the framework of the U.N. Charter, the United Nations evidently employs the principle of self-determination instead of the principle of self-defense to designate liberation struggles as legitimate. The next part of our inquiry into the legality of the force employed by the liberation fighters will therefore be concentrated on ways the principle of self-determination has been applied to some liberation movements.

THE USE OF FORCE PURSUANT TO THE PEOPLES' RIGHT OF SELF-DETERMINATION

If there is one thing on which all the organs of the United Nations agree, it is that all struggles for self-determination are legitimate. For, as has been demonstrated in several parts of this study, virtually all U.N. resolutions on self-determination—whether passed in the Security Council, the General Assembly, the Economic and Social Council, any of the specialized agencies, or in advisory opinions of the court—reiterate the notion that struggles for self-determination are legitimate. It may be instructive to address a few of the numerous resolutions. Resolutions on a wide variety of struggles—ranging from struggles against the racist minority regimes: Rhodesia, Namibia, and South Africa, to those against traditional colonial masters: the struggles by Angola, Mozambique, Guinea Bissau, and East Timor against the Portuguese, and others such as those of Spanish Sahara and East Timor against Morocco and Indonesia, respectively, which do not fall under colonialism—have branded them all legitimate.

For Namibia, it suffices to remember Security Council Resolutions 269 of 1969, 301 of 1971, and 447 of 1979, and General Assembly Resolutions 34/94 of 1979 and 36/68 of 1981. In paragraph 4 of Resolution S/269 the Council "recognizes the legitimacy of the struggles of the people of Namibia against the illegal presence of the South African authority in that country."[56] Likewise, in Resolution S/301 the Security Council recognizes "the legitimacy of the movement of the people of Namibia against the illegal occupation of their territory by the South African authorities and their right to self-determination."[57]

In General Assembly Resolution 34/94 and 36/68 concerning the Implementation of the Declaration on the Granting of Independence to Colonial Countries and Peoples, the support for liberation movements, particularly those in Namibia, is again sounded: The General Assembly "affirms once again its recognition of the legitimacy of the struggle of the peoples under colonial and alien domination to exercise their right to self-determination and independence by all the necessary means at their disposal."[58]

For South Africa, Resolutions S/282 of 1970 and S/473 of 1980 and A/31/L.14 concerning the Programme of Action Against Apartheid are revealing. In S/282 the council recognizes "the legitimacy of the struggle of the oppressed people of South Africa"[59] in pursuance of their human and political rights as set forth in the Charter of the United Nations and the Universal Declaration of Human Rights. And in Resolution A/31/L.14:

> The General Assembly commends the courageous struggle of the oppressed people of South Africa, under the leadership of their national liberation movements recognized by the Organization of African Unity, to abolish racism. It reaffirms that their struggle for the total eradication of apartheid and the exercise of the right of self-determination by all the inhabitants of the territory is fully legitimate.[60]

For Rhodesia, it is enough to cite resolutions S/403 of 1977,[61] and S/445[62] and S/448 of 1979.[63]

An element of force is an essential component of virtually all the liberation movements studied herein. Given the consistency with which the resolutions applaud liberation movements by referring to some as "courageous," it is obvious that they uphold the element of force as legitimate. But this conclusion requires further analysis.

First, in virtually all these resolutions, the emphasis is on the illegality of colonialism and the legality of the struggles for its eradication. Can the conclusion drawn from the resolutions be applied to noncolonial cases, too? In other words, one faces the dilemma of whether it is legitimate for noncolonial cases also to use force against their adversaries. According to the maxim *expressio unius est exclusio alterius*, since the resolutions do not mention any noncolonial cases, the provisions may not extend beyond the colonial cases. But this difficulty can be surmounted easily. The maxim is not to be applied automatically in every situation; it is to be applied where the circumstances of individual cases warrant. The important factor to consider is the purpose for which the resolutions were passed. Essentially, they are aimed at condemning and eradicating colonialism, which is the reason for their silence on noncolonial cases. Besides, it is impossible to apply the resolutions solely to the colonial cases because not only do all the provisions accept the view that self-determination is a universal right to be exercised by all people, but they emphasize the need to observe democratic and humanitarian values without any discrimination against any class of people in any given society.

The second difficulty with the resolutions is whether the suggestion that they sanction the legitimacy of the use of force by liberation movements is absolutely sustainable. On the basis of the Charter's failure to mention the use of force as an element of the principle of self-determination, some scholars have contended that the use of force by liberation movements is illegal.[64] The crux of the matter is that, although the resolutions cite the U.N. Charter as their basis for considering liberation movements as legitimate, the Charter's provision is so equivocal on whether force can be used for self-determination that the emphasis on that document as the raison d'être for the resolutions' position on the use of force seems at best inadequate, at least at first. But, again, this argument cannot be sustained within the framework of the Charter, nor is it borne out by the practice. As a document that merely states the main principles to be followed in international relations, the Charter cannot make an exhaustive list of all the rules it wants to postulate. Even though the Charter does not expressly say anything about force in its provisions on the principle of self-determination, the use of force is so incidental to the principle that citing it as a basis for branding liberation movements as illegitimate would be offensive to the principle of effective construction.

Finally, it is necessary to consider the organs that passed the resolutions. Not only do these organs have full power to interpret and apply the Charter, they are also the main bodies by which the Charter's provisions are rendered meaningful. Obviously, if the use of force is a legitimate tool for the pursuit of the people's right of self-determination, then that notion, by its reiteration and the near unanimity with which it is adumbrated, amounts to a customary international law. But, do the resolutions really support the notion that force can be used for self-determination?

The most important argument against the legitimacy of force in liberation movements is the fact that none of these resolutions mentions "force" *expressis verbis*. But further consideration makes it clear that this apparent deficiency cannot affect the obvious conclusion that the use of force by liberation movements is legitimate.

First, virtually all the resolutions suggest that the "evil" against which the struggles are directed is sustained only by force—an instrument that is so brutally employed against the strugglers that it kills or maims them or, if they are lucky, causes their incarceration with little possibility that they may be released and be able to resume their struggles as recently epitomized by Mandela's experience under South African Prime Minister De Klerk. Since such brutality knows no distinction between a peaceful demonstration and an armed struggle, and since it would be ludicrous as well as hypocritical to expect an unarmed person to fight against an armed oppressor, it is difficult to see any substance in the argument that the resolutions support the liberation movements but at the same time disapprove of the only means by which such movements can be pursued. Second, most of the resolutions mince no words in commending successful liberation movements. Can it be suggested that the resolutions applaud the success of the movements but frown upon the means by which they succeed? If their silence on the use of force is the main basis for the argument that the resolutions do not sanction the use of force by liberation movements, then, *proprio vigore*, their failure to condemn the use of force in liberation movements also can lead to the conclusion that the use of force by liberation movements is legitimate.

But there are more direct supports for use of force by the movements. In most U.N. resolutions, for example, the authorities against whom the struggles are directed are enjoined to apply the laws of war—laws that apply solely to armed conflicts—to the strugglers. Resolution 3103 (XXVIII), titled "Basic Principles of the Legal Status of Combatants Struggling Against Colonial and Alien Domination and Racist Regimes," reads in part:

> The General Assembly . . . Reaffirming that the continuation of colonialism in all its forms and manifestation . . . is a crime and that *colonial peoples have the inherent right to struggle by all necessary means at their disposal against colonial Powers* and alien domination in exercise of their right of self-determination. . . .
>
> Recalling numerous appeals of the General Assembly to the colonial Powers and those occupying foreign territories as well as to the racist regimes . . . to ensure the application to the fighters for freedom and self-determination of the provisions of the Geneva Convention relative to the Treatment of Prisoners of War, of 12 August 1949, and the Geneva Convention relative to the Protection of Civilian Persons in Time of War of 12 August 1949.[65]

In Resolution 35/206 K concerning the campaign for the release of political prisoners in South Africa, the General Assembly . . .

> Recalling and reaffirming its resolutions concerning political prisoners in South Africa, in particular resolution 34/93 H of 12 Dec. 1979 . . .

Cognizant of the provisions of Additional Protocol 1 to the Geneva Conventions of 1949, whereby freedom fighters in wars of national liberation are entitled to prisoner-of-war status . . .

3. Calls upon parties to the Geneva Convention of 12 August 1949 and the Additional Protocols thereto to ensure respect by the South African regime for the Conventions and Additional Protocols;
4. Condemns the death sentences imposed on those freedom fighters on 22 November 1980.[66]

Again, in Resolution 36/172 on the Situation in South Africa, the Assembly . . .

Commending the liberation movements, particularly the African National Congress, and the oppressed people of South Africa for intensifying the armed struggle against the racist regime . . .
Reaffirming that freedom fighters of South Africa are entitled to prisoner-of-war status under Additional Protocol 1 to the Geneva Conventions of 12 August 1949, . . . 14. Demands that the apartheid regime treat captured freedom fighters as prisoners of war under the Geneva Conventions of 12 August 1949 and Additional Protocol 1 thereto.[67]

Another direct support for the force used by liberation movements is evident from many recent resolutions that definitely put to rest any lingering doubts about the U.N. position. For example, Resolution A/34/92 G expressly supports the use of armed force:

The General Assembly . . . *Reaffirming its full support for the armed struggle of the Namibian people* under the leadership of the South West Africa People's Organization . . .

4. Reaffirms the inalienable right of the people of Namibia to self-determination, freedom, and national independence in a united Namibia . . . *and the legitimacy of their struggle by any means at their disposal, including armed struggle against the illegal occupation of their Territory by South Africa*;
12. Supports the armed struggle of the Namibian people, led by the South West Africa People's Organization, to achieve self-determination, freedom and national independence in a united Namibia.[68]

Again, in Resolution 35/227 A of 1981,

the General Assembly . . . *Reaffirming its full support for the armed struggle of the Namibian people* under the leadership of the South West Africa People's Organization . . .

3. Reaffirms the inalienable right of the people of Namibia to self-determination, freedom and national independence in a united Namibia . . . and the
legitimacy of their struggle by all means at their disposal, including armed
struggle, against the illegal occupation of their Territory by South Africa, . . .
5. Supports the armed struggle of the Namibian people, under the leadership
of the South West Africa People's Organization, to achieve self-determination,
freedom and national independence in a united Namibia.[69]

Finally, in Resolution 36/8 of 1981 concerning the Implementation of the
Programme for the Decade for Action to Combat Racism and Racial Discrimination, the assembly reaffirms "its support for the national liberation struggle
against racism, racial discrimination, apartheid, colonialism and foreign domination and for self-determination *by all available means, including armed
struggle.*"[70]

Considering the uniform wording and thought in these resolutions, it is
impossible to deny their legal force. It may be unquestionable, therefore, that
the use of force by liberation movements is legitimate under the present U.N.
system, but may the resolutions be construed and applied literally? For instance, when the carte blanche permission for liberation movements to use "any
means at their disposal" against their enemies is taken to mean that the strugglers can also use armed force, does the illegality of the actions of the enemies
of the liberation fighters release the movements from the prescriptions of the
laws of war? Interesting as this question might be, it is not within the scope of
this study. The next chapter, however, elucidates one of the other questions
arising from the literal implications of some of the resolutions: the issue of
intervention in favor of the strugglers.

Chapter

11

Foreign Intervention in Liberation Movements

INTERNATIONAL RESPONSIBILITIES TOWARD THE PROTAGONISTS IN LIBERATION MOVEMENTS

One intriguing issue about the U.N. resolutions as they pertain to liberation struggles is the posture that third parties are required to take vis-à-vis the protagonists. Evidently, whereas all the recent resolutions forbid any assistance to the beleaguered authorities, states are encouraged to support and assist the liberation fighters.

We begin with the way the law is elucidated in Security Council resolutions. Consider Resolution S/227 of March 8, 1970:

> The Security Council . . . Noting with grave concern that . . . (b) Some states, contrary to resolutions 232 (1966) and 253 (1968) of the Security Council and to their obligation under Article 25 of the Charter of the United Nations, have failed to prevent trade with the illegal regime of Southern Rhodesia . . .
>
> 2. Decides that Member States shall refrain from recognizing this illegal regime or from rendering any assistance to it . . .
> (a) Immediately sever all diplomatic consular, trade, military, and other relations that they may have with the illegal regime in Southern Rhodesia, and terminate any representation that they maintain in the territory . . .
> (14) Urges Member States to increase moral and material assistance to the people of Southern Rhodesia and their legitimate struggle to achieve freedom and independence.[1]

Again, in Resolution S/445 of March 8, 1975, the council

> 2. Commends the People's Republic of Angola, the People's Republic of Mozambique and the Republic of Zambia and other front-line States for their

287

288   *Foreign Intervention*

support of the people of Zimbabwe in their just and legitimate struggle for the attainment of freedom and independence . . .
3. *Requests all States to give immediate and substantial material assistance* to enable the Governments of the front-line States to strengthen defense capability in order to safeguard effectively their sovereignty and territorial integrity.[2]

The same pattern is evident in numerous General Assembly resolutions. In Resolution 3328 (XXIX):

The General Assembly . . .

7. Urges all States and specialized agencies and other organizations within the United Nations system *to provide moral and material assistance to all peoples under colonial and alien domination struggling for their freedom and independence*, in particular to the national liberation movements of the territories in Africa.[3]

In Resolution 2787, concerning the Importance of the Universal Realization of the Right of Peoples to Self-Determination, the General Assembly

3. Calls upon all States dedicated to the ideals of freedom and peace to give all their political, moral and material assistance to the peoples struggling for liberation, self-determination and independence against colonial and alien domination.[4]

Finally, in Resolution A/36/L.20, the assembly

9. Requests all States, directly and through their action in the specialized agencies and other organizations of the United Nations system, to withhold assistance of any kind from the Government of South Africa until the inalienable right of the people of Namibia to self-determination and independence . . .
11. Urges all States, directly and through their action in the specialized agencies and other organizations of the United Nations system to provide all moral and material assistance to the oppressed people of Namibia and in respect of the other Territories.[5]

Is it possible that the United Nations passed all these resolutions without intending that they be observed? Considering the documents' consistent reiteration of the injunction to abstain from assisting the incumbent authorities and their authorization of assistance to the liberation movements, an affirmative response to this question would be unsustainable. Indeed, any other position by the General Assembly and the Security Council would be a betrayal of the principle that the United Nations must observe and implement the provisions of the Charter in good faith. But what are the meaning and implications of the injunction to abstain from assisting the incumbent authorities and the encouragement of states to assist the liberation movements by "all necessary means"— "moral," "substantial," and "material" assistance?

Evidently, there is no unanimity on what constitutes intervention by one state in the affairs of another. Thus, whereas one view considers any type of unsolicited interference[6] as interventionist, another—the view that seems to enjoy majority support[7]—adopts a more restrictive position, considering as intervention only acts that "dictatorially" interfere with "the affairs of another state for the purpose of maintaining or altering the actual condition of things."[8] Although it is unnecessary to evaluate the two positions, it is obvious that regardless of which definition is preferred, the injunction against dealing with the incumbent authorities and the call for states to give assistance to liberation movements fully authorize intervention in the affairs of the affected states. It suffices merely to note that what is demanded of the incumbent authorities is that they dismantle certain aspects of their sociopolitical, legal, and economic lives—a demand that is patently interventionist.

Granted the soundness of this construction, it would be unnecessary to consider what form the resolutions require the intervention to take, since the law of intervention does not prescribe the different means by which a state may intervene in the affairs of another.[9] The meaning of the expression "moral and material assistance" is not difficult to find. In all the situations to which the resolutions apply, the incumbent authorities oppress and suppress the strugglers by the use of armed force. The strugglers are always so poorly armed that even minor confrontations with their adversaries result in death for many of them. The call on states to assist the strugglers cannot have any practical meaning if it excludes assistance in the form of arms.[10] Any other construction of the resolutions would be hypocrisy on the part of the international community. Nor would it tally with the express injunction on states to support and assist the movements by "all necessary means," "all moral and material" or "moral and substantial assistance." What is more, not only is assistance to the incumbent authorities prohibited, but states and organizations like the O.A.U. that assist the movements with arms or troops are praised in the resolutions.

Indeed, the more recent resolutions of the United Nations are very specific: they state expressly that military assistance is not excluded from the ways that liberation movements may be assisted. Thus, in Resolution 35/227 A of 1981, the General Assembly . . .

Calls upon Member States, specialized agencies and other international organizations to render increased and sustained support and material, financial, military and other assistance to the South West Africa People's Organization to enable it to intensify its struggle for the liberation of Namibia.[11]

In Resolution 35/227 J the assembly

renews its call to the international community to render all material, financial, military, political and diplomatic assistance to that organization for the immediate termination of South Africa's illegal and racist colonial occupation of the Territory.[12]

Again, in Resolution 36/121 of December 1981, not only does the assembly reaffirm "its full support for the armed struggle of the Namibian people under the leadership of the South West Africa People's Organization," but it also calls "upon Member States, specialized agencies and other international organizations to render sustained and increased support and material, financial, military and other assistance to the South West Africa People's Organization to enable it to intensify its struggle for the liberation of Namibia."[13]

The only question about the resolutions is whether the authorization extends to assistance to any kind of movement professedly undertaken for self-determination. Since virtually all the resolutions mention "authentic representatives" of the oppressed, it is somewhat difficult to extend their application to any other movements. But legal documents do not have to exhaust all the subjects and objects about which they stand. Yet the problem is not simple; states do not always agree on what constitutes a fight for self-determination, let alone what constitutes a legitimate liberation movement. In most cases, states accord recognition and assistance to different belligerent factions, arguing that the factions they recognize are the champions for self-determination. Indeed, not even the United Nations' labeling some movements as the authentic representatives of their compatriots could bring the problem under control. In the Angolan situation, although the M.P.L.A. is recognized by the United Nations and most members of the international community, that recognition has not precluded other countries from recognizing the opposing F.N.L.A. and U.N.I.T.A. Thus the United Nations' failure to label certain movements as authentic does not necessarily mean that those movements cannot be recognized and assisted by other states. Obviously, the law is at best inadequate. To the extent that recognition is often accompanied by assistance, the encouragement of states to give assistance to movements for self-determination is inconsistent with the international commitment to maintain peace, since it provides a comfortable excuse for states to form alliances and counteralliances to fight against each other on the pretext of aiding liberation movements.

RECONCILING THE RESOLUTIONS WITH OTHER LAWS RELATING TO INTERVENTION

The Resolutions and the Traditional Law

Another conceivable difficulty with construing the resolutions as encouraging states to intervene on behalf of liberation movements is that it runs counter to many other laws of the international system. Under the traditional law, for instance, the legitimacy of foreign intervention in any intrastate conflict depends on whether that situation has reached the stage of belligerency.[14] If it has not, assistance to the incumbent authorities but not to the "rebels" or "insurgents" is legitimate. Conversely, if it has reached that stage, all states are by law enjoined to be neutral.[15] Since the position of the resolutions is obviously different from this, and given the priority of the U.N. commitments over commitments under any other system, the only way to understand the present position is to examine the resolutions vis-à-vis the traditional law, at least to see whether the latter has survived, or has been superseded by, the laws in the U.N. system.

Authorities are generally skeptical about the relevance of the traditional law to contemporary international law. Farer, for instance, has urged that the conditions that necessitated assistance to the incumbent authorities in the traditional system are no longer important in international relations.[16] In a critique, bearing essentially on similar considerations, Brownlie sees the traditional law as having been supplanted by the principles of self-determination and human rights.[17] Again, on the basis of the extensive leeway by which the traditional norm is applied,[18] Lauterpacht, Higgins, Dhokalia, Falk, and Friedmann have expressed grave doubts about the suitability of the traditional law to the present system. Falk's critique runs thus:

> The real flaw in the traditional system lies not only in its failure to provide objective tests . . . for bestowal of different statuses to a civil war but also in the allocation of authority to sovereign states having maximum discretion to specify their attitude unilaterally. The result of this over-individualized process has been neither stability nor control of the phenomenon of civil war. . . . This freedom given by traditional international law, leaving every state to decide for itself which of the two contestants is in the right, may have been well adopted to the situations which existed when the resort to war was unregulated by law. But, a return to that traditional law in our times would be disastrous for the world community which the UN Charter and the modern law of nations seek to preserve.[19]

These criticisms are so to the point that they need no further analysis.[20] Yet it may be interesting to consider briefly one of the rationales on which the traditional law was based. According to this notion, assistance to a sovereign was compatible with the doctrine of sovereignty in the pre-belligerency stage of a conflict, but incompatible with it when the struggle reached the point when determining who wielded the legitimate authority became impossible. But that notion is equally problematic, because a sovereign that wields control over its people hardly needs any foreign assistance to quell sporadic uprisings. Hall is directly on point:

> Supposing the intervention to be directed against the existing government, independence is violated by an attempt to prevent the regular organs of the state from managing the state affairs in its own way. Supposing it, on the other hand, to be directed against the rebels, the fact that it has been necessary to call in foreign help is enough to show that the issue of the conflict would without it be uncertain, and consequently that there is a doubt as to which side would ultimately establish itself as the legal representative of the state.[21]

Given these ambiguities, can it be argued that the resolutions have superseded the traditional law? Some critics seem to suggest so.[22] However, if this is really what the critics mean, then they are wrong, because ambiguities per se do not vitiate norms, particularly a traditional norm like that on intervention, which is so well established as to warrant its consideration as a peremptory norm. If ambiguities alone can undermine the status of norms in the international system, then most, if not all of the principles of international law (including the U.N. resolutions on intervention) are questionable, for all of them contain ambiguities.

Another argument used to deny the relevance of the traditional law to the contemporary law on intervention is that the law on recognition has been out of use for a considerable length of time.[23] Obviously, this raises the need for inquiry into whether non-use of a law can create a contrary law in place of the one in disuse. However, in the contemporary international system where the United Nations is the highest legal institution, the answer to this issue would be inconclusive unless it was reflected in U.N. practice, too. For U.N. action, either by abrogating or endorsing the traditional law, will be of equal, if not greater, importance in effecting a change in an existing law. It is thus necessary to conduct the discussion on two broad lines: (1) the legal consequences of the non-use of a norm—whether the lapse in the use of a norm always effects a substitution of that norm with that of the contrary persuasion; and (2) whether there is evidence to suggest that the U.N. system has abrogated or superseded the traditional law on intervention.

Desuetude and the Creation of Norms by State Practice

Does the non-use of a norm abrogate it? And if it does, is the non-use of the traditional law on intervention enough to establish a contrary norm in its stead? State practice is a source of customary international law. A practice that is consistently followed for a long time crystalizes into a rule of customary international law. It is therefore logical to infer that a practice that consistently diverges from a previous one may create a contrary norm. The conditions that are generally considered necessary for creating a customary law by practice are: (1) that the practice in question must have been consistently applied over a sufficient period of time to demonstrate its general applicability to designated types of situations; (2) that it must have been accepted, either expressly or implicitly, by a large majority of states having the occasion to express themselves on the issue, including any state that is in a position to frustrate the effectuation of the principle by its unilateral action; and (3) that in pursuing the principle, state policymakers must have believed that they are complying with it because of a binding legal obligation rather than acting out of expediency or purely moral conviction.[24]

Clearly, the privotal question is, can the standards used in establishing a new principle be used to determine whether an out-of-use practice has been abolished? According to McNair, the question as to whether the non-use of a particular custom has matured into a contrary custom depends on

1. whether the disuse is of such duration that it establishes itself as a custom;
2. whether another customary law has been substituted for it;
3. whether the contrary practice approaches universality in its acceptance; and
4. whether opportunities must have presented themselves for the law to have been applied.[25]

Granted that this test is appropriate, the issue is whether the alleged non-use of the traditional law is of such character as to warrant an argument that a new customary law has emerged in its stead. In other words, the crucial issue is whether there has been sufficient time and consistency in the non-use of the preexisting practice, and whether by the nature of the non-use states can be said to have sought to make a contrary norm in its stead.

The question as to how much time is necessary for the creation of law by custom has been addressed by Friedmann:

Not only is it difficult to say at what point a rule of international law, especially customary one, has ceased to be valid, but it is even more difficult to say when a new practice has hardened into law. Between these two stages lie many transitory ones when an old practice, once universally accepted, but gradually abandoned by a large part of international society, fades away and a new practice has not yet spread sufficiently or become definite enough to crystallize into a rule of law.[26]

Yet there are certain considerations that may make the issue less difficult for our purposes. Although it is not clear when the practice leading to the establishment of the traditional law on intervention started unfolding, it is generally agreed that the practice was upheld in the American Revolution of 1776 and was unquestionably applied in 1861.[27] If the period between those two dates was the time taken to develop the law, it is arguable that a comparable length of time, plus the other prerequisites, may suffice in bringing a contrary law into being. It has been suggested that the law on belligerency recognition (which is the line between intervention in favor of an incumbent authority and neutrality) was neglected in the Cuban revolt of 1896 and the Spanish civil war of 1936. It has also been noted that the law on belligerency recognition has rarely been applied since World War I and has been absolutely abandoned since World War II.[28] Comparing the length of time within which the concept was applied—1776 to 1861—with that within which it was abandoned, the argument urges that the old law has fallen into desuetude.[29]

These arguments, in sum, raise many doubts about whether the law on intervention has really been abolished by a contrary norm. Evidently, almost all writers agree that although there has been no recognition of belligerence, many conflicts have been granted the status of insurgency, with the consequence that intervention is withheld.[30] This is undeniably a departure from the traditional law, which calls for neutrality only after the stage of belligerency is reached. But it is also true that the traditional law did not make it mandatory for states to assist any party until the stage of belligerency was reached. Considering this and also that it was within the discretion of each state to determine what the status of a conflict was, the alleged new practice is too equivocal to sustain the argument that the old norm has been superseded by a contrary one. Indeed, in virtually all the cases where insurgency status was accorded instead of belligerency, the recognizing states did not withhold their assistance to the incumbent authorities until they considered the traditional conditions for neutrality to have been reached.[31]

Finally, the traditional law of intervention does not seem to have been discarded, because states often cite the traditional principle of assistance to incumbent authorities to support their intervention in internal conflicts.[32] One has only to recall the arguments presented in the Czechoslovakian, Hungarian, Laotian, Yemeni, Lebanese, and Dominican Republican cases to see the relevance of the traditional law to the practice in the modern system. Admittedly, in some of these cases the governments on behalf of whom the interventions were professedly undertaken were actually not the governments at all. Although it would thus be possible to brand any of them as illegal, it is difficult to see the practical significance of doing so. The law has no objective third party to monitor situations as they arise, and judgments ex post facto may be no less subjective than the original ones. Moreover, in cases where the interventions succeeded, there is often no way to undo the fait accompli.

The U.N. Charter and the Law of Intervention

In situations where the United Nations is taking enforcement or preventive actions, the traditional law on intervention is of no avail to any state.[33] For, as Kelsen has said of article 2(5) of the U.N. Charter: "member states no longer possess, in principle, the freedom either to refrain from actively participating in a war that has taken on the character of a United Nations enforcement action or—should they not be called upon by the Security Council to take military measures—to observe the duty of impartiality as laid down by the traditional law."[34]

What remains uncertain, however, is the status of the traditional law where the United Nations takes no action, either because it is unable to reach a resolution or because it is not apprised of the case. Conceivably, the Charter's provision against the use of force might be applicable here. Yet, because the Charter expressly prohibits the use of force *against* the territorial integrity and political independence of states, writers contend that an intervention *in favor* of an incumbent government is not affected by it. This argument might at first seem plausible, particularly considering that an intervention in favor of an existing system may help to preserve the status quo. A more careful study of the issue, however, raises a number of problems. For, not only can it be difficult to determine who wields the legitimate authority in a conflict-stricken country,[35] but the restriction of the article to its provision on territorial integrity and political independence ignores the clause that the prohibition applies also to acts that may not be consistent with the purposes and principles of the United Nations. To the extent that a struggle may be for self-determination, and to the extent that the violation of a people's right to self-determination may be inconsistent with the purposes and principles of the United Nations, it is arguable that article 2(4) is at best too equivocal to be said to have abrogated the traditional rule.

Another provision of the Charter relating to intervention is article 2(7). By this the United Nations is specifically prohibited from "intervention" in matters that are "essentially within the domestic jurisdiction of any state." The question thus arises as to whether the provision has any relevance to the issue of intervention by individual states. One possible answer for this has been offered by Pinkard: "It should be noted that since Article 2 specifically mentions the United Nations in its prohibition on intervention into matters of 'domestic jurisdiction' this Article refers only to the international organization and may not be extended to include individual states."[36] Since the responsibilities, powers, and duties of the United Nations are certainly not coterminous with those of states, Pinkard's view is supportable. A cumulative reading of the article with the Charter as a whole, however, raises some doubt about whether she is right. For how can a body like the United Nations, whose purpose is the collective security, be precluded from conflicts in which its individual members are free to intervene? It is obvious, then, that the insulation of states from the impact of article 2(7) may not be logically sound. Nor would it be possible to adopt the obverse of that construction as absolute. The ambiguities of the Charter, particularly those of the provision in question, are so conspicuous that it is difficult to find any conclusive solution to the issue in that document.

Examine the scope of the article, for example. Evidently, there are numerous situations where the prohibition does not apply. If the basis for applying the provision to states is the fact that the United Nations is prohibited from intervening in certain cases, is it also sound to say that states are permitted to intervene in cases where the United Nations is not prohibited from intervening? Even a brief scrutiny of the exceptional cases is enough to reveal the enormity of the problem.

The United Nations is authorized to intervene in cases that fall within the scope of chapter VII of the Charter. Admittedly, this power cannot be enjoyed by individual states,[37] except in cases where the United Nations authorizes them by a specific resolution to do so. The difficulty with the article, however, is that the United Nations cannot act under chapter VII unless there at least has been a finding of the existence of threats to the peace. Since the United Nations may be unable to operate under that chapter (either because it cannot attain the requisite votes or because the case may not be brought before it), and since states are equally responsible, either individually or as a collective body, for the maintenance of international peace and security, the question is whether an intervention that seeks to settle a case that the United Nations is not acting on is legally defensible.

Another difficulty with article 2(7) concerns the scope of the intervention the United Nations is forbidden to undertake. According to some scholars, notably Lauterpacht and Wright, who share the view that intervention is unlawful only when it is "dictatorial," the proscription does not apply to recommendations, discussions, inquiries, or investigations, done by or on the authorization of the United Nations.[38] Although not necessarily disagreeing with the argument that discussion is not intervention, others, like Kelsen and Goodrich and Hamboro, insist that the scope of article 2(7) cannot be limited to "dictatorial intervention."[39] For, as they argue, nondictatorial acts like setting up a commission, investigating, and recommending constitute intervention regardless of whether they are pursued as procedural or substantive matters. To support their position they urge that the Charter has forbidden dictatorial intervention elsewhere and, therefore, that a construction that limits the article to "dictatorial intervention" would render that provision superfluous.

Plausible as the broader construction is, it is unsustainable because, apart from being a minority view, it is obvious that a construction that precludes the United Nations from investigating matters under article 2(7) would only lead to absurdities since it would deprive the organization of the only means by which it can determine whether or not there is a threat to the peace and, consequently, whether or not it is forbidden to take measures to control any given situation. Unlike the broader position, the restrictive construction seems to be borne out by the practice of both states and the United Nations. One need only remember the U.N. position in the Greek Frontier Question, where the U.S. rebuff of the Soviet contention that the establishment of a commission to investigate the alleged infiltration through the borders of the neighbors of Greece would be a form of intervention was applauded and endorsed by most of the members of the organization. It may be necessary to quote the U.S. statement: "the Council could not be frustrated in making an investigation simply by the will of one member of the United Nations who does not desire to be investigated. It can, however, determine what violation has taken place, and it may choose to do so by an investigation."[40]

If article 2(7) forbids dictatorial intervention alone, does that mean that states can intervene nondictatorially? Because of the ambiguities in article 2(4), it is difficult to answer this question. Moreover, there is some controversy about who determines whether a matter is within the domestic jurisdiction of states. Since states are not obligated to bring an action to the United Nations for the determination of this issue, it is at least arguable that until a case is finally determined, individual states may be justified in intervening to help preserve the territorial integrity or political independence of another.

Given the ambiguities of the Charter's provisions on intervention, no matter how plausible an argument is, it cannot provide conclusive information on the status and implications of the law in the present system. It is, of course, conceded that as a mere document whose value rests mainly on how it is applied by the relevant institutions, the consistency with which the United Nations calls for assistance for liberation movements and condemns dealings with incumbent authorities can be taken as a strong indication of what is permissible intervention and what is not, at least in relation to the subject of liberation movements. But the question is whether the United Nations' practice is as consistent as it appears from the documents studied in this work.

The Law of Intervention as Seen through U.N. Resolutions

The practice of the United Nations gives the impression that the organization has no sympathy at all for interference by one state in the affairs of another. In the Resolution on Peace Through the Deeds, for instance, the General Assembly,

> Condemning the intervention of a state in the internal affairs of another State for the purpose of changing its legally established government by the threat or use of force,

> (1) Solemnly reaffirms that, whatever the weapons used, any aggression, whether committed openly, or by fomenting civil strife in the interest of a foreign power, or otherwise, is the gravest of all crimes against peace and security of the world.[41]

Similarly, the U.N. Declaration on Inadmissibility of Intervention reads:

> (1) No State has the right to intervene, directly or indirectly, for any reason whatever, in the internal or external affairs of any other State. Consequently, armed intervention and all other forms of interference or attempted threats against the personality of the State or against its political, economic and cultural elements are condemned.
> (2) No State may use or encourage the use of economic, political or any other type of measures to coerce another State in order to obtain from it advantages of any kind. Also, no State shall organize, assist, foment, finance, incite or tolerate subversive, terrorist or armed activities directed towards the overthrow of the regime of another State, or interfere in civil strife in another State.[42]

In Resolution 36/102 on the Implementation of the Declaration on the Strengthening of International Security, the General Assembly Urges all States

> (a) To refrain from any threat or use of force, intervention, interference, aggression, foreign occupation or measures of political and economic coercion which violate the sovereignty, territorial integrity, independence and security of other States or their right freely to dispose of their resources.[43]

Finally, in Resolution 36/103, Annex, on the Declaration on the Inadmissibility of Intervention and Interference in the Internal Affairs of States:

> The General Assembly . . .
> Reaffirming, in accordance with the Charter of the United Nations, that no State has the right to intervene directly or indirectly for any reason whatsoever in the internal or external affairs of any other State . . .
> Solemnly declares that:
>
> 1. No State or group of States has the right to intervene or interfere in any form or for any reason whatsoever in the internal and external affairs of other States.
> 2. The Principle of non-intervention and non-interference in the internal and external affairs of States comprehends the following rights and duties:
>
> I
> (a) Sovereignty, political independence, territorial integrity, national unity and security of all States, as well as national identity and cultural heritage of their peoples;
>
> II
> (a) The duty of States to refrain in their international relations from the threat or use of force in any form whatsoever to violate the existing internationally recognized boundaries of another State, or disrupt the political, social or economic order of other States, to overthrow or change the political system of another State or its Government . . .
>
> III
> (b) The right and duty of States fully to support the right to self-determination, freedom and independence of peoples under colonial domination, foreign occupation or racist regimes, as well as the right of these people to wage both political and armed struggle to that end, in accordance with the purposes and principles of the Charter . . .
> 4. Nothing in this Declaration shall prejudice in any manner the right to self-determination, freedom and independence of peoples under colonial domination, foreign occupation or racist regimes, and the right to seek and receive support in accordance with the purposes and principles of the Charter.[44]

Is it possible to reconcile these resolutions with those that warrant intervention in favor of liberation fighters? Surely, at the superficial level it is not, because virtually all resolutions seem to prohibit any interference, regardless of how noble the intervenor's intentions are. Yet, although their basic concern is about the preservation of the peace, it is also clear from the documents, particularly the most recent ones, that intervention is impermissible only if the state against which it is perpetrated does not deprive its subjects of their rights to self-determination. Indeed, this construction is echoed in the famous Declaration on Friendly Relations, where the international community urges that "in their actions against, and resistance to, such forcible action in pursuit of the exercise of their right to self-determination, *such people are entitled to seek and receive support in accordance with the principles of the Charter*."[45] Nor would a contrary construction agree with the corresponding provision in the draft resolution II on the Declaration on the Inadmissibility of Intervention and Interference in the Internal Affairs of States. The resolutions focus principally on the territorial integrity, political independence, and sovereignty of states. To the extent that intervention to assist in the realization of a people's right of self-determination may not necessarily impair any of these "sacred" rights of states, it is certainly not impossible to reconcile the notion of inadmissibility of intervention with that calling for assistance to people struggling for self-determination. Even in the recent definition of aggression, where the express prohibition of the use of armed force by one state against another poses a serious question as to whether the U.N. resolutions on liberation movements cannot be construed as having excluded the use of armed force, the right of liberation movements to get armed assistance is not denied. For although states are expressly forbidden to use armed force against "the sovereignty, territorial integrity or political independence, or in any manner inconsistent with the Charter," the resolution affirms the main mechanism for realizing peoples' right of self-determination:

> Nothing in the Definition, and in particular article 3, could in any way prejudice the right to self-determination, freedom and independence, as derived from the Charter, of peoples *forcibly deprived of that right* and referred to in the Declaration on Principles of International Law Concerning Friendly Relations and Co-Operation among States in accordance with the Charter of the United Nations, particularly peoples under colonial and racist regimes or other forms of alien domination; nor the right of these peoples to struggle to that end and to seek and receive support in accordance with the principles of the Charter and in conformity with the above mentioned Declaration.[46]

Since the primary objective of the definition is to prohibit the use of force by one state against another, the reference to people's struggling against forcible repression of their right of self-determination is susceptible to no other interpretation than one that authorizes assistance to the liberation movements.

CONCLUSIONS AND RECOMMENDATIONS

Liberation struggles are one of the most thought-provoking subjects of contemporary international relations. The cause of liberty has changed, or at least immensely contributed to changing, the position of the individual under international law. Accordingly, people—whether colonial or otherwise—now have a full legal backing to rise up against established systems and governments to liberate themselves from colonialism or oppression. Moreover, although the use of force in international relations has been outlawed categorically, not only are liberation movements now entitled to use force, arguably any type of force, but they are to be assisted by any state, and any attempt to suppress any liberation movement is illegal. Many privileges are accorded to liberation movements but perhaps the most significant manifestation of them is the impressive record of new states whose liberation from colonialism or oppression has been effected largely via direct assistance from the international community, encouragement from new developments in international law, and support from states claiming justification from the present law.

Yet the legal significance of liberation movements is not simple. The so-called new status of liberation movements raises several difficult questions, ultimately causing doubt about whether the significance of liberation movements has really changed. Because the term "liberty" defies definition, lawyers and politicians find it difficult to determine which conflicts are liberation oriented and which are not. In practice, this lack of precision invariably provides opportunities for actors, influenced by personal biases, idiosyncrasies, or self-interest, to recognize and assist those they want to support. Needless to say, this tendency sometimes makes the so-called privileges given to liberation movements go to factions other than liberation movements. Moreover, insofar as the internationally created privileges for liberation movements include the right of the strugglers to receive any form of assistance from any state and to use any means, including armed force, against their adversaries, the question is whether liberation movements do not represent a new loophole in the Charter's prohibition of the use of force and thereby revert the international system to the past, when alliances and counteralliances were formed and used to fight adversaries.

Another paradox arising from the present law concerns the doctrine of sovereignty. This doctrine still forms the basis of contemporary international relations, and among its attributes are the duties of states to preserve their independence and territorial integrity; to abstain from intervening in each other's affairs; and to render assistance to each other in prebelligerent stages of intrastate conflict or, at any other stage, to intervene to counter an illegal intervention. The paradox is that the same legal system encouraging people to fight for their freedom and calling upon states to assist freedom fighters is at the same time sanctioning suppression of the movements by the beleaguered states, either by the beleaguered states themselves or with the assistance of other states.

One, of course, may find plausible arguments to deny that the law is contradictory. For instance, the development of the principles of self-determination and human rights can be used to challenge the legality of any assistance to any state confronted with a movement within its borders. But the fallacy in any such argument is self-evident. The fact is that the beleaguered states and those assisting them do not see the strugglers as liberation fighters but as subversives, terrorists, or rebels. To expose the paradox by illustration, one need mention only the struggles in El Salvador and Nicaragua. How do states visualize the contras in the two countries? Obviously, to each of the beleaguered governments the issue is nothing else than a conflict between an established government and a bunch of terrorists or rebels. Can governments be condemned for suppressing rebels and terrorists? Obviously not.

Nor is the picture different if perceived from the point of view of states that assist other states. Such states can claim legal support for their assistance from treaty provisions or even from friendly relations between themselves and others. Perjorative terms like those used by the beleaguered authorities are also useful. A good example is the U.S. government's support of the incumbent regime against the El Salvadoran "rebels." In the Nicaraguan situation the chips are the same but the players are labeled differently. Thus the supporters and the opponents of the government and "rebels" in El Salvador, respectively, become opponents and supporters of the government and "rebels" in Nicaragua. The records reveal similar situations again and again. The Nigerian crisis, the conflict in the Horn of Africa, the conflict in Angola, the unfortunate situation in Afghanistan, and even the brutal war between the Bengalis and their East Pakistani compatriots—all demonstrate how elusive the concept of liberty is, especially as the international system is yet to devise an objective definition for it.

One inference to draw from the so-called newly created rights for liberation movements, then, is that the liberation movements are probably put into a worse state than their counterparts of the past. In the past when any movement could claim no legitimacy except through its success, any group of people getting up to fight any system voluntarily assumed the risk and had itself to blame if it failed to succeed. But now that the encouragement to fight for liberty makes it doubtful whether liberation movements deserve all the credit for their success, the law seems to have created false hopes that put the strugglers into a worse situation: After starting their struggles, they are left in the cold to fight for themselves, or are at best encouraged by words while they perish under the unmatched force of their adversaries. One needs only recall that regardless of how noble the cause of any liberation movement is, the international community does not attempt to rescue any liberation fighter who is caught, maltreated under inhuman conditions, and tried and "executed" for treason or terrorism by their states. The best the system does for them is to call for the application of the laws of war to give them a war prisoner's status—a stance that in practice does not benefit the liberation movements in any way.

Since one of the factors occasioning the inception of the present law of liberation is the need to preserve international peace and security, and since that peace and security is the most important value cherished by the international community, we should evaluate the present status of liberation movements by studying how they promote or impede the preservation of the peace.

The interrelatedness of liberty and peace is unquestionable. It was no accident that in all the steps leading to the U.N. Charter—from the Inter-Allied Declaration, the Atlantic Charter, the Declaration by United Nations, the Moscow and Teheran conferences, and the Dumbarton Oaks and Yalta conferences to the San Francisco conference—the causes of freedom and peace were bracketed together. In the Inter-Allied Declaration of June 1941, the equation reads: "the only true basis of enduring peace is the willing co-operation of free peoples in a world in which, relieved of menace and aggression, all may enjoy economic and social security." The participants then made the commitment "to work together to this end." But we must ask: If the international community believes in freedom and sees it as the safest route to its cherished destination—peace—why is it apparently more interested in pursuing liberty and a fortiori peace by words rather than deeds? This question is important, because by making liberation movements the exceptions to the provisions against the use of force and intervention while at the same time leaving states with the freedom to determine what is liberationist, the system only provides opportunities for the formation of the sort of alliances and counteralliances that in the past have always threatened world peace. Ironically, the peace is perhaps even more endangered than it was in the past, when there were no false hopes that people could be assisted in their fight for the cause of liberty.

But the question of how to determine what constitutes a genuine liberation movement is not our only problem, as we evaluate the significance of liberation movements vis à vis the present commitment to preserve global peace and security. As a regime made of a multiplicity of rules and institutions with little or no indication as to how one rule should be chosen over the other, the international system cannot provide easy, let alone conclusive, answers to issues posed by liberation movements. Nor does its attitude to particular cases enhance the credibility of its laws relating to liberation. The tongue-in-cheek approach of the United Nations to the Congo crisis, its colorless stance in the Bengali situation, its failure to invoke its extensive powers to bring the recalcitrant apartheid authorities to justice, its near insignificance in Vietnam, the Falklands, the Spanish Sahara, East Timor, and Afghanistan, or its failure even to assess what the cause of liberty was in Grenada and Nigeria—all raise important questions about the seriousness of the international commitment to preserve the peace by promoting the cause of liberty. It is obvious, then, that unless the international community devises a more credible system to pursue its commitment to liberty objectively and by means other than words, not only will its credibility be in serious question, but the peace will be greatly jeopardized.

How could the international system solve the problem? Let us consider a few possibilities.

The first issue is how to define liberty and a fortiori liberation movements collectively, rather than allow the defining to be done unilaterally by the individual states. Related to this is how to make the laws more precise and consistent with one another. Since the international system is fortunate to have a body representing the whole community, the United Nations, it is possible to use the U.N. machinery to do this work. It is conceded that solutions to issues like these have always proven elusive. The difficulty of defining aggression until the ambiguous definition in Resolution 3313 was accomplished is but one example of the problem. Another difficulty, encountered at the Hostages Convention, is whether liberation movements could be treated as terroristic if they resort to certain means. But these problems should not be a reason for the system to be inactive and irresponsible about its commitments. The system operates by law, and its credibility therefore lies mainly on its ability to give meaning to its laws by making its subjects comply with its behests. If it is unable to do this merely because of difficulties with regulating the conduct of its subjects, its usefulness would indeed, be questionable. It is necessary, then, for the United Nations to be firm: It should employ the decision-making process, namely, inviting all members and experts alike to participate in debates on some of the pressing issues and taking decisions by a designated formula, making it clear that whatever decision is made is final.

Attention should be given also to how rules are ascertained and applied. Although it is reasonable to retain the right of states to construe norms unilaterally, it is important to reduce that right by encouraging greater reliance on the collective process and less on the resources of the individual states. One possible way of doing this is by ruling that if a state makes a unilateral determination of any issue and is later found to have acted wrongly, it be held accountable and at least made to repair the wrong. The political and judicial organs of the United Nations can have an important role in this exercise. Under the present arrangement the International Court can exercise jurisdiction over states only when they consent; how can the role of the Court be made stronger? If the suggestion to make states accountable for their acts was followed, states would be more cautious and at least much more inclined to precede their actions by declaratory judgments of the court.

But perhaps the most practical way of using the international judicial process is to employ the "Step by Step Acceptance of the Jurisdiction of the International Court of Justice" along the lines suggested by Sohn. Since this approach presupposes that the court cannot exercise jurisdiction except with the consent of the parties before it, there may, of course, be skepticism as to whether it does not perpetuate the dilemma it is supposed to solve, especially considering that the court would not assume jurisdiction over cases in which consent was withheld. But the proposal is not entirely useless. By its "carrot and stick" approach, not only does it accord with the all-important tradition of consensual basis of jurisdiction, but it encourages states to give up the apprehension that their sovereignty would be encroached upon if they consent to jurisdiction. Under piece-by-piece acceptance of jurisdiction, the proposition invites states to taste international adjudication on nonpolitical matters on which they accord jurisdiction; the hope is that after being convinced that jurisdiction is not all that erosive of their rights, they will thereby be encouraged to use the international judicial machinery more frequently.

Of course, the problem may still continue insofar as a state that accepts jurisdiction can add reservations to preclude the court from acting on some cases. Yet, by the piece-by-piece accession to the court's jurisdiction, states that might be apprehensive about the court's intrusion may, by encouragement from the results of others' experiences, become more open to using the adjudicatory processes instead of resources that might threaten the peace.

But the extension of the role of the court cannot have much credibility unless it entails greater coordination between that body and the political organs of the United Nations. Although the world community might reconsider the question as to whether the court should have the power to construe norms conclusively, perhaps the easier method would be to revise the present law that advisory opinions are not automatically binding on anyone, including even the body that requests the court to render them. Since the decision to put an issue before the court presupposes that the requesting body is not only incapable of reaching a decision but has faith in the court to handle the matter expeditiously, the nonbindingness of the court's advisory opinion should be the exception rather than the rule. The only instance where a requesting body can be justified in disregarding an advisory opinion is if the opinion is patently outrageous or seriously violates the rules of natural justice, particularly the *nemo judex* rule. If opinions of experts like the distinguished judges of the International Court should continue to be treated lightly, not only will the court be brought to disrepute by the incessant divergence from its opinions, but its credibility will be greatly reduced, thereby also discouraging states from using the peaceful process to settle their disputes.

The usefulness of precision and of coherence among rules in enhancing the credibility of any legal system cannot be overemphasized. But the mere precision and comprehensiveness of rules cannot guarantee the effectiveness of a system. Notwithstanding the unanimity with which the U.N. Declaration on Friendly Relations was adopted, its supposedly most authoritative provisions have done little to promote conclusive determination of issues, let alone greater observance of the laws.

It is obvious, then, that in addition to making the rules more definite and devising means of solving issues conclusively, ways should be explored to achieve greater compliance with the rules. States should be made to support rules more by deeds than by words. Since by their predisposition to preserve their sovereignties the states normally put national interest ahead of international norms, it may be difficult to imagine how this can be done. Yet, a few suggestions are worth considering. First, there can be comprehensive efforts by the international system to disseminate information about the cause of liberty and how valuable it is for the peace. By this exercise, governments can be made to join together to put pressure on those who have little regard for the cause of liberty. It is conceded, of course, that depending on how governments value their friendship and interest with others, the so-called pressure may be ineffective. However, it is clear from some recent cases, notably developments relating to the apartheid system in Pretoria, that if people are fully cognizant of the offenses committed by a regime, even the strongest governments can be induced by public opinion to issue threats to isolate those disregarding the cause of liberty. A case in point is the threat by President Ronald Reagan, who faced with intense pressure from the well-informed American public about the situation in South Africa, had no other choice than to be tough on the Pretoria regime. Pretoria's immediate response, to eradicate some of the harsh laws of the apartheid system—a move culminating in the release of Nelson Mandela and the concomitant arrangement for negotiation between him and South African Prime Minister De Klerk—is a strong indication of how useful the indirect process of disseminating information can be in promoting compliance with the laws relating to liberty.

Another way of using the information media is to publicize the laws of war and their values. Most of the conflicts in the present system are pursued in developing countries by irregular armies who, by the randomness of their recruitment, lack knowledge of the law and its values; such combatants often display a gross disregard of the laws of war. The carnage against the U.N. force, particularly of the Ghanaian soldiers in the Congo operation, exemplifies this problem. Not only would extensive use of the media to expose people to the values of the laws of war encourage combatants to use their conscience and perhaps fight in less inhuman ways, but it would also promote post-war reconciliation of combatants.

Finally, more direct is the use of coercive measures to enforce compliance with the established law. If recourse to force by individual states is really to be reduced, collective means of enforcing the law and redressing wrongful acts should be resorted to. Presently, there are two arrangements for law enforcement by collective means. These are the U.N. security measures under chapter

VII of the Charter and measures that may be taken by regional bodies under chapter VI.

Given the many technicalities surrounding coercive intervention by the United Nations, notably, the occasional use of the veto and the requirement that intervention cannot take place until there is a threat to or breach of the peace, it is tempting to give preference to the regional processes. This alternative seems all the more reasonable, considering that the regional bodies are often more familiar with the problems in their regions. But regional processes are not the better choice. First, a regional body like the O.A.U. is unable to mobilize force to combat a problem like that in South Africa. Moreover, in many cases— notably the partial position of the O.A.U. in the Nigerian conflict, the manipulation of the O.A.S. by the United States in the case of the Dominican Republic, and the Soviet's preemption of its commitment to the Warsaw Pact by the so-called Brezhnev Doctrine—demonstrate how seriously the credibility of any regional intervention can be questioned if that course is taken to enforce the present law relating to liberty and the peace.

On the other hand, the advantages of using the U.N. machinery are enormous. Thanks to the "Uniting for Peace" resolution, the veto cannot pose the difficulty it once did, in the period before the Korean crisis. Of course, the U.N. system may not always be blessed with an abstention of a superpower that enables it to invoke the resolution. But it is possible for the United Nations to trim that technicality if it proves to be an impediment to keeping the peace. What makes the use of the U.N. machinery even more attractive is that, apart from the credibility it enjoys by virtue of its universality, it is difficult for any state to counter-intervene against the United Nations. The Korean crisis clearly illustrates this advantage. Since the question of what constitutes intervention and counterintervention and that of how to determine the legitimacy of any faction is elusive, particularly in view of the Cold War context in which that case erupted, it is impossible to say what would have happened if either of the two interested superpowers, the United States and the Soviets, had intervened in favor of its allies. Yet when the United Nations decided to send a United States–led force under the U.N. flag, all the Soviets could do was to sit and shout. Similarly, in the Congo situation where states were ideologically split on whether Lumumba should be assisted by the U.N. force, the pro-Western position of the United Nations could only be criticized by the supporters of the Communist bloc. Finally, even in the ongoing Persian Gulf conflict where pro-Iraqi countries such as Lybia and Yemen are very critical of the U.S. mobilization of troops in the area, arch enemies of the United States like Qaddafi have indicated clearly that they will send out troops against Iraq if that is requested by the U.N.

The few U.N. operations make it clear, then, that the U.N. machinery is the best means by which coercive intervention can be pursued to promote liberty and the peace. Given the difficulties surrrounding some of the cases—for example, the serious financial problems arising from the Congo situation—it is of course possible to be skeptical about whether the intervention of the United Nations is very useful. A careful study of the situation, especially by matching the value of liberty and the peace against the possible financial problems, reduces that skepticism to insignificance. But even if the financial problems were serious, it is still obvious that if an intervention is well planned and launched at the nascent stages of a conflict, when superpower interests are yet to develop fully, the crisis will be easier to avoid. The final question, then, is how the United Nations can be developed to handle all the numerous cases arising around the globe. One way would be to establish subsidiaries of the United Nations in all the different parts of the world and entrust them with the duty of monitoring cases and possibly sending in emergency troops to observe and keep conflicts from escalating.

Liberation struggles thus are of practical value to the contemporary international system. Although the system has been unable to provide full answers to questions arising from them, or to assist the strugglers in the way it professes to do, only extreme cynicism can cause one to question the seriousness of the international commitment to the cause of liberty. The record is clear—from those liberated from colonialism, to the United Nations' participation in the creation of states, notably Israel, or even to its role in determining how people who do not want to be part of nascent states should be integrated into others of their choice—it is impossible to downplay the U.N. commitment of the present system to liberty. Admittedly, the system has played little role in difficult conflicts like those in Nigeria and Pakistan. Nor has it done much for the displaced Palestinians. As a dynamic system faced with growing problems, shortcomings like these are to be expected. The system must face its challenges squarely and with vigilance. It is hoped that a development on the lines suggested in this book will do much to obviate some of the problems undermining the efficiency and credibility of the present international system.

Notes

ABBREVIATIONS

A.C.	Appeal Cases
AKRON L. REV.	Akron Law Review
AM. J.I.L.	American Journal of International Law
AM. POL. SCI. REV.	American Political Science Review
B.Y.B.I.L.	British Year Book of International Law
CAN. Y.B.I.L.	Canadian Year Book of International Law
C.C.	Current Cases (Ghana)
C.L.P.	Current Legal Problems
COLUM. J. TRANSNAT'L L.	Columbia Journal of Transnational Law
COLUM. L. REV.	Columbia Law Review
DEN. J.I.L.	Denver Journal of International Law and Policy
DUKE L.J.	Duke University Law Journal
E. AFR. L. REV.	East African Law Review
E. AFR. PROV. L. REP.	East African Provinces Law Report
FOREIGN AFF.	Foreign Affairs
G.L. REP.	Ghana Law Reports
GA. J.I.C.L.	Georgia Journal of International and Comparative Law
G.Y.B.I.L.	German Year Book of International Law
HARV. INT'L L.J.	Harvard International Law Journal
HARV. INT'L REV.	Harvard International Review
HARV. L. REV.	Harvard Law Review
INDIAN J.I.L.	Indian Journal of International Law
INT'L AFF.	International Affairs
INT'L & COMP. L.Q.	International and Comparative Law Quarterly
INT'L L.M.	International Legal Materials
INT'L ORG.	International Organizations
IS. L. REV.	Israel Law Review
IS. Y.B.I.L.	Israel Year Book of International Law

J.I.L.E.	Journal of International Law and Economics
J.I.L.P.	Journal of International Law and Policy
LAW & CONTEMP. PROBS.	Law and Contemporary Problems
L.N.T.S.	Law of Nations Treaty Series
L.Q.R.	Law Quarterly Review
NETH. Y.B.I.L.	Netherlands Year Book of International Law
NIG. L.J.	Nigeria Law Journal
N.L.R.	Netherlands Law Review
N.Y.U.J.I.L.P.	New York University Journal of International Law and Politics
PROC. A.S.I.L.	Proceedings of the American Society of International Law
REV. G.L.	Review of Ghana Law
R.I.A.A.	Reports of International Arbitral Awards
S.A.	South African Reports
S.A.J.I.L.	South African Journal of International Law
S.A.L.J.	South African Law Journal
S.J.I.S.	Stanford Journal of International Studies
TEXAS INT'L L.J.	Texas International Law Journal
TOWSON S.J.I.L.	Towson State Journal of International Law
U.G.L.J.	University of Ghana Law Journal
W.N.L.R.	Western Nigeria Law Reports
Y.B. INT'L L.C.	Yearbook of the International Law Commission
Y.L.R.	Yale Law Review
ZAMBIA L.J.	Zambia Law Journal

CHAPTER 1

1. First, there is the issue of whether liberation struggles are international conflicts—a question on which opinions vary widely. Similarly, authorities do not seem to agree on what constitutes a liberation movement. Some, notably Ronzitti, limit the subject to anticolonial cases; others, like Cassese and Tyner, extend it to noncolonial cases. Authorities like Baxter see only a part of the laws of war—those embodied in common article 3 of the Geneva Conventions of 1949—as applicable to most liberation movements; others, notably Abi-Saab, maintain that the entirety of the laws of war may apply to any liberation movement. For full appreciation of the controversy, see Tyner, *Wars of National Liberation in Africa and Palestine: Self-Determination for Peoples or for Territories*, 5 YALE STUDIES IN WORLD PUBLIC ORDER, 235–49 (1979); Ronzitti, *Wars of National Liberation—A Legal Definition*, 1 ITALIAN Y.B.I.L. 192–97 (1975); Abi-Saab, *Wars of National Liberation and the Laws of War*, 3 ANNALES D'ETUDES INTERNATIONALES 93, 94–116 (1972); Baxter, *Humanitarian Law or Humanitarian Politics? The 1974 Diplomatic Conference on Humanitarian Law*, 16 HARV. INT'L L.J. 1, 11–15 (1975); Cassese, *The Status of Rebels Under the 1977 Geneva Protocol on Non-International Armed Conflicts*, 30 INT'L & COMP. L.Q. 416, 417 (1980).

2. See the U.N. CHARTER, arts. 2(4) and 51. Reprinted in L. SOHN, BASIC DOCUMENTS OF THE UNITED NATIONS 1 (2d ed. 1956).

3. Baxter, *The Geneva Convention of 1949 and Wars of National Liberation*, 56 RIVISTA DI DIRITTO INTERNAZIONALE 193, 195 (1974).

4. Tyner, supra note 1, at 236.

5. In the 1974 Geneva Diplomatic Conference, the U.S. representative, for instance, urged that the Provisional Revolutionary Government (P.R.G.) of South Vietnam could not be considered "a national liberation movement, since its activities were not directed against a colonial power." See Dip. Conf. 1974 CDDH/SR.5, at 43, cited in Ronzitti, supra note 1, at 197. See also Dugard, *The Organization of African Unity and Colonialism: An Inquiry into the Plea of Self-Defence as a Justification for the use of Force in the Eradication of Colonialism*, 16 INT'L & COMP. L.Q. 157, 157–58 (1967).

6. Baxter, supra note 3, at 193. See also Abi-Saab, supra note 1, at 93, n. 1, and Schachter, *The United Nations and Internal Conflict*, in LAW AND CIVIL WAR IN THE MODERN WORLD 401, 406–07 (E. Moore ed. 1974).

7. See the U.N. CHARTER, arts. 1, paras. 2 and 55, and Res. 2625:

All peoples have the right freely to determine without external interference, their political status and to pursue their economic, social, and cultural development, and every State has the duty to respect this right in accordance with the provisions of the Charter. . . . Nothing in the foregoing shall be construed as authorizing or encouraging any action which would dismember or impair . . . the territorial integrity or political unity of . . . States conducting themselves in compliance with the principle of equal rights and self-determination of peoples . . . possessed of a government representing the whole people belonging to the territory without distinction as to race, creed, or color.

Declaration on Principles of International Law Concerning Friendly Relations and Co-Operation Among States in Accordance With the Charter of the U.N., G.A. Res. 2625, 25 U.N. GAOR Supp. (28) at 122, U.N. Doc. A/8028 (1970).

8. Cassese, supra note 1, at 417.

9. See the Protocol Additional to the Geneva Conventions of August 12, 1949, and Relating to the Protection of Victims of International Armed Conflicts, (Protocol I) (1977), reprinted in 72 AM. J.I.L. 457, at 458 (1978). Emphasis added.

10. G.A. Res. 1514, 15 U.N. GAOR Supp. (16) at 66, U.N. Doc. A/4684 (1960).

11. Res. 2625, supra note 7.

12. It was adopted by experts specifically entrusted with the responsibility of finding the meaning of certain terms in the Charter—terms that include the principle of self-determination. The committee that dealt with the issue adopted the proposals of the experts unanimously. And when the document was brought before the General Assembly, it was adopted by acclamation. See Rosenstock, *The Declaration of Principles of International Law Concerning Friendly Relations: A Survey*, in 65 AM. J.I.L. 712 (1971); Johnson, *Toward Self Determination—A Reappraisal as Reflected in the Declaration on Friendly Relations*, 3 GA. J.I.C.L. 145 (1973).

13. Although doubts may exist as to whether the two declarations are treaties, there will be no offense to the provisions of the Vienna Convention on the Law of Treaties, whose article 30 provides that a later treaty should have priority over an earlier one that does not fully agree with it. It is arguable, of course, that some difficulty would be encountered in reconciling this construction with the articles' express deference to the U.N. Charter's supremacy clause—article 103. Yet considering that the Declaration on Friendly Relations was adopted as the most authoritative interpretation of the Charter and by a committee specifically set up by the organ entrusted with the responsibility to initiate studies for progressive development of the law, it is suggested that any such problem would be tenuous at best. See the VIENNA CONVENTION ON THE LAW OF TREATIES, art. 30, U.N. Doc. A/CONF. 39/27 (1969).

14. It is important to note that the Palestinian-Israeli conflict has been bracketed with the anticolonial cases in some U.N. resolutions. It may thus not be entirely inappropriate to treat them also as colonial cases. See U.N. Res. 2787, 26 U.N. GAOR Supp. (29) at 16, U.N. Doc. A/8429 (1972).

15. This list is adopted merely for this preliminary analysis; it is not a complete definition of liberation movements. For more information, see infra Chapter 7.

16. Leiser, *Terrorism, Guerilla Warfare and International Morality*, 12 S.J.I.S. 39, 47–48 (1977).

17. J. LEE, AFRICAN ARMIES AND CIVIL ORDER 184 (1969 ed.).

18. Zolberg, *The Military Decade in Africa*, 25 WORLD POLITICS 309, 319 (1972–73).

19. Infra, this chapter, "Complications in Defining Liberation Movements."

20. Cohen, *Legal Problems Arising From the Dissolution of the Mali Federation*, 36 B.Y.B.I.L. 375 (1960). On the Malaysian Federation, see 15 KEESING'S CONTEMPORARY ARCHIVES (1965–66) 20891 (Aug. 7–14, 1965).

21. Abu-Lughod, *Unconditional Warfare and International Politics*, in TERRORISM AND POLITICAL CRIMES IN INTERNATIONAL LAW, 67 PROC. A.S.I.L. 100, 102 (1973).

22. See the U.N. CHARTER arts. 2(3) and 2(4).

23. I. Blishchenko, however, refers to the provision on the use of force as one that is expressed with the "utmost clarity." See Blishchenko, *The Use of Force in International Relations and the Role of Prohibition of Certain Weapons*, 60 CURRENT PROBLEMS OF INTERNATIONAL LAW 157, 161 (A. Cassese ed. 1975). For more detailed discussion of the confusion with the law, see infra Chapter 10.

24. It reads in part: "Nothing in the present Charter shall impair the inherent right of individual or collective self-defense if an armed attack occurs against a Member of the United Nations, until the Security Council has taken measures necessary to maintain international peace and security." U.N. CHARTER art. 51.

25. See infra Chapter 10.

26. See 22 TRIAL OF MAJOR WAR CRIMINALS BEFORE THE INTERNATIONAL MILITARY TRIBUNAL, PROCEEDINGS 411, 427–63 (1948), cited in INTERNATIONAL LAW IN A CHANGING WORLD: CASES DOCUMENTS AND READINGS 337–38 (E. Collins, Jr., ed. 1970).

27. In the South-West African Peoples' struggles against the South African government, this argument has been echoed on several occasions. One notable instance was the International Conference on Namibia and Human Rights, where the South-West

Africa People's Organization (S.W.A.P.O.) traced the illegality of the South African overlordship back to the beginning of the Namibian colonial situation. Although the argument is supported overwhelmingly by many countries, there are questions as to its validity. First, it is not clear whether the illegality is traced to the first time Namibia was colonized—its colonial history from the time when it was under the German overlordship—or merely from the time it was placed under the South African mandate. It is suggested that unless some qualification is added, their argument cannot be right because, apart from the transformation of the German overlordship to that of South Africa—a transformation effected legitimately under the League system—there is no connection between the initial "illegal" occupation and the arrangement that put the territory under the South African administration. Thus the only period for which the South African overlordship can be considered illegal is that dating from the United Nations' termination of the mandate. For the S.W.A.P.O. statement, see the International Conference on Namibia and Human Rights, CONF. DAKAR (1976) at 9 (published by the International Institute of Human Rights, Strasbourg, 1976), quoted in T. Kuhn, Terrorism in International Law 86, January 1980 (unpublished S.J.D. thesis located in Harvard Law Library).

28. See Wright, *The Goa Incident*, 56 AM. J.I.L. 617, 622 (1962).

29. W. HALL, INTERNATIONAL LAW 143 (8th ed.). See also J. BRIERLY, THE LAW OF NATIONS 167–70 (6th ed. 1963); cf. the Indian commissioner's ruling in the Ladakh boundary case, 1 INDIAN J.I.L. 545 (1961), cited in Wright, supra note 28, at 622–23.

30. See the *Caroline* case, 4 THE WORKS OF DANIEL WEBSTER 261 (1851), cited in E. COLLINS, supra note 26, at 336.

31. An otherwise critical resolution of the Security Council was prevented from passing by a Soviet veto. See Wright, supra note 28, at 617.

32. See infra Chapter 9.

33. See I. BROWNLIE, INTERNATIONAL LAW AND THE USE OF FORCE BY STATES 403–23 (1963).

34. *Id.* at 412.

35. See Abu-Lughod, supra note 21, at 103.

36. Infra, Chapters 10, 11.

37. J. CRAWFORD, THE CREATION OF STATES IN INTERNATIONAL LAW 108–09 (1979).

38. Dugard, supra note 5, at 168–75; T. KUHN, supra note 27, at 84; Schwebel, *Wars of Liberation as Fought in U.N. Organs*, in E. MOORE, supra note 6, 447 at 449–51.

39. J. BRIERLY, supra note 29, at 402.

40. See Milte, *Extradition and the Terrorist*, 11 AUSTRALIAN AND NEW ZEALAND JOURNAL OF CRIMINOLOGY 89, 92 (1978).

41. Recently there have been several efforts to curb the incidence of terrorism. Among the most crucial is the abolition or at least the circumscription of the "political offenses" rule, which, in most extradition treaties, is the main exception to the *aut dedere aut punire* concept. See the proceedings of the International Conference on the Repression of Terrorism, League of Nations Doc. C.94.M.47.1938.V, 49, 49–50 (a938.V.3), Annex 1, at 1 (1938).

42. Baxter, supra note 3. As Connor O'Brien has aptly stated: "in such struggles each side sees itself as upholding the cause of liberty, but the idea of liberty is differently defined by each side—with a varying degree of precision and intensity." O'Brien, *International Security and Terrorism*, 2 INTERNATIONAL SECURITY 56, at 56 (1977–78).

43. Falk, *The Beirut Raid and the International Law of Retaliation*, 63 AM. J.I.L. 415, 420–22 (1969).

44. See Blum, *The Beirut Raid and the International Double Standard: A Reply to Professor Richard A. Falk*, 64 AM. J.I.L. 73, 74–75 (1970).

45. A. RENEGARD, INTERNATIONAL TERRORISM IN A LEGAL CONTEXT 11 (1978).

46. Haradsveit, *Role of International Terrorism in the Middle East Conflict and Its Implications for Conflict Resolution*, in TERRORISM AND WORLD SECURITY 93, at 93 (D. Carlton and C. Schaeff eds. 1975). See also B. JENKINS, INTERNATIONAL TERRORISM: A NEW MODE OF CONFLICT 2 (1975).

47. See the statement by the Tanzanian delegate. Cited in Verwey, *The International Hostages Convention and National Liberation Movements*, 75 AM. J.I.L. 69, 70–71.

48. According to them, "no goal or cause was so noble that it would justify all possible means." See, particularly, the statement by the U.S. delegate, U.N. Doc. A/32[*sic*]/39, at 53, cited in Verwey, supra note 47, at 74–75 (1981). For similar statements, see those of the French, the Dutch, and the British, *id*.

49. Webster defines it as a "method of government by inspiring terror by acts of brutality and savagery." WEBSTER DICTIONARY AND HOME REFERENCE LIBRARY (international ed. 1963). Paust defines it as "a form of violent strategy used to alter the freedom of choice of others." Paust, *Response to Terrorism: A Prologue to Decision Concerning Private Measures of Sanction*, 12 S.J.I.S. 39, at 39 (1977). According to Dinstein terrorism is the "use of violence with an emphasis on the three a's: Assassination, assault and arson." Dinstein, *Terrorism and Wars of Liberation as Applied to the Arab-Israeli Conflict: An Israeli Perspective*, 3 Is. Y.B.I.L. 78, 85 (1973). And Leiser defines it as "any organized set of acts of violence designed to create an atmosphere of despair or fear, to shake the faith of ordinary citizens in their government and its representatives, to destroy their structure of authority which normally stands for security or to reinforce and perpetuate a governmental regime whose support is shaky." Leiser, *Terrorism, Guerilla Warfare and International Morality*, 12 S.J.I.S. 39, 39 (1977).

50. The Final Document: Conclusions and Recommendations from the Conference on Terrorism and Political Crimes, held in Syracuse, Italy, June 4–16, 1973, in INTERNATIONAL TERRORISM AND POLITICAL CRIMES 14 (M. Bassiouni ed. 1975).

51. See the definition given at the Convention for the Prevention and Punishment of Terrorism of 1937, cited in Verwey, supra note 47, particularly art. 1, para. 2. But see the Convention to Prevent and Punish Acts of Terrorism Taking the Form of Crimes Against Persons and Related Extortion that are of International Significance, O.A.S. Doc. AG/88 Rev. 1, Feb. 2, 1971. Reprinted in 10 INT'L L.M. 255.

52. The term, first used during the Reign of Terror in the French Revolution, referred to the intimidating practices of the government between 1789 and 1794. Frank & Lockwood, *Preliminary Thoughts Toward an International Convention on Terrorism*, 68 AM. J.I.L. 69, 73 (1974).

53. See, e.g., the argument of the Nigerian delegate. According to him, "parts of the African continent were in a stage of siege, and whole peoples were being held hostage, whether they knew it or not." Verwey, supra note 47, at 70.

54. *Id.* at 70. See also the observations to the Ad Hoc Committee on International Terrorism submitted by the Syrian Arab Republic, U.N. Doc. A/AC. 160/1, at 36 (1973); the statement of the Yemen Arab Republic, U.N. Doc. A/AC. 160/1, Add. 1 at 29 (1973); and the draft proposal submitted to the subcommittee by the nonaligned group in the Ad Hoc Committee, U.N. Doc. A/AC. 1690/L.3/ Add. 1 and Corr. 1 (1973).

55. See Verwey, supra note 47, at 70–72.

56. Abu-Lughod, supra note 21, at 100.

57. See U.N. Doc. A/AC.160 /L.3 /Add. 1. and Corr. 1.

58. Jackson, *Terrorism as a Weapon in International Politics*, in INTERNATIONAL TERRORISM: CHALLENGE AND REPORTS, PROC. OF THE JERUSALEM CONFERENCE ON INTERNATIONAL TERRORISM 33, 36 (B. Netanyanu ed. 1975).

59. Lador-Lederer, *A Legal Approach to International Terrorism*, 9 Is. L. REV. 194, 200 (1974).

60. Frank & Lockwood, supra note 52, at 80.

61. Jenkins, *International Terrorism: A New Mode of Conflict*, in 17 SURVIVAL 158, 160 (1975).

62. Slomanson, *I.C.J. Damages: Tort Remedy for Failure to Punish or Extradite International Terrorists*, 5 CALIFORNIA WESTERN INT'L L.J. 121, 121–23 (1974–75).

63. Beres, *International Terrorism and World Order: The Nuclear Threat*, 12 S.A.J.I.L. 131, 135 (1977).

64. Green, *International Terrorism and Its Control*, 21 CHITTY'S LAW JOURNAL, 289, 294 (1973).

65. For full appreciation of the confusion here, see Knisbacher, *The Entebbe Operation: A Legal Analysis of Israel's Rescue Action*, 12 J.I.L.E. 57, at 68–70 (1977).

66. Frank & Lockwood, supra note 52, at 78–80.

67. 27 U.N. GAOR Supp. (10), at 94, U.N. Doc. A/8710/Rev. 1 (1972).

68. *Id.* at 95.

69. O.A.S. Off. Records, Ser. G, CP/Doc. 54/70 Rev. 1 (1970); 65 AM. J.I.L. 898 (1971). Emphasis added.

70. Paust, *Selected Terrorism Claims Arising from the Arab-Israeli Conflict*, 7 AKRON L. REV. 404, 405 (1974).

71. Nwogugu, *The Nigerian Civil War: A Case Study in the Law of War*, 14 INDIAN J.I.L. 13, 17–27 (1974).

72. Forsythe, *Legal Management of Internal War: The 1977 Protocol on Non-International Armed Conflict*, 72 AM. J.I.L. 272, 288 (1978).

73. It reads in part: "an impartial humanitarian body, such as the International Committee of the Red Cross *may offer* its services to the parties to the Conflict." See common article 3 to the 1949 Geneva Convention, 75 U.N.T.S. 85 (1950). Emphasis added.

74. Rusk, *The Control of Force in International Law*, 1 THE VIETNAM WAR AND INTERNATIONAL LAW 338 (R. Falk ed. 1968), cited in E. Firmage, *National Liberation and the Third World*, in E. MOORE, supra note 6, at 309 n. 15.

75. Higgins, *Internal War and International Law*, 3 FUTURE OF INTERNATIONAL LEGAL ORDER 81, 105 (1971).

76. B. SCHWARTZ, COMMUNISM AND CHINA: IDEOLOGY IN FLUX 191 (1968).

77. STALIN, THE FOUNDATIONS OF LENINISM (1924), quoted in F. SCHALTEN: COMMUNISM IN AFRICA 66 (1966).

78. See Tyner, supra note 1, at 243.

79. This doctrine was enunciated on March 12, 1947, by the United States "to support free people who are resisting attempted subjugation by armed minorities or outside pressures." See L. SOHN, CASES ON UNITED NATIONS LAW 347 (2d ed. 1967).

80. Korolyov, *El Salvador: The "Hot Spot" in Latin America*, INT'L AFF. 58 (Moscow 1981). See also Grachyov, *Extremism and Terrorism in the Service of World Reaction*, in *id.*, at 67–74.

81. Friedman, *Intervention in Civil War and the Role of International Law*, PROC. A.S.I.L. (59th mtg.) 67, 67–70 (1965). But see the Spanish Question wherein it was urged that the Franco government could not be admitted to the United Nations because it had been helped into power by the Axis powers. See L. SOHN, supra note 79, at 291.

82. Art. 38(b) of the I.C.J. Statute lists "international custom, as evidence of a general practice accepted as law" as one of the sources of law to be considered by the I.C.J. in its determination of issues brought before it. See THE STATUTE OF THE INTERNATIONAL COURT OF JUSTICE (I.C.J.), art. 38, para. (b) 59 STAT. 1055, T.S. 993, 3 BEVANS 1179, reprinted in L. SOHN, supra note 2, at 221, 228.

83. Falk, *Janus Tormented: The International Law of Internal War*, INTERNATIONAL ASPECTS OF CIVIL STRIFE 185, 197–203 (J. Rosenau ed. 1964). See also, Dhokalia, *Civil Wars and International Law*, 11 INDIAN J.I.L. 219, 226 (1971).

84. L. KOTZSCH, THE CONCEPT OF WAR IN CONTEMPORARY HISTORY AND INTERNATIONAL LAW 230 (Geneva 1956). See also H. LAUTERPACHT, RECOGNITION IN INTERNATIONAL LAW 240 (1947).

85. Dhokalia, supra note 83, at 225–26.

86. See the Ambrose Light case, C. FENWICK, CASES ON INTERNATIONAL LAW 362 (1935).

87. See Falk, supra note 83, at 198; Lauterpacht, *Revolutionary Activities by Private Persons against Foreign States*, 22 AM. J.I.L. 105–30 (1928).

88. Falk, supra note 83, at 205–06; H. LAUTERPACHT, supra note 84, at 176; Dhokalia, supra note 83, at 226–27.

89. Higgins, *International Law and Civil Conflict*, in INTERNATIONAL REGULATION OF CIVIL WAR 169, 170 (E. Luard ed. 1972).

90. H. LAUTERPACHT, supra note 84, at 276–77.

CHAPTER 2

1. The present international system is premised on "sovereign equality of states," and (full) membership in the United Nations is open solely to states. U.N. CHARTER arts. 2, para. 1, and 4, para. 1. See also art. 2, para. 7.

2. U. UMOZURIKE, INTERNATIONAL LAW AND COLONIALISM IN AFRICA 17–38 (1979); Nawaz, *Colonies, Self-Government and the United Nations*, 11 INDIAN Y.B. INT'L AFF. 3, 4–7 (1962).

3. The Dutch used it in Indonesia; the Portuguese used it in Angola, Guinea Bissau, and Mozambique; the Spaniards used it in the Spanish Sahara; and the French used it in Algeria. See Mushkat, *The Process of African Decolonization* 6 INDIAN J.I.L. 483, 500 (1966). For the Dutch position in Indonesia, see L. SOHN, CASES ON UNITED NATIONS LAW 352–70 (1967).

4. It reads in part: "The territory of a colony or other Non-Self-Governing Territory has, under the Charter of the United Nations, a status separate and distinct from the territory of the State administering it." G.A. Res. 2625, 25 GAOR Supp. (28) at 121, U.N. Doc. A/8028 (1970).

5. It provides that "any attempt aimed at the partial or total disruption of the national unity and the territorial integrity of a country is incompatible with the purposes and principles of the Charter of the United Nations." G.A. Res. 1514, 15 GAOR Supp. (16), at 66, U.N. Doc. A/4684 (1960).

6. For the Bengali situation, see Nanda, *Self-Determination in International Law—A Tragic Tale of Two Cities—Islamabad (West Pakistan) and Decca (East Pakistan)*, 66 AM. J.I.L. 321–36 (1972); Nawaz, *Bangladesh and International Law*, 11 INDIAN J.I.L. 251–68 (1971); Mani, *The 1971 War on the Indian Sub-Continent and International Law*, 12 INDIAN J.I.L. 83–99 (1972); L. BUCCHEIT, SECESSION, THE LEGITIMACY OF SELF-DETERMINATION 198–216 (1978).

7. See L. SOHN, supra note 3, at 416.

8. See J. BRIERLY, LAW OF NATIONS 139–40 (1963). Cf. H. LAUTERPACHT, RECOGNITION IN INTERNATIONAL LAW 78 (1947).

9. See G.A. Res. 2787, 27 U.N. GAOR Supp. (29) at 16, U.N. Doc. A/8429 (1972).

10. Krauss, *Internal Conflicts and Foreign States: In Search of the State of Law*, 5 YALE STUDIES IN WORLD PUBLIC ORDER 173, 174 (1979); Luard, *Civil Conflicts in Modern International Relations*, in INTERNATIONAL REGULATION OF CIVIL WAR 7, 7–8 (E. Luard ed. 1972); E. Firmage, *The War of National Liberation and the Third World*, in LAW AND CIVIL WAR IN THE MODERN WORLD 304, 305 (J. Moore ed. 1974).

11. Luard, supra note 10; Firmage, supra note 10; Krauss, supra note 10.

12. The weakness of art. 51 has been well described by Hoffman: "What was supposed to be an exception not much larger than a needle's eye has become a loophole through which armies have passed." Hoffman, *International Law and the Control of Force*, in RELEVANCE OF INTERNATIONAL LAW (D. Hoffman ed. 1968).

13. See the Legal Memorandum prepared by Leonard C. Meeker, Legal Advisor of the U.S. Department of State, reproduced in 60 AM. J.I.L. 565, 566–67 (1966). Emphasis added.

14. The Goa debate, in Official Records of the Security Council, 987th mtg. at 9 (Dec. 18, 1961).

15. Firmage, supra note 10, at 305.

16. Luard, supra note 10, at 9.

17. *Id.*; Firmage, supra note 10, at 305–7.

18. For the legal implications of the importation of the missile and the U.S.-imposed quarantine, see Wright, *The Cuban Quarantine*, 57 AM. J.I.L. 546 (1963); cf. Meeker, *Defensive Quarantine and the Law, id.* at 515.

19. The INTER-AMERICAN TREATY OF RECIPROCAL ASSISTANCE, 1947 (Rio Pact). Reprinted in 17 U.S. DEP'T STATE BULL. 565 (1947).

20. Resolution Adopted by the Organization of American States, Oct. 23, 1962, in 74 U.S. DEP'T STATE BULL. 722 (1963). Emphasis added.

21. For the inappropriateness of the concept of pacific blockade to the Cuban missile crisis, see Wright, supra note 18.

22. Proclamation No. 3504, 47 DEP'T STATE BULL. 717 (1962), 27 Fed. Reg. 10401 (1962), reprinted in W. FRIEDMANN, O. LISSITZYN & R. PUGH, INTERNATIONAL LAW CASES AND MATERIALS 896 (1965). Emphasis added.

23. Luard, supra note 10, at 9–10.

24. Firmage, supra note 10, at 306–7.

25. Pinkard, *Force, Intervention, and Neutrality in Contemporary International Law*, 3 TOWSON S.J.I.L. 66, 68 (1968).

26. D. NINCIC, THE PROBLEM OF SOVEREIGNTY IN THE CHARTER AND IN THE PRACTICE OF THE UNITED NATIONS 70–71 (1970).

27. Firmage, supra note 10; Luard, supra note 10.

28. Luard, supra note 10, at 11–13.

29. R. FALK, THE INTERNATIONAL LAW OF CIVIL WAR 2 (1971).

30. Luard, supra note 10, at 17–23.

31. Baxter, *The Geneva Convention of 1949 and Wars of National Liberation*, 56 RIVISTA DI DIRITTO INTERNAZIONALE 193, 195–99 (1974); *Humanitarian War or Humanitarian Politics? The 1974 Diplomatic Conference on Humanitarian Law*, 16 HARV. INT'L L.J. 1, 11–16 (1975).

32. Compare all the provisions of the 1949 Geneva Convention with the so-called common article 3, which was inserted specifically to apply to the "conflicts of non-international character." See the Convention for the Amelioration of the Condition of the Wounded and Sick in Armed Forces in the Field (Aug. 12, 1949), 3 U.S.T. 3114, T.I.A.S. No. 3362, 75 U.N.T.S. 31 (1955); Convention for the Amelioration of the Condition of the Wounded, Sick, and Shipwrecked Members of Armed Forces at Sea (?), 3 U.S.T. 3217, T.I.A.S. No. 3363, 75 U.N.T.S. 85 (1955); Convention Relative to the Treatment of Prisoners of War (?), 3 U.S.T. 3316, T.I.A.S. No. 3364, 75 U.N.T.S. 135 (1955); and the Convention Relative to the Protection of Civilian Persons in Time of War (?), 3 U.S.T. 3516, T.I.A.S. No. 3365, 75 U.N.T.S. 287 (1955).

33. L. OPPENHEIM, INTERNATIONAL LAW para. 289–90, p. 344 (1903). See also L. SOHN & T. BUERGENTHAL, INTERNATIONAL PROTECTION OF HUMAN RIGHTS 1 (1973). Emphasis added.

34. See C. NORGAARD, THE POSITION OF THE INDIVIDUAL IN INTERNATIONAL LAW 1–78 (1962).

35. *Id.* at 33.

36. INTERNATIONAL LAW IN A CHANGING WORLD: CASES DOCUMENTS AND READINGS 72 (E. Collins, Jr., ed. 1970).

37. 5 Wheat. 161–62 (1820). Emphasis added.

38. 22 Trial of the Major War Criminals before the International Military Tribunal, Proceedings, 16 at 878 (1948).

39. See Convention on Rights and Duties of States, 49 STAT. 3097, T.S. 881, 165 L.N.T.S. 19.

40. See U.N. CHARTER arts. 1, para. 3; 55, para. c; and 56.

41. The Universal Declaration of Human Rights, G.A. Res. 217, 3 U.N. GAOR, the preamble, U.N. Doc. 1/777 (1948).

42. The U.S. position is an example:

In giving our approval to the Declaration today, it is of primary importance that we keep clearly in mind the basic character of the document. It is and does not purport to be a statement of law or of legal obligation. It is a declaration of basic principles of human rights and freedoms, to be stamped with the approval of the General Assembly by formal vote of its members, and to serve as a common standard of achievement for all peoples of all nations.

19 U.S. DEP'T STATE BULL. 751 (1948).

43. See G.A. Res. 1514, supra note 5.

44. G.A. Res. 1904 (XXVII), Nov. 20, 1963, art. 11, 18 GAOR Supp. (No. 15)(A/5515) at 35.

45. For the texts of the two covenants, see 61 AM. J.I.L. 51 (1967).

46. See L. SOHN & T. BUERGENTHAL, supra note 33, at 556, 596, 617.

47. 1928 P.C.I.J. (ser. B) No. 15.

48. The Mavrommatis Palestine Concessions, 1924 P.C.I.J. (ser. A) No. 2.

49. The Case Concerning the Barcelona Traction, Light and Power Company, Limited (New Application: 1962) (Belgium v. Spain), 1970 I.C.J. Rep. 4. Cited in H. STEINER & D. VAGTS, TRANSNATIONAL LEGAL PROBLEMS, MATERIALS AND TEXT 222, 231 (1978). Emphasis added.

50. United States ex rel. Keefe v. Dulles, 22 F.2d 390 (D.C. Cir. 1954).

51. Quoted in 1 M. WHITEMAN, DIGEST OF INTERNATIONAL LAW 57–58. Emphasis added.

52. 1966 I.C.J. Rep. 6.

53. Dissenting, Judge P. Jessup referred to the judgment as "completely unfounded in law." *Id.* at 323. Cf. the separate opinion of Judge Van Wyk, who urged, "It is true that a great deal of the reasoning of the present judgment is in conflict with the reasoning of the 1962 judgment." *Id.* at 65.

54. The I.C.J., in a long line of cases, starting from 1950, had held repeatedly that the racial policies of South Africa violated the South-West African mandate, the U.N. Charter, and such other documents as the Universal Declaration of Human Rights. See L. SOHN & T. BUERGENTHAL, supra note 33, at 373 et seq.

55. See The Interhandel case (Switzerland v. U.S.A.) (Preliminary Objections), 1959 I.C.J. Rep. 6; the Ambitielos Claim (Greece v. U.K.) 1941 INT'L L. REP. 306.

56. On the practice of the European Community and the operation of the convention see L. SOHN & T BUERGENTHAL, supra note 33, at 1222.

CHAPTER 3

1. See T. HOBBES, LEVIATHAN chs. 13 and 14 (H. Schneider ed. 1958); Fuller, *Human Interaction and the Law*, in THE RULE OF LAW 171 (L. Wolf ed. 1971).
2. 2 Ex. D. 63, 153, 154 (1876).
3. In the case of *New Jersey v. Delaware* Justice Cardozo elucidated the nexus between morality and law—whether in the domestic systems or otherwise—when he held: "International law . . . has, at times, like the common law within states, a twilight existence during which it is hardly distinguishable from morality or justice, till at length the *imprimatur* of a court attests to its jural quality." 291 U.S. 366 (1934). See also Kaplan & Katzenbach, *States Obey International Law Because They Have an Interest in Doing So*, reprinted in INTERNATIONAL LAW AND THE CHANGING WORLD 39 (E. Collins ed. 1970).
4. WEBSTER'S NEW COLLEGIATE DICTIONARY (G. & C. Merriam, 1981).
5. H. HART, THE CONCEPT OF LAW 24 (1961). See also J. BRIERLY, THE LAW OF NATIONS: AN INTRODUCTION TO THE INTERNATIONAL LAW OF PEACE 70–71 (6th ed. 1963).
6. 2 Hong Kong L. Rep. 207, 225 (1906).
7. According to art. 59 of the I.C.J. Statute, "the decision of the Court has no binding force except between the parties and in respect of that particular case."
8. For more information on the United Nations Emergency Forces (U.N.E.F.) precedent, see infra, Chapter 8.
9. See infra, Chapter 8.
10. The United Nations condemned it for violating the Loi Fondamentale and imposed economic sanctions against the secessionists.
11. See infra, Chapter 8.
12. See The South West African Cases (Preliminary Objections), 1962 I.C.J. REP. 319, 425. See also L. SOHN & T. BUERGENTHAL, INTERNATIONAL PROTECTION OF HUMAN RIGHTS 412 (1973).
13. South West African Cases (2d phase), 1966 I.C.J. Rep. 6, 51, L. SOHN & T. BUERGENTHAL, supra note 12, at 418.
14. This position seems to be the majority view, at least in the contemporary system. See infra, Chapter 8.
15. Schachter, *The United Nations and International Conflict*, in LAW AND CIVIL WAR IN THE MODERN WORLD 401, 414 (J. Moore ed. 1974). See also Mcleod v. United States, 229 U.S. 434 (1913).
16. Neither resolutions of the United Nations nor those of other international and regional organizations are included in the list of sources of law under the I.C.J. Statute. Although the list has been described by some writers as a complete statement of the sources of international law—see M. HUDSON, THE PERMANENT COURT OF INTERNATIONAL JUSTICE 601, cited in I. BROWNLIE, PRINCIPLES OF PUBLIC INTERNATIONAL LAW 3 (3d ed. 1979)—others, notably Blaine, argue that it is not exhaustive. See Blaine, *The Binding Force of a "Recommendation" of the General Assembly of the United Nations*, 25 B.Y.B.I.L. 1, 2 (1948).
17. See infra, Chapters 10–11.

18. The Statute of the International Court of Justice, art. 38, 59 STAT. 1055, T.S. 993, 3 BEAVANS 1179.

19. For detailed discussion of this article, see the history of its predecessor in M. HUDSON, THE PERMANENT COURT OF INTERNATIONAL JUSTICE, 1920–1942, at 606–20 (1943).

20. According to art. 10, "*In the absence of any agreement between the parties* concerning the law to be applied, the tribunal shall apply." 2 Y.B. INT'L L.C. 83 (1958). Emphasis added.

21. M. HUDSON, supra note 19, at 619–20.

22. J. CRAWFORD, THE CREATION OF STATES IN INTERNATIONAL LAW 80 (1977). I. BROWNLIE, PRINCIPLES OF PUBLIC INTERNATIONAL LAW 4, 512–15 (3d ed. 1979).

23. VIENNA CONVENTION ON THE LAW OF TREATIES, arts. 53 & 64, U.N. Doc. A/Conf. 39/27 (1969), 63 AM. J.I.L. 875 (1969).

24. *Id.* art. 64.

25. One way of clarifying the problem is by looking at what the International Law Commission said in its commentary on article 53: "This provision makes it plain that nullity attaches to a treaty under the article *only if the rule with which it conflicts is a peremptory norm of general international law from which no derogation is permitted* even by agreement between the particular states." This observation literally suggests that the test cannot apply in a conflict between norms that are anything but peremptory. See United Nations Conference on the Law of Treaties, First and Second Sessions: Vienna 26 March–24 May 1968 and 9 April–22 May 1969, Official Records, Documents of the Conference 68, see Ciobanu, *Impact of the Characteristics of the Charter Upon Its Interpretation*, in 60 CURRENT PROBLEMS OF INTERNATIONAL LAW 13 (A. Cassese ed. 1975).

26. See, e.g., the statement made on June 5, 1945, in Committee 1/1 by the British delegate that art. 2(6) imposes an obligation on the organization to get nonmembers to comply with its principles, Doc. 810, 1/1/30, June 6, 1945, 6 U.N.C.I.O. Doc. 348 (1945). Cf. the observation by the Venezuelan delegation that the article "which would obligate the non-member states to obey the rules of the institution and carry out their obligations would be found contrary to legal postulates, at least as long as no disturbance of peace occurred, and would occasion controversies difficult to decide in the present state of international law." Doc. 2, G/7 (d) (1), 3 U.N.C.I.O. Docs. 193–94 (1945).

27. VIENNA CONVENTION ON THE LAW OF TREATIES, supra note 23, art. 53.

28. See 1 Y.B. INT'L L.C. 63 (1963).

29. He notes at one point "that general international law continues to be valid while the Charter of the United Nations forms only particular international law, binding on the basis and within the framework of general international law." Verdross, *The Charter of the United Nations and General International Law*, in LAW AND POLITICS IN THE WORLD COMMUNITY: ESSAYS ON HANS KELSEN'S PURE THEORY AND RELATED PROBLEMS IN INTERNATIONAL LAW 153–54 (1953).

30. Tunkin, *Co-existence and International Law*, 95 RECUEIL DES COURS 65 (1958). Cf. Wright, *Effects of the League of Nations Covenant* 13 AM. POL. SCI. REV.

556 (1919). Lauterpacht, *The Covenant as the Higher Law*, 17 B.Y.B.I.L. 54, at 58 (1936).

31. I. BROWNLIE, supra note 16, at 515.

32. See the Case of Reparation for Injuries Suffered in the Service of the United Nations, 1949 I.C.J. REP. 179.

33. See Ciobanu, *Impact of the Characteristics of the Charter Upon Its Interpretation*, in CURRENT PROBLEMS OF INTERNATIONAL LAW 3, 9 n. 14 (A. Cassese ed. 1975).

34. See Doc. WD 441, CO/205, 17 U.N.C.I.O. Docs. 382 (1945).

35. It reads: "The Organization *shall ensure that* states which are not Members of the United Nations act in accordance with these Principles so far as may be necessary for the maintenance of international peace and security." U.N. CHARTER art. 2, para. 6. Emphasis added.

36. Doc. 933, IV/2/42 (2), 13 U.N.C.I.O. Docs. 708 (1945).

37. B. COHEN, THE UNITED NATIONS: CONSTITUTIONAL DEVELOPMENTS, GROWTH, AND POSSIBILITIES 5–6 (1961).

38. *Id.* at 2–5. This is obvious from the preamble. The United Nations is committed inter alia to save succeeding generations from the scourge of war, reaffirm faith in fundamental human rights, and advance dignity and welfare of humankind by establishing and maintaining peace under international justice, and insure that the members of the international community practice tolerance and live together with one another as good neighbors. See the U.N. CHARTER, preamble. The preamble generally carries as much weight as any other part of the document. Cf. VIENNA CONVENTION ON THE LAW OF TREATIES, supra note 23, art. 31, para. 2. This approach may be the most sound, if it is considered that the Charter is widely acknowledged as a treaty. See the Case of the Certain Expenses of the United Nations, 1962 I.C.J. REP. 151, 163.

39. U.N. Doc. 944 1/I/34(1), 6 U.N.C.I.O. Docs. 446–47 (1945).

40. U.N. CHARTER art. 2, para. 2.

41. See Schachter, supra note 15, at 403–4.

42. See the position of the Harvard Research on the Law of Treaties, in 29 AM. J.I.L. SUPP. 938 (1935).

43. Fitzmaurice, *The Law and Procedure of the International Court of Justice: Treaty Interpretation and Certain Other Treaty Points*, 28 B.Y.B.I.L. 1, 1 (1951).

44. Kelsen, *Legal Technique in International Law: A Textual Critique of the League Covenant*, 10 GENEVA STUDIES 12 (1939).

45. Fitzmaurice, supra note 43.

46. The Expenses Case, supra note 38, at 184. Emphasis added. The Competence of the General Assembly Regarding Admission to the United Nations, I.C.J. REP. 4, 8, 23–24 (1950).

47. VIENNA CONVENTION ON THE LAW OF TREATIES, supra note 23, art. 32. See also Judge Alvarez in the Competence Case, 1950 I.C.J. REP. 4, at 23–24. Cited in L. SOHN, CASES ON UNITED NATIONS LAW 25, 27–28 (1967).

48. Wright, *The Interpretation of Multilateral Treaties*, 23 AM. J.I.L. 104 (1929). See also McNair, *The Functions and Differing Legal Character of Treaties*, 11 B.Y.B.I.L. 100 at 107 (1930).

49. Case Concerning the Aerial Incident of July 27th, 1955, 1959 I.C.J. REP. 176.

50. Pollux, *The Interpretation of the Charter*, 23 B.Y.B.I.L. 54, 72 (1946).

51. VIENNA CONVENTION ON THE LAW OF TREATIES, supra note 23, art. 31. Emphasis added.

52. The Certain Expenses case, supra note 38, at 185. Emphasis added. See also Judge Viniarski's opinion, *id*. at 230.

53. Competence case, supra note 46, at 17. Emphasis added.

54. See U.N. CHARTER art. 108.

55. Certain Expenses case, supra note 38, at 196.

56. *Id*. at 223–25.

57. *Id*. at 189–90.

58. The Competence case, supra note 47, at 18.

59. Competence case, supra note 46, at 23.

60. See Brierly, *The Covenant and the Charter*, 23 B.Y.B.I.L. 83 (1946).

61. Quoted with approval by Dhokalia, in *Civil Wars and International Law*, 11 INDIAN J.I.L. 249 (1971).

62. 1971 I.C.J. REP. 16, 31.

63. Doc. 933, IV/2/42 (2), 8; 13 U.N.C.I.O. Docs. 709–10 (1945). See also U.N. Doc. A/474, Nov. 13, 1947.

64. The Peace Treaties case, 1950 I.C.J. REP. 65, 71 (1950).

65. Supra, note 63.

66. The court is listed as the principal judicial organ of the United Nations, and a fortiori of the entire world community (see art. 92 of the U.N. CHARTER); though its decisions are not subject to review (arts. 60 and 94 of the I.C.J. Statute and U.N. CHARTER, respectively), it enjoys supervisory jurisdiction over almost all international judicial and arbitral bodies. See art. 1; 3, para. 2; 27; and 33 of the MODEL RULES, reproduced in 53 AM. J.I.L. 239 (1959).

67. See art. 7 of the SOUTH WEST AFRICA MANDATE. League of Nations Doc. 21/31/140 (Dec. 17, 1920).

68. See LEAGUE OF NATIONS O.J. Spec. Supp. 194, 21st Ass. 32–33 (plenary 1946).

69. See Report of the Committee on South West Africa, 14 U.N. GAOR Supp. (No. 12) at 32–33, U.N. Doc. A/4191 (1959).

70. G.A. Res. 1565, 15 U.N. GAOR Supp. (No. 16) at 31–32, U.N. Doc. A/4684 (1960). See also Res. 1361 (XIV), 14 GAOR Supp. (No. 16) at 29, U.N. Doc. A/4354 (1959).

71. See South West African Cases, Preliminary Objections, supra note 12, 319, 347.

72. Advisory Opinion of the International Court of Justice, July 11, 1950, 1950 I.C.J. REP. 128, reprinted in L. SOHN & T. BUERGENTHAL, supra note 12, at 375, 382. Emphasis added.

73. See G.A. Res. 449(V) A and B, 5 U.N. GAOR Supp. (No. 20) at 55–56, U.N. Doc. A/1775 (1950). See also Res. 1361, supra note 70.

74. South West African Cases, Preliminary Objections, supra note 12, 319–34. L. SOHN & T. BUERGENTHAL, supra note 12, at 413–15.

75. "In the event of an equality of votes, the President . . . shall have a casting vote." I.C.J. Statute, art. 55(2).

76. South West African Cases, Second Phase, I.C.J. REP. supra note 13, at 17–18.

77. In a statement issued after the 1966 judgment Judge Zafrullah indicated that he was forced by the president—Spender—not to sit solely because he had at one time been nominated a judge ad hoc by the Applicant States though he never sat in that capacity. According to him, "I disagreed entirely with that view and gave the President my reasons which I still consider very good reasons."

78. South West African Cases (2d phase), supra note 13, at 323, 382.

79. See U.N. Doc. A/ 6300, Rev. 1, 21 U.N. GAOR Annexes (No. 23) Add. 1, at 290–91, reprinted in L. SOHN & T. BUERGENTHAL, supra note 12, at 423–24. Emphasis added.

80. It provides that any decision of the court binds only the contentious parties and applies solely to the particular issue for which it is made.

81. See the *Case Concerning Certain German Interests in Polish Upper Silesia*, where, in following an identical provision of the Statute of the P.C.I.J., the court held that the legal principles accepted by the court in a particular case could not be binding on parties in other disputes. 1926 P.C.I.J. (ser. A) No. 7 at 4, 19.

82. Cited in *Impact of the Characteristics of the Charter Upon Its Interpretation*, in 60 CURRENT PROBLEMS OF INTERNATIONAL LAW 3, 57–58 n. 135 (A. Cassese ed. 1975).

83. See W. FRIEDMANN, O. LISSITZYN & R. PUGH, INTERNATIONAL LAW CASES AND MATERIALS 82 (1969). Emphasis added.

84. The court may decide *ex aequo et bono* if the parties agree. I.C.J. Statute, art. 38(d).

85. See art. 36(1) of the I.C.J. Statute. See also the Status of the Eastern Carelia case, 1923 P.C.I.J. (ser. B) No. 5, at 27, cited in H. STEINER & D. VAGTS, TRANSNATIONAL LEGAL PROBLEMS, MATERIALS AND TEXT 198 (1978) and the Case Concerning the Aerial Incident of September 4th, 1954 (United States v. Union of Soviet Socialist Republics), 1958 I.C.J. REP. 158. In the latter, it was observed that although membership of the United Nations automatically makes any member of the organization a party to the court, the court's compulsory jurisdiction cannot apply unless it is expressly or impliedly granted by a state in respect of which a case has been instituted.

86. See the U.S. Declaration, cited in W. FRIEDMANN, O. LISSITZYN & R. PUGH, supra note 83, at 279–80. For more detailed recitation, see L. SOHN, BASIC DOCUMENTS OF THE UNITED NATIONS 272 (2d ed. 1956).

87. See the British Declaration, in W. FRIEDMANN, O. LISSITZYN & R. PUGH, supra note 83, at 278; L. SOHN, supra note 86, at 271. Emphasis added.

88. See, for instance, the Portuguese Declaration, cited in W. FRIEDMANN, O. LISSITZYN & R. PUGH, supra note 83, at 284.

89. Certain *Norwegian Loans* case (France v. Norway), 1957 I.C.J. REP. 9, cited in *id.* at 280, 282.

90. In the *Norwegian Loans* case, where Norway sought to invoke its Connally-type reservation against France, the court declined to hold on the validity of the reservation but ironically used that as a basis for invoking and applying the principle of reciprocity against the French. In the *Interhandel* case, although the issue recurred, the court premised its decision on the basis that one of the parties did not exhaust the available domestic remedies. For the two cases, see *id.* at 280–85.

91. Cited in Ofosu-Amaah, *Observance on Exception Clauses in Treaties*, 1 U.G.L.J. 110, 114 (1964).

92. Sohn, *Step-by-Step Acceptance of the Jurisdiction of the International Court of Justice*, in PROC. A.S.I.L. 131 (1964).

93. Schachter, *The Enforcement of International Judicial and Arbitral Decisions*, 54 AM. J.I.L. 1, 5 (1960).

94. It cannot, however, proceed with a case if the Security Council is considering it. U.N. CHARTER art. 12.

95. See Baxter, *The Geneva Convention of 1949 and Wars of National Liberation*, 56 RIVISTA DI DIRITTO INTERNAZIONALE 193, 198 (1974).

96. See Doc. 507, II/2/22, 9 U.N.C.I.O. Doc. 70, at 2 (1945). Significantly, the question whether the General Assembly should have power to impose conventions was also rejected. See Doc. 571, II/2/27, *id.*, at 80–81.

97. U.N. CHARTER art. 13.

98. Schreuer, *Recommendations and Traditional Sources of International Law*, 20 G.Y.B.I.L. 103, 112–15 (1977).

99. Blaine, supra note 16, at 6.

100. U.N. Doc. E/CN/4/L.610 (1962), cited in Bleicher, *The Legal Significance of Re-Citation of General Assembly Resolutions*, 63 AM. J.I.L. 444, 450 (1969). Emphasis added.

101. Schreuer, supra note 98, at 117. See also Bleicher, supra note 100, at 450.

CHAPTER 4

1. See U. UMORZURIKE, INTERNATIONAL LAW AND COLONIALISM IN AFRICA 22 (1979); Mushkat, *The Process of African Decolonization*, 6 INDIAN J.I.L. 483–85 (1966). According to some writers, the colonies were intimidated by show of force immediately before the so-called treaties were entered into. In one instance, the account reads:

Sir Frederick Lugard of Northern Nigeria preceded negotiations with short military actions in order to place himself in a position of strength. Consul Ralph Moor of the Niger Coast Protectorate moved up and down the Cross River with troops shelling and destroying villages before settling down to make "treaties of friendship" with the frightened people.

See Ukpabi, *Military Considerations in African Foreign Policies*, 6 TRANSITION 31, 33–40 (June–July 1967). See also U. UMORZURIKE, supra, at 19; Umorzurike, *International Law and Colonialism in Africa*, 3 E. AFR. L. REV. 95–100 (1970).

2. See U. UMORZURIKE, supra note 1, at 40.

3. F. WHITE, MANDATES 129 (1926).

4. Cited in Umorzurike, supra note 1, at 98.

5. See CONGO FREE STATE BULLETIN OFFICIET 191 (Sept.–Oct. 1905), cited in *id.* at 98.

6. See also Chapters 2 and 10.

7. UMORZURIKE, supra note 1, at 99. Emphasis added.

8. This was evident from the experiences of leaders who sought to enforce the terms of the so-called treaties against the colonizers. In *Ol Le Njogo et al. v. A. G. for Eastern Africa*, a British colonial case, King Farlow, J., ruled: "I agree with the view expressed by the respondents that it (the so-called treaty) imposed moral obligations on both the contracting parties; *these however are not cognizable in a Court of law.*" See *Ol Le Njogo et al. v. A. G. for Eastern Africa* (the Massai case), 5 E. AFR. PROV. L. REP. 70 (1913–14), cited in U. UMORZURIKE, supra note 1, at 43. Emphasis added. See also the *Sahaba* case, cited in U. UMORZURIKE, supra note 1, at 48–49.

9. UMORZURIKE, supra note 1, at 98.

10. See E. HERTSLET, THE MAP OF AFRICA BY TREATIES 468 (1967). See also Chukwurah, *The Organization of African Unity and African Territorial and Boundary Problems*, 13 INDIAN J.I.L. 176–206 (1973).

11. The treaty for the renunciation of war (Kellogg-Briand Pact), 46 STAT. 2343, 94 L.N.T.S. 57 (1928), arts. 1 and 2. Reprinted in W. FRIEDMANN, O. LISSITZYN & R. PUGH, INTERNATIONAL LAW CASES AND MATERIALS 883 (1978).

12. Manchester Guardian, Oct. 13, 1936, cited in Umorzurike, supra note 1, at 107.

13. *Id.*, at 111.

14. Hansard, col. 29300–31 (1935).

15. CH. D. 182 (1939). See also CH. D. 545 (1938).

16. See the LEAGUE OF NATIONS COVENANT art. 22, para. 1, 1 HUDSON, INTERNATIONAL LEGISLATION 19–42, reprinted in L. SOHN, BASIC DOCUMENTS OF THE U.N. 295 (1956).

17. *Id.* at para. 3.

18. *Id.* at para. 4.

19. *Id.* at para. 5.

20. *Id.* at para. 6.

21. G. PADMORE, AFRICA AND WORLD POLITICS 178 (1937). See U. UMORZURIKE, supra note 1, at 61.

22. UMORZURIKE, supra note 1, at 102.

23. For more detailed information, see U. UMORZURIKE, supra note 1, at 59–60.

24. *Id.* at 60–61.

25. M. MUSHKAT, THEORY AND PRACTICE IN INTERNATIONAL RELATIONS 242–44 (1959).

26. U.N. CHARTER art. 77.

27. *Id.* at art. 76(b).

28. *Id.* at arts. 83, 87, and 88.

29. In opposing efforts to subject colonies to U.N. supervision, the administering powers sought to rely on the difference between the provisions in chs. XI and XII–XIII. Their strategies included citing statements issued at the San Francisco conference. Thus, in one instance, they argued: "The obligations under Chapter XI were entirely different from those of Chapters XII–XIII (the trusteeship provisions) in that they conferred no supervisory rights upon the United Nations." 1(2) U.N. GAOR 4th Comm., pt. 1, at 66.

30. 1950 I.C.J. REP. 128.

31. See U.N. CHARTER, arts. 77(2), 79, and 80.

32. 1955 I.C.J. REP. 67.

33. U.N. CHARTER art. 73.

34. Cited in Nawaz, *Colonies, Self-Government, and the United Nations*, 11 IN-
DIAN Y.B.I.L. 3, 7 (1962). In echoing the same idea, Portugal contends: "The title of
the chapter is 'Declaration regarding Non-Self-Governing Territories' and any declaration made by Member States under this heading is a unilateral act of which the General
Assembly can merely take note, as has always been the practice in the United Nations."
U.N. Doc. A/P.V.855/26, cited in Nawaz, *id.*, at 7 n. 12. Again, as the New Zealand's
delegate put it in 1948, the declaration in article 73 "was a unilateral declaration of
policy and . . . could not therefore be construed as a formal obligation to the United
Nations." 3 U.N. GAOR, 4th Comm., at 35. See Nawaz, supra, p. 7 nn 12 and 13.

35. Cited in H. KELSEN, LAW OF THE UNITED NATIONS 554 (1950).

36. Asbeck, *International Law and Colonial Administration*, TRANSACTIONS OF
THE GROTIUS SOCIETY FOR 1953, 5 at 23 (1946). See also U.N. Doc. A/AC.58/1/Add.
4, at 7, and H. KELSEN, supra note 35, at 554.

37. Nawaz, supra note 34, at 8.

38. See U.N. Doc. A/AC100/2 Add. 1, at 4–5. See Nawaz, supra note 34, at
9 n. 20.

39. *Id.* at 12.

40. *Id.* at 12.

41. Committee II/4, Verbatim minutes of the 11th mtg., Running No. 31H, cited
in *id.* at 13.

42. Doc. II/4/A/2, U.N.C.I.O. Docs. 727 (June 1, 1945).

43. A/74, June 29, 1946, authorized by G.A. Res. 9(1). Cited in J. CRAWFORD,
THE CREATION OF STATES IN INTERNATIONAL LAW, 360 (1979).

44. See G.A. Res. 66(1) of Dec. 13, 1946. The only objections to it were from
states claiming sovereignty over some of those territories (Guatemala over British Honduras, Panama over the Panama Canal Zone, and Argentina over the Falkland Islands).
See J. CRAWFORD, THE CREATION OF STATES IN INTERNATIONAL LAW 360 (1979).

45. U.N. Doc. A/AC100/2, supra note 38, p. 24.

46. U.N. Doc. A/C/4/52, quoted in 2 U.N. GAOR, 4th Comm. at 1–27.

47. It reads:

Non-Self-Governing territories may . . . be defined to mean and to include
territories where the rights of the inhabitants, their economic status and social
privileges are regulated by another state in charge of the administration of such
a Territory. A territory in which there are internal executive authorities and
legislative bodies representing the inhabitants of the territory themselves,
which are free to regulate the economic conditions and social rights of their
people cannot be said to be non-self-governing even though in some aspects,
such as the conduct of foreign relations, the territory must be subject to the
direction and control of another State. It is suggested, therefore, that the criterion should be whether in any particular territory, there is or is not an institution legally established which is responsible for the internal administration and

control of the territory; where there is no such institution, the territory should be defined as non-self-governing.

48. *Id.*, at 274. U.N. Doc. A/AC58/1, supra note 36, at 4–5.
49. According to it, its "overseas territory has no more and no less in its status than any other (metropolitan) territory." U.N. Doc. A/AC100/2, supra note 38, at 37. See also U.N. Doc. A/AC.4/347 and G.A. XI, 4th Comm., 616th mtg.
50. U.N. GAOR Supp. (No. 16) at 29–30, U.N. Doc. A/4684.
51. *Id.*, at 30–31. See also U.N. REPERTORY, Supp. III, vol. 3, art. 73, paras. 105–29.
52. Doc. 404, II/4/17, U.N.C.I.O. Docs., Summary Report of 6th mtg. of Comm. II/4, at 2 (Doc. X, p. 453), cited in Nawaz, supra note 34, at 37 n. 93.
53. See Nawaz, supra note 34, at 37.
54. 6 FOREIGN AFFAIRS RECORD (Ministry of External Affairs, Gov't of India, New Delhi) 192 (1950), cited in Nawaz, supra note 34, at 38–39.
55. According to this article:

Immediate steps shall be taken, in Trust *and Non-Self-Governing Territories* or all other territories which have not yet attained independence, to transfer all powers to the peoples of those territories, without any conditions or reservations, in accordance with their freely expressed will and desire, without any distinction as to race, creed or color, *in order to enable them to enjoy complete independence and freedom.*

The declaration on the granting of independence to colonial countries and peoples, G.A. Res. 1514, 15 U.N. GAOR Supp. (No. 16) at 66, U.N. Doc. A/4684 (1960). Emphasis added.

56. 1975 I.C.J. REP. 12, 32. See infra ch. 6, "Western Sahara before the World Court."
57. G.A. Res 1541, 15 U.N. GAOR U.N. Doc. A/4651 (1960). Cf. the development of the concept of association in G.A. Res. 567 (VI), 648 (VII), and 742(VII).
58. U.N. CHARTER art. 73e.
59. *Id.* at art. 88. See also art. 83, para. 3.
60. T. KUNZ, TERRORISM IN INTERNATIONAL LAW 82 (1974).
61. Dugard, *The Organization of African Unity and Colonialism: An Inquiry into the Plea of Self-Defence as a Justification for the Use of Force in the Eradication of Colonialism*, 16 I.C.L.Q. 157, 172 n. 86 (1967).
62. 18 U.N. SCOR (1043d mtg.), para 4. Cited in *id.* at 172, n. 86.
63. See U.N. CHARTER arts. 73 & 76.
64. See O.A.U. CHARTER arts. 2, para 1(d), and 3, para 6.
65. By art. 103 of the U.N. Charter, whenever there is a conflict between the obligations under the Charter and those assumed under other international agreements, the obligations under the Charter will prevail.
66. O.A.U. CHARTER, preamble.
67. *Id.* at art. 2, para. e.

68. T. ELIAS, AFRICA AND THE DEVELOPMENT OF INTERNATIONAL LAW 125 (1972). See also Akindele, *The Organization of African Unity and the United Nations: The Organization and Maintenance of International Peace and Security*, 9 CAN. Y.B.I.L. 30–58 (1971).

69. G.A. Res. 35/227, U.N. GAOR Supp. (No. 48) at 40, U.N. Doc. A/35/48 (Mar. 1981).

70. G.A. Res. 34/94, 34 U.N. GAOR Supp. (No. 46) at 39–40, U.N. Doc. A/34/46 (Dec. 1979).

71. See the statement by Quayson Sackey, 18 U.N. SCOR (1042d mtg.), para. 77. Cited in Dugard, supra note 61, at 174.

72. J. MOORE, LAW AND THE INDO-CHINA WAR 187 (1972).

73. E. SCHWELB, HUMAN RIGHTS AND THE INTERNATIONAL COMMUNITY (1964), cited and discussed in *id.* at 187.

74. R. HIGGINS, THE DEVELOPMENT OF INTERNATIONAL LAW THROUGH THE POLITICAL ORGANS OF THE UNITED NATIONS 100 (1963).

75. These include South Africa, Portugal, France, the United Kingdom, and the United States.

76. G.A. Res. 1514, 15 U.N. GAOR Supp. (No. 16) at 66, U.N. Doc. A/4684 (1960), preamble. Emphasis added.

77. *Id.* at arts. 1 & 2.

78. G.A. Res. 2625, 25 U.N. GAOR Supp. (No. 28) at 121, U.N. Doc. A/8028 (1970).

79. See Tyner, *Wars of National Liberation in Africa and Palestine: Self-Determination for Peoples or Territories?* 5 YALE STUDIES IN WORLD PUBLIC ORDER 234, 274 (1979).

80. G.A. Res. 2625, supra note 78.

81. Tyner, supra note 79, at 274.

82. S/473 of June 13, 1980, S/INF/36, at 18 (1980).

83. S/445 of March 8, 1979, S/INF/35, at 13–14 (1979).

84. Res. 311 of Feb. 4, 1972, S/INF/28, at 10 (1972).

85. See U.N. CHARTER art. 7

86. Res. 1450, 47 U.N. ECOSOC Supp. (No. 1) at 10, U.N. Doc. E/4735 (1965).

87. Res. 1543, 49 U.N. ECOSOC Supp. (No. 1) at 26, U.N. Doc. E/4904 (1970).

88. Res. 1892, 57 U.N. ECOSOC Supp. (No. 1) at 29, U.N. Doc. E/5570 (1974).

89. C.H.R. Res. 19 (XXX), 54 U.N. ECOSOC Supp. (No. 6) at 82–85, U.N. Doc. E/5265 (1973).

90. Dugard, supra note 61, at 174–75. Emphasis added.

91. Tyner, supra note 79, at 272.

92. Dugard, supra note 61 at 174–75.

93. B. COHEN, THE UNITED NATIONS: CONSTITUTIONAL DEVELOPMENTS, GROWTH, AND POSSIBILITIES 5–6 (1961).

94. See the separate opinion of Judge Spender in the *Certain Expenses* case and the dissenting view of Judge Winiarski on the same case. I.C.J. REP. 151, 197, 229 (1962).

95. See infra, ch. 9.

96. See infra, ch. 9.
97. Dugard, supra note 61, 175–76. Emphasis added.
98. See the Wimbledon case, 1923 P.C.I.J. (ser. A), No. 1, at 20.
99. Infra, Chapter 6, "Western Saharan Decolonization after the I.C.J. Action." According to the I.C.J., a customary rule is inapplicable against a state that has "always opposed any attempt to apply it." The *Anglo-Norwegian Fisheries* case. Cf. the Asylum case, I.C.J. REP. 266, 266–78 (1950).
100. 23 U.N. GAOR, 4th Comm. (1793d mtg.), para. 20.
101. U.N. Doc. A/8010, para. 232. See Ronzitti, *Resort to Force in Wars of National Liberation*, in CURRENT PROBLEMS OF INFORMATIONAL LAW, 319, 339–40 (A. Cassese, ed., 1973).
102. S/PV. 1677, at 29–30 (1972), cited in N. Ronzitti, *id.*
103. S/PV. 1639, at 67 (1972). See also U.N. Doc. A/C6/SR. 1179, at 6e, A/8018, para. 151. Considering France's position in the Algerian decolonization struggle—the position from which it did not change till it was defeated in shame after hundreds of thousands of people had perished—it is difficult to deny the seriousness of this new stand of the French.
104. See U.N. Doc. S/SP./1634, at 43, and S/PV./1674 (1972), at 34–35 (Belgium); A/C.6/SR.1180, at 7; S/PV./1677 (1972), at 37 (United States) cited in Ronzitti, supra note 101, at 339–40.

CHAPTER 5

1. See International Convention on the Suppression and Punishment of the Crime of Apartheid, G.A. Res. 3068 (XXVII), 28 U.N. GAOR Supp. (No. 30) at 75, U.N. Doc. A/9030 (1974), reprinted in 13 INT'L L. MAT. 50 (1974); Res. 2671 (XXV), 25 U.N. GAOR Supp. (No. 28) U.N. Doc. A/8028 (1970); G.A. Res. 1761, 17 U.N. GAOR Supp. (No. 17), 9 U.N. Doc. A/5217 (1962); S.C. Res. 182, 18 U.N. SCOR, Resolutions and Decisions of the Security Council, 8 U.N. Doc. A/INF/18 Rev. 1 (1960); S.C. Res. 181, *id.* at 7–8; G.A. Res. 2307, 22 U.N. GAOR Supp. (No. 16) 19, U.N. Doc. A/6716 (1967).
2. See G.A. Res. 2145 (XXI) of 1966. It reads in part: "South Africa has no other right to administer the Territory and . . . henceforth South West Africa comes under the direct responsibility of the United Nations." 21 U.N. GAOR Supp. (No. 16) at 2–3, U.N. Doc. A/6316 (1966). The resolution was affirmed by Security Council Resolution 264 of 1969 at 1–2, U.N. Doc. S/INF/24/Rev. 1. It received the I.C.J. imprimatur in the case of the Legal Consequences for States of the Continued Presence of South Africa in Namibia—1971 I.C.J. REP. 16—and has subsequently been confirmed in several recent U.N. resolutions. See G.A. Res. 35/227, G.A. Res. 34/92 A–G of Dec. 6, 1979; 35/206 and S.C. Res. 539 of Oct. 1983.
3. Although there is temptation to rationalize the situation on the basis of the constitutive limitations of the United Nations, it may be misleading to place much emphasis on those factors because, given the extensive powers of the United Nations and the unanimity against apartheid, the technical limitations of the United Nations can be

surmounted with little difficulty. And there are good precedents for these. In the Korean and Congolese crises, when almost all the members of the United Nations agreed on intervention to maintain the peace, the theoretical prescriptions of the Charter could not pose serious impediments to U.N. action. There are, of course, arguments that can be made against the application of these precedents to the apartheid situation. In the Korean example, for instance, one can doubt whether the world would always be blessed with an abstention of a superpower in the Security Council to enable the General Assembly to take action under a "Uniting for Peace Resolution." But who says an abstention of a superpower should be the only opportunity for the United Nations to meet its challenges, particularly those relating to the maintenance of the peace? Recall that the "Uniting for Peace Resolution" was not contemplated until after the veto had incessantly frustrated the United Nations in its efforts to prevent the rupture of the peace. It was only fortuitous that the Soviets abstained at the time they did. Since the maintenance of peace is very important for the survival of the United Nations, it is difficult to imagine why the United Nations should be deterred by the technicality that characterized the Korean situation. This is especially important in the instance of apartheid, for the principles threatened by apartheid are as important as, if not more important than, those in the Korean case. It is, of course, arguable that with the untold financial problems that attended the later cases—the operations in Egypt and the Congo, for instance—the failure of the United Nations to take enforcement measures might not be without foundation. Yet the possibility of financial difficulty cannot rationalize the organization's failure to take strong economic sanctions against apartheid—sanctions that, even if they require the use of force for compliance, would obviously not raise as much financial difficulty as the one the United Nations encountered in the Congo situation.

4. See Table 2.

5. For instance, long before the beginning of the twentieth century, the whites in South Africa had enacted draconian laws requiring blacks to carry passes at all times, forbidding them to own land in their own country, and punishing them for vagrancy. See P. FRENKEL, THE NAMIBIANS OF SOUTH WEST AFRICA, MINORITY RIGHTS GROUP REPORT No. 19, at 10–26 (1974).

6. H. BIERMONN, THE CASE FOR SOUTH AFRICA 147 (1963), cited in Kaipi, *The Status of Apartheid in International Law*, 17 INDIAN J.I.L. 57, 58 (1977). Emphasis added.

7. South Africa House of Assembly Debates, col. 579, Feb. 7, 1978, cited in Dugard, *South Africa's "Independent Homelands": An Exercise in Denationalization*. 10 (1) DENV. J.I.L. 11, 16 (1980).

8. House of Assembly Debates, cols. 3278–79, Mar. 21, 1980.

9. In 1964 a group of experts—physical anthropologists and geneticists—in reviewing scientific facts about races under the auspices of UNESCO, affirmed the finding of an earlier group that "it is not possible from a biological point of view to speak in any way whatsoever of a general inferiority or superiority of this or that race." Likewise in 1967, another UNESCO Committee of Experts declared:

Current biological knowledge does not permit us to impute cultural achievements in genetic potential. Differences in the achievements of different peoples should be attributed solely to their cultural history. The peoples of the world today appear to possess equal biological potentialities for attaining any level of civilization.

See the analysis of professor of biology J. Hiernaux, *Biological Aspects of the Racial Question*, 3 (1) OBJECTIVE: JUSTICE 17 (1971).

10. See infra, Chapter 7.

11. This assumption is based on the numerous U.N. resolutions that brand apartheid as posing serious threats to international peace and security.

12. See Richardson, *Constitutive Questions in the Negotiations for Namibian Independence*, 78 AM. J.I.L. 76, 77–89 (1984).

13. Crocker, *The Search for Regional Security in Southern Africa*, U.S. DEP'T STATE BULL. No. 2073, at 50, 52 [Statement before Sub-Committee on Africa of House Foreign Affairs Comm., Feb. 15, 1983] (Apr. 1983).

14. APARTHEID THE FACTS (Publication of International Defense Aid for Southern Africa, in Co-Operation with the U.N. Center Against Apartheid) 75 (1983) [hereinafter APARTHEID THE FACTS].

15. Res. 36/172 C.

16. Because South Africa is recognized by almost the whole world as independent and South-West Africa is dependent and administered as a "trust" on behalf of the international community, the principle of sovereignty may insulate the former but not the latter from international regulation. This apparent distinction is, however, unsustainable in the contemporary international system, because South Africa is a member of the United Nations and is therefore governed by U.N. standards relating to human rights and self-determination; its apartheid policy is therefore internationally challengeable.

17. L. THOMPSON, POLITICS IN THE REPUBLIC OF SOUTH AFRICA 3 (1966).

18. *Id.* at 4. Emphasis added.

19. This trial was of doubtful legality. It was instituted under the South Africa Terrorist Act, which was to operate not only retroactively but on Namibia at the time when South Africa's authority to administer Namibia had been terminated by the United Nations.

20. See A TRUST BETRAYED: NAMIBIA, U.N. DEP'T OF PUBLIC INFORMATION, at 42–43, U.N. Sales No. E.74/1.19 (1974). Emphasis added.

21. APARTHEID THE FACTS, supra note 14, at 16–34. See also P. FRENKEL, supra note 5, at 31, and the testimony before the *Ad Hoc* Working Group of Experts of the U.N. Commission of Human Rights, quoted in A TRUST BETRAYED: NAMIBIA, supra note 20, at 10.

22. P. FRENKEL, supra note 5, at 15–16.

23. See A TRUST BETRAYED: NAMIBIA, supra note 20, at 7. Although the Group Areas Act has been amended over the years, it is as reprehensible, if not more reprehensible, as ever. See APARTHEID THE FACTS, supra note 14, at 16–21 and 18–25.

24. See *Urban Blacks*, FOCUS ON KEY ECONOMIC ISSUES, No. 9 (1977), cited in APARTHEID THE FACTS, supra note 14, at 41.

25. Cited in A. BROOKS & J. BRICKHILL, WHIRLWIND BEFORE THE STORM: THE ORIGINS AND DEVELOPMENT OF THE UPRISING IN SOWETO AND THE REST OF SOUTH AFRICA FROM JUNE TO DEC. 1976, at 169 (1980).

26. *Id.* at 170. The procedure is described well by this account:

Hard hit by unemployment, family men are compelled to leave their wives to come and lead bachelors' lives in the so-called free boarding and lodging compounds. These men have as their assembly point TEBA (The Employment Bureau of Africa Limited) in Johannesburg. Here all mine recruits go through a primitive medical check up, a kind of medical treatment that has no place in a highly developed society like South Africa. Men of all ages are made to strip naked and queue for VD examinations. . . .

When we miners . . . arrive at our various mining companies, we are once more subjected to yet another awful TB check-up. The free striptease show continues, followed by a long injection which goes from chest to chest without any sterilization whatsoever.

APARTHEID THE FACTS, supra note 14, at 37. Another description runs as follows:

The Ovambos, who provide the majority of . . . contract laborers, are . . . given a medical examination including a humiliating anal examination, classified A, B, C, according to physical fitness and then given a contract and identity document. They are labelled with the name and address of their employer-to-be and packed into lorries for the long journey south. . . . Wives and children are not allowed to go with them.

P. FRENKEL, supra note 5, at 35.

27. P. FRENKEL, supra note 5, at 35.

28. *Id.* at 36.

29. A TRUST BETRAYED: NAMIBIA, supra note 20, at 17. Under the Labor Relations Act of 1981, even financial assistance to any striking worker is illegal. See APARTHEID THE FACTS, supra note 14, at 48.

30. A TRUST BETRAYED: NAMIBIA, supra note 20, at 25.

31. APARTHEID THE FACTS, supra note 14, at 40, footnotes omitted. Emphasis added.

32. See P. FRENKEL, supra note 5, at 36.

33. See G. CARTER, THE POLITICS OF INEQUALITY 101 (1958); Commission on Racial Situation in the Union of South Africa, Report, U.N. GAOR Supp. (No. 16) sec. 702, U.N. Doc. A/2505/Add. 1 (1953).

34. Cited in E. JANSEN & T. DONGES, THE GRAVE OF THE MIND 4 (1957).

35. G. CARTER, supra note 33, at 108.

36. J. W. MacQuarrie, *The New Order in the Bantu Education*, 1 AFRICA SOUTH 32 at 34–38 (Oct.–Dec. 1956); G. CARTER, supra note 33, 100–101.

37. G. CARTER, supra note 33, at 106.

38. See sec. 9 of Act No. 47 of 1953, as amended by Act No. 36 of 1956. The definition of "school" is so broad that any type of instruction for one African child or adult is covered. Thus, women have been fined for lecturing children in the fields if a

blackboard was available although no textbooks might be present. See R. v. Tanya, 20 So. Afr. L. Rep. 65 (1957).

39. Commission on Racial Situation, supra note 33, sec. 161.

40. T. B. Davie, Education and Race Relations in South Africa: The Interaction of Educational Policies and Race Relations in South Africa 15–16 (1955). Emphasis added.

41. Act No. 44 of 1950 as amended.

42. It is significant that by the force of this paragraph, any movement, even if it merely calls for the establishment of a democratic system like that in the United States or Britain, would fall under the definition for communism. Challenging its broad sweep, the South African (white) opposition party urged the following:

> May I refer to Clause 2 of the Bill which . . . says—Any reference in the Suppression of Communism Act, 1950, to the objects of communism, shall be construed as a reference to the objects of an organization . . . which is an unlawful organization in terms of a proclamation under sub-section (1) or (2) of this Act.
>   That means that all reference to the objects of communism must be interpreted in the relevant section as applying to the objects of the Pan Africanist movement or the African National Congress. When one looks at Section 11 of the Suppression of Communism Act, which is one of the sections which is now to be applied to these two organizations, one finds
>   Any person who—
>
> (o) performs any act which is calculated to further the achievement of any of the objects of communism . . . shall be guilty of an offense.
>
> Now that must be read when related to the Bill before us in the following terms:
>   *Any person who performs any act which is calculated to further the achievement of any of the objects of the African National Congress or of the Pan Africanist movement, shall be guilty of an offense.*
>   This is ridiculously wide. . . . My party, the Progressive Party, wishes the Pass Laws to be abolished, and that is one of the objects of both the African National Congress and the Pan Africanist movement and, as soon as we advocate the abolition of the Pass Laws, we become guilty of an offense.

H.A. Deb., Mar. 30, 1960, cols. 4575–76. Emphasis added.

43. Act No. 17 of 1956. This replaced an earlier act of the same name—Act No. 27 of 1914.

44. So. Afr. L. Rep. 11, at 37 (1934).

45. Act No. 34 of 1955.

46. Khosi Mbatha, at a press conference in London in Nov. 1982, speaking about her detention. Cited in Apartheid the Facts, supra note 14, at 63.

47. *Id.* at 65.

48. Cited in A Trust Betrayed: Namibia, supra note 20, at 31.

49. *Id.* at 31.

50. See Commission on the Racial Situation in the Union of South Africa, Report, U.N. GAOR Supp. (No. 16) 8th sess., sec. 720, U.N. Doc. A/2505 and A/2505 Add. 1 (1953).

51. For instance, in the case of Namibia, although the I.C.J. 1971 decision suggests that anything done by South Africa in relation to that afflicted country is illegal and null and void, there have been so many interactions and negotiations under the auspices of the United Nations and between the United Nations and South Africa about Namibia that there may be questions about whether the opinion carries any force.

52. Some may wonder if South Africa's intransigence has altered the Charter's provisions teleologically, but for many reasons this doubt cannot be entertained. First, in failing to comply with U.N. entreaties, South Africa never challenged the soundness of the Charter's principles on human rights, self-determination, and commitment to maintain the peace and security—a fact that makes any application of the teleological test to those principles inappropriate. Second, even on the assumption that it disagrees with the resolutions, the law of treaties forbids South Africa to be the sole judge of the scope of its obligations under the Charter. Thus the only way the Charter's provisions can be affected teleologically by South Africa's intransigence is if South Africa's position is shared by almost all the members of the international community.

53. U.N. CHARTER art. 13.

54. G.A. Res. 217, 3 U.N. GAOR, U.N. Doc. 1/777 (1948). This resolution was adopted by a 48-to-0 vote with 8 abstentions. The abstainers included South Africa, the Soviet Union, Saudi Arabia, and Yugoslavia.

55. *Id.* at art. 1.

56. For more detailed information on the Declaration, see L. SOHN & T. BUERGENTHAL, INTERNATIONAL PROTECTION OF HUMAN RIGHTS 514–56 (1972).

57. See *id.* at 514–56.

58. The Convention on the Prevention and Punishment of the Crime of Genocide (1948), 78 U.N.T.S. 277. Although South Africa was not a party to this convention, it is bound by its strictures because, by the convention's close affinity to the Nuremberg principles and the basic values of the U.N. Charter, it is generally taken as a peremptory norm of international law and hence binding on all, regardless of whether a state is a party.

59. *Id.*, arts. 1 & 2.

60. At the Nuremberg trials where an attempt was made to use orders from superiors as a defense against criminal liability, the tribunal ruled:

> It was submitted that international law is concerned with the actions of sovereign states, and provides no punishment for individuals; and further, that where the act in question is an act of state, those who carry it out are not personally responsible, but are protected by the doctrine of sovereignty of the state. In the opinion of the Tribunal, both these submissions must be rejected. That international law imposes duties and liabilities upon individuals as well as upon states had long been recognized . . . enough has been said to show

that individuals can be punished for violations of international law. Crimes against international law are committed by men, not by abstract entities, and only by punishing individuals who commit such crimes can the provisions of international law be enforced.

See Proceedings of the Nuremberg Tribunal, reprinted in 41 AM. J.I.L. 172, 220–21 (1947).

61. See the Genocide Convention, supra note 58, art. 7.

62. See Tiewul, *Apartheid: Steps Toward International Legal Control* 6 ZAMBIA L.J. 101, 122 no. 81 (1974).

63. It is idle to talk about how the 1983 constitutional changes admitted representatives of the 2.5 million Asians and "Coloreds" (the racially mixed descendants of the indigenous people and the first European settlers) into the South African Parliament. It is enough to observe that this so-called constitutional development is no development at all. It was brought about by a vote in which no nonwhite had a say. Besides, it excludes the more than 20 million blacks, thus presenting itself as a mere charitable act to lure away the new entrants and, hence, perpetuate the apartheid strategy of divide and rule. But even if it is contended that the "homelands" nationalization policy is the reason why the blacks are excluded from this deal, how can the continued presence of more than 10 million urban blacks who are not yet assigned to any "homelands" and who are still excluded from benefiting from the scheme be rationalized? Nor is the scheme progressive; it not only perpetuates the racial stratification by putting the new entrants into separate categories in which they are to deal solely with the affairs affecting people of their own racial blocs, it gives whites the ultimate say on what matters are of general interest and how to resolve them, even though it purports to allow nonwhites to participate in making decisions on matters of "general" interest. Nor does the scheme affect the main tenets of apartheid. It does not change the "homelands" policy, it does not improve the laws against mixed political parties, and it does not alter the laws against free movement of blacks. Indeed, even with the so-called beneficiaries of the new system—the Asians and "Coloreds"—almost all the restrictive laws still apply: they are unable to ride white trains or to visit white theaters, and they are banned from taking residence in any of the four South Africa's provinces—the Orange Free State. For more information, see Bates, *A Constitutional Sidestep*, 7 HARV. INT'L REV. 28–30 (May–June 1985).

64. SOUTH AFRICAN TRANSKEI CONSTITUTION ACT, Act No. 48 of 1963.

65. South Africa Status of Transkei Act, No. 100 of 1976, reprinted in 15 INT'L L. MAT. 1175 (1976).

66. The international abhorrence for the policy was sounded long before the "independence" packages were unleashed. By Res. 2775E (XXVI) of Nov. 1971, the General Assembly condemned

the establishment by the Government of South Africa of Bantu homelands "Bantustans" and the forcible removal of African people of South Africa and Namibia to those areas in violation of their inalienable rights, contrary to the principle of self-determination and prejudicial to the territorial integrity of the countries and the unity of their peoples.

G.A. Res. 2775 E., 26 U.N. GAOR Supp. (No. 29) 41–43, U.N. Doc. A/8429 (1971). See also G.A. Res. 34110, 30 U.N. GAOR Supp. (No. 34) 37, U.N. Doc. A/10034 (1975); G.A. Res. 3151 G, 28 U.N. GAOR Supp. (No. 30) 32, U.N. Doc. A/9030 (1973); and Res. 31/6 A, 31 U.N. GAOR Supp. (No. 39) 10, U.N. Doc. A/31/39 (1976). And in the resolution in which the O.A.U. referred to the Transkeian independence scheme as "fraudulent pseudoindependence," invitation was advanced to "all states . . . not to accord recognition to any Bantustan, in particular, Transkei whose so-called independence is scheduled for the 26 October 1976." O.A.U. Res. 493 (XXVII), para. 4, 15 INT'L LEG. MAT. 1221 (1976).

67. Dugard, *South Africa's "Independent" Homelands: An Exercise in Denationalization* 10(1) DENV. J.I.L. 11, 13–14 (1980).

68. 107 House of Assembly Deb., cols. 4191–93, Apr. 10, 1961, cited in *id.* at 14.

69. Res. 395 (V), 5 U.N. GAOR Supp. (No. 20) at 24, U.N. Doc. A/1775 (1950). This resolution was specifically responsive to South Africa's maltreatment of Asians in South Africa.

70. See G.A. Res. 917 (X) of Dec. 6, 1955; Res. 1016 (XI) of Jan. 30, 1955; and Res. 1178 (XII) of Nov. 26, 1957.

71. G.A. Res. 1248 (XIII) of Oct. 30, 1958; Res. 1375 (XIV) of Nov. 17, 1959.

72. G.A. Res. 1761 (XVII), 17 U.N. GAOR Supp. (No. 7) at 9–10, U.N. Doc. A/5217 (1962).

73. S.C. Res. 182, 18 U.N. SCOR, U.N. Doc. S/5471 (Dec. 4, 1963).

74. 19 U.N. SCOR, App. 11, U.N. Doc. S/5658, Corr. 1 and Add. 1 & 2 (1964).

75. S.C. Res. 191, 19 U.N. SCOR at 13–15, U.N. Doc. S/5773 (1964).

76. Dugard, *The Legal Effect of United Nations Resolutions on Apartheid*, 83 S.A.L.J. 44, 46–50 (1966). Emphasis added.

77. On this, it is instructive to note what the South African representative at the United Nations said in 1947:

> I would submit . . . that a recommendation, as the very term itself denotes, is not a rigidly binding injunction, legal or moral. By this, however, I do not mean to convey that a recommendation does not give rise to any obligation at all. I am prepared to admit that it does give rise to an obligation. But the obligation I would submit, is no more than this: It is the duty of every State affected by a recommendation to give that recommendation its bona fide and earnest consideration; to carry out that recommendation if it is at all practicable for it to do so; and not to disregard it on grounds that are clearly insufficient or frivolous.

See 2 U.N. GAOR (105th mtg.), at 637 (1947). Cited in Dugard, supra note 16, at 51.

78. G.A. Res. 35/206 A of Jan. 28, 1981. Emphasis added.

79. See S/14794, incorporated in the record of the 2315th mtg. S/INF/37 (1981). See also G.A. Res. 34/92 G, 34 U.N. GAOR Supp. (No. 43–46) at 33 (1979).

80. The denationalization element in the independence program is discussed below. For present purposes it is enough to consider the following provision in the Status of Transkei Act of 1976: "Every person falling into certain defined categories shall be a citizen of Transkei and shall cease to be a South African citizen." Supra note 65, art. 5.

81. Act No. 68 of 1951.

82. House of Assembly Deb., col. 579, Feb. 7, 1978, cited in Dugard, supra note 67, at 16.

83. House of Assembly Deb., cols. 5737–38, May 7, 1980, cited in Dugard, supra note 67, at 18.

84. Cited in Witkin, *Transkei: An Analysis of the Practice of Recognition—Political or Legal*, 18 HARV. INT'L L.J. 605, 615–17 (1977).

85. LEAGUE OF NATIONS COVENANT art. 10. Emphasis added.

86. See League of Nations O.J. Spec. Supp. 100, at 8 (1932).

87. The following extract from Max Huber's verdict on the *Island of Palmas* case is revealing:

> The title alleged by the United States of America as constituting the immediate foundation of its claim is that of cession, brought about by the treaty of Paris, which cession transferred all rights of sovereignty which Spain may have possessed in the region indicated in Article 3 of the said Treaty and therefore also those concerning the Island of Palmas. *It is evident that Spain could not transfer more rights than she herself possessed.* This principle of law is expressly recognized in a letter dated April 17th, 1900, from the Secretary of State of the United States.

See the Island of Palmas Case, 2 U.N.R.I.A.A. 829. Emphasis added.

88. L. OPPENHEIM, 1 INTERNATIONAL LAW: A TREATISE sec. 219 (8th ed. H. Lauterpacht). Cf. I. BROWNLIE, PRINCIPLES OF PUBLIC INTERNATIONAL LAW 174 (2d ed. 1973).

89. Chen & Reisman, *Who Owns Taiwan: A Search for International Title*, 81 YALE L.J. 599, 638 (1972). See also H. JOHNSON, SELF-DETERMINATION WITHIN THE COMMUNITY OF NATIONS 59–61 (1967).

90. Schedule B of the Status of Transkei Act, No. 100 of 1976, supra note 65. Emphasis added.

91. Rand Daily Mail (Johannesburg), May 1, 1976, at 6.

92. Liechtenstein v. Guatemala, 1955 I.C.J. REP. 4, cited in W. FRIEDMANN, O. LISSITZYN & R. PUGH, INTERNATIONAL LAW CASES AND MATERIALS 502, 503 (1978).

93. 1923 P.C.I.J. (ser. B) No. 4; 1 HUDSON, WORLD CT. REP. 143 (1923), cited in W. FRIEDMANN, O. LISSITZYN & R. PUGH, supra note 92, at 498. Emphasis added.

94. Reprinted in 5 INT'L L.M. 352 (1966); L. SOHN & T. BUERGENTHAL, BASIC DOCUMENTS ON INTERNATIONAL PROTECTION OF HUMAN RIGHTS 79, 83 (1973).

95. Convention on the Reduction of Statelessness (Aug. 29, 1961), art. 9, U.N. Doc. Conf. 9/15 (1961).

96. See Mann, *The Present Validity of Nazi Nationality Laws*, 89 L.Q.R. 194 at 199 (1973).

97. Convention Relating to the Status of Stateless Persons (Sept. 28, 1954), 360 U.N.T.S. 117 (1954).

98. Convention Relating to the Status of Refugees (July 28, 1951), 189 U.N.T.S. 137 (1951).

99. Protocol Relating to the Status of Refugees (Jan. 31, 1961), 19 U.S.T.S. 6223, T.I.A. No. 6577; 606 U.N.T.S. 267 (1967).

100. Of all these, South Africa is a party to only the Convention Relating to the Status of Stateless Persons.

101. Convention on the Reduction of Statelessness, supra note 95.

102. See J. BRIERLY, THE LAW OF NATIONS 139 (6th ed. 1963).

103. See W. FRIEDMANN, O. LISSITZYN & R. PUGH, supra note 92, at 164. L. OPPENHEIM, supra note 88, at 18. For more information on the two theories, see J. CRAWFORD, THE CREATION OF STATES IN INTERNATIONAL LAW 13–25 (1979).

104. The Convention on the Rights and Duties of States (Dec. 26, 1933) 165 U.N.T.S. 19 (1936). W. FRIEDMANN, O. LISSITZYN & R. PUGH, supra note 92, at 153.

105. See 5 ANNUAL DIGEST OF PUBLIC INTERNATIONAL LAW CASES 11, 15 (Case No. 5) (1929–30). J. CRAWFORD, supra note 103, at 38.

106. 1969 I.C.J. REP. 3, 32. See J. CRAWFORD, supra note 103, at 38.

107. For the recognition of Israel, see Jessup, *The Conditions of Statehood*, 3 U.N. SCOR (383d mtg.) at 9–12, U.N. Doc. S/109 3 (Dec. 1948). Cited in W. FRIEDMANN, O. LISSITZYN & R. PUGH, supra note 92, at 153. See also Ijalaye, *Was "Biafra" at Any Time a State in International Law*, 65 AM. J.I.L. 551, 552 (1971).

108. J. CRAWFORD, supra note 103, at 42.

109. I. BROWNLIE, supra note 88, at 75.

110. *Id*. at 75.

111. A. C. 797 [1924], cited in W. FRIEDMANN, O. LISSITZYN & R. PUGH, supra note 92, at 158.

112. *Id*. at 814, in FRIEDMANN, *id*.

113. See J. CRAWFORD, supra note 103, at 42–44.

114. See W. FRIEDMANN, O. LISSITZYN & R. PUGH, supra note 92, at 155.

115. I.C.J. Statute, art. 34.

116. See the Status of Transkei Act, art. 1, para. 2, reprinted in 15 INT'L L.M. 1175 (1976). TRANSKEI CONSTITUTION, art. 2, para. 3, *id*. at 1136. See also Dugard, supra note 67, at 19–21.

117. See D. Heydt, *Nonrecognition of the Independence of Transkei* 10 CASE W. RES. J.I.L. 167, 184 (1978).

118. Cited in W. FRIEDMANN, O. LISSITZYN & R. PUGH, supra note 92, at 499.

119. *Id*. at 145–46, in FRIEDMANN, *id*. at 500.

120. *Id*. at 500.

121. *Id*. at 501.

122. *Id*. at 499–500.

123. Quoted in *id*. at 502 & 505.

CHAPTER 6

1. Consider, for instance, Gibraltar, one of the cases in this category. Its inhabitants have indicated time and again that they do not like being part of Spain—the country that claims it as an integral part. In the referendum of 1967 involving 12,182 voters, 12,138 voted to maintain their present association with Britain, their so-called colonial master. See 22 U.N. GAOR Annexes (Agenda Item 23) at 5–6, U.N. Doc. A/6876 (1967). Pressured by the Spanish claim predicated on the reversionary clause in the Treaty of Utrecht of 1713, Britain expressed willingness to give up the territory if Spain would abdicate its rights under the treaty: "Would the Spanish Government be ready to release the United Kingdom Government from that provision of the Treaty of Utrecht, so that it should become possible for the United Kingdom Government to decolonize Gibraltar in the normal way, i.e., by granting independence." See 23 U.N. GAOR (1799th mtg.) at 14, cited in T. Franck & P. Hoffman, *The Right of Self-Determination in Very Small Places*, 8 N.Y.U.J.I.L.P 331, 375 (1976). But the question is whether, by "independence," Britain meant statehood. If so, further legal questions could be raised as to the significance of that statement because Gibraltar is so small—about 2.3 square miles with about 29,000 people—that it is doubtful whether it could satisfy the conditions for statehood.

2. A classic manifestation of this dilemma is the Djibouti situation. Although Ethiopia was willing to uphold the principle of self-determination for Djibouti as might be expressed freely by all the inhabitants of that territory—the Afars and Issas alike, Somalia, which indeed had more to gain if Djibouti were independent, qualified the principle of self-determination by echoing the practical question raised in the Israeli-Palestinian conflict. It urged that the only way the principle of self-determination could be observed in Djibouti was if the thousands of Djibouti (Issa) refugees now living in Somalia were repatriated into Djibouti and if those new entrants were treated by the French as Djiboutis rather than as foreigners and were consequently allowed to participate in the referendum. The crux of the matter was that with the close affinity between the Issas and their kin in Somalia, it was not possible to determine which Somalis were Djiboutis and were to be allowed to participate in the exercise of their right of self-determination. Nor could the Somali claim be upheld in disregard of Ethiopia's connection with the Afars—a factor that would practically have made the issue one of self-determination between Ethiopians and Somalis. For the Somali position, see Franck & Hoffman, supra note 1, at 356.

3. In the Falklands, for instance, almost all the inhabitants are British. The Argentine claim over the territory thus raises knotty questions as to whose right of self-determination is at stake: Is it the right of the inhabitants, in which case the criterion for determining would be the majority who are British and prefer association with Britain, or should it be a territorial right, in which case the outcome would have favored Argentina, the state with geographical contiguity to the island? Similar problems were encountered in relation to Gibraltar, where Spain, the claimant of the territory, placed more emphasis on the principle of territorial integrity, arguing that the Charter must be interpreted to restrict the right to "indigenous populations . . . to those who had their roots in the Territory" rather than to make it mean that "a few settlers, established in a Territory from which the original inhabitants had been expelled, could one day take over the

territory." See 23 U.N. GAOR 4th Comm. (1799th mtg.) at 14 (1968), cited in Franck & Hoffman, supra note 1, at 376.

4. T. Franck, *The Stealing of the Sahara*, 70 Am. J.I.L. 694, 698 (1976). Franck & Hoffman, supra note 1, at 351.

5. For instance, the Declaration on Colonialism provides: "Any attempt aimed at the partial or total disruption of the national unity and territorial integrity of a country is incompatible with the purposes and principles of the Charter of the United Nations." G.A. Res. 1514, art. 6, 15 U.N. GAOR Supp. (No. 16) at 66–67, U.N. Doc. A/4684 (1960).

6. See the Declaration on Friendly Relations, Res. 2625:

> Nothing in the foregoing paragraphs shall be construed as authorizing or encouraging any action which would dismember or impair, totally or in part, the territorial integrity or political unity of sovereign and independent States conducting themselves in compliance with the principle of equal rights and self-determination of peoples . . . possessed of a government representing the whole people belonging to the territory without distinction as to race, creed or color.

25 U.N. GAOR Supp. (No. 28) at 121, U.N. Doc. A/8028 (1970).

7. See U.N. Doc. A/PV.2431, 37, at 41 (Mar. 1975), cited in Franck & Hoffman, supra note 1, at 366.

8. See G.A. Res. 2353, 22 U.N. GAOR Supp. (No. 16) at 53, U.N. Doc. A/6716 (1967). Cf. the results of the referendum over Gibraltar, supra note 1, and the opinion of Judge Dillard in the *Spanish Sahara* case: "It is for the people to determine the destiny of their territory and not the territory the destiny of the people." I.C.J. Rep. 3, at 122 (1975).

9. Statement by George Thompson, Commonwealth Secretary, House of Commons Parliamentary Debates, vol. 764, May 1968, col. 271, cited in Franck & Hoffman, supra note 1, at 374.

10. One of the first resolutions on Spanish Sahara was in 1964. See 19 U.N. GAOR Annex (No. 8) (Part 1) at 290–91, U.N. Doc. A/5800/Rev. 1 (1964). Subsequently, G.A. Res. 2072, 20 U.N. GAOR Supp. (No. 14) at 59–60, U.N. Doc. A/6014 (1965); G.A. Res. 2229, 21 U.N. GAOR Supp. (No. 16) at 72–73, U.N. Doc. 6316 (1966); G.A. Res. 2354, 22 U.N. GAOR Supp. (No. 16) at 53–54, U.N. Doc. A/6716 (1967).

11. It regarded its colonies as extensions of its metropolis and considered any attempt to control its relationship with any of them as intervention in its domestic affairs. See the Report of the Special Committee on the Situation with Regard to the Implementation of the Declaration on the Granting of Independence to Colonial Countries and Peoples, U.N. Doc. A/10023/Add, Annex 17–21 (Nov. 1975).

12. See Letter from the Permanent Representative of Spain to the U.N. to the Secretary General, Aug. 20, 1974, U.N. Doc. A/9714 (1974).

13. Franck, supra note 4, 703–06 (1976); E. Riedel, *Confrontation in Western Sahara in the Light of the Advisory Opinion of the International Court of Justice of 16 October 1975: A Critical Appraisal*, 19 G.Y.B.I.L. 405, at 412 (1976); Janis, *The*

International Court of Justice: Advisory Opinion on the Western Sahara, 17(3) HARV. INT'L L.J. 609 n. 2 (1976).

14. G.A. Res. 1541, 15 U.N. GAOR Supp. (No. 16) at 29–30, U.N. Doc. A/4684 (1960).

15. *Id*. at 29–30.

16. G.A. Res. 2625, supra note 6.

17. See Doc. A/36/679 of 1981, adopted in Res. A/36/50; 36 U.N. GAOR Supp. (No. 51) (1981).

18. G.A. Res. 3162, 28 U.N. GAOR Supp. (No. 30) at 110–11, U.N. Doc. A/9030 (1973).

19. G.A. Res. 3292, 29 U.N. GAOR Supp. (No. 31) at 103–04, U.N. Doc. A/9631 (1974).

20. *Id*. at 103–04.

21. U.N. CHARTER art. 96, para. 1. Emphasis added.

22. I.C.J. Statute art. 65, paras. 1 & 2. Emphasis added.

23. 1975 I.C.J. REP. 12, 69, 77.

24. *Id*. at 78.

25. 1962 I.C.J. REP. 155.

26. In previous years, virtually all resolutions on the Sahara had been taken with little opposition, but this time nearly one-third of the members abstained, clearly indicating the "uneasiness aroused by Morocco's and Mauritania's changed positions." See Riedel, supra note 13, at 417.

27. I.C.J. REP., supra note 23, at 18–19.

28. 1923 P.C.I.J. (ser. B) No. 5, at 27 (1923).

29. 1950 I.C.J. REP. 65.

30. It reads:

The Court is aware of the fact that it is not requested to decide a dispute, but to give an advisory opinion. This circumstance, however, does not especially modify the above considerations. The question put to the Court is not one of abstract law, but concerns directly the main point of the controversy between Finland and Russia, and can only be decided by an investigation into the facts underlying the case. Answering the question would be substantially equivalent to deciding the dispute between the parties. The Court being a Court of Justice, cannot, even in giving advisory opinions depart from the essential rules guiding their activity as a Court.

P.C.I.J. (ser. B), supra note 28, at 27–28. Emphasis added.

31. It thus distinguished between the *Carelia* case and the case of the *Peace Treaties* by observing that the former "related to the main point of a dispute actually pending between two states" whereas the *Peace Treaties* case was "solely concerned with the applicability of certain disputes of procedure for settlement instituted by the Peace Treaties." I.C.J. REP., supra note 29, at 72. Cited in M. Janis, supra note 13, at 612–13 n. 20.

32. Hudson, *The Twenty-Ninth Year of the World Court*, 45 AM. J.I.L. 1, 5 (1951), cited in Janis, supra note 13, at 612–13.

33. As he puts it, "Western Sahara has now completely dealt with Eastern Carelia." *Id.* at 612–13.

34. I.C.J. REP., supra note 23, at 48–53.

35. *Id.* 162–63.

36. Yet Morocco construed the confirmation of the link between it and the colony as an endorsement of its claim for revindication of the colony and used that as the basis for the so-called Green March. It stated:

> The opinion of the Court can mean one thing: the so-called Western Sahara was part of Minimum territory over which the sovereignty was exercised by the Kings of Morocco and that the population of this territory considered themselves and were considered to be Moroccans. *To-day Minimum demands have been recognized by the legal advisory organ of the United Nations.*

Press Release of the Permanent Mission of Morocco to the United Nations on Oct. 16, 1975, quoted in U.N. Doc. S/PV/1849, at 11 (1975). Emphasis added.

37. Nor did it disregard the few instances where some of the principal modes of exercising self-determination have been departed from. Yet it did not hesitate to distinguish those situations:

> The validity of the principle of self-determination defined as the need to pay regard to the freely expressed will of peoples, is not affected by the fact that in certain cases the General Assembly has dispensed with the requirement of consulting the inhabitants of a given territory. Those instances were based either on the consideration that a certain population did not constitute a "people" entitled to self-determination or on the conviction that a consultation was totally unnecessary, in view of special circumstances.

1975 I.C.J. REP. 32, para. 59, cited in Riedel, supra note 13, at 423.

38. *Id.* at 48–49.

39. *Id.* at 434.

40. See the Administrative Tribunal case, 1973 I.C.J. REP. 166, 172.

41. See the Report of the United Nations Visiting Mission to Spanish Sahara (1975), U.N. Doc. A/10023/Add. 5, Annex, at 26 (1975). Cited in Franck, supra note 4, at 706–7. Emphasis added.

42. See supra note 36.

43. Spain, for instance, made it clear that it would forcibly defend the territory, if necessary. See Franck, supra note 4, at 713.

44. See S.C. Res. 380 (1975), 30 U.N. SCOR at 9, U.N. Doc. S/INF/31 (Nov. 1975).

45. Algeria was invited to the meeting, but it boycotted it and declared that it would accord no validity to the agreement. See U.N. Doc. S/11880, Annex IV, at 2–3 (1975).

46. *Id.* at 1.

47. Franck, supra note 4.

48. Franck & Hoffman, supra note 1, at 342.

49. Res. 3458A (XXX), U.N. Doc. GA/5438, at 254–55 (1975); Res. 3458B, U.N. Doc. GA/5438, at 256 (1975). See Franck, supra note 4, at 717.

50. This time by a revolution.

51. Report of the Special Committee, U.N. Doc. A/10023/Add. 1, chap. VII Annex B, at 41 (1975).

52. See Franck & Hoffman, supra note 1, at 345.

53. See P. Elliott, *Shorter Articles, Comments and Notes, The East Timor Dispute*, 27 I.C.L.Q. 238 at 239–40 (Jan. 1978).

54. See the letter dated July 8, 1976, from José Ramos Horta addressed to the Secretary General. U.N. Doc. S/12133. Cited in Elliott, *id.* at 240.

55. See letter from the Permanent Representative of Indonesia to the Secretary-General, Dec. 4, 1975, U.N. Doc. A/C.4/808, Annex, at 1 (1975). See also Franck & Hoffman, supra note 1, at 348–49.

56. A/Res. 3485 (XXX), U.N. Doc. GA/5438 at 262.

57. See Report of the Security Council of June 16, 1975–June 15, 1976, 31 GAOR Supp. (No. 2) ch. 4, U.N. Doc. A/31/2 (1976).

58. U.N. Doc. S/12011, 1, 12 (1976). See Elliott, supra note 53, at 240.

59. Franck & Hoffman, supra note 1, at 349.

CHAPTER 7

1. For recent discussion of the subject, see Ginsburgs, *Wars of National Liberation and the Modern Law of Nations—A Soviet Thesis*, 29 LAW AND CONTEMPORARY PROBLEMS 910, 910–11 (1964); Ronzitti, *Resort to Force in Wars of National Liberation*, in CURRENT PROBLEMS OF INTERNATIONAL LAW 318, 319 n. 1 (A. Cassese ed. 1975); Tyner, *Wars of National Liberation in Africa and Palestine: Self- Determination for Peoples or Territories?* 5 YALE STUDIES IN WORLD PUBLIC ORDER 235, 238 (1975); Ronzitti, *Wars of National Liberation: A Legal Definition*, 1 ITALIAN Y.B.I.L. 193, 196–205 (1975); Abi-Saab, *Wars of National Liberation and the Laws of War*, 3 ANNALES D'ETUDES INTERNATIONALES 93 (1972). But see Wright, *United States Intervention in Lebanon*, 53 AM. J.I.L. 112, 121 (1959).

2. 175 U.S. 677 20 S.Ct. 290, 44 L.Ed. 320 (1900).

3. I.C.J. Statute art. 38, paras. (c) & (d), 59 STAT. 1055, T.S. 993, 3 BEVANS 1179.

4. "The decision of the Court has no binding force except between the parties and in respect of that particular case." *Id.* art. 59.

5. Abi-Saab, supra note 1, at 93. Emphasis added.

6. Ronzitti, *Resort to Force*, supra note 1, at 319, n. 1.

7. Ronzitti, *Wars of National Liberation*, supra note 1, at 196.

8. *Id.* at 196.

9. Supra Chapter 1, "What Is a Liberation Movement?"

10. Cassese, *The Status of Rebels under the 1977 Geneva Protocol on Non-International Armed Conflicts*, 30 INT'L & COMP. L.Q. 416, 417 (1981).

11. Discussed in Verwey, *The International Hostages Convention and National*

Liberation Movements, 75 AM. J.I.L. 69–79 (1981); see also Cassese, supra note 10, at 416–20.

12. Before 1963, military intervention in politics had been confined to the independent countries in Asia, Latin America, and the Middle East—the only exceptions in Africa being Egypt (1952) and Sudan (1958). See B. NWABUEZE, CONSTITUTIONALISM IN THE EMERGENT STATES 219–24 (1973).

13. The only exceptions to this are the 1966 and 1970 coups in Uganda and Lesotho, respectively. In these cases, the leaders of the civilian regimes overthrew the preexisting systems. *Id*. at 227.

14. Hunter, *A Decade of Unrest: What's the Cause of African Coups?* in Christian Science Monitor, Apr. 1969, at 9, reprinted in 42 (6) WEST AFRICA TODAY 36, 37 (1971) [hereinafter WEST AFRICA TODAY]. Emphasis added.

15. Gutteridge, *African Military Rulers: An Assessment*, 62 CONFLICT STUDIES 1 (Oct. 1975).

16. *Id*. See also D. AUSTIN, THE UNDERLYING PROBLEMS OF THE ARMY COUP D'ETAT IN EAST AFRICA 65–72 (1966); R. FIRST, POWER IN AFRICA 86–140 (1970); S. DECALLO, COUPS AND ARMY RULE IN AFRICA—STUDIES IN MILITARY STYLE 5–35 (1979); B. NWABUEZE, supra note 12, at 219–55; A. Zolberg, *The Military Decade in Africa*, 25 WORLD TODAY 309, 315–19 (1972–73). For more general discussion, see J. LEE, AFRICAN ARMIES AND CIVIL ORDER (1969); S. PANTER-BRICK, NIGERIAN POLITICS AND MILITARY RULE: PRELUDE TO CIVIL WAR (1970); C. WELSH, SOLDIER AND STATE IN AFRICA: A COMPARATIVE ANALYSIS OF MILITARY INTERVENTION AND POLITICAL CHANGE 95–125 (1970); S. HUNTINGTON, POLITICAL ORDER IN THE CHANGING SOCIETIES 66–75 (1968).

17. M. LEVY, MODERNIZATION AND STUDIES OF SOCIETIES 603 (1966).

18. Pye, *Armies in the Process of Political Modernization*, in THE ROLE OF THE MILITARY IN UNDERDEVELOPED COUNTRIES 69, 70–79 (J. Johnson ed. 1962).

19. S. DECALLO, supra note 16, at 13–14.

20. In the struggle against Idi Amin in Uganda, three of the movements had these names: Save Uganda Movement (S.U.M.), Forces for National Redress (F.N.R.), and Ugandan Liberation Front (U.L.F.).

21. Reprinted in WEST AFRICA TODAY, supra note 14, at 47. Emphasis added.

22. B. NWABUEZE, supra note 12, at 220.

23. Gutteridge, supra note 15, at 5.

24. R. FIRST, supra note 16, at 20.

25. D. AUSTIN, supra note 16, at 65–72.

26. Fadugba, *The Military Factor in Nigerian Politics*, in 150 AFRICA 17, 17 (monthly ed. 1984).

27. See *Upper Volta—The Law According to Sankara*, in 150 AFRICA (monthly ed. 1984).

28. See Ross Hoyle, *A Continent Gone Wrong*, in TIME, Jan. 16, 1984, at 24–34.

29. S. DECALLO, supra note 16, at 28. See also Nelkin, *The Economic and Social Setting of Military Takeovers in Africa*, 2 JOURNAL OF ASIAN AND AFRICAN STUDIES 231, 250, and Malan, *Africa's Quest for Economic Freedom—Objectives and Problems*, in AFRICAN FREEDOM ANNUAL 37–64 (F. Metrowich ed. 1979).

30. S. DECALLO, supra note 16, at 28.

31. Nordlinger, *Soldier in Mufti: The Impact of Military Rule upon Economic and Social Change in the Non-Western States*, 64 AM. POL. SCI. REV. 1131, 1133 (Dec. 1970).

32. See Hunter, *After Nkrumah: Ghana Puts the Pieces Together Again*, 20 Christian Science Monitor 9 (1969), reprinted in 42(6) WEST AFRICA TODAY, at 60 (1971); S. DECALLO, supra note 16.

33. See Nwogugu, *The Nigerian Civil War: A Case Study in the Law of War*, 14 INDIAN J.I.L. 13, 16 (1974); B. DUDLEY, AN INTRODUCTION TO NIGERIAN GOVERNMENT AND POLITICS 79–85 (1980).

34. B. DUDLEY, supra note 33, at 79–85.

35. S. DECALLO, supra note 16, at 194–206.

36. *Id.* at 194–206.

37. Kraus, *Arms and Politics in Ghana*, in SOLDIER AND STATE IN AFRICA 50, 52 (C. Welch ed. 1970). See also Price, *Military and Political Leadership: The Ghanaian Case*, COMPARATIVE POLITICS 361–79 (Apr. 1971).

38. In an interview broadcast by the West German television networks, General Kotoka, the architect of the coup, attributed it to President Nkrumah's plan to send them to fight in Rhodesia. See East African Standard, Mar. 16, 1966, cited in A. AJALA, PAN AFRICANISM: EVOLUTION, PROGRESS, AND PROSPECTS 247–48 (1973). Likewise, Colonel Afrifa said in his book: "Could it be that we had been sent to the Congo to foster the ambition of Kwame Nkrumah?" See A. AFRIFA, THE GHANA COUP, 24 Feb. 1966, at 66 (1967).

39. Ocran, another participant in the coup, referred to the P.O.G.R. as a plot "to gradually strangulate the Army to death." A. OCRAN, A MYTH IS BROKEN 35 (1966).

40. Bennett, *The Military Under Busia Government*, 91 WEST AFRICA 22 (weekly ed. Feb. 15, 1972).

41. S. DECALLO, supra note 16, at 5. See also B. NWABUEZE, supra note 12, at 226.

42. S. DECALLO, supra note 16, at 6–20.

43. Supra Chapter 7, "The Struggles for Overthrow of Existing Governments."

44. UGANDA, THE PUBLIC ACCOUNTS OF THE REPUBLIC OF UGANDA FOR THE YEAR ENDED 30TH JUNE, 1969. ENTEBBE 3–25 (1970); J. LISTOWELL, AMIN 69–71 (1976).

45. See Uganda, in AFRICA CONTEMPORARY RECORD B187 at B188 (1970–71) cited in S. DECALLO, supra note 16, at 210.

46. *Id.* at 210.

47. *Id.* at 7–40.

48. S. DECALLO, POLITICS OF INSTABILITY IN DAHOMEY 18–19 (1968).

49. S. DECALLO, supra note 16, at 28.

50. *Id.* at 28.

51. These policies, however, attracted strong criticism from all over the world, especially Africa. The leader of Nigeria, President Shehu Shagari, for example, strongly deplored the "wanton execution and humiliation to which the family of President William Tolbert had been subjected." See New Nigerian, May 29, 1980, at 2, col. 1.

52. See 27(5) Africa Report at 26 (bimonthly ed. Sept.–Oct. 1982).

53. See 3413 West Africa 66 (weekly ed. Jan. 10, 1983).

54. *Id.* at 6.

55. Gutteridge, supra note 15, at 7–8.

56. *Id.* at 7–8.

57. *Id.* at 7–8.

58. S. Decallo, supra note 16, at 31; Bennett, *The Non-Politicians Take Over*, 17 Africa Report 19–22 (bimonthly ed. Apr. 1972).

59. S. Decallo, supra note 16, at 31.

60. *Id.* at 31–32.

61. *Id.* at 32.

62. *Id.* at 32.

63. See Hoyle, supra note 28, at 27–28.

64. See J. Strate, *Post Military Coup Strategy in Uganda: Amin's Early Attempts to Consolidate Political Support*, Papers in International Studies: African Series 25, 30–39 (1972).

65. Uganda Argus, May 3, 1971, at 1, col. 2.

66. S. Decallo, supra note 16, at 222–24.

67. See Uganda, in Contemporary Africa Record, B269, at B281 (1972–73); Shaw, *Uganda Under Amin: The Costs of Confronting Dependence*, 20 Africa Today 41 (1973).

68. S. Decallo, supra note 16, at 226.

69. See Short, *Uganda: Putting it in Perspective*, 20(1) Africa Report 37 (Mar.–Apr. 1973); Parson, *Africanizing Trade In Uganda: The Final Solution*, 20(1) Africa Today 70 (1973).

70. Short, supra note 69, at 37.

71. Ghana Constitution of 1979, art. 1, para. 2.

72. Nigeria Constitution of 1963, sect. 1, para. 1.

73. Nigeria Constitution of 1979, art. 1, para. 2.

74. B. Dudley, An Introduction to Nigerian Government and Politics 74 (1982).

75. H. Chand, Nigerian Constitutional Law 5–7 (1981).

76. See State v. Otchere, 2 G.L.R. 463 (1963); 2 G.&G., A Source Book of Constitutional Law in Ghana 277 (1970) [hereinafter G.&G.]; In re Okine, 1 G.L.R. 84 (1959); In re Akoto, G.L.R. 523 (1961), 2 G.&G. 160; State v. Isaac Boro, S.C. 377/1966 (Nig.) of Dec. 5, 1966 (unreported). See also Elias, *The Nigerian Crisis in International Law*, 5 Nig. L.J. 1, 3 (1971); O. Achike, Groundwork of Military Law in Nigeria 136–38 (1978).

77. Ghana Constitution of 1979, supra note 1, arts. 1 & 2.

78. The National Liberation Council (N.L.C.) Establishment Proclamation Decree, N.L.C.D. No. 1 (1966) (Ghana). Art. 2, para. 3 reads:

Notwithstanding the suspension of the Constitution of the Republic of Ghana and subject to any decree that may be made by the National Liberation Council, all courts in existence immediately before the 24th day of February 1966,

shall, on and after that date continue in existence with the same powers as they
had immediately before the said date and also all judges and every other person holding any office or post in the Judicial Service immediately before the
24th day of February 1966, shall on or after the said date continue in that
office or post upon the same terms and conditions as before.

Cf. the National Redemption Council (N.R.C.) Establishment Proclamation Decree of
1972, sect. 2, and the Nigerian Decree No. 1, entitled "Constitution (Suspension Modification) Decree 1966.

79. E. WADE & G. PHILLIPS, CONSTITUTIONAL LAW 665–66 (1970).

80. Onyia v. Governor in Council, 2 All Nig. L.R. 174 (1962); W.N.L.R. 89
(1962).

81. Vajesingji Joravarsingji v. Secretary of State for India, L.R. 51 Ind. App.
357, quoted with approval in the Privy Council in Hoani te Heuheu Tukin v. Aotea
District Maori Land Board, A.C. 308 [1941]. Emphasis added. For discussion of more
cases on this issue, see B. NWABUEZE, CONSTITUTIONAL LAW OF THE NIGERIAN RE-
PUBLIC 26 (1962); B. NWABUEZE, MACHINERY OF JUSTICE IN NIGERIA 3–4 (1963).

82. H. KELSEN, GENERAL THEORY OF LAW AND STATE 119 (1961 ed.).

83. State v. Dosso, 2 Pakistani Supreme Court Reports 180 (1958).

84. Uganda v. Commissioner of Prisons, Ex parte Matovu, E. AFR. L. REV. 514
(1966).

85. *Id.* at 538. Emphasis added.

86. 2 G.&G., supra note 76, at 493.

87. Executive Instrument 203.

88. Legislative Instrument 395.

89. See the following ruling of Judge Apaloo:

It seems to me highly artificial and I cannot believe that with the known
pragmatism that informs judicial attitudes towards questions of legislative interpretation, the Attorney General can have thought an argument such as this
was likely to carry seasoned judicial minds. We should fail in our duty to
effectuate the will of the Constituent Assembly if we interpreted the Constitution not in accordance with its letter and spirit but in accordance with some
doctrinaire juristic theory. . . . Without disrespect to them, I think Kelsen's
theory of the pure science of law would have given them as much interest as a
lecture in metaphysics would have given to a child of ten. I believe members
of the Constituent Assembly approached and performed their task as practical
men of business guided by the experience of our recent past and informed by
an understanding of ordinary English words. I cannot accept that in using the
word 'establish' in section 9(1) they had in mind any juristic theories on the
principle of legitimacy.

2 G.&G., supra note 76, at 508–9.

90. *Id.* at 508–9.

91. Date-Bah, *Jurisprudence Day in Court in Ghana*, 20 INT'L & COMP. L.Q. 315, 316 (1971).

92. In a typical encroachment on the independence of the judiciary, the leader of the government stated in a radio and television broadcast: "My Government will exercise its right to employ only those whom it wishes to employ. No Court can enforce any decision that seeks to compel the Government to reemploy anyone. That would be a futile exercise." See Busia, *Fair Trial for all in Ghana*, a radio and television broadcast on Monday, April 20, 1970, cited in THE CONTRIBUTION OF THE COURTS TO GOVERNMENT: A WEST AFRICAN VIEW 302 (A. Amissah ed. 1981).

93. 2 G.&G., supra note 76, at 442.

94. *Id.* at 444. Emphasis added.

95. Justice Azu Crabbe's dissenting ruling in the *Gbedemah* case was very insightful. Briefly, Gbedemah's case involved the right of a successful candidate in the 1969 elections to his seat in Parliament. Before the elections Gbedemah had been found guilty of corruption by a commission set under a decree of the N.L.C. He persistently challenged the findings, but the N.L.C. government failed to allow him a hearing. Following Gbedemah's victory in the 1969 elections, the losing candidate opposed his membership in Parliament by invoking article 71 of the constitution, which stipulated that any person who had been "adjudged or otherwise declared" guilty of corruption could not be a parliamentarian. Under article 102, however, not only was the judicial power of the state vested in the judiciary, but there was also an express provision that no organ or agency of the executive should be given a final judicial power. Gbedemah challenged the finding, arguing that they could not bar him from taking his seat in Parliament. The court rejected the argument and held that it had been effectively precluded from going into the case. Whereupon Justice Crabbe rendered his seasoned opinion with illustration:

> Supposing Mr. X is "declared" (using the word in its broad meaning, as canvassed by the plaintiff) by the report of a commission of inquiry that while being a public officer he acquired assets unlawfully. . . . And supposing the Commission makes a recommendation, as Commissions of inquiries often do, that Mr. X should be prosecuted. Now, supposing the report is published, together with a Government White Paper in which the Government signifies its acceptance of the recommendation. Upon the publication of the report Mr. X becomes, by virtue of Article 71(2)(b)(ii), disqualified to a member of the National Assembly for five years. Supposing that Mr. X is subsequently tried in the High Court on charges of stealing or defrauding or abuse of office under the Criminal Code, 1960 (Act 29), or on a charge of dissipation of public funds under the Public Property (Protection) and Corrupt Practices (Prevention) Act, 1962 (Act 121). And supposing that Mr. X is acquitted by the High Court. If the plaintiff's interpretation is accepted it will mean that the disqualification from membership of the National Assembly still attaches to Mr. X, even though a Superior Court of the land has declared him innocent of the charges. Surely this would be absurd.

Id. at 451. For discussion of the Crabbe opinion, see Read, *Judicial Power and the Constitution of Ghana*, REV. G.L. 107 (1971). See also A. AMISSAH, supra note 92, at 274–75.

96. S.C. 58/96 (Nig. West) of April 24, 1970 (unreported), discussed in Ojo, *The Search for a Grundnorm in Nigeria—The Lakanmi Case*, 20 INT'L & COMP. L.Q. 119 (Jan. 1971); B. ILLUYOMADE & B. EKA, CASES AND MATERIALS ON ADMINISTRATIVE LAW IN NIGERIA 5–19 (1980); Elias, *Military Decrees in Nigeria and Ghana*, 5 NIG. L.J. 128 (1971); Bundu, *Recognition of Revolutionary Authorities: Law and Practice of States*, 27 INT'L & COMP. L.Q. 18, at 32–33 (1978); Elias, *The Nigerian Crisis in International Law*, supra note 76, at 1.

97. Ogunlesi v. A.G. L.D./28/19 (1970). Unreported; discussed, however, in Bundu, supra note 96. See also Ojo, supra note 96.

98. Adamolekun v. The Council of the University of Ibadan, S.C. 378/1966 (1967). Unreported, but discussed in Ojo, supra note 96, at 132–38.

99. *Id.* at 132–38.

100. See infra, Chapter 7, "The *Lakanmi* Case."

101. Decree No. 1, "Constitution (Suspension and Modification) Decree No. 1. 1966," sec. 1, para. 1, supra note 78.

102. Decree No. 14 of 1967.

103. B. ILLUYOMADE & B. EKA, supra note 96, at 5–9.

104. See Ojo, supra note 96, at 132.

105. *Id.* at 126–30. See also Elias, supra note 96, at 128–30.

106. Ojo, supra note 96, at 130–33.

107. *Id.* at 130–33. See also Elias, supra note 96, at 129 (1971).

108. See Bundu, supra note 96, at 32–33; Elias, supra note 76, at 4–5; Ojo, supra note 96, at 119.

109. Bundu, supra note 96, at 33–34. Emphasis added.

110. H. KELSEN, supra note 82, at 117–18, 120.

111. State v. Dosso, supra note 83, at 538–39. Emphasis added.

112. Elias, supra note 76, at 5.

113. *Id.* at 5.

114. Elias has pointed out certain useful criteria for finding out whether an upheaval is a coup d'état:

1. There must have been an abrupt political change; i.e. a coup d'état or a revolution;
2. The change must not have been within the contemplation of an existing constitution;
3. The change must destroy the entire legal order except what is preserved;
4. The new constitution and government must be effective.

Elias, *Military Decrees*, supra note 96, at 130. See also Ojo, supra note 96, at 131.

CHAPTER 8

1. W. HALL, A TREATISE ON INTERNATIONAL LAW 55–60 (8th ed. 1924); T. LAWRENCE, PRINCIPLES OF INTERNATIONAL LAW 56 (1904).
2. Higgins, *International Law and Civil Conflicts*, in INTERNATIONAL REGULATION OF CIVIL WAR 169 (E. Luard ed. 1972).
3. U.N. CHARTER art. 1, paras. 2 and 55.
4. Art. 21(3), G.A. Res. 217, U.N. Doc. A/810, at 71, 75 (1948).
5. G.A. Res. 1514, 15 U.N. GAOR Supp. (No. 16) at 166, U.N. Doc. A/4684 (1960).
6. Annex to G.A. Res. 2200, 21 U.N. GAOR Supp. (No. 16), at 52, U.N. Doc. A/6316 (1966).
7. G.A. Res. 3314, 29 U.N. GAOR Supp. (No. 31) at 142, U.N. Doc. A/9631 (1974).
8. Declaration on Friendly Relations, G.A. Res. 2625, Annex, 25 U.N. GAOR Supp. (No. 17) at 66, U.N. Doc. A/5217 (1970).
9. *Id.* at 66.
10. Annex to G.A. Res. 2200, supra note 6.
11. The fifth point of this document reads: "A free, open minded, and impartial adjustment of all colonial claims, based upon a strict observance of the principle that in determining all such questions of sovereignty the interests of the populations concerned must have equal weight with the equitable claims of the government whose title is to be determined." See 5 WHITEMAN, DIGEST OF INTERNATIONAL LAW 42. In his message to Congress on Feb. 11, 1918, President Wilson noted that "national aspirations must be respected, peoples may now be dominated and governed only by their own consent. . . . The right of nations to free self-determination is not a mere phrase, it is an imperative principle of action which will be disregarded by statesmen in the future only at their own risk." Official statements of War Aims and Peace Proposals, Dec. 1916 to Nov. 1918, at 268, cited in SELF-DETERMINATION: FROM BIAFRA TO BANGLA DESH 3–4 (J. Saxena ed. 1978).
12. WHITEMAN, supra note 11, at 44.
13. Supra, Chapter 2.
14. Art. 27(b)(3), I.L.C. Rep. 2d. pt., 17th sess., at 52–53 U.N. Doc. A/6309/Rev. 1.
15. R. EMERSON, SELF-DETERMINATION REVISITED IN THE ERA OF DECOLONIZATION 27 (Occasional Papers No. 9, Center for International Affairs, Harvard University (Dec. 1964).
16. See the discussion in Chapters 2 to 4.
17. Supra, Chapter 6.
18. G.A. Res. 2625, supra note 8.
19. In its consideration of when a territory attains a full measure of self-government, the General Assembly approved a list of criteria for these resolutions: (1) factors indicative of the attainment of independence; (2) factors indicative of the free association of a territory on equal footing with the metropolitan or other country as an integral

part of that country or in any other form; and (3) factors indicative of the attainment of other separate system of self-government.

20. R. GIBSON, AFRICAN LIBERATION MOVEMENTS: CONTEMPORARY STRUGGLES AGAINST MINORITY RULE 20–55 (1972).

21. There is the question as to whether this practice is not tantamount to an impairment of the right of the people to decide the issue freely by themselves.

22. Often the strength is determined by international assistance rather than the capabilities of the belligerent parties. In Angola, for instance, it has been pointed out that the U.S. support for the F.N.L.A. was surpassed by that given by the Soviet-sponsored Cubans to the M.P.L.A. See Yusuf-Abdi, *Cuba's Role in Africa: Revolutionary or Reactionary*, in 1 HORN OF AFRICA 17, 19–27 (Oct.–Dec. 1978).

23. Sinha, *Is Self-Determination Passe?* 12 COLUM. J. TRANSNAT'L L. 260, 271 (1973).

24. See also U.N. CHARTER arts. 1(2) and 55.

25. *Id.* at art. 2, paras. 1 and 4.

26. VIENNA CONVENTION ON THE LAW OF TREATIES, art. 31, U.N. Doc. A/Conf. 39/27 (1969).

27. R. RUSSEL, A HISTORY OF THE UNITED NATIONS CHARTER: THE ROLE OF THE UNITED STATES 1940–1945, at 810–11 (1958).

28. Doc. 343 I/1/16, 6 U.N.C.I.O. Doc. 296 (1945).

29. Eagleton contends that "the term 'self-determination' was crowded into Article 1 of the Charter without relevance and without explanation." Eagleton, *Excesses of Self-Determination*, 31 FOREIGN AFF. 592 (1953).

30. Doc. 343, I/1/16, 6 U.N.C.I.O. Doc. 296 (1945).

31. Doc. WD381, Co/156, 18 U.N.C.I.O. Docs. 657–58 (1945).

32. Sinha, *Self-Determination in International Law and Its Applicability to the Baltic Peoples*, RES BALTICA 256–57 (1968) quoted in SECESSION: THE LEGITIMACY OF SELF-DETERMINATION 23 (L. Buchheit ed. 1978).

33. H. KELSEN, THE LAW OF THE UNITED NATIONS 51–53 (1950).

34. Emerson, *"Self-Determination,"* PROC. A.S.I.L. 136–37 (Apr. 1966).

35. *Id.* at 137.

36. *Id.* at 139; see also Emerson, *"Self-Determination,"* 65 PROC. A.S.I.L. 459, 464–66 (1971).

37. R. EMERSON, supra note 15, at 64. See also Emerson, supra note 34, at 136.

38. Chowdhury, *The Status and Norms of Self-Determination in Contemporary International Law*, 24 N.L.R. 72, 74–75 (1977).

39. *Id.* at 79–80. Emphasis added.

40. According to one brilliant critique: "The United Nations would be in an extremely difficult position if it were to interpret the right of self-determination in such a way as to invite or justify attacks on the territorial integrity of its own members." VAN DYKE, HUMAN RIGHTS, THE UNITED STATES AND THE WORLD COMMUNITY 102 (1970); see also the O.A.U. Resolution on Border Disputes of 1964, which stated that the borders of African states on the day of their independence constitute a "tangible reality." Cited in BASIC DOCUMENTS ON AFRICAN AFFAIRS 360–61 (I. Brownlie ed. 1971); A. MCEWEN, INTERNATIONAL BOUNDARIES IN EAST AFRICA 23–24 (1971).

41. See C. LEGUM, PAN AFRICANISM: A SHORT POLITICAL GUIDE 254–55 (1962).

42. See U.N. CHARTER art. 2, para. 1.

43. C. OJUKWU, BIAFRA: SELECTED SPEECHES AND RANDOM THOUGHTS 190 (1969).

44. Tiewul, *Relations Between the United Nations Organization and the Organization of African Unity in the Settlement of Secessionist Conflicts*, 16 HARV. INT'L L.J. 259, 263 (1975).

45. J. WORONOFF, ORGANIZATION OF AFRICAN UNITY 404–9 (1979); B. NWABUEZE, CONSTITUTIONALISM IN THE EMERGENT STATES 257–68 (1973).

46. Nayar, *Self-Determination Beyond the Colonial Context: Biafra in Retrospect*, 10 TEXAS INT'L L.J. 321, 333 (1975). Emphasis added.

47. Chowdhury, supra note 38, at 80. Emphasis added.

48. See Doc. 343 I/1/16, 6 U.N.C.I.O. Docs. 396, at 455 (1945).

49. H. LAUTERPACHT, INTERNATIONAL LAW AND HUMAN RIGHTS 178–86 (1950).

50. McDougal and Reisman, *Rhodesia and the United Nations: The Lawfulness of International Concern*, 62 AM. J.I.L. 1, 12 n. 50 (1968).

51. See B. NWABUEZE, supra note 45, at 256–65.

52. See the BURMESE CONSTITUTION 1947, reprinted in M. MAUNG, BURMA'S CONSTITUTION 258–301 (1961). See also SOVIET CONSTITUTION, art. 17, reprinted in 13 CONSTITUTIONS OF THE COUNTRIES OF THE MODERN WORLD, U.S.S.R. (1974); the (pre-1975) CONSTITUTION OF THE PEOPLES REPUBLIC OF CHINA, 3 *id*. at PEOPLES REPUBLIC OF CHINA 14–15 (1975), cited in L. BUCHHEIT, supra note 32, at 100–103.

53. The limitations of the Burmese Constitution are obvious from art. 10, where the right to secede is so carefully circumscribed as to make it practically inoperable. See also L. BUCHHEIT, supra note 32, at 99–100. In the Communist countries, apart from the qualification that the right is exercisable only if it is compatible with communist principles as construed by the "proletariat," experiences in Hungary and Czechoslovakia, where mere switches in ideological positions triggered implacable responses from the Soviet Union, leave no room to doubt that attempts to secede would be unacceptable—the opposite provisions of their constitution notwithstanding. For discussion of the Brezhnev Doctrine, see Firmage, *Summary and Interpretation*, in THE INTERNATIONAL LAW OF CIVIL WAR 405, 409 (R. Falk ed. 1971). See also L. BUCHHEIT, supra note 32, at 100–20 and the discussion of the Soviet practice below.

54. Examples of these are the federations between Mali and Senegal, the United Arab Republic and Syria, and Malaysia and Singapore. All these are discussed in L. BUCHHEIT, supra note 32, at 97–99; B. NWABUEZE, supra note 45, at 179–86. For a discussion of the legal significance of the Mali Federation, see Cohen, *Legal Problems Arising from the Dissolution of the Mali Federation*, 36 B.Y.B.I.L. 375 (1960).

55. Infra Chapter 8, "The Congo-Katanga Conflict."

56. Makinda, *Conflict and the Super Powers in the Horn of Africa*, 4(1) THIRD WORLD QUARTERLY 92, 98 (Jan. 1982).

57. Quoted in THE UNFINISHED QUEST FOR UNITY 71 (Z. Cervenka ed. 1977).

58. For more detailed discussion of the politics in the area, see A. Selassie, *The Evolution of the Principle of Self-Determination*, 1 HORN OF AFRICA 3, 5–7 (Oct.–Dec.

1978); Abdi, *Cuba's Role in Africa: Revolutionary or Reactionary?* *id.* at 17–25; Makinda, supra note 56, at 94–101.

59. See L. BUCHHEIT, supra note 32, at 121–37.
60. 19 U.N. SCOR (1088th mtg.) at 27, para. 70 (1964).
61. 19 U.N. SCOR (1089th mtg.) at 2, para. 77 (1964).
62. 27 U.N. SCOR (161th mtg.) at 21, para. 192 (1971).
63. O.A.U. CHARTER, para. 7 of the preamble, and arts. II, para. 1 (C), and III, para. 3. Reprinted in J. WORONOFF, supra note 45, at 642–43.
64. *Id.*, arts. III, paras. 1, 2, 3, and 5.
65. O. OJUKWU, supra note 43, at 328.
66. S. TOUVAL, THE BOUNDARY POLITICS OF INDEPENDENT AFRICA 83–86 (1972).
67. J. WORONOFF, supra note 45, at 139–40. Emphasis added.
68. *Id.* at 140.
69. Supra note 40.
70. Since its formation in 1963, it became an important instrument by which the United Nations brought the rebellion to an end. E. LEFEVER, UNCERTAIN MANDATE: POLITICS OF THE U.N. CONGO OPERATION 159–70 (1967).
71. S. TOUVAL, supra note 66, at 118, 154.
72. Cited in Nayar, supra note 46, at 328. Emphasis added.
73. See F. FORSYTHE, THE BIAFRA STORY 203–6, 286 (1969); O.A.U. Secretariat, Addis Ababa Resolution on Nigeria, AGH/RES 3 (VI) 1969.
74. See O.A.U. Resolution on Situation in Nigeria, AHG/RES 51 (IV), s. 3. On the whole, only four African countries—Tanzania, Gabon, Ivory Coast, and Zambia—and one non-African (Haiti) recognized the Biafran movement. And it appears the recognition was premised more on humanitarian considerations than on whether secessionist movements were legitimate. For more detailed discussion of the Nigerian case, see Nayer, supra note 46; L. BUCHHEIT, supra note 32, at 162. Ijalaye, *Was Biafra at Any Time a State in International Law?* 65 AM. J.I.L. 551, 553–55 (1971).
75. U.N. CHARTER art. 103. But see art. 52.
76. See S.C. Res. S/4387; 15 U.N. SCOR Supp. (July–Sept. 1950), at 16 (1960); Res. S/4405 (July 22, 1960), *id.* at 34; and Res. S/4426 (Aug. 9, 1960), *id.* at 91–92. Reprinted in L. SOHN, CASES ON UNITED NATIONS LAW 712, 725, and 731 (1967).
77. As will be seen momentarily, O.N.U.C. was initially forbidden to use force except in self-defense. This inhibition was partially removed when the Tsombe forces persistently refused to allow the O.N.U.C. entry into the Katanga area. See L. SOHN, supra note 76, at 746–53.
78. The rationale and implications of the economic measures were explained in the Secretary-General's Report on the Implementation of the Resolution of Feb. 4, 1963. It must be quoted *in extenso*:

At the beginning of 1962, there was hope, following Mr. Tsombe's declaration at Kiltona, that the problem of the secession of Katanga might be speedily settled. That hope was quickly dispelled, however, when Mr. Tsombe, in effect disavowed his promises as soon as he returned to Katanga. A subsequent six months of dilatory "negotiating" . . . served only to waste time and to raise questions of bad faith. . . . It was imperative that the problem of attempted Katangese secession, which not only caused impoverishment and instability in the rest of the Congo, but also threatened the peace of the African continent . . . , be finally settled. I myself, therefore, following consultations with a number of Governments, proposed in August 1962 the Plan of National Reconstruction. This plan was accepted by Prime Minister Adoula and Mr. Tsombe. . . . The failure of the Katangese provincial authorities, after more than three months, to take any practical steps to implement this plan, and their continued lack of co-operation with other activities of the United Nations, led me in December 1962 to advance certain measures designed to bring economic pressure to bear on the Katangan provincial authorities and thereby to lead the Katangese problem to an early and peaceful solution. The Government of Belgium was thus asked to exert every possible influence on the Union Minière du Haut-Katanga, a Belgian corporation, which is part of a powerful international financial complex, to induce it to desist from paying to Katanga province revenues and taxes due to the Government of the Congo. States which had jurisdiction over territories through which Katanga copper was exported, namely Portugal, the Union of South Africa, and the United Kingdom were requested to take measures to prohibit the shipment of such copper. . . . Other interested Governments were requested by the Central Government of the Congo, with my support, not to permit the import of copper and cobalt from Katanga into their territories.

See S/5240 (Feb. 4, 1963), 18 U.N. SCOR Supp. (Jan.–Mar., 1963) at 92–104, reprinted in L. Sohn, supra note 76, at 746, 746–47.

    79. S/5002 (Nov. 24, 1961), 16 U.N. SCOR Supp. (Oct.–Dec. 1961) at 148–50; reprinted in L. Sohn, supra note 76, at 744–46. See also Res. S/199 (Dec. 30, 1964) 19 U.N. SCOR (1964) at 18–19, U.N. Doc. S/INF/19/Rev. 1, also reprinted in *id.* at 760.

    80. R. Higgins, The Development of International Law Through the Political Organs of the United Nations 109 (1969).

    81. See the cablegram from the Prime Minister and the President of the Republic to the Secretary-General of the U.N., S/4382 (July 13, 1960), at 1; 15 U.N. SCOR Supp. (July–Sept. 1960) at 11, cited in L. Sohn, supra note 76, at 706.

    82. See S/4389 (July 18, 1960), 15 U.N. SCOR Supp. (July–Sept. 1950) at 16–24, reprinted in *id.* at 713, 715–16.

    83. S/4417/Add. 6 (Aug. 12, 1960), 15 U.N. SCOR Supp. (July–Sept. 1960) at 64–65, 70–71, reprinted in *id.* at 732–34.

    84. Thus in Resolution S/4741 of Feb. 21, 1961, the Security Council authorized the O.N.U.C., for the first time, to use force to prevent the occurrence of civil war. Significantly, not only was this qualified by the condition that the force should only be used as a "last resort," but it was also construed by the secretary general as having not derogated from the original mandate that enjoined the United Nations from taking sides in the conflict. See Res. S/4741A of Feb. 21, 1961, 16 U.N. SCOR Supp. (Jan.–Mar.

1961) at 147–48, in *id.* at 742–44. For the secretary general's interpretation of the resolution see S/4752 (Feb. 27, 1961) Annex II, 16 U.N. SCOR Supp. (Jan.–Mar. 1961) at 176, 188, *id.* at 743–44; Hoffmann, *In Search of a Thread: The UN in the Congo Labyrinth*, 16 INT'L ORG. 331, 343–46 (1962).

85. See Letter from Mr. P. Lumumba, Prime Minister of the Republic of Congo to the Secretary-General, Aug. 14, 1960; S/4417/Add. 7 (Aug. 15, 1960); 15 U.N. SCOR Supp. (July–Sept. 1960) at 71–73; reprinted in L. SOHN, supra note 76, at 735.

86. See Hoffmann, supra note 84, at 336–42.

87. Res. S/4387, 15 U.N. SCOR Supp. (July–Sept. 1960) at 16; L. SOHN, supra note 76, at 712.

88. Res. S/4405 (July 22, 1960), 15 U.N. SCOR Supp. (July–Sept. 1960) at 34, in *id.* at 725–26.

89. Extracts from translation of the Loi Fondamentale may be found in T. FRANK & J. CAREY, THE LEGAL ASPECTS OF THE UNITED NATIONS ACTION IN THE CONGO 5–10 (1963).

90. See the cables of July 12 and July 13, 1960, from the President and Prime Minister of the Congo to the Secretary-General of the U.N., S/4382 and S/4381, supra note 81, at 11; L. SOHN, supra note 76, at 707–8.

91. See 15 U.N. SCOR (873d mtg.) at 3–45, in L. SOHN, supra note 76, at 707–9.

92. See S. Hoffmann, supra note 84.

93. Res. S/4387, supra note 87. The secretary general's understanding of the implications of the resolution is stated in S/4389: "The resolution of the Security Council was adopted in response to my initial statement to the Council. Therefore, that statement may be regarded as a basic mandate." S/4389 (July 18); 15 U.N. SCOR Supp. (July–Sept. 1950) at 16–24, in L. SOHN, supra note 76, at 713.

94. This development was not anticipated at the San Francisco conference. Nor was it embodied in the Charter. It was a principle that emerged in the Korean crisis. Essentially, it permits the General Assembly to authorize the use of force in situations of emergency where a use of the veto by a permanent member precludes the Security Council from reaching a resolution. For the history and implications of the resolution, see B. COHEN, THE UNITED NATIONS—CONSTITUTIONAL DEVELOPMENTS, GROWTH AND POSSIBILITIES 15–30 (1961).

95. L. BUCHHEIT, supra note 32, at 149–50.

96. *Id.* at 149–50.

97. See his report of Feb. 4, 1963, S/5240, supra note 78.

98. Not only did it occur many years after Nigeria had been independent, but also there was no constitutional crisis between the leaders in power; nor was there any external involvement like the one that necessitated the U.N. intervention in the Congo situation.

99. 7 U.N. MONTHLY CHRONICLE, Feb. 1970, at 37, cited in L. BUCHHEIT, supra note 32, at 168–69.

100. According to the article, "The Secretary-General may bring to the attention of the Security Council any matter which in his opinion may threaten the maintenance of

international peace and security." It is significant that the article does not make the introduction of the conflict in the United Nations by any member state a sine qua non for the exercise of the secretary general's responsibilities under the provision. U.N. CHAR-TER art. 99.

101. U.N. Press Release S.C/S.M./998, Sept. 13, 1968, cited in J. SAXENA, supra note 11, at 44.

102. *Id.* at 44.

103. 7 U.N. MONTHLY CHRONICLE, supra note 99, at 36; L. BUCHHEIT, supra note 32, at 87.

104. U.N. MONTHLY CHRONICLE, supra note 99, at 39. See also L. BUCHHEIT, supra note 32, at 87–88.

105. Before the partition of India into India and Pakistan in 1947, the two were a single entity—India. On the partition, which followed mainly religious lines, the predominantly Hindu population formed the state of India, and the Muslim portion fell under Pakistan.

106. L. BUCHHEIT, supra note 32, at 198–99.

107. J. SAXENA, supra note 11, at 89 (1978).

108. Without reference to any of the political aspects of the situation, one may do well to mention the position of the United States as expressed in the statement of Secretary of State Rogers: "we did favor, we do favor unity as a principle, and we do not favor secession as a principle, because once you start down that road it could be destabilizing." See President Nixon's foreign policy report to Congress, Feb. 9, 1972, 66 U.S. DEP'T STATE BULL. 54 (1972). Again, on India's refusal to withdraw its troops from East Pakistan in defiance of the G.A. Res. 2793, the U.S. representative in the United Nations, George Bush, stated: "In view of India's defiance of world opinion, expressed by such an overwhelming majority, the United States is now returning the issue to the Security Council. With East Pakistan virtually occupied by Indian troops, a continuation of the war would take on increasingly the character of armed attack on the very existence of a Member State of the United Nations." 26 U.N. SCOR (1611th mtg.) at 2, para. 16 (1961). In the Kurdish situation it was abundantly clear that the U.S. attitude was influenced more by its political interests than whether or not secession would have a devastating effect on the country in which it is pursued. Thus, according to recent reports, the U.S. military assistance to the Kurds was not prompted by any commitment to the ideal of self-government for a distinct national group, but rather as a convenient way of weakening Iraq—a country from whom Iran, an American ally, bore no affection. A document purportedly drafted by the U.S. House of Representatives Intelligence Committee was quoted as having summarized the U.S. Kurdish policy as not hoping for a complete Kurdish victory but preferring instead "that the insurgents simply continue a level of hostilities sufficient to sap the resources of our ally's [Iran] neighboring country [Iraq]. This policy was not imparted to our clients [the Kurds], who were encouraged to continue fighting." See Shawcross, *Banned Report Says American Left Kurds in Lurch*, The Sunday Times (London), Feb. 15, 1976, at 6, col. 6. See also *Mr. Nixon 'told C.I.A. to send arms to Kurds'*, Times (London), Nov. 3, 1975, at 6, col. 8. To top it all, it is interesting to realize that whatever assistance was being provided by the United

States to the Kurds was suddenly terminated as soon as a new government with Western sympathies ousted the preceding administration. See Shawcross, supra. See also L. BUCHHEIT, supra note 32, at 119.

109. One notable argument of the Indians was that based on the principle of self-defense. Thus, the Indian representative in the Sixth Committee of the General Assembly argued:

> For example, there could be a unique type of bloodless aggression from a vast and incessant flow of millions of human beings forced to flee into another State. If this invasion of unarmed men in totally unmanageable proportion were to not only impair the economic and political well-being of the receiving victim state but to threaten its very existence . . . it could have to be categorized as aggression. In such a case, there may not be use of armed force across the frontier since the use of force may be totally confined within one's territorial boundary, but if this results in inundating the neighboring State by millions of fleeing citizens of the offending State, there could be an aggression of a worst order.

Reprinted in 11 INDIAN J.I.L. 724, at 28 (1971). Obviously, India's main concern was about the influx of East Pakistani refugees. On the whole, the number of refugees who fled to India was estimated in the neighborhood of ten million. One might wonder why a country like India, which had more than five hundred million people, could be troubled by the addition of this relatively insignificant number of refugees. Considering the fact that as a developing country India has enormous problems, including those of clothing and feeding its citizens, it is readily evident that the refugee situation would have seriously affected India's security if not managed properly.

110. This resolution was passed at the earlier stages of the conflict—when the disagreement between the Soviets and the United States over whether to include the political issues of how to achieve a ceasefire between the belligerents resulted in the resolution that moved the matter from the Council to the General Assembly. See 26 U.N. SCOR (1608th mtg.) at 15–16, para. 137 (1971). See also G.A. Res. 2793, 26 U.N. GAOR (2003rd mtg.) at 44–45, para. 490 (1971).

111. B. NWABUEZE, supra note 45, at 266.

112. L. BUCHHEIT, supra note 32, at 199. See also Nawaz, *Bangla Desh and International Law*, 11 INDIAN J.I.L. 251, 251–54 (1971); Mani, *The 1971 War on the Indian Sub- Continent and International Law*, 12 INDIAN J.I.L. 83, 84 (1972).

113. J. CRAWFORD, THE CREATION OF STATES IN INTERNATIONAL LAW 116 (1979). Footnotes omitted.

114. L. BUCHHEIT, supra note 32, at 201.

115. B. NWABUEZE, supra note 45, at 266–67.

116. See the International Commission of Jurists Report of 1972 entitled, "The events in East Pakistan, 1971," A LEGAL STUDY BY THE SECRETARIAT OF THE INTERNATIONAL COMMISSION OF JURISTS 26–27 (1972).

117. The Declaration on Friendly Relations, supra note 8. See the seventh paragraph of the provision headed "The principle of equal rights and self-determination of peoples."

118. A. COBBAN, THE NATION STATE AND NATIONAL SELF-DETERMINATION 138 (1970). Emphasis added. See also J. SAXENA, supra note 11, at 13–26; L. BUCHHEIT, supra note 32, at 93–96; Nayar, supra note 46, at 342–43.

119. Although in the *Aaland Island* case the International Commission of Jurists rejected the right of minorities to secede from established states—an opinion to which the Committee of Rapporteurs concurred—the rapporteurs went further to say that minorities could secede under certain exceptional situations, including instances where they are not justly treated:

> To concede to minorities, either of language or religion, or to any fraction of a population the right of withdrawing from the community to which they belong, because it is their wish or their good pleasure, would be to destroy order and stability within states and to inaugurate anarchy in international life; it would be to uphold a theory incompatible with the very idea of the state as a territorial and political unity. . . . *The separation of a minority from the State of which it forms a part and its incorporation in another State can only be considered an altogether exceptional solution, a last resort when the state lacks either the will or the power to enact and apply just and effective guarantees.*

Report of the Committee of Rapporteurs, League of Nations Council Doc. B/21/68/106 [VII] 22–23 (Apr. 16, 1921). Emphasis added.

120. See "The Events in East Pakistan," supra note 116 at 67.

121. *Id.* at 68. Emphasis added.

122. L. BUCHHEIT, supra note 32, at 207; J. CRAWFORD, supra note 113.

123. According to this treaty the Belgian government was not to bring Belgian metropolitan troops into the Congo unless it was expressly requested to do so by the Congolese minister of defense. See L. BUCHHEIT, supra note 32, at 144.

124. Cited in Mani, supra note 112, at 98.

125. Indeed, it was because of this disagreement, most particularly that between the Soviet Union, on the one hand, and the Chinese and the United States, on the other, about whether the secessionist issues should be explored that the matter was taken to the General Assembly under the "Uniting for Peace Resolution" proposed by the Somali representative. See 26 U.N. SCOR (1608th mtg.) at 15–16, para. 137 (1971); G.A. Res. 2793, 26 U.N. GAOR (2003rd mtg.) at 44–45, para. 490.

126. 26 U.N. SCOR (1613th mtg.) at 9, paras. 92–93.

127. 26 U.N. GAOR Supp. (No. 1A) at para. 148, U.N. Doc. A/8401/Add. 1 (1971).

128. B. NWABUEZE, supra note 45, at 226.

129. See Abbey Maine, The Sunday Times of Zambia, Mar. 28, 1971, cited in B.

NWABUEZE, supra note 45, at 227; O. ACHIKE, GROUNDWORK OF MILITARY LAW AND MILITARY RULE IN NIGERIA 113 (1978).

130. See Afriscope 6 (Jan. 1966), cited in F. R. Metrowich, AFRICAN FREEDOM ANNUAL 24 (F. R. Metrowich ed. 1979).

131. W. GUTTERIDGE, THE MILITARY IN AFRICAN POLITICS 100 (1969). Colonel Afrifa also echoed the tendency in his book on the 1966 Ghana coup: "where there was no constitutional means of offering political opposition to the one-party government the armed forces were automatically made to become the official opposition to the Government." A. AFRIFA, THE GHANA COUP, 24th Feb., 1966, at 31 (1967).

CHAPTER 9

1. See Chapter 7, "The Noncolonial Cases under their Municipal Systems," supra.

2. H. KELSEN, GENERAL THEORY OF LAW AND STATE 120 (1961 ed.).

3. See L. OPPENHEIM, INTERNATIONAL LAW, A TREATISE, Vol. 1, PEACE, 121–28 (H. Lauterpacht ed. 1947); T. CHEN, THE INTERNATIONAL LAW OF RECOGNITION 283 (1966 ed.); 1 O'CONNELL, INTERNATIONAL LAW 136–37 (1970); R. DHOKALIA, INTERNATIONAL LAW 207–10 (1963).

4. L. OPPENHEIM, supra note 3, at 130–34.

5. Yrisarri v. Clement, 2 G.&P. at 233 (1825); 1 BRITISH INTERNATIONAL LAW CASES 71.

6. L. OPPENHEIM, supra note 3, at 130–34.

7. R. DHOKALIA, supra note 3, at 210.

8. L. OPPENHEIM, supra note 3, at 124.

9. See the Canadian prime minister's response to the issue of recognition of the regime that ousted President Kwame Nkrumah of Ghana, 5 CAN. Y.B.I.L. 331–32.

10. H.C. DEB. Vol. 811, col. 580, Written Answers (Feb. 19, 1977), cited in A. Bundu, *Recognition of Revolutionary Activities: Law and Practice of States*, 27 INT'L & COMP. L.Q. 18, 37 (1978).

11. Discussed in *id.* at 37–40.

12. H.C. DEB., Vol. 712, col. 91, Written Answers, May 12, 1965. A similar answer was given on May 17, 1965, *id.*, col. 166.

13. See 5 CAN. Y.B.I.L., supra note 9, at 322.

14. This view may be anchored by the principle that foreign states can go to the assistance of the ruling government. Although the assistance can be given so long as the conflict is below insurgency, states are so free in determining the accrual of the various stages that any state seeking to support any faction easily finds justification from the argument that the conflict is in the stage of belligerency or insurgency or rebellion. Higgins has elucidated the contemporary practice very clearly by pointing out that in most cases, including the Nigerian, states accord recognition to their favorites even when some of the requisite conditions have not been met. Higgins, *International Law and Civil Conflicts*, in INTERNATIONAL REGULATION OF CIVIL WAR 169, 171 (E. Luard ed. 1972); R. HIGGINS, THE DEVELOPMENT OF INTERNATIONAL LAW THROUGH THE PO-

LITICAL ORGANS OF THE UNITED NATIONS 210–13 (1963). Cf. Ijalaye, *Was "Biafra" at Any Time a State in International Law?* 65 AM. J.I.L. 551, 553–54 (1971).

15. 769 PARL. DEB. H.C. (5th Ser.) 1146 (1968). Cited in L. BUCHHEIT, SECESSION: THE LEGITIMACY OF SELF-DETERMINATION 171 (1978). Higgins, *Internal War and Internatiodnal Law*, 3 FUTURE OF INTERNATIONAL LEGAL ORDER, 79, 98 (R. Falk & C. Black ed. 1971). It seems to imply that all Commonwealth governments may expect to be assisted by Britain in times of internal conflicts, regardless of whether they are in control.

16. HANSARD, Aug. 27, 1968, col. 1448; cited in Higgins, supra note 15, at 101. It is, of course, arguable that the British statement can be defended by the principle that a state can intervene in the affairs of another if there has been an illegal intervention in favor of any of the factions. But the British did not label the Russian intervention as illegal. Besides, the law seems to indicate that the second intervention must be to counter the previous one. Since the British intervention was in favor of the same side assisted by the Russians, it is doubtful whether that second intervention can be defended by the principle of counterintervention.

17. The case was originally decided in the General Division of the Rhodesian High Court and later in the Appellate Division. See G.D./CIV/23/66, Sept. 9, 1966, reported in the RHODESIAN GOVERNMENT BLUE BOOK. An extract thereof is reprinted in 2 S.A. 284 (1968). The Appellate Division refused to grant appeal to the Judicial Committee of the Privy Council, whereupon the latter unilaterally assumed jurisdiction over the case and issued the judgment in question. See *id.* at 457.

18. 1 A.C. (P.C.) 645, 725, 1250 (1969).

19. See Southern Rhodesia (Annexation) Order in Council [1923], 21 STAT. R.&O. 369; STAT. INSTR. 1948, No. 21 (rev.). See also Cummings, *The Rhodesian Unilateral Declaration of Independence and the Position of the International Community*, 6(28) INT'L L. & POL. 56, 59 (1973); McDougal & Reisman, *Rhodesia and the United Nations: The Lawfulness of International Concern*, 62 AM. J.I.L. 1, 1 (1968); Cefkin, *The Rhodesian Question at the United Nations*, 22 INT'L ORG. 640, 641 (1968); J. COZETZEE, THE SOVEREIGNTY OF RHODESIA AND THE LAW OF NATIONS 28 (1970).

20. As Prime Minister Wilson put it in the British Parliament, "This Government has a solemn duty to be satisfied that before granting independence it would be acceptable to the people of the country as a whole." 701 PARL. DEB. 67 (5th ser.). Earlier, the secretary for Commonwealth relations, Duncan Sandys, had stated that "the British Government would not feel able to give up its reserve powers unless there was a significant alteration of the franchise and a substantial increase in African representation in the Legislature." 644 PARL. DEB., col. 171.

21. For the text of the Unilateral Declaration of Independence, see 5 INT'L L.M. 230–31 (1966); see also A. QUENTIN-BAXTER, RHODESIA AND THE LAW 3 (1970).

22. In the *Madzimbamuto* case, the decision of the General Division of the Rhodesian High Court was upheld by all the judges. Quenet and McDonald, JJ.A., thought the government was not only de facto but also de jure and therefore that its constitution was binding. See 2 S.A. 375, 416. Beadle, C.J., and Jarvis, A.J.A., thought the government was in effective control, and that that trend was likely to continue. *Id.* at 359, 422. Fieldsend thought it was in de facto control, *id.* at 444.

23. It is significant that when the British government commuted certain sentences passed by the Rhodesian court, the revolutionary government went ahead to implement the Rhodesian decision without impediment. See Dhlamini and Others v. Carter N.O. and Another, *id.* at 445.

24. See Res. S/216 of 1965, S/INF/26, reprinted in 60 AM. J.I.L. 924 (1966) at 23; Res. 217 of Nov. 20, 1965, *id.*, at 25, reprinted in 60 AM. J.I.L. 924; Res. 221 of Apr. 9, 1966, *id.* at 26–27 reprinted in 60 AM. J.I.L. 925 and Res. 232 of Dec. 16, 1966, *id.* at 27–29.

25. See Statement of Prime Minister Wilson, reproduced in U.N. Doc. A/6300/ Add. 1 (part 1).

26. W. HALL, A TREATISE ON INTERNATIONAL LAW 108 (8th ed. 1924).

27. H. LAUTERPACHT, RECOGNITION IN INTERNATIONAL LAW 26, 55 (1947).

28. J. BRIERLY, THE LAW OF NATIONS 138 (1963).

29. The Tinocco Concession Case, 1 R.I.A.A. 369, 381–82 (1923).

30. Evidently, Britain was not alone in thinking that the sanctions might have a positive effect on the rebels. The Canadian prime minister took a similar position: "I feel strongly and hope I am right in this feeling; I hope the results will justify my feeling— that the overthrow of the illegal regime can be achieved by economic and financial measures without the use of military force." 1 H.C. DEB. (Can.) 1966 (Jan. 20, 1966), reprinted in *Canadian Practice in International Law, 1965–66*, 5 CAN. Y.B.I.L. 331, 335.

31. The force was not to be used to back all the sanctions; it was to be used exclusively against the "Joanna V" and was to be used solely by the British, the state that had expressly ruled out the use of force. See U.N. Doc. SC/Res. 221, Apr. 9, 1966, discussed in Higgins, *International Law, Rhodesia, and the Law*, WORLD TODAY 94, 95–98 (1976).

32. See R. v. Ndhlovu and Others, 4 S.A. 515, 536.

33. See A. QUENTIN-BAXTER, supra note 21, at 18.

34. It is significant that the declaration did not make any reference to the effective-control test. It reads: "reaffirmed their previous statement that they were irrevocably opposed to the Unilateral Declaration of Independence by the Government of Rhodesia and further reaffirmed their insistence on the principle of Majority rule." See the *Office of the Prime Minister Press Release on Oct. 14, 1965*, 5 CAN. Y.B.I.L., supra note 30, at 334.

35. See Boals, *The Relevance of International Law to the Internal War in Yemen* in THE INTERNATIONAL LAW OF CIVIL WAR 303, 306–14 (R. Falk ed. 1971).

36. Higgins, *International Law and Civil Conflicts*, supra note 14, at 176.

37. *Id.* at 176–77.

38. Res. 216 of 1965, supra note 24.

39. Res. 217 (1965), Nov. 20, 1965, supra note 24. See also Res. 2024 of Nov. 11, 1965, reprinted in 60 AM. J.I.L. 924 (1966).

40. Thus Representative Selden of Alabama questioned in the U.S. Congress: "But what crime has Rhodesia committed? Whose borders has Rhodesia invaded? What sections of the Charter of the United Nations has this small African nation violated? On what basis does Great Britain argue that Rhodesia has become a threat to the peace?"

CONG. REC., H4029 (daily ed. Apr. 12, 1967), cited in M. McDougal & W. Reisman, supra note 19, at 5–6. See also the statements of Representative Gurney of Florida, H4035, and Representative Bray of Indiana, H4031, both cited in *id.* at 5–6. For a more detailed list of the critics, see *id.*

    41. 12 U.N.C.I.O. Doc. 505.
    42. 1962 I.C.J. Rep. 151, 168.
    43. U.N. CHARTER, art. 39
    44. According to art. 2(7) of the U.N. CHARTER,

> Nothing contained in the present Charter shall authorize the United Nations to intervene in matters which are essentially within the domestic jurisdiction of any state *or shall require the Members to submit such matters to settlement under the present Charter*; but this principle shall not prejudice the application of enforcement measures under Chapter VII.

Emphasis added.

    45. H. LAUTERPACHT, OPPENHEIM'S INTERNATIONAL LAW 414, 415 (1955).
    46. See the Indonesian Question, the Tunis-Morocco Nationality Decree, the *Russian Wives* case, the case of *Human Rights of Indians in South Africa*, and that of the *Violation of Human Rights in Bulgaria, Hungary and Roumania*, cited supra in Chapter 2.
    47. The new text, which amended the 1945 version, came into force on Aug. 30, 1965. It increased the membership of the Security Council from eleven to fifteen and the votes required for the adoption of decisions on matters of substance from seven to nine. See U.N. CHARTER, art. 27.
    48. South Africa and Portugal, for instance, claimed that the abstention of the French and the Soviets from voting on resolutions 221 and 232 amounted to negative votes and therefore prevented their respective decisions from being adopted. See McDougal and Reisman, *Rhodesia and the United Nations: The Lawfulness of International Concern*, 62 AM. J.I.L. 1 at 9, note 35 (1968).
    49. At the San Francisco conference the issue was discussed by Committee IV/III. The answer given in the "Statement of the Four Sponsoring Governments" was not absolutely clear: "Therefore if a majority voting in the Security Council is to be made possible, the only practicable method is to provide, in respect of non-procedural decisions, for unanimity of the permanent members plus the concurring votes of at least two of the non-permanent members." See 11 U.N.C.I.O. Docs. 707, 713 (1945).
    50. *Id.* at 610–11. Emphasis added.
    51. Stavropoulos, *The Practice of Voluntary Abstention by Permanent Members of the Security Council under Article 27 Paragraph 3 of the Charter of the United Nations*, 61 AM. J.I.L. 737, 740–42 (1967).
    52. B. COHEN, THE UNITED NATIONS CONSTITUTIONAL DEVELOPMENTS, GROWTH, POSSIBILITIES, AND PROSPECTS 9–10 (1961).
    53. See REPERTOIRE OF THE PRACTICE OF THE SECURITY COUNCIL, 1946–51, ch. IV, pt. III, at 173, case 180, U.N. Doc. ST/PSCA/1.
    54. *Id.* at 173–74, case 182.

55. *Id.* at 174, case 183. According to Higgins, she has personally witnessed a confirmation of this practice of the Security Council on 107 separate occasions. Higgins, supra note 31, at 97.

56. 1971 I.C.J. Rep. 22. Emphasis added.

57. Higgins, supra note 31, at 97–98.

58. See text in 1 HACKWORTH, DIGEST OF INTERNATIONAL LAW 186; 2 AM. J.I.L. 299 (1908).

59. 1 HACKWORTH, supra note 58, at 188; 17 AM. J.I.L. Supp. 177.

60. 1 HACKWORTH, supra note 58, art. 2.

61. See U.N. CHARTER art. 103. See also art. 53 of the VIENNA CONVENTION ON THE LAW OF TREATIES, U.N. Doc. A. Conf. 32/ 27 (1969); 63 AM. J.I.L. 875 (1969).

62. VIENNA CONVENTION, supra note 61, arts. 4 and 28.

63. Ser. A, No. 7, p. 29 (1926), cited in A. MCNAIR, THE LAW OF TREATIES 309–22 (1961).

64. 1926 P.C.I.J. (ser. A) No. 7, at 29.

65. See VIENNA CONVENTION, supra note 61, arts. 37 and 38. See also the Case of the Free Zones of Upper Savoy and the District of Gez, 1932 P.C.I.J. (ser. A-B) No. 46, at 147.

66. VIENNA CONVENTION, supra note 61; see also arts. 12, 13, 14, and 15.

67. *Id.* at art. 1.

68. 1 HACKWORTH, supra note 58, at 298; Woolsey, *The Recognition of the Government of El Salvador,* 28 AM. J.I.L. 325, 327–28 (1934). See also the official statement of Secretary of State Kellogg, wherein it was noted that the United States was in "hearty accord" with the concept embodied in the treaty. 1 HACKWORTH, supra note 58, at 298.

69. Woolsey, supra note 68, at 328.

70. *Id.* at 326.

71. The U.S. practice on the issue is described by Whiteman:

In fairly recent years the United States, in determining whether or not to extend recognition to . . . governments, has considered the following criteria (not always uniformly described):

(1) Whether the government is in *de facto* control of the territory and in possession of the machinery of the State;

(2) Whether it is administering the government with the assent or consent of the people, without substantial resistance to its authority; ie., whether there is public acquiescence in the authority of the government; and

(3) Whether the new government has indicated its willingness to comply with international obligations under treaties and international law.

Other factors borne in mind, as appropriate, for example, are the existence or non-existence of evidence of foreign intervention in the establishment of the new regime; the political orientation of the government and its leaders; evidence of intention to observe democratic principles . . . the attitude of the new government towards private investment. . . . These, and other criteria, depending on the international situation at the time, have been considered with varying weight.

2 WHITEMAN, DIGEST 72–73 (1963).

72. VIENNA CONVENTION, supra note 61, arts. 1 and 11.

73. See the Legal Status of Eastern Greenland case (Denmark v. Norway) 1933 P.C.I.J. (ser. A-B) No. 53, 3 HUDSON, WORLD CT. REP. 148 (1938); W. FRIEDMANN, O. LISSITZYN & R. PUGH, INTERNATIONAL LAW CASES AND MATERIALS 338–41 (1969).

74. See Harvard Research on International Law, Draft Convention on the Law of Treaties, art. 20, printed in 29 AM. J.I.L. Supp. 653, 999–1002 (1935); 2 C. HYDE, INTERNATIONAL LAW AS CHIEFLY APPLIED BY THE UNITED STATES 9 (1922). See also VIENNA CONVENTION, supra note 61, arts. 46 and 47.

75. If a party to the treaty exceeds its authority and the other party knowingly goes ahead to conclude the treaty but later seeks to exploit the defect to its advantage, the law conceivably would not favor the second party. At best, the treaty will be voidable at the instance of the state whose law was violated.

76. See 25 AM. J.I.L. Supp. 203 (1931); 2 WHITEMAN DIGEST 85.

77. See U.N. Res. 2131 on Inadmissibility of Intervention 20 U.N. GAOR (Supp. No. 14) at 11, U.N. Doc. A/6014 (1965). But see the numerous U.N. resolutions that permit assistance to peoples struggling for their rights of self-determination, infra Chapter 11.

78. L. Woolsey, supra note 68, at 329.

79. Vienna Convention, arts. 60 and 62.

80. J. BRIERLY, supra note 28, at 335–42.

81. *Id.* at 335–42.

82. See the statement of the U.S. delegation at the Hostages Convention, U.N. Doc. A/32/39, at 53. See also the Netherlands' statement, *id.*, and the statement of the chairman *ad interim*, which reads: "Even the proponents of safeguards for the rights of national liberation movements had maintained that they were in no way suggesting that those movements should be granted an open license to take hostages." *Id.* at 58, cited in W. Verwey, *The International Hostages Convention and National Liberation Movements*, 75 AM. J.I.L. 69, 77 (1981).

83. "Nothing is better settled, as a canon of interpretation in all systems of law, than that a clause must be so interpreted as to give a meaning rather than so as to deprive it of meaning." See the Cayuga Indian Claims, 6 R.I.A.A. 173 (1926); A. MCNAIR, THE LAW OF TREATIES 383–85 (1961).

CHAPTER 10

1. See Blishchenko, *The Use of Force in International Relations and the Role of Prohibition of Certain Weapons*, in CURRENT PROBLEMS OF INTERNATIONAL LAW 157–

58 (A. Cassese ed. 1975). See also Waldock, *The Use of Force in International Law*, ACADEMIE DE DROIT INTERNATIONAL, 2 RECUEIL DES COURS 455, 455–57.

2. See 1 HUDSON, INTERNATIONAL LEGISLATION 1 (1931), reprinted in L. SOHN, BASIC DOCUMENTS OF THE UNITED NATIONS 295 (1956).

3. 94 L.N.T.S. 57 (1929).

4. Convention Respecting the Limitation of Employment of Force for the Recovery of Contract Debts. Reprinted in 2 AM. J.I.L. Supp. 81 (1908).

5. Although the League Covenant proclaimed the "obligation not to resort to war" and urged members to "respect and preserve as against external aggression the territorial integrity and political independence of all Members of the League," there were many loopholes in the Covenant that suggest that war was still permissible. For instance, there was a cooling-off period of three months during which efforts could be made to settle disputes pacifically but after which war could be waged. Besides, any kind of force, including armed force, was permissible provided it was short of war. See LEAGUE OF NATIONS COVENANT preamble and arts. 10; 12; 13, para. 4; and 15, para. 7. 12 LEAGUE OF NATIONS O.J. (1931). Likewise, the pact that forbade settlement of contractual debts by the instrument of force had many limitations. It was limited to the parties thereof; it was inapplicable to cases not involving contractual debts; and even in cases involving contractual debts, a party that failed to settle its debt after demand could not hide behind it. Of the three, the Paris Pact is the widest in scope. For, although its specific prohibition of war raises some problems as to what "war" is and, indeed, provides a loophole by which war could be started, its art. 2 made it clear that even force short of war was unlawful. Yet, as an instrument outlawing the use of force and war among states, the pact was not foolproof. It did not apply to nonsignatories, nor did it fully terminate the right of states to use force when they deem it necessary to do so in self-defense, for it allowed the parties to attach reservations enabling them to use force in "self-defense." See W. FRIEDMANN, O. LISSITZYN & R. PUGH, INTERNATIONAL LAW, CASES AND MATERIALS 883 (1969). See also Waldock, supra note 1, at 468–75.

6. U.N. CHARTER art. 2(4). See also preamble and art. 2(3).

7. Doc. 933, IV/2/42, 13 U.N.C.I.O. Doc. 710 (1945).

8. Pinkard, *Force, Intervention and Neutrality in Contemporary International Law*, 3(1) TOWSON S.J.I.L. 66, 68 (1968).

9. Ronzitti, *Resort to Force in Wars of National Liberation*, in CURRENT PROBLEMS OF INTERNATIONAL LAW 319 (A. Cassese ed.).

10. Waldock, supra note 1, at 487, 492.

11. Ronzitti, supra note 9, at 320–28; Waldock, supra note 1, at 487, 492.

12. Ronzitti, supra note 9, 320–22.

13. Waldock, supra note 1, at 492–93.

14. See G.A. Res. 2625, 25 U.N. GAOR Supp. (No. 28) at 121, U.N. Doc. A/8028 (1970).

15. C. HYDE, 1 INTERNATIONAL LAW 106 (1922); Kunz, *Individual and Collective Self-Defense in Article 51 of the Charter of the United Nations*, 41 AM. J.I.L. 872, 877 (1947).

16. H. KELSEN, PRINCIPLES OF INTERNATIONAL LAW 41 (1966).

17. E. Goodrich & H. Hambro, Charter of the United Nations 35–50 (1949).

18. J. Brierly, The Law of Nations 416 (1963).

19. Waldock, supra note 1, at 492.

20. *Id.* at 492–94. See also the British position at the proceedings of the Committee on Friendly Relations, U.N. Doc. A/AC/119/SR.5, at 12–13, and the Report of the Special Committee on the Principles of International Law Concerning Friendly Relations and Co-Operation Among States, U.N. Doc. A/6230, at 40–41 (1969).

21. Wright, *The Outlawry of War and the Law of War*, 47 Am. J.I.L. 365–76 (1953). See also P. Jessup, A Modern Law of Nations 173 (1956); the "Individual Opinion" of Judge Alvarez in the Corfu Channel Conflict, 1949 I.C.J. Rep. 42; and the Report of the Special Committee on the Principles of International Law Concerning Friendly Relations and Co-Operation Among States, supra note 20.

22. U.N. Doc. A/AC/125/L.2.

23. U.N. Doc. A/AC/125/L.3.

24. U.N. Doc. A/AC/125/L.12.

25. D. Nincic, The Problem of Sovereignty in the Charter and in the Practice of the United Nations 65–66 (1970).

26. See Convention Concerning the Duties and Rights of States in the Event of Civil Strife, 134 L.N.T.S. 47, No. 3082 (1932); 22 Am. J.I.L. Supp. 159 (1928).

27. See G.A. Res. 2131, 20 U.N. GAOR Supp. (No. 14) at 11, U.N. Doc. A/6014 (1965); 60 Am. J.I.L. 662 (1966).

28. Wright, *The Goa Incident*, 56 Am. J.I.L. 617, 620 (1956).

29. "Namibia and the International Rule of Law," Conf. Dakar (NDH 76) IVa, published by the International Institute of Human Rights, Strasbourg (1976). Cf. J. Dugard, "Namibia and Human Rights. A Report on the Dakar Conference and Its Implications for the South West African issue and Detente," South African Institute of International Affairs (Jan. 1976).

30. Kunz, supra note 15, at 876–77.

31. *Id.*; Knisbacher, *The Entebbe Operation: A Legal Analysis of Israel's Rescue Action*, 12 J.I.L.E. 57, 61–65 (1977); Wright, *United States Intervention in Lebanon*, 53 Am. J.I.L. 112, 116–19 (1959).

32. But see Kunz, supra note 15, at 875–77.

33. 30 Brit. & Foreign St. Papers 193 (1843); Jennings, *The Caroline and McLeod Cases*, 32 Am. J.I.L. 82 (1938); Knisbacher, supra note 31, at 61. Cf. the *Naulilaa* case where the main tests—imminence of attack and proportionality—were used in justifying an otherwise illegal use of force. See 8 Recueil of Decisions of the Mixed Arbitral Tribunals 409 (1928); 2 R.I.A.A. 1012 (1928).

34. The concept of collective self-defense is beyond the scope of this discussion. Suffice it to note, however, that although the practice is rich in cases where states have based their intervention on the right of collective self-defense, authorities, notably Bowett and Kunz, have urged that collective self-defense cannot be legitimate unless the state claiming to use it is also under attack by a common aggressor. This position clearly is not illogical, especially within the international system where serious efforts are being

made to eradicate flimsy excuses for international armed conflicts. It runs into diffi-
culties, however, with defensive treaties like the Rio Pact and that between the
N.A.T.O. powers. See Kunz, supra note 15, at 875–77; Bowett, *The Interrelation of
Theories of Intervention and Self-Defense*, in LAW AND CIVIL WAR IN THE MODERN
WORLD 38, 46–50 (J. Moore ed. 1974).

35. Wright, supra note 28, at 320–23. A similar argument was advanced by Indonesia to support its invasion of East Timor.

36. See Dugard, *The Organization of African Unity and Colonialism: An Inquiry
into the Plea of Self-Defense as a Justification for the Use of Force in Eradication of
Colonialism*, INT'L & COMP. L.Q. 157, 172 (1967).

37. R. JENNINGS, THE ACQUISITION OF TERRITORIES IN INTERNATIONAL LAW 28–
31 (1963).

38. See 1 INDIAN J.I.L. 545 (1961), cited in Wright, supra note 28, at 623–24.

39. *Id.* at 623–24.

40. U.N. CHARTER art. 51.

41. Dugard, supra note 36, at 172.

42. U.N. CHARTER art. 2, para. 6.

43. I. BROWNLIE, INTERNATIONAL LAW AND THE USE OF FORCE BY STATES 266
(1963).

44. *Id.* at 265–78; Henkin, *Force, Intervention and Neutrality in Contemporary
International Law*, 57 PROC. A.S.I.L. 147, 166 (1963); Brownlie, *The Use of Force in
Self-Defense*, 37 B.Y.B.I.L. 183, 240 (1961); Pedersen, *Comment: Controlling International Terrorism, An Analysis of Unilateral Force and Proposals for Multilateral Co-
operation*, 8 TOLEDO L. REV. 209, 217 (1976).

45. See W. FRIEDMANN, O. LISSITZYN & R. PUGH, supra note 5, at 889.

46. D. BOWETT, SELF-DEFENSE IN INTERNATIONAL LAW 187–93 (1958); McDou-
gal and Feliciano, *Legal Regulation of Resort to International Coercion: Aggression and
Self-Defense in Policy Perspective*, 68 Y.L.R. 1144–50; J. BRIERLY, THE LAW OF
NATIONS 413, 421 (1963); Knisbacher, supra note 31, at 64; Bowett, *The Interrelation
of Theories of Intervention and Self-Defense* in LAW AND CIVIL WAR IN THE MODERN
WORLD 38, 39 (J. Moore ed. 1974); W. O'BRIEN, THE LAW OF LIMITED INTERNA-
TIONAL CONFLICT 23–32 (1965).

47. J. BRIERLY, supra note 46, 416–19. Emphasis in original.

48. See D. MILLER, THE PEACE PACT OF PARIS 198–99, 203, 211, 213–14
(1928).

49. *Id.* at 213–14.

50. THE TRIAL OF GERMAN MAJOR WAR CRIMINALS. THE JUDGMENT (COMMAND
PAPER NO. 6964) at 30 (1946).

51. J. BRIERLY, supra note 46, at 420; Knisbacher, supra note 31, at 65.

52. See, e.g., T. KUHN, TERRORISM IN INTERNATIONAL LAW 82–90 (1980).

53. The case of the *"Lotus,"* Series A, No. 10, at 18 (1927). Emphasis added. See
also the *Free Zones* case, where it was held that "in case of doubt, a limitation on
sovereignty must be construed restrictively." 1932 P.C.I.J. (ser. A/B) No. 46, at 167.

54. The Wimbledon case, 1923 P.C.I.J. (ser. A) No. 1, at 20.

55. The Oder Commission case, 1929 P.C.I.J. (ser. A) No. 23, 5, 26.

56. Res. S/269, 24 U.N. SCOR at 2, U.N. Doc. S/INF/24/Rev. 1 (Aug. 1969). See also Res. 264 of 1969, *id.* at 2.

57. Res. S/301, 26 U.N. SCOR at 7, U.N. Doc. S/INF/27 (Oct. 1971). See also Res. S/309, 25 U.N. SCOR at 4, U.N. Doc. S/INF/28 (Feb. 1972).

58. G.A. Res. 34/94, 34 U.N. GAOR Supp. (No. 46) at 88, U.N. Doc. A/34/46 (1979). See also G.A. Res. A/36/68, 36 U.N. GAOR Supp. (No. 51) at 20, U.N. Doc. A/36/51 (1981).

59. Res. S/282, 25 U.N. SCOR (1549th mtg.) at 12, U.N. Doc. S/INF/25 (July 1970). See also Res. S/417, 32 U.N. SCOR at 4, U.N. Doc. S/INF/33 (Oct. 1977); Res. S/473, 35 U.N. SCOR at 18, U.N. Doc. S/INF/36 (June 1980).

60. Doc. A/31/L.14 and Add. 1–3, Annex, Nov. 2, 1976. See also 31 U.N. GAOR, Doc. A/31/L.13 and Add. 1–3, Nov. 1976.

61. It reads in part:

The Security Council . . . Reaffirming the inalienable right of the people of Southern Rhodesia to self-determination and independence in accordance with General Assembly resolution 1514 (XV) of 14 December 1960, and the legitimacy of their struggle to secure the enjoyment of such rights as set forth in the Charter of the United Nations.

Res. S/403, 35 U.N. SCOR at 1, U.N. Doc. S/INF/33 (Jan. 1977). See also Res. S/232, 21 U.N. SCOR at 7, U.N. Doc. S/INF/21/Rev. 1 (Dec. 1966).

62. Res. S/445, 34 U.N. SCOR at 13, U.N. Doc. S/INF/35 (Mar. 1979).

63. Res. S/448, *id.* at 15. See also Res. S/424 of 1978, 33 U.N. SCOR at 3–4, U.N. Doc. S/INF/34 (Mar. 1978).

64. According to one account, "the illegality of forcible maintenance of colonialism or indeed 'subjection' has been proclaimed. But what has not been accorded to the exponents of wars of liberation is the doctrine that . . . force can be used if the cause is that of war of liberation, if the cause is just." Schwebel, *Wars of Liberation—as Fought in U.N. Organs,* in LAW AND CIVIL WAR IN THE MODERN WORLD 446, 457 (J. Moore ed. 1974).

65. Res. 3103 (XXVII), 28 U.N. GAOR Supp. (No. 30) at 142–43, U.N. Doc. A/9030 (1974), reprinted in 68 AM. J.I.L. 380–82 (1974). Emphasis added.

66. See G.A. Res. A/35/206, 35 U.N. GAOR Supp. (No. 48) at 28, U.N. Doc. A/35/48 (1981). Footnotes omitted.

67. G.A. Res. 36/172 A, 36 U.N. GAOR Supp. (No. 51) at 38, U.N. Doc. A/36/51 (1981). Footnotes omitted.

68. G.A. Res. 34/92 G, 34 U.N. GAOR Supp. (No. 46) at 26, U.N. Doc. A/34/46 (Dec. 1979). Emphasis added.

69. G.A. Res. 35/227 A, 35 U.N. GAOR Supp. (No. 48) at 40, U.N. Doc. A/35/48 (Mar. 1981). Emphasis added. See also G.A. Res. 34/93 A, 35/206 A, supra note 66, and 35/206 O, supra note 66 at 38. See also G.A. Res. 36/121 A, 36 U.N. GAOR Supp. (No. 51) at 29–30, U.N. Doc. A/36/51 (Dec. 1981), and G.A. Res. 36/172, *id.* at 38–40.

70. G.A. Res. 36/8, 36 U.N. GAOR Supp. (No. 51), at 158, 159, U.N. Doc. A/36/51. Emphasis added. See also G.A. Res. 36/9, *id.* at 160.

CHAPTER 11

1. Res. S/277, 25 U.N SCOR at 5, U.N. Doc. S/INF/25 (Mar. 1970).

2. Res. S/445, 34 U.N. SCOR at 13, U.N. Doc. S/INF/35 (Mar. 1979).

3. Res. 3328 (XXIX), 29 U.N. GAOR Supp. (No. 31) at 7, U.N. Doc. A/9631 (Dec. 1974). Emphasis added.

4. G.A. Res. 2787, 26 U.N. GAOR Supp. (No. 29), 82 U.N. Doc. A/8429, reprinted in H. CATTAN, PALESTINE AND INTERNATIONAL LAW 215–16 (1973).

5. G.A. Res. 136/68 (A/36/L.20 and Add. 1), U.N. GAOR Supp. (No. 51) at 20, U.N. Doc. A/36/51 (Dec. 1981).

6. By "unsolicited," reference is made to a state against whom the interference is directed.

7. J. BRIERLY, THE LAW OF NATIONS 402 (1963).

8. L. OPPENHEIM, INTERNATIONAL LAW 305 (8th ed.).

9. Yet the issue is not entirely without academic importance. The term "intervention" is loaded with ambiguities, causing authorities to question its place in the present legal system. Farer, for instance, urges that intervention is permissible if it is short of tactical support. Farer, *Intervention in Civil Wars: A Modest Proposal*, 67 COLUM. L. REV. 267, 273–79 (1967); Farer, *Harnessing the Rogue Elephants: A Short Discourse on Foreign Intervention in Civil Wars*, 82 HARV. L. REV. 511, 522–36 (1969). Though it is not very clear what he meant by a nontactical support, a careful reading of this thesis suggests that his emphasis is against the deployment of foreign troops, technical advisers, and the like to assist any faction in any intrastate conflict. Furthermore, he shows some opposition even to economic assistance. Although he should be applauded for trying to find a way by which the murky but practically unavoidable concept of intervention could be developed to cope with the pacific objectives of the international community, his thesis is not entirely without flaw. First, although it forbids assistance on the battlefield, it permits assistance by training outside the beleaguered territory. The problem here is that, apart from the fact that a state may not be able to train belligerents without also providing them with equipment or sometimes even sending its own troops to the place, not only would the training on the particular venue make that place an object of attack, at least in the name of the dubious concept of self-defense and thus lead to the escalation of the conflict beyond its natural terrain, but it may offer an excuse to any country to go to the assistance of the other faction on the pretext of launching a counterintervention. Indeed, the theory is even more dangerous and less convincing because it considers it permissible for the assistance to be given to either the incumbent authorities or the liberation fighters or rebels, as the case may be. Nor does it set up any standard by which states should determine which faction to assist. Obviously, not only does this make it possible for any state to go to the assitance of a government like that in South Africa or even the defunct one of Idi Amin and thus undermine the principle of self- determination, which has become one of the most important principles of interna-

tional law, but it affords states the opportunity to form alliances with the opposite factions in any conflict, thus producing the very problem that the theory seeks to avoid—undermining the commitment to maintain international peace and security.

10. In supporting this interpretation, Mani has gone even further to suggest that the provision to assist the liberation fighters is mandatory for all states. Mani, *The 1971 War on the Indian Sub-Continent and International Law*, 12 INDIAN J.I.L. 83, 94 (1972).

11. G.A. Res. A/35/227 A, U.N. GAOR Supp. (No. 48) at 42, U.N. Doc. A/35/48 (1980), paras. 5 & 6.

12. *Id.* at J, para. 7.

13. G.A. Res. A/36/121 A, preamble and para. 9, 36 U.N. GAOR Supp. (No. 51) at 29, 30–32, U.N. Doc. A/36/51 (1981).

14. See C. HYDE, INTERNATIONAL LAW AS CHIEFLY APPLIED BY THE UNITED STATES 202 (1945); Falk, *Janus Tormented: The International Law of Internal War*, in INTERNATIONAL ASPECTS OF CIVIL STRIFE 185, 194–97 (J. Rosenau ed. 1964); Higgins, *Internal War and International Law* in 3 FUTURE OF INTERNATIONAL LEGAL ORDER 81, 93 (R. Falk & C. Black ed. 1971), Dhokalia, *Civil Wars and International Law*, 11 INDIAN J.I.L. 219, 245 (1971); Garner, *Questions of International Law in the Spanish Civil War*, 31 AM. J.I.L. 66 (1937); L. KOTZEH, THE CONCEPT OF WAR IN CONTEMPORARY HISTORY AND INTERNATIONAL LAW (1956).

15. Farer, *Harnessing the Rogue Elephants*, supra note 9, at 526–27.

16. *Id.* at 526–27.

17. See I. BROWNLIE, INTERNATIONAL LAW AND THE USE OF FORCE BY STATES 327 (1963).

18. Although the traditional law had an established standard for determining when belligerency should be accorded, it had no means by which the satisfaction of the conditions could be determined. Each state therefore decided for itself and, of course, on the basis of its national interest, whether the conditions had been satisfied. See H. LAUTERPACHT, RECOGNITION IN INTERNATIONAL LAW 270 (1947); Higgins, *International Law and Civil Conflict*, in INTERNATIONAL REGULATION OF CIVIL WAR 169, 170–71 (E. Luard ed. 1972); Dhokalia, supra note 14, at 227; Nawas, *Bangla Desh and International Law*, 11 INDIAN J.I.L. 251, 258 (1971); Friedmann, *Intervention, Civil War and the Role of International Law*, PROC. A.S.I.L. 66, 73–74 (59th mtg.) (1965).

19. See Falk, *International Law of International War: Problems and Prospects*, in LEGAL ORDER IN A VIOLENT WORLD 109, 123 (R. Falk ed. 1968).

20. The apprehension about the relationship between the traditional law and international peace and security is vindicated by the ways that norm has been invoked in such recent cases as the Yemeni crisis, the Hungarian and Czechoslovakian questions, and the conflicts in Laos and the Dominican Republic. See the discussion above, Chapters 1, 9.

21. W. HALL, TREATISE ON INTERNATIONAL LAW 347 (1924).

22. See R. OGLESBY, INTERNAL WAR AND THE SEARCH FOR NORMATIVE ORDER, 101–2, 108–14 (1971); A. MCNAIR, THE LAW OF TREATIES 516–48 (1961); Friedmann, *International Law and the Present War*, 3 MOD. L. REV. 177, 179–80 (1940).

23. OGLESBY, supra note 22, at 101–2.

24. McNAIR, supra note 22, at 518.
25. *Id.* at 518.
26. Friedmann, supra note 22, at 180.
27. See OGLESBY, supra note 22, at 112–13.
28. *Id.* at 113–18.
29. *Id.* at 118.
30. *Id.* at 118.
31. Thus in the case of *The Three Friends* where the U.S. Supreme Court had to decide on the legality of the United States, withdrawal of its assistance to the Cuban government, U.S. neutrality was upheld on the basis of the following consideration:

> We are thus judicially informed of the existence of an actual conflict of arms in resistance to the authority of a Government with which the United States are on terms of peace and amity, although acknowledgement of the insurgents as belligerents by the political department has not taken place; and it can not be doubted that this being so the act in question (i.e., the neutrality act) is applicable.

106 U.S. 1, 63 (1897), cited in *id.* at 118.

32. For continuing validity of the practice, see Moore, *The Lawfulness of Military Assistance to the Republic of Viet Nam*, in THE VIET NAM WAR AND INTERNATIONAL LAW 237, 265 (R. Falk ed. 1968). But see C. HYDE, INTERNATIONAL LAW AS CHIEFLY APPLIED AND INTERPRETED BY THE UNITED STATES 253 (1945).
33. Art. 2(5) of the U.N. CHARTER.
34. H. KELSEN, PRINCIPLES OF INTERNATIONAL LAW 169 (R. Tucker ed. 1966).
35. See Baxter, *Ius in Bello Interno: The Present and Future Law*, in LAW AND CIVIL WAR IN THE MODERN WORLD 518, 525 (J. Moore ed. 1974).
36. Pinkard, *Force, Intervention, and Neutrality in Contemporary International Law*, 3 TOWSON S.J.I.L. 66, 73 n. 25 (1968).
37. *Id.* at 74; H. KELSEN, supra note 34, at 295–97.
38. See Wright, *Is Discussion Intervention?* 50 AM. J.I.L. 106 (1956).
39. KELSEN, supra note 34 at 298; L. M. GOODRICH & E. HAMBRO, THE CHARTER OF THE UNITED NATIONS 61 (1949).
40. See the argument of the U.S. delegate, cited in Pinkard, supra note 36, at 75.
41. The Resolution on Peace Through the Deeds, G.A. Res. 380(V), 5 U.N. GAOR Supp. (No. 20), at 13–14, U.N. Doc. A/1775 (Nov. 1975). See also the Essentials of Peace Resolution, G.A. Res. 290 (IV), 4 U.N. GAOR at 13, U.N. Doc. A/1251 (Dec. 1, 1949); and the Draft Declaration on Rights and Duties of States, 4 U.N. GAOR Supp. (No. 10), at 7–10, U.N. Doc. A/925 (June 9, 1949).
42. G.A. Res. 2131 (XX), 20 U.N. GAOR Supp. (No. 14) at 11–12, U.N. Doc. A/6014 (Dec. 12, 1965).
43. G.A. Res. 36/102, 36 U.N. GAOR Supp. (Nos. 46–51), at 77 (1981).
44. G.A. Res. 36/103. See 36 U.N. GAOR Supp. (No. 51), at 78–80 (Dec. 1981). Cf. the provisions of the Declaration on Friendly Relations, Res. 2625, 25 U.N. GAOR Supp. (No. 28), at 121, U.N. Doc. A/8028 (1970).

45. Res. 2625, supra note 44. Emphasis added.

46. The Definition of Aggression, Resolution 3314, 29 U.N. GAOR Supp. (No. 31), at 142, U.N. Doc. A/9631 (1974). Emphasis added. See also Res. 2625, supra note 44.

Index

Acquisition of territories: by force, 12–13, 88, 92, 273; by prescription, 13, 273

Afghanistan: Communists' practice in, 26; Soviet invasion of, 37, 41

Africa: cold war in, 6; incidence of coups in, 186–95; regional organizations in (*see* Organization for African Unity)

Aggression: fruits of, 12–13; in Goa, 12, 273; Italian invasion of Ethiopia by, 13; Kellogg-Briand Pact on, 13, 91; League of Nations Covenant on, 13, 93; Stimson Doctrine on, 13, 40

Algeria. *See* Anticolonial struggles

Allende, Salvador, 44

Angola: communists' and non-communists' assistance in, 27–28; Cuban troops in, 128, 129; liberation movements in, 27, 128–29; right to choose own destiny, 129; South African aggression in, 129

Anticolonial struggles: against racist regimes, 9–10; Algerian War of Independence by, 9, 44–45, 126, 215; Angolan War of Independence by, 9, 126, 215; and the domestic jurisdiction concept, 32, 212; Guinea Bissau War of Independence by, 9, 126, 215; and League of Nations mandate system, 9, 93–96; legality of, 88–90, 108–15, 120–23, 199; as liberation movements, 5, 6, 9, 185, 186; Mozambique War of Independence by, 9, 126, 215; Namibian War of Independence by, 10; Rhodesian War of Independence by, 10, 126; self-defense of, 12–13, 272–74; status of, 32; use of force in, 272–74; Western Saharan War of Independence by, 10. *See also* Spanish Sahara

Apartheid, 124; anti-communist propaganda for, 28, 127; Bantustans, 131, 145, 149 (*see also* Homelands); Bophuthatswana, 145, 155; Ciskei, 145, 155; communism under, 137; Contact Group proposals for, 127–28; criminal justice system, 139; definition of, 125, 130, 131, 150; development of, 145; educational system, 136–37; employment under, 133–35; features of, 130–31, 132, 133, 134, 136, 137, 141; Group Areas Act, 131–33; human rights under, 142, 155; implications under Genocide Convention, 144–45; implications under U.N. Charter, 142 (*see also* U.N. resolutions); implications under the Universal Declaration of Human Rights, 143–44; internal security laws, 137, 138, 139; international pressure against, 145–47; justification of, 125–27, 129; legal and institutional framework of, 131–34, 137; migrant labor system, 133, 134, 135, 150, 163; O.A.U. support against, 149–50; pass system, 131, 133; police torture, 138–39, 140; presumption of guilt under, 139; prosecuting evidence, 139–40; racial composition, 131, 132; racial separation, 131, 137; recent development of, 145; the Riotous Assemblies Act, 137; in South Africa, 28, 131, 142; in South-West Africa (Namibia), 131, 132, 142; South-West Africa mandate termination, 124, 128, 142; the Suppression of Communism Act under, 137; the Terrorism Act under, 137, 138; terrorism under, 138; terrorist trial under, 130, 131, 139–40; trade unions under, 134–35; Transkei, 145, 155, 162; the Unlawful Or-